7 $\frac{00}{6/0}$

Democracy for the Few

Sixth Edition

Democracy for the Few

Sixth Edition

Michael Parenti

St. Martin's Press

New York

Executive editor: Don Reisman
Manager, publishing services: Emily Berleth
Publishing services associate: Kalea Chapman
Project management: Omega Publishing Services, Inc.
Art director: Sheree Goodman
Cover design: Henry Sene Yee
Cover photo: Philip Jones Griffiths/Magnum Photos, Inc.

Manufactured in the United States of America.
987
fe

For information, write:
St. Martin's Press, Inc.
175 Fifth Avenue
New York, NY 10010

Acknowledgments

Page 11: Drawing by Dana Fradon; © 1974 The New Yorker Magazine, Inc. **Page 21:** Fred Wright/UE NEWS. **Page 26:** TOLES copyright 1991 *The Buffalo News.* Reprinted with permission of UNIVERSAL PRESS SYNDICATE. All rights reserved. **Page 38:** Drawing by D. Reilly; © 1974 The New Yorker Magazine, Inc. **Page 54:** By Tom Meyer. © *San Francisco Chronicle.* Reprinted by permission. **Page 79:** © 1985 by Herblock in *The Washington Post.* **Page 94:** By permission of Johnny Hart and Creators Syndicate, Inc. **Page 114:** © 1993 by Herblock in *The Washington Post.* **Page 122:** By permission of Johnny Hart and Creators Syndicate, Inc. **Page 126:** Drawing by Handelsman; © 1973 The New Yorker Magazine, Inc. **Page 135:** FEIFFER copyright Jules Feiffer. Reprinted with permission of UNIVERSAL PRESS SYNDICATE. All rights reserved. **Page 152:** © 1976 by Herblock in *The Washington Post.* **Page 159:** Gary Huck—UE/Huck/Konopacki Cartoons. **Page 194:** *Dunagin's People* by Ralph Dunagin © Field Enterprises, Inc., 1980, by permission of North America Syndicate, Inc. **Page 233:** Drawing by Dana Fradon; © 1976 The New Yorker Magazine, Inc. **Page 245:** Reprinted by permission: Tribune Media Services. **Page 292:** Drawing by Dana Fradon; © 1973 The New Yorker Magazine, Inc. **Page 328:** TOLES copyright 1993 *The Buffalo News.* Reprinted with permission of UNIVERSAL PRESS SYNDICATE. All rights reserved. **Page 334:** TOLES copyright 1993 *The Buffalo News.* Reprinted with permission of UNIVERSAL PRESS SYNDICATE. All rights reserved.

For my son, Christian

Preface to the Sixth Edition

The study of politics is itself a political act, containing little that is neutral. True, we can all agree on certain neutral facts about the structure of government and the like. However, the book that does not venture much beyond these minimal descriptions will offend few readers but also will interest few. Any determined pursuit of how and why things happen draws us into highly controversial areas. Most textbooks pretend to a neutrality they do not really possess. While claiming to be objective, they are merely conventional. They depict the status quo in implicitly accepting terms, propagating fairly orthodox notions about American politics.

For decades, mainstream political scientists and other apologists for the existing social order have tried to transform practically every deficiency in our political system into a strength. They would have us believe that the millions who are nonvoters are content with present social conditions, that high-powered lobbyists are nothing to worry about because they perform an information function vital to representative government, and that the growing concentration of executive power is a good thing because the president is democratically responsive to broad national interests. The apologists have argued that the exclusion of third parties is really for the best because too many parties (that is, more than two) would fractionalize and destabilize our political system, and besides, the major parties eventually incorporate into their platforms the positions raised by minor parties (which is news to a number of socialist parties whose views have remained unincorporated throughout this entire century).

Reacting to the mainstream tendency to turn every vice into a virtue, left critics of the status quo have felt compelled to turn every virtue into a vice. Thus they have argued that electoral struggle is meaningless, that our civil liberties are a charade, that federal programs for the needy are next to worthless, that reforms are mostly sops to the oppressed, and labor unions are all complacent, corrupt, and conservative. The left critics have been a much needed antidote to the happy pluralists who painted a silver lining around every murky cloud. But they were wrong in seeing no victories, no "real" progress in the democratic struggles fought and won. *Democracy for the Few* tries to strike a balance; it tries to explain how democracy is incongruous with modern-day capitalism and is consistently violated by a capitalist social order, and yet how democracy refuses to die and continues to fight back and even make gains despite the great odds against popular forces.

Democracy for the Few offers an interpretation that students are not likely to get in elementary school, high school, or most of their college courses, nor in the mass media or mainstream political literature. There are political scientists who for thirty years have written about American government, the presidency, and public policy without ever once mentioning capitalism, a feat of omission that would be judged extraordinary were it not so commonplace. In this book I talk about that forbidden subject, capitalism, so better to comprehend the underpinnings of the political system we are studying. It may come as a surprise to some academics, but there is a marked relationship between economic power and political power.

I have attempted to blend several approaches. Attention is given to traditional political *institutions* such as the Congress, the presidency, the bureaucracy, the Supreme Court, political parties, elections, and the law enforcement system. But these institutional, formalistic features of American government are placed in an overall framework that relates them to the realities of class power and interest.

In addition, the book devotes attention to the *foundations and historical development* of American politics, particularly in regard to the making of the Constitution, the growing role of government, and the political culture. The major eras of reform are investigated with the intent of developing a more critical understanding of the class dimension in American politics, the struggle waged by democratic forces, and the difficulties of reform.

Herein we will give critical attention not only to the existing practices and institutional arrangements of the American political system (who governs, what governs, and how?), but also to the outputs of the system (who gets what?). Instead of concentrating solely on the process of government, as do many texts, I also give attention to the content of actual government practices. Thus a major emphasis is placed throughout the book on the *political economy* of public policy. The significance of government, after all, lies not in its abstracted structure as such, but in what it does and how its policies affect people at home and abroad. I have included a good deal of public-policy information of a kind not ordinarily found in the standard texts, first, because students tend to be poorly informed about politico-economic issues, and second, because it makes little sense to talk about the "policy process" as something abstracted from actual issues and content, divorced from questions of power and interest. This descriptive information, however, is presented with the intent of drawing the reader to an analysis and an overall synthesis of American political reality.

This book takes what some would call a "structural" approach. Rather than treating political developments as the result of happenstance or the contrivances of particular personalities or idiosyncratic events, I try to show that most (but not necessarily all) of what occurs is the outcome of broader configurations of power, wealth, class, and institution as structured into the dominant political organizations, the economy, and the society itself. Unfortunately there are some individuals who believe that a structural analysis forbids us from thinking that conspiracies are anything but imaginary or ephemeral things. They go so far as to argue that we are all now divided into two camps, which they call the "structuralists" and the "conspiracists." In this book I consider conspiracies (by which I mean secret, unlawful, consciously planned crimes by persons in high places) to be part of the arsenal of structural rule. No structure and no system exists without the help of human agency. The larger social formation and broader forces do not operate like mystical abstracted entities. They are directed by people who deliberately pursue certain goals, using all sorts of methods of state, including propaganda, persuasion, elections, fraud, lies, fear, incitements, coercion, concessions, and sometimes even secrecy and concerted violence and other criminal ploys. Watergate and Iran-contra are only two of the better publicized instances of this kind of criminal conspiracy in high places—utilized in the service of structural interests. Rather than seeing conspiracy and structure as mutually exclusive, we might consider how the former is one of the instruments of the latter. Some conspiracies are imagined, some are real. Some of the real ones are part of the existing political structure, not exceptions to it.

Almost every page of this edition has been revised, not only for the purpose of updating but also in an attempt to deepen the book's informative function and advance its analysis. My hope is that this new edition proves as useful to students and lay readers as were the earlier ones.

An expression of gratitude goes to my research assistant, Peggy Noton, for her efforts in hunting down sources and for her most helpful and valuable reading of the final manuscript. My warm thanks also to Sally Soriano who once again offered generous assistance. I also benefited from the conscientious efforts of the staff at St. Martin's Press, especially that superb gentleman, Don Reisman, who singlehandedly has done so much to improve my opinion of editors. My thanks also to Mary Hugh Lester of St. Martin's and Rich Wright of Omega Publishing Services.

This sixth edition is dedicated to the author and social scientist Christian Parenti because no father could wish for a nicer, finer son.

MICHAEL PARENTI

Contents

14 The President: Guardian of the System 242

15 The Political Economy of Bureaucracy 266

16 The Supremely Political Court 289

17 Democracy for the Few 312

1

Partisan Politics

How does the U.S. political system work and for what purpose? What are the major forces shaping political life and how do they operate? Who governs in the United States? Who gets what, when, how, and why? Who pays and in what ways? These are the central questions investigated in this book.

BEYOND TEXTBOOKS

Many of us were taught a somewhat idealized textbook version of American government, which might be summarized as follows:

1. The United States was founded upon a Constitution fashioned to limit political authority and check abuses of power. Over the generations it has proven to be a "living document," which, through reinterpretation and amendment, has served us well.

2. The people's desires are registered through elections, political parties, and a free press. Decisions are made by persons within the various circles of government, but these decision makers are kept in check by each other's power and by their need to satisfy the electorate in order to remain in office. The people do not rule directly but they select those who do. Thus, government decisions are grounded in majority rule—subject to the restraints imposed by the Constitution for the protection of minority rights.

3. The United States is a nation of varied social, economic, ethnic, and regional groups. The role of government is to mediate the conflicting demands of these groups, formulating policies that benefit the public. Although most decisions are compromises that seldom satisfy all

1

interested parties, they usually allow for a working consensus. Hence, every significant group has a say and no one chronically dominates.

4. These institutional arrangements have given us a government of laws and not of individuals, which, while far from perfect, allows for a fairly high degree of popular participation. Our political system is part of a free and prosperous society that is the envy of peoples throughout the world.

This view of the United States as a happy, pluralistic polity assumes that existing social, economic, and political institutions operate with benign effect; that power is not highly concentrated nor heavily skewed toward those who control vast wealth; that capitalism is not to be treated as of critical concern when discussing American government; and that the state is a neutral entity with no special class relationship to those who own the land, technology, resources, and capital of this and other societies. These enormous assumptions will be challenged in the pages ahead.

The theme of this book is that our government often represents the privileged few rather than the needy many, and that elections and the activities of political parties are insufficient measures against the influences of corporate wealth. The laws of our polity are written principally to advance the interests of the haves at the expense of the rest of us. Even when equitable as written, they usually are enforced in highly discriminatory ways. Furthermore, it will be argued that this "democracy for the few" is a product not only of the venality of particular officeholders but a reflection of the entire politico-economic system, the way the resources of power are distributed within it, and the interests that are served by it.

The American people have not always been the passive victims to all this (nor the willing accomplices). The democratic forces of society—the mass of ordinary working people, oppressed minorities, women, and persons from other social groups—have won important gains in political rights and in economic and social betterment, forcing—often after long and bitter struggles that went beyond the electoral process—important concessions from the politico-economic hierarchy. This democratic struggle is an important part of the story that will be given more attention in the pages ahead.

This book recognizes the linkages between various components of the whole politico-economic system. When we study any part of that system, be it the media, lobbying, criminal justice, overseas intervention, or environmental policy, we will see how that part reflects the nature of the whole and how in its particular way it serves, for the most part, to maintain the larger system—especially the system's overriding class interests. We will see that seemingly distinct issues and problems are often interrelated. This will become more evident as we investigate the actual components of the political system in some detail.

The political system comprises the various branches of government along with the political parties, laws, lobbyists, and private interest groups that affect public policy. By public policy, I mean the decisions made by government. Policy decisions are seldom neutral. They usually benefit some interests more than others, entailing social costs that are rarely equally distributed. The shaping of a budget, the passage of a piece of legislation, and the development of an administrative program are all policy decisions, all *political* decisions, and there is no way to execute them with neutral effect. If the wants of all persons could be automatically satisfied, there would be no need to set priorities and give some interests precedence over others; indeed, there would be no need for policies or politics as the words have just been used.

Politics extends even beyond the actions of state. Decisions that keep certain matters within "private" systems of power—such as leaving rental costs or health care to the private market—are highly political even if seldom recognized as such. Power in the private realm is generally inequitable and undemocratic and often the source of struggles that spill over into the public arena (e.g., management-labor disputes, race and sex discrimination).

Someone once defined a politician as a person who receives votes from the poor and money from the rich on the promise of protecting each from the other. And President Jimmy Carter observed: "Politics is the world's second oldest profession, closely related to the first." Many people share this view. For them, politics is little more than the art of manipulating appearances in order to sell oneself, with the politician as a kind of prostitute. While not denying the measure of truth in such observations, I take a broader view. Politics is more than just something politicians do. It is the process of struggle over conflicting interests carried into the public arena. It also involves muting and suppressing conflicting interests. Politics involves not only the competition among groups within the system but the struggle to change the system itself, not only the desire to achieve predefined ends but the struggle to redefine ends and to pose alternatives to the existing politico-economic structure.

THE POLITICO-ECONOMIC SYSTEM

Along with discussing the political system, I frequently refer to "the politico-economic system." Politics today covers every kind of issue, from abortion to school prayers, but the bulk of public policy is concerned with economic matters. The most important document the government produces each year is the budget. Probably the most vital functions of government are taxing and spending. Certainly they are necessary for everything else it does, from delivering the mail to making war. The very organization of the federal government reflects its close involvement with the economy: thus, one finds the departments of Commerce, Labor, Agriculture, Interior, Transportation, and Treasury, and the Federal Trade Commission, the National Labor Relations Board, the Interstate Commerce Commission, the Securities and Exchange Commission, and numerous other agencies involved in regulating economic activity. Most of the committees in Congress can be identified according to their economic functions, the most important having to do with taxation and appropriations.

Politics and economics are but two sides of the same coin. Economics is concerned with the allocation of scarce resources for competing ends, involving conflicts between social classes and among groups and individuals within classes. Much of politics is a carryover of this struggle. Both politics and economics deal with the survival and material well-being of millions of people; both deal with the first conditions of social life itself.

This close relationship between politics and economics is neither neutral nor coincidental. Large governments evolve through history in order to protect large accumulations of property and wealth. In nomadic and hunting societies, where there is little surplus wealth, government is rudimentary and usually communal. In societies where wealth and property are controlled by a select class of persons, a state develops to protect the interests of the haves from the have-nots. As wrote John Locke in 1689: "The great and chief end . . . of Men's uniting into Commonwealths, and putting themselves under Government, is the Preservation of their Property." And Adam Smith, who is above suspicion in his dedication to capitalism, wrote in 1776: "The necessity of civil government grows up with the acquisition of valuable property." And "Till there be property there can be no government, the very end of which is to secure wealth, and to defend the rich from the poor."[1]

Many political scientists manage to ignore the relationship between government and wealth, treating the corporate giants, if at all, as if they were but one of a number of interest groups. Most often this evasion is accomplished by labeling any approach that links class, wealth, and capitalism to politics as "Marxist." To be sure, Karl Marx saw such a relationship, but so did more conservative theorists like Thomas Hobbes, John Locke, Adam Smith and, in America, Alexander Hamilton and James Madison. Indeed, just about every theorist and practitioner of politics in the seventeenth, eighteenth, and early nineteenth centuries saw the linkage between political organization and economic interest, and between state and class, as not only important but desirable and essential to the well-being of the polity.

---

1. John Locke, *Treatise of Civil Government* (New York: Appleton-Century-Croft, 1937), p. 82. Adam Smith, *An Inquiry into the Nature and Causes of the Wealth of Nations* (Chicago: Encyclopaedia Britannica, 1952), pp. 309 and 311.

"The people who own the country ought to govern it," declared John Jay. A permanent check over the populace should be exercised by "the rich and the well-born," urged Alexander Hamilton. Unlike most theorists before him, Marx was one of the first in the modern era to see the existing relationship between property and power as undesirable and exploitative, and this was his unforgivable sin. The tendency to avoid critical analysis of American capitalism persists to this day among business people, journalists, lawyers, and academics.[2]

Power is no less political because it is economic. By "power," I mean the ability to get what one wants, either by having one's interests prevail in conflicts with others or by preventing others from raising their demands. Power presumes the ability to manipulate the social environment to one's advantage. Power belongs to those who possess the resources that enable them to shape the political agenda and control the actions and beliefs of others, such as jobs, organization, technology, publicity, media, social legitimacy, expertise, essential goods and services, and—the ingredient that often determines the availability of these things—money.

Some people say our politico-economic system does not work and should be changed or overthrown; others say it does work or, in any case, we can't fight it and should work within it. Some argue that the existing system is "the only one we have" and imply that it is the only one we ever *could* have. They fear that a breakdown in this system's social order would mean a breakdown in all social order, an end to society itself or, in any case, a creation of something far worse. These fearful notions keep many people not only from entertaining ideas about new social arrangements but also from taking a critical look at existing ones.

Sometimes the complaint is made: "You're good at criticizing the system, but what would you put in its place?" the implication being that unless you have a finished blueprint for a better society, you should refrain from pointing out existing deficiencies and injustices. But this book is predicated on the notion that it is desirable and necessary for human beings to examine the society in which they live, possibly as a step toward making fundamental improvements. It is unreasonable to demand that we refrain from making a diagnosis of an illness until we have perfected a cure. For how can we hope to find solutions unless we really understand the problem. (In any case, suggestions for fundamental changes are offered in the closing chapter and in other parts of the book.)

---

2. See William Appleman Williams, *The Great Evasion* (Chicago: Quadrangle Books, 1964) for an analysis of the way Marxist thought has been stigmatized or ignored by American intellectuals and those who pay their salaries. Also Sidney Fine, *Laissez-Faire and the General-Welfare State* (Ann Arbor: University of Michigan Press, 1964) for a description of capitalist, anti-Marxist orthodoxy in the United States in the late nineteenth century and its control over business, law, economics, university teaching, and religion.

Political life is replete with deceit, corruption, and plunder. Small wonder that many people seek to remove themselves from it. But whether we like it or not, politics and government play a crucial role in determining the conditions of our lives. People can leave political life alone, but it will not leave them alone. They can escape its noise and its pretensions but not some of its worst effects. One ignores the doings of the state only at one's own risk.

If the picture that emerges in the pages ahead is not pretty, this *should not be taken as an attack on the United States,* for this country and the American people are greater than the abuses perpetrated upon them by those who live for power and profit. *To expose these abuses is not to denigrate the nation that is a victim of them.* The greatness of a country is to be measured by something more than its rulers, its military budget, its instruments of dominance and destruction, and its profiteering giant corporations. A nation's greatness can be measured by its ability to create a society free of poverty, racism, sexism, imperialism, and social and environmental devastation, and by the democratic nature of its institutions. Albert Camus once said, "I would like to love my country and justice too." In fact, there is no better way to love one's country, no better way to strive for the fulfillment of its greatness, than to entertain critical ideas and engage in the pursuit of social justice at home and abroad.

2

Wealth and Want in the United States

Most scholars and journalists who write about the American political system never mention capitalism. But the capitalist economy creates imperatives that bear urgently upon political life. In this chapter we will consider how wealth is distributed and used in the United States.

WEALTH AND CLASS

One should distinguish between those who own the wealth of the society, specifically the very rich families and individuals whom we might call "the owning class," and those who are dependent on that class for their employment, "the working class." The latter includes not only blue-collar workers but just about everyone else who is not independently wealthy. The distinction between owners and employees is blurred somewhat by the range of affluence within the owning and working classes. "Owners" include both the wealthy stockholders of giant corporations and the proprietors of small stores. But the latter control a relatively small portion of the wealth and hardly qualify as part of the *corporate* owning class. While glorified as the purveyors of the entrepreneurial spirit, small businesses are really just so many squirrels dancing among the elephants. Small owners often are stamped out when markets decline or bigger competitors move in. By the 1980s, over 600 small and medium-sized businesses were going bankrupt every week in the United States.[1]

---

1. *Washington Post*, March 5, 1984; S. N. Nadel, *Contemporary Capitalism and the Middle Classes* (New York: International Publishers, 1983).

7

Among the employee class are professionals and middle-level executives who in income, education, and life-style tend to be identified as "middle class." Then there are some entertainment and sports figures, lawyers, doctors, and top executives who earn such lavish incomes that they become in part, or eventually in whole, members of the owning class by investing their surplus wealth and living mostly off the profits of their investments.

You are a member of the owning class when your income is very large and comes mostly from the labor of other people—that is, when others work for you, either in a company you own, or by creating the wealth that allows your money and realty investments to increase in value. Hard work seldom makes anyone rich. The secret to wealth is to have others work hard for you. This explains why workers who spend their lives toiling in factories or offices retire with little or no wealth to speak of, while the owners of these businesses, who do not work in them at all, can amass riches from such enterprises.

Wealth is created by the labor power of workers. As Adam Smith noted, "Labor . . . is alone the ultimate and real standard by which the value of all commodities can at all times and places be estimated and compared. It is their real price; money is their nominal price only."[2] What transforms a tree into a profitable commodity such as paper or furniture is the labor that goes into harvesting the timber, cutting the lumber, and manufacturing, shipping, advertising, and selling the commodity (along with the labor that goes into making the tools, trucks, and whatever else is needed in the production process). For their efforts, workers are paid wages that represent only a portion of the wealth created by their labor. The unpaid portion is expropriated by the owners for personal consumption and further investment.

Workers endure an exploitation of their labor as certainly as do slaves and serfs. Under slavery, it is obvious that the chattel works for the enrichment of the master and receives only a bare subsistence. Under feudalism, when serfs work numerous days for the lord without compensation, again the exploitation is readily apparent. So with sharecroppers who must give a third or half their crop to the landowner. Under capitalism, however, the portion taken from the worker is not visible. All one sees is five days' pay for five days' work. If wages did represent the total value created by labor, there would be no surplus wealth, no profits for the owner, no great fortunes for those who do not labor.

But don't managers and executives make a contribution to production for which they should be compensated? Yes, if they are performing productive and useful labor for the enterprise, and usually they are paid very well indeed. But income from ownership is apart from salary and apart

2. Adam Smith, *An Inquiry into the Nature and Causes of the Wealth of Nations* (New York: Modern Library, 1937, originally published 1776), p. 33.

from labor; it is money you are paid *when not working*. The author of a book, for instance, does not make "profits" on his book; he *earns* an income from the labor of writing it, proportionately much less than the sum going to those who own the publishing house and who do none of the writing, editing, printing, and marketing of books. The sum going to the owners is profits; it is *unearned* income. Profits are what you make when not working.

While corporations are often called "producers," the truth is they produce nothing. They are organizational devices for the expropriation of labor and for the accumulation of capital. The real producers are those who apply their brawn, brains, and talents to the creation of goods and services. The primacy of labor was noted years ago by a Republican president. In a message to Congress, Abraham Lincoln stated: "Labor is prior to and independent of capital. Capital is only the fruit of labor and could not have existed had not labor first existed. Labor is the superior of capital and deserves much the higher consideration." Lincoln's words went largely unheeded. The dominance of capital over labor remains the essence of the American economic system, bringing ever greater concentrations of wealth and power into the hands of a small moneyed class.

WHO OWNS AMERICA?

Contrary to a widely propagated myth, this country's wealth does not belong to a broad middle class. The top 10 percent of American households own 98 percent of the tax-exempt state and local bonds, 94 percent of business assets, 95 percent of the value of all trusts. The richest 1 percent own 60 percent of all corporate stock, and fully 60 percent of all business assets; while 90 percent of American families have little or no net assets. The greatest source of individual wealth is inheritance. If you are not rich, it is probably because you lacked the initiative to pick the right parents at birth.[3]

The trend is toward greater economic inequality. In the last fifteen years, income from investments and property (interest, dividends, rents, land and mineral royalties) has been growing two to three times faster than

---

3. *Internal Revenue Service, Statistics of Income Bulletin,* Spring 1990; Stephen Rose, *The American Profile Poster: Who Owns What* (New York: Pantheon, 1986), p. 31; *Colorado Labor Advocate* (AFL-CIO), February 20, 1987, p. 4. Of IRS returns listing over $1 million in adjusted gross income (i.e., income after tax deductions are taken), only 16 percent of earnings was derived from wages and salaries; the rest was from ownership of capital: Benjamin Page, *Who Gets What from Government* (Berkeley: University of California Press, 1983), p. 15. Recent studies show that "rags-to-riches" is a rare exception. Be they rich or poor, virtually everyone dies in the class to which they were born: *New York Times,* May 18, 1992.

income from work (wages, salaries). By 1988, there were 65,000 million-aires in the United States with combined incomes of $173 billion. The top 800,000 people have more money and wealth than the other 184,000,000 combined (over age sixteen). The top 1 percent saw their average in-comes soar by 85.4 percent after taxes in the decade up to 1990, while the incomes of the bottom fifth declined by 10 percent. Income and wealth disparities are greater today than at any time since such information was first collected in 1947.[4] As one economist put it: "If we made an income pyramid out of a child's blocks, with each layer portraying $1,000 of income, the peak would be far higher than the Eiffel Tower, but almost all of us would be within a yard of the ground."[5]

Less than 1 percent of all corporations account for over 80 percent of the total output of the private sector. In 1992 the combined sales of goods and services of the corporate giants totaled $4 trillion. Forty-nine of the biggest banks hold a controlling interest in the 500 largest corporations. American Express, ITT, IBM, Citicorp, and others can claim J. P. Morgan, Inc. as one of their top investors. J. P. Morgan is the nation's largest stock-holder, with more than $15 billion invested in the stock market.[6] The trend is toward ever greater concentrations of corporate wealth as giant compa-nies are bought up by supergiants. The ten largest corporate mergers in U.S. history occurred in the last dozen years. Texaco engulfed Getty Oil; Philip Morris inhaled Miller Brewing; Coca-Cola swallowed Columbia Pic-tures. In 1989, Time, Inc. joined Warner Communications in a $14 billion merger, the largest in history.

The many billions spent on mergers absorb money that could be better spent on new technologies and jobs. A corporation has to procure large sums to buy a dominant share of its own stock if it wishes to ward off a hostile takeover by corporate raiders. Or if acquiring another company, it usually needs money to buy up that firm's stock. In either case, cash re-serves are seldom sufficient and the company must borrow huge sums from

---

4. *The Chairman's Report,* Joint Economic Committee of the Congress, Washington, D.C., December 28, 1989, pp. 12–15; *Background Material and Data on Programs within the Jurisdiction of the Committee of Ways and Means* (Washington, D.C.: Government Printing Office, 1989). *New York Times,* July 20, 1992; Lawrence Mishel and Jacqueline Simon, *The State of Working America* (Washington, D.C.: Economic Policy Institute, 1988); Ramon McLeod, "Gulf Widening between Rich and Poor in U.S.," *San Francisco Chronicle,* July 29, 1991; Isaac Shapiro, *Selective Prosperity,* report by the Center of Budget and Policy Priorities: Washington, D.C., July 1991.

5. Paul Samuelson quoted in Sam Pizzigati, *The Maximum Wage* (New York: Apex Press, 1992).

6. Labor Research Associates, *Economic Notes,* May/June 1991, p. 11 and February 1991, p. 15; *Forbes* various issues through 1992; Lester Thurow, "The Leverage of Our Wealthiest 400," *New York Times,* October 11, 1984.

"The Duke and Duchess of A.T. & T., the Count and Countess of Citicorp, the Earl of Exxon, and the Marchioness of Avco. The Duke of Warnaco . . ."

banks. Then, to meet its debt obligations, it must lay off workers, enforce speedups, break labor unions, reduce wages and benefits, sell off productive plants for quick cash, move to cheaper labor markets abroad, and take other such measures that fail to create new assets and diminish existing ones for quick paper profits. The owner-managers borrow enormous sums not to build factories or invest in research but to merge, raid, and buy one another, issuing new stock and walking away with enormous profits for themselves, leaving the company and the community of employees in worse shape than ever. Because of leveraged buyouts and other such factors, U.S. businesses increased their borrowing 50 percent in the last decade, emerging with debts of $3.5 *trillion.* Currently, U.S. corporations expend about half their earnings just on interest payments—all of which are tax deductible. "Never before has so much money changed hands so quickly and produced so little."[7]

We are taught that the economy consists of a wide array of independent producers. We refer to "farmers" as an interest group apart from business, at a time when Bank of America has a multimillion dollar stake in California farmlands; Beatrice Foods has absorbed more than four hundred companies; and R. J. Reynolds, with vast holdings in cigarettes, transportation, and petroleum, owns Del Monte—itself a multinational agribusiness. A handful of agribusiness firms control most of our farmland. Just 1 percent of all food corporations control 80 percent of the industry's assets and close to 90 percent of the profits. Six multinational firms handle 90 percent of all the grain shipped in the world market.[8]

This centralized food industry represents an American success story—for the big companies. Independent family farms are going deeper into debt or completely out of business. Today, the combined farm debt is many times greater than net farm income. With the growth of corporate agribusiness, regional self-sufficiency in food has virtually vanished. The Northeast, for instance, imports more than 70 percent of its food from other regions. For every $2 spent to grow food in the United States, another $1 is spent to move it. Giant agribusiness farms rely on intensive row crop farming and heavy use of toxic spraying and artificial fertilizers, all of which cause massive damage to ecosystems. The nation's ability to feed itself is being jeopardized, as each year more and more land is eroded by large-scale, quick-profit commercial farming.[9] This is not to mention the harmful effects on people's health resulting from the consumption of food produced by these methods.

Many corporations are owned by stockholders who have little say over the management of their holdings. From this fact, it has been incorrectly inferred that control of most firms has passed into the hands of corporate managers who run their companies with a regard for the public interest that is not shared by their profit-hungry stockholders. Since 1932, when A. A.

---

7. Editorial, *Dollars and Sense*, May 1990, p. 2; also Donald Barlett and James Steele, *America: What Went Wrong?* (Kansas City: Andrews & McMeel, 1992), pp. 27–30; *New York Times*, September 25, 1990. On how corporate greed led to the decline of the steel industry, see Mark Reutter, *Sparrows Point: Making Steel—The Rise and Ruin of American Industrial Might* (New York: Summit, 1988).

8. Jay Staten, *The Embattled Farmer* (Golden, Colo.: Fulcrum Inc., 1987); Frances Moore Lappe and Joseph Collins, *World Hunger: Ten Myths*, 4th ed. (San Francisco: Institute for Food and Development Policy, 1979).

9. Gary Comstock (ed.), *Is There a Moral Obligation to Save the Family Farm?* (Ames, Iowa: Iowa State University, 1987); Staten, *The Embattled Farmer;* Brian Ahlberg, "Farm Debate Plows Under Families," *Extra!* January/February 1991, p. 11; *New York Times*, March 17, 1986. Millions of acres of topsoil are blown away each month, an effect of intensive chemicalized commercial farming: *September Wheat*, documentary film produced by Peter Krieg, New Times Films, New York.

Berle and Gardner Means first portrayed the giant firms as developing "into a purely neutral technocracy," controlled by disinterested managers who allocated resources on the basis of public need "rather than private cupidity,"[10] many observers have come to treat this fantasy as a reality. In fact, the decline of family capitalism has not led to widespread ownership among the general public. The diffusion of stock ownership has not cut across class lines but has occurred within the upper class itself. In an earlier day, three families might have owned companies A, B, and C, respectively, whereas today all three have holdings in all three companies, giving "the upper class an ever greater community of interest than they had in the past."[11]

Some "family enterprises" are of colossal size. Indeed, a small number of the wealthiest families, such as the Mellons, Morgans, Du Ponts, and Rockefellers, dominate the American economy. The Du Ponts control ten corporations, each worth billions of dollars, including General Motors, Coca-Cola, and United Brands, along with many smaller firms. The Du Ponts serve as trustees of scores of colleges. They own about forty manorial estates and private museums in Delaware alone and have set up thirty-one tax-exempt foundations. The family is frequently the largest contributor to Republican presidential campaigns and has financed right-wing and anti-labor causes.[12]

Another powerful family enterprise, that of the Rockefellers, extends into just about every industry in every state of the Union and every nation in the world. The Rockefellers control five of the twelve largest oil companies and four of the largest banks in the world. At one time or another, they or their close associates have occupied the offices of the president, vice-president, secretaries of State, Commerce, Defense, and other cabinet posts, the Federal Reserve Board, the governorships of several states, key positions in the Central Intelligence Agency (CIA), the U.S. Senate and House, and the Council on Foreign Relations.[13]

Whether companies are or are not under family control, their corporate heads prove to be anything but "public-minded," showing far less interest in developing new technologies and creating jobs than in feathering their

---

10. A. A. Berle Jr. and Gardner Means, *The Modern Corporation and Private Property* (New York: Harcourt, Brace, 1932), p. 356.

11. G. William Domhoff, *Who Rules America?* (Englewood Cliffs, N.J.: Prentice-Hall, 1967), p. 40; also Domhoff's *Who Rules America Now?* (New York: Simon and Schuster, 1983).

12. Gerald Colby, *Du Pont Dynasty: Behind the Nylon Curtain* (New York: Lyle Stuart, 1985).

13. Ferdinand Lundberg, *The Rockefeller Syndrome* (Secaucus, N.J.: Lyle Stuart, 1975); William Minter and Laurence Shoup, *Imperial Brain Trust* (New York: Monthly Review Press, 1977).

own nests. During the 1990–93 recession, while corporate profits fell and workers were being laid off or were taking pay cuts, compensation for CEOs rose sharply. In 1990, the chief executive officer (CEO) of Time-Warner, a company that was facing harrowing debt payments, took home $78.2 million in salary and bonuses, making more in one day than most of his employees made in five years. The ten highest paid Wall Street executives, investment bankers, and money managers were paid between $30 million to $125 million a year. In 1992, the ten top-paid corporate CEOs made from $24.6 million to $127 million in salaries, bonuses, and long-term incentive payouts. CEOs are voted sumptuous raises by their directors—most of whom are themselves CEOs for other firms. The directors thereby lift the income floor for themselves. Japanese CEOs earn only one-fifth as much as their U.S. counterparts (still outrageously high sums), yet they perform just as well—if not better.[14]

CEO Richard Munro admitted: "Corporate managers lead just about the most privileged lives in our society."[15] Far from being neutral technocrats dedicated to the public welfare, they are self-enriching members of the owning class. Their social and political power rests not in their personal holdings but in their corporate positions. "Not great fortunes, but great corporations are the important units of wealth, to which individuals of property are variously attached."[16]

THE DYNAMIC OF CAPITALISM

There is something more to capitalism than just the concentration of wealth. Vast fortunes existed in ancient Egypt, feudal Europe, and other early class societies. What is unique about capitalism is its perpetual dynamic of capital accumulation and expansion—and the dominant role this process plays in the economic order.

Capitalists like to say they are "putting their money to work," but money as such cannot create more wealth. What capitalists really mean is that they are putting more human labor power to work, paying workers less in wages than they produce in value, thereby siphoning off more profit for themselves. That's how money "grows." The average private-sector employee works a little over two hours for himself or herself and almost six hours for

---

14. *New York Times,* March 31, 1993; *Wall Street Journal,* April 17, 1991; *Washington Post,* September 1 and 24, 1991; *Economic Notes* (publication of Labor Research Association) June 1993, p. 7. Chrysler's Lee Iacocca pocketed a 15 percent raise while his company's profits plunged 81 percent and its workers were being let go: *Press Democrat* (Santa Rosa), April 13, 1991.

15. *Washington Post,* February 11, 1982.

16. C. Wright Mills, *The Power Elite* (New York: Oxford University Press, 1956), p. 116.

the boss. That latter portion is the "surplus value," which Marx described as the source of the owner's wealth. Sometimes non-Marxists will acknowledge the existence of surplus value as in this advertisement to lure investments: "New York's manufacturing workers produce $4.25 in value over and above every dollar they get in wages."[17] Workers in Texas produce $5 in surplus value for every wage dollar. The percentage is vastly higher in most Third World nations.

All of Rockefeller's capital could not build a house nor a machine, only human labor can do that. Of itself, capital cannot produce anything; it is the thing that is produced by labor. Under capitalism, the ultimate purpose of work is not to produce goods and services but to make money for the investor. Money harnesses labor in order to convert itself into goods and services that will produce still more money. Capital annexes living labor in order to create more capital.[18]

The function of the corporation is not to perform public services or engage in philanthropy but to make as large a profit as possible. The social uses of the product and its effects upon human well-being and the natural environment win consideration in capitalist production, if at all, only to the extent that they do not violate the profit goals of the corporation. As David Roderick, the president of U.S. Steel (now USX) put it: "United States Steel Corporation is not in the business of making steel. We're in the business of making profits."[19]

This relentless pursuit of profit results from something more than just greed—although there is enough of that. Under capitalism, enterprises must expand in order to survive. To stand still amidst growth is to decline, not only relatively but absolutely. A slow-growth firm is less able to move into new markets, hold onto old ones, command investment capital, and control suppliers. A decline in the rate of production eventually cuts into profits and leads to a company's decline. Even the biggest corporations, enjoying a relatively secure oligopolistic control over markets, are beset by a ceaseless drive to expand, to find new ways of making money. Ultimately, the only certainty, even for the giants, is uncertainty. Larger size, greater reserves, and better organizational control might bring security were it not that all other companies are pursuing these same goals. So survival can never be taken for granted.

---

17. Quoted in Gus Hall, *Karl Marx: Beacon for Our Times* (New York: International Publishers, 1983), pp. 24–25.

18. For the great statement on the nature of capitalism, see Karl Marx, *Capital*, vol. 1, available in various editions. For introductory treatments, see Marx's *Wages, Price, and Profit* (Peking: Foreign Language Press, 1969), and his *A contribution to the Critique of Political Economy* (New York: International Publishers, 1970).

19. Quoted in Pat Barile, "Where Production Benefits Workers," *Daily World*, September 20, 1984, p. 4.

Recession and Stagnation

Business leaders admit that they could not survive if they tried to feed or house the poor, or invested in nonprofit projects for the environment, or in something so nebulous as a desire to "get the economy moving again." Nor can they invest simply to "create more jobs." In fact, many of their labor-saving devices and overseas investments are designed to lower wages and eliminate jobs. By holding down wages capitalists increase profits, but they also reduce the buying power of the very public that consumes their services and commodities. Every owner would prefer to pay employees as little as possible while selling goods to better-paid workers from other companies. "For the system as a whole, no such solution is possible; the dilemma is basic to capitalism. Wages, a cost of production, must be kept down; wages, a source of consumer spending, must be kept up."[20] This contradiction creates a tendency toward overproduction and stagnation.

As unemployment climbs, buying power and sales decline, inventories accumulate, investment opportunities recede, more layoffs are imposed, and the recession deepens. For the big capitalists, however, recessions are not unmitigated gloom. Weaker competitors are weeded out and business is better able to resist labor demands, forcing workers to accept wage and benefit cutbacks in order to hang onto their jobs. A reserve supply of unemployed workers helps to deflate wages further. Unions are weakened and often broken; strike activity declines, and profits rise faster than wages. The idea that all Americans are in the same boat, experiencing good and bad times together, should be put to rest. Even as the economy declines, the rich grow richer—not by producing a bigger pie but by grabbing a bigger-than-ever slice of whatever exists. Thus, during the recession of 1992, corporate profits grew to record levels, as companies squeezed more output from each employee and paid less in wages and benefits.[21]

Inflation

A common problem of modern capitalism is inflation. The 4 to 5 percent inflation rate that has regularly plagued our economy can, in a few years, substantially reduce the buying power of wage earners and persons on fixed incomes. Corporation leaders maintain that inflation is caused by the wage demands of labor unions. In fact, wages have not kept pace with prices and

---

20. "Economy in Review," *Dollars and Sense,* March 1976, p. 3.
21. *San Francisco Chronicle,* August 8, 1992. On the growing divergence of income between management and worker, see Jerry Kloby, "The Top-Heavy Economy: Managerial Greed and Unproductive Labor," *Critical Sociology,* 15, Fall 1988, pp. 53–69.

profits. "Except for a few brief intervals, inflation has risen faster than wages for nearly two decades, leaving workers less well off."[22]

Hardest hit by inflation are the four essentials, which devour 70 percent of the average family income: food, fuel, housing, and health care. But in these necessities, the share of costs going to labor has been dropping. For instance, labor costs in home construction have declined as construction unions have failed to win contracts and have been broken. Nor can the astronomical costs of the health industry be blamed on the low wages paid to health-care workers. Medical costs have been outpacing inflation not because of wage increases but as a result of price gouging by hospital corporations, insurance companies, and the drug industry.[23] In most industries the portion of production costs going to workers over the last decade has been shrinking, while the share taken by executive salaries and interest payments to bankers has multiplied dramatically.[24] The "wage-price" spiral is more often a profit-price spiral, with the worker more the victim than the cause of inflation.

As financial power is concentrated in fewer and fewer hands, supplies, markets—and prices—are more easily manipulated. Instead of lowering prices when sales drop, the big monopoly firms often raise them to compensate for sales losses. The same with agribusiness: whether crops are poor or plentiful, food prices tend to go only in an upward direction. Prices are pushed up also by limiting production, as when the petroleum cartels repeatedly create artificial scarcities in oil supplies, which mysteriously disappear after the companies get price increases.[25]

Other inflationary expenditures include the billions spent on unemployment payments and welfare expenditures to assist the poor, the jobless, and others who fall by the wayside under capitalism. There are also hundreds of thousands of able-bodied adults who do not work but who consume a substantial portion of the surplus value because they are wealthy. While not all the rich are idle, practically all live parasitically, largely off their trust funds or other "private incomes."

Massive military expenditures "happen to be a particularly inflation-producing type of federal spending," admits the *Wall Street Journal*.[26] The Civil War, the First and Second World Wars, the Korean War, and the Viet-

---

22. *New York Times*, June 12, 1983; *Solidarity* (publication of United Auto Workers) August 1993, p. 11.

23. *San Francisco Chronicle*, February 4, 1993.

24. *Economic Notes*, September 1985, pp. 1–2; Victor Perlo's report in *Daily World*, July 21, 1983. Comparisons of wages and profits almost always deal with wages *before* taxes and profits *after* taxes thereby exaggerating the portion going to wages.

25. Howard Sherman, "Inflation, Unemployment, and Monopoly Capital," *Monthly Review*, March 1976, pp. 34–35.

26. *Wall Street Journal*, August 30, 1978.

nam War all produced periods of extreme inflation. Aggregate demand—mostly government demand for military goods and payments to military personnel—far exceed supply during wartime and are not usually covered by increased taxes. Even during "peacetime," assuming that's what we have today, huge defense outlays help create inflationary scarcities, as the military consumes vast amounts of labor power and material resources. (For instance, it is the largest single consumer of fuel in the United States.) The resulting excess of demand over supply generates an upward pressure on prices, especially since the defense budget is funded mostly through deficit spending—that is, by the government's spending more than it collects in taxes.

PRODUCTIVITY AND HUMAN NEEDS

Those who insist that private enterprise can answer our needs seem to overlook the fact that private enterprise has no such interest, its function being to produce the biggest profits possible for the owners. People may *need* food, but they offer no market until their need (or want) is coupled with buying power to become a market *demand*. When asked by the Citizens Board what they were doing about the widespread hunger in the United States, one food manufacturer responded: "If we saw evidence of profitability, we might look into this."[27]

The difference between need and demand shows up on the international market also. When buying power rather than human need determines how resources are used, poor nations feed rich ones. Much of the beef, fish, and other protein products consumed by North Americans (and their livestock and domestic pets) comes from Peru, Mexico, Panama, India, and other Third World countries. These foods find their way to profitable U.S. markets rather than feed the children in these countries who suffer from protein deficiencies. In Guatemala alone, 55,000 children die before the age of five each year because of illnesses connected to malnutrition. Yet, the dairy farmers of countries like Guatemala are converting to more profitable beef cattle for the North American market. The children *need* milk, but they lack the money; hence, there is no market. In the "free market," money is invested only where money is to be made.

Capitalism's defenders claim that the pursuit of profit is ultimately beneficial to all since corporate productivity creates prosperity. This argument overlooks several things: high productivity frequently detracts from the common prosperity even while making fortunes for the few, and it not only fails to answer to certain social needs but may generate new ones. The

---

27. Quoted in *Hunger, U.S.A.*, a report by the Citizens Board of Inquiry into Hunger and Malnutrition in the United States (Boston: Beacon Press, 1968), p. 46.

coal-mining companies in Appalachia, for example, created many miseries, swindling the Appalachians out of their land, forcing them to work under dangerous conditions, destroying their countryside, and refusing to pay for any of the resulting social costs.

Furthermore, an increase in productivity, as measured by a gross national product (GNP) of more than $6 trillion a year, may mean *less* efficient use of social resources and more waste. The GNP, the total value of all goods and services produced in a given year, contains some hidden values in its measurements. Important nonmarket services like housework and child rearing go uncounted, while many things of negative social value are tabulated. Thus, highway accidents, which lead to increased insurance, hospital, and police costs, add quite a bit to the GNP but take a lot out of life.

The *human* value of productivity rests in its social purpose. Is the purpose to plunder the environment without regard to ecological needs, fabricate endless consumer desires, produce shoddy goods designed to wear out quickly, create wasteful forms of consumption, pander to snobbism and acquisitiveness, squeeze as much compulsive toil as possible out of workers while paying them as little as possible, create artificial scarcities in order to jack up prices—all in order to grab as big a profit as one can? Or is productivity geared to satisfying the communal needs of the populace in an equitable manner? Is it organized to serve essential needs first and superfluous wants last, to care for the natural environment and the health and safety of citizens and workers? Is it organized to maximize the capabilities, responsibilities, and participation of its people?

Capitalist productivity-for-profit gives little consideration to the latter set of goals. What is called productivity, as measured quantitatively, may actually represent a decline in the quality of life—for example, the relationship between the increasing quantity of automotive and industrial usage and the decreasing quality of our environment. Under capitalism, there is a glut of nonessential goods and services for those with money and a shortage of essential ones for those without money. Stores groan with unsold items while millions of people are ill-housed and ill-fed.

It is argued that the accumulation of great fortunes is a necessary condition for economic growth, for only the wealthy can provide the huge sums needed for the capitalization of new enterprises. Yet in many industries, from railroads to aeronautics to nuclear energy, much of the funding has come from the government—that is, from the taxpayer—and most of the growth has come from sales to the public—from consumers and from the wealth created by the labor power of workers. It is one thing to say that large-scale production requires capital accumulation but something else to presume that the source of accumulation must be the purses of the rich.

It is also argued that the concentration of corporate wealth is a necessary condition for progress because only big companies are capable of carrying out modern technological innovations. Actually, giant companies leave a good deal of the pioneering research to smaller businesses and individual entrepreneurs. The inventiveness record of the biggest oil companies, Exxon and Shell, is strikingly undistinguished. Referring to electric appliances, one General Electric vice-president noted: "I know of no original product invention, not even electric shavers or heating pads, made by any of the giant laboratories or corporations. . . . The record of the giants is one of moving in, buying out, and absorbing the small creators."[28]

Defenders of the present system claim that big production units are more efficient than smaller ones. In fact, huge firms tend to become less efficient and more bureaucratized with size, and after a certain point in growth there is a diminishing return in productivity. Moreover, bigness is less the result of technological advance than of profit growth. When the same corporation has holdings in manufacturing, insurance, utilities, amusement parks, and publishing, it becomes clear that giantism is not a technological necessity that brings greater efficiency but the outcome of capital concentration.

The long-term survival of an enterprise is of less concern to the investor than the margin of profit to be gained from it. Mines, factories, and housing complexes have been bought and sold like so many game pieces for the sole purpose of extracting as much profit as possible, often with little regard for maintaining their functional capacity. Railroads shipping lines, aerospace companies, and banks have often tottered on the edge of ruin, to be rescued by generous infusions of government funds—even as these enterprises were being milked for millions in profits.

When times are good, the capitalists sing praise to the wonders of their free-market system. When times are bad, they blame labor for capitalism's ills. Inflation is supposedly labor's fault because wage demands drive up prices.[29] If we are to believe management, recession, too, is labor's fault. Workers must learn to work harder for less in order to stay competitive in the global economy. If they did so, business would not move to cheaper labor markets in Third World countries. In fact, studies show that U.S. full-time workers were 30 percent more productive than their opposite numbers in Japan and 12 percent more than in Germany, yet they received less in wages and benefits than Japanese and German full-time workers. In the last two decades, U.S. real wages fell 19 percent, despite a 25 percent growth in productivity.[30]

If there is low productivity, it is among U.S. corporate executives. Business administrative costs are upwards of $1 trillion, of which the lion's share

---

28. Quoted in Paul Baran and Paul Sweezy, *Monopoly Capital* (New York: Monthly Review Press, 1966), p. 49.

29. A different view on inflation was just noted: see pp. 16–18.

30. Study by Andrew Sum, cited in *Dollars and Sense,* July/August 1992; *Economic Notes* (publication of Labor Research Association), January/February 1992 and May 1993; William

goes to executives and corporate professionals. Yet as little as one-fourth of an executive's time is actually spent working, that is, developing, analyzing, or executing company policies.[31]

Baumol and Edward Wolff, "Comparative U.S. Productivity Performance and the State of Manufacturing," *CV Starr Center for Applied Economics Newsletter,* 10, 1992, pp. 1–5.

31. Josh Martin, "Managers Are the Main Reason for Poor Productivity," *In These Times,* October 14–20, 1981, p. 17 and the study conducted by management consultants referred to therein.

Another cause of low productivity is technological obsolescence. Unwilling to spend their own money to modernize their plants, big companies cry poverty and call for federal funds to finance technological innovation—supposedly to help them compete against foreign firms. Yet, these same companies sometimes will produce huge cash reserves for mergers. For example, after laying off 20,000 workers, refusing to modernize its aging plants, and milking the government of hundreds of millions of dollars in subsidies and tax write-offs, U.S. Steel came up with $6.2 billion to purchase Marathon Oil.[32]

Unemployment

In capitalist societies, unlike socialist ones, people have no guaranteed right to employment. If they cannot find work, that's their tough luck. No free-market economy has ever attained full employment. If anything, unemployment is functional to capitalism. Without a reserve army of unemployed to compete for jobs and deflate wages, labor would cut more deeply into profits. In recent years official unemployment has ranged above 7 percent, or over 9 million people. But this figure does not count the many who have given up looking for work or who have exhausted their unemployment compensation and left the rolls, nor the millions of part-time or reduced-time workers who want full-time jobs, nor the many forced into early retirement, nor those who have joined the armed forces because they could not find work (and who are thereby listed as "employed.")

The real unemployment figure in 1992 was over 14 percent, or more than 18 million people. In 1991, according to the Department of Labor, about 21.3 million people experienced some unemployment. Moreover, people are finding it harder to get back into the work force and are remaining unemployed for longer periods. More than in any previous recession, workers have been permanently rather than temporarily laid off.[33]

Some conservatives say there are plenty of jobs; unemployment results because some people are just lazy. But when unemployment jumped by a half-million in the early 1990s, was it really because a mass of people suddenly found work too irksome and preferred to lose their income, homes, cars, medical coverage, and pensions? In fact, a perusal of the help wanted

---

32. On the steel industry, see David Bensman and Roberta Lynch, *Rusted Dreams, Hard Times in a Steel Community* (New York: McGraw-Hill, 1987).

33. *San Francisco Examiner,* November 17, 1991; *Economic Notes,* November/December 1992, p. 14; David Moberg, "The Jobless Recovery," *In These Times,* March 22, 1993, pp. 25–27; economists Lawrence Mishel and Jared Bernstein, quoted in Z *Magazine,* February 1993, p. 31; Kim Moody, "A Clash of 'Economic Miracles,'" *Extra!,* May/June 1988, p. 3; *Washington Post,* February 11, 1988.

ads shows that the great majority of available positions require college training or special skills. For entry level openings, it is another story: in various parts of the country, thousands of people show up for a handful of job openings. Even among the more skilled positions, firms receive hundreds of applications for a few scarce openings.

Another myth is that union wages cause unemployment by pricing workers out of the market. Actually, in states where labor unions are weakest and wages lowest, like Mississippi and Alabama, unemployment is among the highest.[34] For the country as a whole, the decline in both unions and real wages in the last decade has been accompanied by a higher, not lower, rate of unemployment.

It is corporate "restructuring," not high wages, that causes unemployment. Nowadays, unemployment and economic stagnation seem more structural than cyclical, showing no self-correcting upturn. As companies expand their productivity through computers and automation, this no longer creates a commensurate gain in jobs.[35] In 1992 Chrysler announced an investment of $225 million for a new line of Dodge trucks that created only seventy jobs, while the company as a whole continued to lay off workers.[36] As constant capital (machinery, technologies, fuels and the like) outstrips variable capital (labor), fixed costs become proportionately higher, creating a still greater pressure to increase productivity in order to maintain and expand profit levels. Proportionately more capital is needed to attain any given return. Thus there exists a continual tendency toward a falling rate of profit.

Unable to raise profitability rates sufficiently through capital investment, the capitalist raises it through downsizing (laying off workers), speedups (making the diminished work force toil faster and harder), downgrading (reclassifying jobs to lower-wage categories), and part-time and contract labor (hiring people who receive no benefits, seniority, or steady employment). Tens of thousands of workers have been laid off across the country in recent times, many of them from profitable companies. In the last dozen years some 14 percent of manufacturing jobs have disappeared. There also has been a substantial drop in white-collar openings and salaries for college-educated people. Between 1990 and 1992, 2.2 million jobs were lost through mergers and layoffs.[37]

---

34. *Daily World,* June 4, 1982.
35. *New York Times,* July 5, 1992.
36. *News and Letters,* August/September 1992.
37. *USA Today,* June 4, 1992; *Hartford Courant,* March 20, 1988; *U.S. News and World Report,* April 22, 1991; CNN news report, March 23, 1992; *Time,* July 20, 1992. Over five million workers are involuntary part-time: "Working Scared," NBC-TV special report, April 16, 1992. A typical example of layoffs in a profitable company: in 1992 Exxon enjoyed $4.77 billion in profits yet reduced its U.S. work force by 3,000 positions: *New York Times,* April 26, 1993.

It is widely believed that the United States can compensate for losses in manufacturing by expanding its service sector. But much service production—such as construction engineering, transportation, and telecommunications—is linked to manufacturing. As the manufacturing base declines, so does the entire economy.[38] Another cause of decline is the runaway shop; U.S. firms move to cheaper Third World labor markets, supposedly to maintain their competitiveness in the "global economy." As one corporate executive put it: "Until we get [U.S.] real wages down much closer to those of the Brazils and South Koreas, we cannot pass along productivity gains to wages and still be competitive."[39] In other words, working people must continue to sacrifice until they are reduced to poverty and corporate profit rates are as high as they are in the Third World.

The power of the business class is like no other group in our society. The giant corporations control the rate of technological development and the terms of production. They fix prices and determine the availability of livelihoods. They create new standards of consumption and popular taste. They decide which labor markets to explore and which to abandon, sometimes relegating whole communities to destitution in the process. They devour environmental resources, toxifying the land, water, and air. They command an enormous surplus wealth while helping to create and perpetuate conditions of scarcity for millions of people at home and abroad. And as we shall see, they enjoy a predominating voice in the highest councils of government.

THE HARDSHIPS OF WORKING AMERICA

By 1994, in the midst of a deep recession, the U.S. economy was going through what some called "a jobless recovery." Business failures and bankruptcy rates were still high; real wages had declined; consumer spending was down; over a thousand jobs were being eliminated daily; and poverty was on the rise. We were witnessing the gradual Third-Worldization of the United States, involving the abolition of high-wage jobs, a growth in low-wage and part-time employment, an increase in permanent unemployment, a shrinking middle-income population, a growing number of mortgage delinquencies, greater concentrations of wealth for the few and more poverty and privation for the many.

One hears much talk from politicians and media pundits about the middle class. In fact, most Americans are working class; their income source is

---

38. Stephen Cohen and John Zysman, *Manufacturing Matters, The Myth of the Post-Industrial Economy* (New York: Basic Books, 1987).

39. Stanley Mihelick, Goodyear Rubber, quoted in *New York Times,* December 12, 1989.

hourly wages and their labor is manual, unskilled, or semiskilled. Even among white-collar service employees, 87 percent were nonsupervisory, earning less than $20,000 in 1990 in full-time jobs.[40] Compared to twenty years earlier, U.S. workers put in an average 158 more hours in job related activities—the equivalent of an extra month of toil. They had fewer paid days off, fewer benefits, less sick leave, shorter vacations, and less discretionary income.[41] In short, people are experiencing a declining standard of living.

Millions do not earn enough to live in any comfort or security. Almost two-thirds of the families below the government's official poverty line have a member who is fully employed.[42] They work for a living but not for a living wage. The Census Bureau reports that some 14.4 million (18 percent) full-time, year-round workers earned wages below the poverty level in 1990—up from 6.6 million (12.3 percent) in 1974. Two-thirds of them were high school or college educated and half were over thirty-three years old. Over a quarter of our labor force, some 30 million, are employed in part-time, temporary, and low-paid "contingent work."[43] It is not laziness that keeps so many in poverty; it is the low wages their bosses pay them and the high prices, rents, and taxes they must pay others. Of the 13 million jobs created in the last decade, 8.2 million paid less than $7,000 annually.[44] To make ends meet, millions are obliged to hold down two jobs.[45] Underemployment was hurting even middle-level managers, engineers, technicians, lawyers, and other usually well-off professionals.

By 1993, the number of people living in poverty had climbed to 37 million, or 14.5 percent of the U.S. population.[46] The Census Bureau's poverty line for a family of four in that year was $13,920, but some 26 million additional people in families that made upwards of $20,000 still lived in serious deprivation, lacking medical insurance, unable to pay utility

---

40. Vicente Navarro, "The Middle Class—A Useful Myth," *Nation*, March 23, 1992, pp. 1, 381; *Economic Notes*, September/October 1989, p. 2.

41. Juliet Schor and Laura Leete-Guy, *The Great American Time-Squeeze* (Washington, D.C.: Economic Policy Institute, 1992); Juliet Schor, *The Overworked American* (New York: Basic Books, 1991).

42. *America's Middle Class Under Siege*, report by AFL-CIO Maritime Trades Department, Washington D.C., November 1991, p. 9.

43. Bruce Klein and Philip Rones, "A Profile of the Working Poor," *Monthly Labor Review*, 112, October 1989, pp. 3–13; Sar Levitan and Isaac Shapiro, *Working but Poor* (Baltimore: Johns Hopkins Press, 1987); Richard Cloward and Frances Piven, "The Fraud of Workfare," *Nation*, May 24, 1993, p. 693.

44. According to the Joint Economic Committee of Congress: *New York Times*, February 25, 1989.

45. The Bureau of Labor Statistics found that the number of women with two or more jobs had quintupled from 636,000 in 1970 to 3.1 million in 1990: *New York Times*, February 15, 1990.

46. NPR news report, October 4, 1993.

bills or keep up car payments, even lacking sufficient funds for food during certain times in the month. They were officially above the poverty line but still poor.[47]

Americans have been taught that they are the most prosperous and fortunate people in the world. The truth is, of twenty major industrial countries, the United States has the highest infant death rate and the highest rate of youth deaths due to accidents, homicide, and other violence. In

---

47. The poverty level is regularly adjusted by the Consumer Price Index to account for inflation. For those of modest means, a disproportionately larger part of their income goes to basic necessities such as housing, food, fuel, and medical care than to other items. The cost of these necessities rose much more rapidly than the general price index. If the Census Bureau had applied the same formula for measuring the cost of necessities that was used to calculate the original poverty line in the early 1960s, they would have discovered that a family of four needed at least 50 percent more than $13,920. The bureau's measurement in effect defined away nearly half the nation's poor: John Schwarz and Thomas Volgy, "Above the Poverty Line—But Poor," *Nation,* February 15, 1993, pp. 191–192; also *Real Life Poverty in America,* a report by Families USA, Center on Budget and Policy Priorities, and Population Reference Bureau, Washington, D.C., July 1990.

addition, poverty is more widespread, severe, and long-lasting than in most other developed nations.[48] Low-income communities are a source of great profit for price-gouging merchants and rent-gouging slumlords. The poor pay more for most commodities, including food.[49] When able to find work, they often perform the toughest, grimiest, lowest-paying jobs, serving as a reserve army of underemployed labor that helps deflate wages and keeps profits up.

Especially hard hit have been people of color. In the early 1990s, African Americans had a declining life expectancy, an infant mortality rate twice as high as Whites, a school drop-out rate of more than 50 percent in some cities, a poverty rate that was 300 percent higher than Caucasians, and an unemployment rate 176 percent higher (compared to 86 percent in 1970). African Americans who were employed took home an overall income that was only 56 percent of White income. Black people continued to suffer racial discrimination in employment and other areas of life.[50]

Women also number among the superexploited. Of the more than 53 million women who work, a disproportionately high number are concentrated in low-paying secretarial and clerking jobs. Although 20 million mothers are working, 44 percent of single mothers remain below the poverty level. Women with college degrees earn about the same as men with one to three years of high school. Two out of three adults in poverty are women.[51]

---

48. U.S. Congress, House of Representatives, Report of the Select Committee on Children, Youth, and Families, *Childrens' Well-Being: An International Comparison* (Washington, D.C.: Government Printing Office, 1990); Dana Hughes et al., *Health of America's Children* (Washington, D.C.: Children's Defense Fund, 1989); (report on poverty by Joint Center for Political and Economic Studies in *San Francisco Chronicle*, September 19, 1991.

49. House Select Committee on Hunger, *Obtaining Food: Shopping Constraints on the Poor* (Washington, D.C.: Government Printing Office, January 1988; Herbert Gans, *More Equality* (New York: Pantheon, 1973).

50. William O'Hare et al., *African Americans in the 1990s*, report by Population Reference Bureau, Washington, D.C., August 1991; National Resource Council, *A Common Destiny: Blacks and American Society* (Washington, D.C.: National Academy Press, 1989); *San Francisco Chronicle*, April 9, 1991. One experiment showed that when Whites and African Americans, who were deliberately matched in qualifications, applied for the same jobs, the Whites were three times more likely to be hired; African Americans were more likely to encounter discouragements and slighting treatment: Michael Fix, Raymond Struyk, Marjorie Turner, *Opportunities Denied, Opportunities Diminished* (Washington, D.C.: Urban Institute, 1991). On racial discrimination in mortgage lending, see *Washington Post*, October 22, 1991. One study shows that infant mortality for African Americans, Latinos and other minorities has been greatly underestimated: Robert Hahn, "The State of Federal Health Statistics on Racial and Ethnic Groups," *Journal of the American Medical Association*, 267, January 8, 1992, pp. 268–271.

51. Bureau of the Census, *Statistical Abstract of the United States 1992* (112th edition), Washington, D.C.; Barbara Gelpi et al. (eds.), *Women and Poverty* (Chicago: University of Chicago Press, 1986); study by National Association of Working Women reported in *People's Weekly World*, April 22, 1987.

By the mid-1990s, one out of every five children in the USA lived in poverty.[52] Official investigations found a dramatic increase in child labor violations, with millions of minors illegally working long hours that interfere with their education or toiling at hazardous jobs in sweatshops, mills, fast food restaurants, and on farms. Employers often seek out child workers because they can pay them less and take advantage of them. The American Academy of Pediatrics estimates that 100,000 minors are injured on the job each year. At least several hundred are killed yearly; many more suffering burns, deep cuts, and amputations. The federal government had relatively few inspectors to check workplaces for child-labor violations. The average fine in cases involving death or permanent injury was $750—a measure of the value placed on the life of low-income children.[53]

As of 1992, about thirty million Americans were not getting enough to eat—up from twenty million in 1985—as hunger spread from the inner cities to the heartland. The number of families lining up for emergency food assistance has increased sharply over the last two decades. Many of those experiencing hunger were regularly employed in the free market. The poorest households spent 60 percent of their incomes on housing, cutting deeply into food budgets. Among those below the poverty line, average outlay per individual meal was only sixty-eight cents. In major cities and small towns, there were people who picked their food out of garbage cans and dumps.[54] As one columnist noted, "If the president on his visit to China had witnessed Chinese peasants eating from garbage cans, he almost certainly would have cited it as proof that communism doesn't work. What does it prove when it happens in the capitalist success called America?"[55]

A team of doctors investigating rural poverty found children plagued with diseases of the heart, lungs, and kidneys, and other serious ailments that would normally warrant immediate hospitalization. One in eight children in the nation suffered from hunger, with millions more facing insuffi-

52. U.S. Census Bureau data reported in *New York Times,* May 29, 1992; *Kids Count Data Book,* annual profile by Center for the Study of Social Policy, Washington, D.C., March 1993; *Opening Doors for America's Children,* interim report by National Commission on Children, Washington, D.C.: Government Printing Office, April 1990. In recent years there has been a rapid increase in impoverishment among Caucasian and Latino children: Isaac Shapiro, *White Poverty in America* (Washington, D.C.: Center on Budget and Policy Priorities, 1992); *New York Times,* August 18, 1992.

53. *New York Times,* June 21, 1992; *Link, Health and Development Report,* Fall 1992, pp. 5–7; *Washington Post,* March 6, 1991 and April 20, 1992; *Sweatshops in the U.S.,* report by General Accounting Office (Washington, D.C.: Government Printing Office, 1988).

54. *Oakland Tribune,* September 10, 1992; *Washington Post,* March 27, 1991; Laura Waxman and Lilia Reyes, *Status Report on Hunger and Homelessness in America's Cities,* U.S. Conference of Mayors, Washington, D.C., January 1989; Dale Maharidge, "And the Rural Poor Get Poorer," *Nation,* January 6/13, 1992, pp. 10–12.

55. William Rasberry, "Garbage Eaters," *Washington Post,* May 2, 1984.

cient nutrition. Such children are preoccupied with desires for food and medical care for their illnesses. They show signs of lethargy, "stunting," "wasting," and Third World diseases such as kwashiorkor and marasmus.[56]

One of every five American adults is functionally illiterate.[57] One of four individuals lives in substandard housing without adequate plumbing, heat, or other facilities. Housing is the largest single expenditure for most families. Due to realty speculations, gentrification, condominium conversions, and unemployment, people of modest means have been squeezed out of the housing market in greater numbers than ever. Affordable housing has become so scarce that more and more working-class families have been forced to double- and triple-up, imposing hardships and severe strains on family relations.[58]

Current estimates of homelessness vary from 250,000 to three million, almost a third of whom are families with children. Half the homeless in major cities are single men. Homelessness is something more than being without shelter. It is the most desperate condition of poverty, offering a life of hunger, filth, destitution, mental depression, unattended illness, and violent victimization. Even among the housed there are millions who are doubled up with family and friends or who are only a paycheck away from the streets.[59] One study found that 20 percent to 82 percent of persons who stayed in homeless shelters held jobs (employment varying according to particular shelters). Most worked full time but with rents so high and pay so low, they could not afford a place to live.[60]

Despite all the talk about the affluent elderly, almost half of the Americans who live below the poverty line are aged. More than three million senior citizens experienced chronic hunger in 1990. Every winter hundreds of people, mostly the very old and very young, freeze to death in unheated

---

56. Judy Rakowsky, "Tufts Study Finds 12 Million Children in U.S. Go Hungry," *Boston Globe,* June 16, 1993, Waxman and Reyes, *Status Report on Hunger and Homelessness in America's Cities; San Francisco Chronicle,* March 27, 1991.

57. Jonathan Kozol, *Illiterate America* (New York: Anchor Press, 1985).

58. *New York Times,* September 25, 1990.

59. Joel Blau, *The Visible Poor, Homelessness in the United States* (New York: Oxford University Press, 1992); Michael Lang, *Homelessness amid Affluence* (New York: Praeger, 1989); David Schwartz and John Glascock, *Combating Homelessness* (Rutgers, N.J.: American Affordable Housing Institute, 1989). Peter Rossi, *Down and Out in America, The Origins of Homelessness* (Chicago: University of Chicago Press, 1989); *Children and Youth,* General Accounting Office report on Homeless Youth, Washington, D.C., June 15, 1989. One study found that 62 percent of teenagers living on the street and 39 percent living in shelters have attempted suicide; more than half have been physically abused: *Washington Post,* November 19, 1991. One study found that over 13.5 million Americans have been on the streets or in homeless shelters at some point in their lives: Dr. Bruce Link, Columbia University, reported in *Food for Thought,* 13, January–February 1994, p. 2.

60. Study by Virginia Coalition for the Homeless, reported in *Washington Post,* August 19, 1988.

apartments or perish in fires caused by unsafe gas stoves (used to compensate for heat cutoffs). Not more than 3 percent of senior citizens have coverage for nursing homes or long-term care. Despite Medicare assistance, the elderly face the highest out-of-pocket health-care costs. Millions are finding that Social Security, pensions, and savings are insufficient. Almost half of all seniors have returned to work or are looking for work.[61]

It is difficult for those who have never known serious economic want to imagine the misery and social pathology it can cause. Studies indicate that even small rises in unemployment bring noticeable increases in illness, mental problems, substance addictions, suicide, and crime.[62] Tuberculosis, a disease much associated with poverty, has risen to a rate unseen in over half a century in the United States.[63]

This country is beset by the greatest illegal drug epidemic in its history, with annual consumption estimated at nearly $150 *billion*. With only 6 percent of the world's population, the U.S. consumes 70 percent of the world's illicit drugs. Some 6.5 million U.S. citizens use heroin, crack, cocaine, or some other narcotic.[64] Millions more are addicted to legal drugs such as amphetamines and barbiturates. The pushers are the doctors; the suppliers are the drug industry; the profits are stupendous. About 32 percent of Americans have experienced some form of mental "disorder" such as serious depression.[65] One out of every four families is affected by alcohol-related problems, a 100 percent increase since 1974. An estimated four in ten Americans suffer some direct or indirect effect of alcohol abuse.[66]

Suicide has become the third leading cause of death among U.S. youth. Each year, some 25,000 to 27,000 Americans take their own lives. Another 23,000 to 24,000 are murdered. An estimated 135,000 children take guns to school, with more than two dozen a day being killed. About 30 percent of American households experience a crime of violence or theft each year, the

---

61. *Washington Post,* January 22, and August 31, September 19, 1989; *New York Times,* October 10, 1992.

62. M. Harvey Brenner, *Economy, Society and Health* (Washington, D.C.: Economic Policy Institute, 1992); Mary Merva and Richard Fowles, *Effect of Diminished Opportunities on Social Stress* (Washington, D.C.: Economic Policy Institute, 1992).

63. *New York Times,* October 14, 1992; *Washington Post,* September 23, 1990. The increase in drug abuse and poverty has also brought an increasing incidence of syphilis, along with a continuing acceleration of AIDS among low-income people: *Washington Post,* September 19, 1990.

64. Clarence Lusane and Dennis Desmond, "Bush Drug Plan Not What It's Cracked up to Be," *Guardian,* September 27, 1989, p. 12.

65. Report by National Institute of Mental Health, November 3, 1988; Marc Miringoff, *The Index of Social Health* (Tarrytown, N.Y.: Fordham Institute for Innovation in Social Policy, 1992).

66. Charlotte Schoenborn, *Exposure to Alcoholism in the Family* (Washington, D.C.: National Center for Health Statistics, 1991); *New York Times,* April 26, 1987.

highest rates being in the poorest neighborhoods.[67] Over the last two decades serious crimes almost doubled and the prison population has tripled. With more than 1.2 million people in prison, or one out of every 180 persons over the age of sixteen, the United States has the highest incarceration rate in the world. Over 40 percent of inmates have an alcohol or drug abuse problem. In an average year, almost ten million are admitted to local jails, with some people entering and getting released several times in one year. More and more prisons are being built to ease overcrowding; in the midst of recession, prison construction remains a boom industry.[68]

With economic adversity there has come a skyrocketing increase in family violence and abuse. Millions of U.S. women are battered by men; almost five million sustain serious injury each year.[69] Over two million children—predominantly but not exclusively from lower income families—are battered, abused, or abandoned each year. Over 30,000 children annually are left permanently physically handicapped from abuse and neglect. Child abuse kills more children than leukemia, automobile accidents, and infectious diseases combined. Every year 150,000 children are reported missing, of whom some 50,000 are never found. Ten to thirteen youngsters are stabbed, raped, beaten, or burned to death by parents or surrogates every day.[70] One in four women and almost one in six men report having been sexually abused as children by adults.[71] An estimated 1.5 million elderly are subjected to serious abuse, such as forced confinement and beatings. Like child abuse, the mistreatment of elderly parents increases dramatically when economic conditions worsen.[72]

---

67. There are approximately 34,000 gunshot deaths in the U.S. each year: *New York Times,* May 26, 1993. In 1990, according to the FBI, there were 1,810,000 violent crimes, including murder, rape, and aggravated assaults, along with 12,532,000 burglaries and larceny thefts—and these were only the offenses reported to authorities: see estimates in *Los Angeles Times,* April 29, 1991; on suicides, see *New York Times,* September 11, 1986; on child killings: NBC-TV evening news report, March 16, 1993, and *Seattle Times,* March 23, 1993.

68. House Judiciary Subcommittee on Criminal Justice: The Sentencing Project, 1990 report, Washington, D.C.; General Accounting Office report on prison overcrowding, reported in *Washington Post,* December 4, 1989; Franklin Zimring, "The Great American Lockup," *Washington Post,* February 28, 1991.

69. *Violence Against Women,* Congressional Caucus for Women's Issues, Washington, D.C., July 1992; Maya Pines, "Recession Is Linked to Far-Reaching Psychological Harm," *New York Times,* April 6, 1982.

70. See report by the Children's Defense Fund: *New York Times,* August 18, 1992; report by U.S. Advisory Board on Child Abuse and Neglect: *Washington Post,* June 27, 1990; *Z Magazine,* February 1993, p. 50; and recent reports by the National Committee for Prevention of Child Abuse, Chicago, Ill.

71. John Crewdson, *By Silence Betrayed: Sexual Abuse of Children in America* (Boston: Little, Brown, 1988): Jane Ashley, "When Incest Haunts Love," *Washington Post,* August 27, 1990.

72. *New York Times,* May 1, 1990.

In sum, the story of the United States' great "affluence" has a darker side involving want, misery, and social pathology in what is becoming an increasingly exploitative and inequitable system. The free market is very good for winners, offering all the rewards that money can command. But it is exceedingly harsh on those who lack the financial means, family connections, and opportunity to share in the affluence. It is not enough to denounce the inequities that exist between the wealthy and the majority of the population; it is also necessary to understand the connection between them. By its very nature, the capitalist system squanders our natural resources, exploits and underpays our labor, creates privation and social needs and then neglects these social needs in service to an accumulation process that serves the few at great cost to the many.

If we love our country, then we should also care for the people who inhabit it and not want to see them victimized. The data presented in this chapter are not an attack on the United States but on the untrammeled market system that victimizes our people.

3

The Plutocratic Culture: Institutions and Ideologies

In trying to understand the American political system we would do well to look at the wider society in which it operates. What can be said about the predominant social institutions, values, and ideologies and their relationship to the distribution of power within American society?

AMERICAN PLUTOCRACY AND CULTURAL HEGEMONY

American capitalism represents more than just an economic system; it is an entire cultural and social order, a plutocracy, a system of rule that is mostly by and for the rich. Most universities and colleges, publishing houses, mass circulation magazines, newspapers, television and radio stations, professional sports teams, foundations, churches, private museums, charity organizations, and hospitals are organized as corporations, ruled by boards of trustees (or directors or regents) composed overwhelmingly of affluent businesspeople. These boards exercise final judgment over all institutional matters.[1]

Consider the university: institutions of higher education are public or private corporations (e.g., the Harvard Corporation, the Yale Corporation) run by boards of trustees with authority over all matters of capital funding and budget; curriculum, scholarships, and tuition; hiring, firing, and pro-

---

1. On the ruling class, see chapter 11; also Michael Parenti, *Power and the Powerless* (New York: St. Martin's Press, 1978) for a discussion of business power within social and cultural institutions.

motion of faculty and staff; degree awards; student fees; and so on. Most of the tasks related to these activities have been delegated to administrators, but the power can be easily recalled by the trustees, and in times of controversy it usually is. Trustees have legal control of the property of the institution, not because of their academic experience but because as successful businesspeople they supposedly have proven themselves to be the responsible leaders of the community.[2]

This, then, is a feature of real significance in any understanding of political power in America: almost all the social institutions existing in this society, along with the immense material and vocational resources they possess, are under plutocratic control, ruled by nonelected, self-selected, self-perpetuating groups of affluent corporate representatives who are answerable to no one but themselves. These institutions shape many of our everyday experiences and much of our social consciousness; yet we have no vote, no portion of the ownership, and no legal decision-making power within them. The power they exercise over us is hierarchical and nondemocratic.

The existing social order and culture are not independent of the business system. Nor are social institutions independent of each other, being controlled by the more active members of the business class in what amounts to a system of interlocking and often interchanging directorates. Through this institutional control, the business elites are able to exercise a good deal of influence over the flow of mainstream ideas and over the actions of broad constituencies.

The agencies of culture, namely the media, the schools, the politicians, and others, associate the capitalist system with the symbols of democracy, Americanism, and prosperity. Criticisms of the system are equated with un-Americanism. Capitalism is treated as an inherent part of democracy, although, in truth, capitalism also flourishes under the most brutally repressive regimes, and capitalist interests have supported the overthrow of democracies in numerous Third World countries and the installation of right-wing dictators who make their lands safe for corporate investments. The private enterprise system, it is taught, creates equality of opportunity, rewards those who show ability and initiative, relegates the parasitic and slothful to the bottom of the ladder, provides a national prosperity that is the envy of other lands, and safeguards (through unspecified means) personal liberties and political freedom.

---

2. Parenti, *Power and the Powerless*, pp. 156–163; also David N. Smith, *Who Rules the Universities?* (New York: Monthly Review Press, 1974). Most trustees are businesspeople who have no administrative or scholarly experience in higher education. They are transients who make monthly visits to the campus for board meetings. Their decisions are covered by insurance paid out of the university budget. On most fiduciary questions they rely on accountants. In short, they take none of the financial risks and offer no special expertise. Their main function seems to be to exercise oligarchic, ideological control over the institution.

The private enterprise system places a great deal of emphasis on commercial worth: how to sell, compete, and get ahead. As Ralph Nader notes, the free market system "only stimulates one value in society—the acquisitive, materialistic, profit value. How about the justice value? the health value? the safety value? the heritage-for-future-generations value? the accountability-in-government value? the enforcement-of-consumer-environmental-worker-laws value?"[3]

Among the institutions of plutocratic culture, our educational system looms as one of the more influential purveyors of dominant values. From the earliest school years, children are taught to compete individually rather than work cooperatively for mutual benefit. Grade-school students are fed stories of their nation's exploits that might be more valued for their inspirational nationalism than for their historical accuracy. Students are instructed to believe in America's global virtue and moral superiority and to hold a rather uncritical view of American politico-economic institutions. One nationwide survey of 12,000 children (grades two to eight) found that most youngsters believe "the government and its representatives are wise, benevolent and infallible, that whatever the government does is for the best." The study found that teachers concentrate on the formal aspects of representative government and accord scant attention to the influences that wealthy, powerful groups exercise over political life.[4] Teachers in primary and secondary schools who wish to introduce critiques of American politico-economic institutions do so often at the risk of jeopardizing their careers. High-school students who attempt to sponsor unpopular speakers and explore controversial views in student newspapers have frequently been overruled by administrators and threatened with disciplinary action.[5]

School texts at the elementary, high-school, and even college levels seldom give more than passing mention to the history of labor struggle and the corporate exploitation of working people at home and abroad. Almost nothing is said of the struggles of Native American Indians, indentured servants, small farmers, and Latino, Asian, and European immigrant labor. The history of resistance to slavery, racism, and U.S. expansionist wars is largely untaught in U.S. schools at any level.[6]

---

3. Nader quoted in *Home and Gardens,* August 1991, p. 144.

4. A Carnegie Institute three-year study: *New York Times,* September 23, 1970; also Joel Spring, *Education and the Rise of the Corporate State* (Boston: Beacon Press, 1972).

5. Commission of Inquiry into High School Journalism, *Captive Voices* (New York: Schocken Books, 1974). A later survey of 500 high-school newspapers found widespread censorship: *Washington Post,* December 30, 1981.

6. On political bias in children's literature and texts, see Betty Bacon (ed.), *How Much Truth Do We Tell the Children?* (Minneapolis: MEP Publications, 1988), and William Griffen and John Marciano, *Lessons of the Vietnam War: A Critical Examination of School Texts* (Totowa, N.J.: Rowman & Allanheld, 1979).

For decades, teaching about the "evils of communism" has been required by law in many state education curricula.[7] Schools are inundated with millions of dollars worth of printed materials, films, and tapes provided by the Pentagon and various corporations at no cost, to promote a glorified view of the military and to argue for tax subsidies to business and deregulation of industry. Pro-business propaganda on nutrition (boosting commercial junk foods), nuclear power, environmental issues, and the wonders of free enterprise are also widely distributed in schools and communities.[8]

Colleges and graduate and professional schools offer a more sophisticated extension of this same orthodox socialization. Conservative think tanks and academic centers have proliferated, along with conservative journals, conferences, and endowed chairs, all funded by tens of millions of dollars from corporations and right-wing foundations. Progressive faculty, and even students, have been subjected to discriminatory treatment because of their dissenting views and political activities, suffering negative evaluations and loss of scholarships, research grants, and jobs.[9] While sometimes portrayed as being above worldly partisan interests, the average American university performs a wide range of services—from advanced research to specialized personnel training and recruitment—which are essential to military and corporate interests. The "neutral" university also has a direct investment link to the corporate structure in the form of a substantial stock portfolio.[10]

Socialization into the orthodox values of American culture is achieved not only by indoctrination but also by economic sanctions designed to punish dissent and reward political conformity. This is true of the training and advancement of lawyers, doctors, journalists, engineers, managers, bureaucrats, and teachers. To get along in one's career, one learns to go along with things as they are and avoid the espousal of views that conflict with the dominant economic interests of one's profession, institution, and society.

---

7. For instance, Florida has no math, science, or language requirements for a high-school diploma, but it does require every student to complete a thirty-hour course called "Americanism vs. Communism." The Florida law dictates: "No teacher or textual material assigned in this course shall present Communism as preferable to the system of constitutional government and the free-enterprise, competitive economy indigenous to the U.S.": *New York Times*, May 4, 1983.

8. Linda Rocawich, "Education Infiltration: The Pentagon Targets High Schools," *Progressive*, March 1994, pp. 25–27.

9. Philip Meranto et al., *Guarding the Ivory Tower, Repression and Rebellion in Higher Education* (Denver: Lucha Publications, 1985).

10. See *Scholars Inc.: Harvard Academics in Service of Industry and Government*, (a report by Harvard Watch, a Ralph Nader group, Cambridge, Mass., 1988); Kathleen Hart, "Is Academic Freedom Bad for Business?" *Bulletin of the Atomic Scientists*, April 1989, pp. 28–34.

Another agent of political socialization is the government itself. Government officials prevent leaks of potentially embarrassing information and flood the public and the media with press releases and planted information supporting the viewpoints of officialdom, industry, and the military. Hardly a day passes without the president or some White House official feeding us reassuring pronouncements about the economy and alarming assertions about crises abroad.

Although we are often admonished to "think for ourselves," we might wonder if our socialization process allows us to do so. Ideological orthodoxy so permeates the plutocratic culture, masquerading as "pluralism," "democracy," and the "open society," that it is often not felt as indoctrination. The worst forms of tyranny are those so subtle, so deeply ingrained, so thoroughly controlling as not even to be consciously experienced. So, there are Americans who are afraid to entertain contrary notions for fear of jeopardizing their jobs, but who still think they are "free."

In a capitalist society, business tries to get people to consume as much as they can—and sometimes more than they can afford. Mass advertising offers not only commodities but a whole way of life, teaching us that the piling up of possessions is a life goal, a measure of one's worth. In the plutocratic culture, the emphasis is on self-absorption: "do your own thing" and "look out for number one." Born of a market economy, the capitalist culture is essentially a market culture, one that minimizes cooperative efforts and human interdependence and keeps us busily competing as workers and consumers.

We are admonished to "get ahead." Ahead of whom and what? Of others and of one's present material status. This kind of "individualism" is not to be mistaken for the freedom to choose deviant political and economic practices. Each person is expected to operate "individually" but in more or less similar ways and similar directions. Everyone competes against everyone else but for the same things. "Individualism" in the United States refers to privatized ownership, consumption, and recreation. You are individualist in that you are expected to get what you can for yourself and not be too troubled by the problems faced by others. This attitude, considered inhuman in some societies, is labeled approvingly as "ambition" in our own and is treated as a quality of great social value.

Whether or not this "individualism" allows one to have control over one's own life is another story. The decisions about the quality of the food we eat, the goods we buy, the air we breathe, the prices we pay, the wages we earn, the way work tasks are divided, the opinions fed to us by the media—the decisions controlling many of the realities of our lives—are usually made by people other than ourselves.

The plutocratic culture teaches us that proximity to the poor is to be shunned, while wealth is something to be pursued and admired. People

"Religious freedom is my immediate goal, but my long-range plan is to go into real estate."

Drawing by Donald Reilly; © 1974 The New Yorker Magazine, Inc.

who occupy privileged positions within the social hierarchy become committed to the hierarchy's preservation and hostile toward demands for greater equalization. According to one study, upper-income people were most opposed to equality of political power for all groups, while lower-income respondents were the firmest supporters of equality.[11] Economically deprived groups are seen as a threat because they want more, and more for the have-nots might mean less for the haves.

A special word should be said about *class* bigotry, which, along with racism and sexism, is one of the widely held forms of prejudice in American

11. William Form and Joan Rytina, "Ideological Beliefs on the Distribution of Power in the United States," *American Sociological Review*, 34, February 1969, pp. 19–31.

society and the least challenged. Working-class people are often presented in movies and television as villains or as uncouth, goofy characters. The message sent is that material success is a measure of one's worth; thus the poor are not worth much and society's resources should not be squandered on them.[12] As the American humorist Will Rogers once said: "It's no disgrace to be poor, but it might as well be."

The emphasis placed on getting ahead and making money is not the outcome of some genetic flaw in the American character. Americans have their doubts about the rat race, and some who are able to, seek an alternative life-style, consuming less and working in less demanding jobs. But the economy does not always allow such a choice. With layoffs, wage cuts, inflation, and growing tax burdens, most people must keep running on the treadmill just to stay in the same place. In a society where money is the overriding determinant of one's life chances, the competitive drive for material success is not merely a symptom of greed but a factor in one's very survival. Rather than grasping for fanciful luxuries, most Americans are still struggling to provide for basic necessities. If they need more money than was essential in earlier days, this is largely because essentials cost so much more.

Because human services are based on ability to pay, money becomes a matter of life and death. To have a low or modest income is to run a higher risk of illness, insufficient medical care, and job exploitation, and to have less opportunity for education, leisure, travel, and comfort. The desire to "make it," even at the expense of others, is not merely a wrong-headed attitude but a reflection of the material conditions of capitalist society wherein no one is ever really economically secure except the superrich.

For those who enjoy the best of everything, the existing politico-economic system is a smashing success. For those who are its most hapless victims, or who are concerned about the well-being of all and not just themselves, the system is something of a failure. Those in between are not sure. They fear losing what they have and want more security. Dreading the decline in earning power and living standards that has afflicted so many, they are absorbed with the struggle to survive.

IDEOLOGY: RIGHT, CENTER, AND LEFT

Political ideologies traditionally have been categorized as rightist, centrist, and leftist. Each of these terms carries ambiguities and within each are variations and differences. Here we will try to draw the broad outlines of

---

12. A number of books discuss the low esteem in which the poor are held, often by the poor themselves, for instance: Martin Robertson, *What Unemployment Means* (New York: Oxford University Press, 1981, pp. 35–57; James Patterson, *America's Struggle Against Poverty* (Cambridge, Mass.: Harvard University Press, 1981).

the three tendencies. What is called the political Right consists of the more conservative and even reactionary individuals, including most corporate elites and many—but not all—persons of high income and wealth. The conservative ideology supports the "free market" of the capitalist system and defends business as the primary mainstay of the good society. Right-wing leaders preach the virtues of individual initiative and self-reliance. They believe that rich and poor pretty much get what they deserve, that people are poor not because of inadequate wages and lack of economic opportunity but because they are lazy, spendthrift, and incapable. The conservative keystone to individual rights is the enjoyment of property rights, especially the right to make a profit off other people's labor and enjoy the privileged conditions of a favored class.

In practice, conservatives are for strong or weak government depending on what interests are being served. They denounce as government "meddling" those policies that move toward an equalization of life chances or attempt to impose regulations upon business. But they advocate strong government measures to restrict dissent and regulate our private lives and personal morals. And they are willing to expend vast public funds and expand state power in order to conduct wars and intervene militarily in other countries.[13]

Conservatives are for or against government handouts depending on whose hand is out. They want to cut spending on human services and aid to lower-income groups, but have supported huge allocations on behalf of that largest of all federal bureaucracies, the Department of Defense. They also vigorously support all sorts of government subsidies and bailouts for large enterprises. Conservatives treat economic recession as just part of a natural cycle. Other than admonishing American workers to work harder for less, they have nothing to say about the deindustrialization of the U.S. economy, the devastating effects of corporate mergers and buyouts, the capital flight to cheap labor markets abroad, the decline of managerial competence, the increase in economic hardship for working people, and the deleterious effects of a massive military buildup.

Not all conservatives are affluent. People of rather modest means, who oppose big government because they do not see it doing anything for them, will call themselves conservatives, for want of an alternative. Many of these are conservative about "cultural issues." They want government to support antigay ordinances in civil and military life and deny equal rights to homosexuals. They want government to outlaw safe and legal abortions because

---

13. Some right-wingers talk tough about military matters but evade the opportunity to go into military service, preferring to have others do the fighting and dying. Such was the case with editor Norman Podhoretz, columnist Robert Novak, journalist Pat Buchanan, Rep. Newt Gingrich and former Vice-President Dan Quayle: *Washington Post*, August 19, 1988; Jack Newfield, "The Rambo Coalition, War Wimps," *Village Voice*, July 23, 1985, pp. 15–17.

they believe a fertilized ovum is a human being. They want the government to impose the death penalty and take stronger measures against criminals. Some conservatives want government to require school prayers and subsidize religious education. They blame the country's ills on decadent morality, the decline of Christian ethics, homosexuality, feminism, legalized abortion, and the loss of family values. The religious Right supports conservative candidates and causes. In turn, big-money conservatives finance the religious Right—including corporations such as Coors, Pepsico, Mobil Oil, Amoco, Heinz, Marriott, and former heads of RCA, Chase Manhattan Bank, and other companies.[14]

To the right of conservatives are former Nazi collaborators, neofascists, and anti-Semitic and racist activists, many of whom have found a home in the Republican party, including David Duke, former member of the American Nazi Party and Ku Klux Klan, who ran for governor of Louisiana on the Republican ticket and then in the 1992 GOP presidential primaries.[15]

More toward the center and left-center of the political spectrum are the "moderates" and liberals, who might be lumped together. Like the conservatives, they accept the capitalist system and its basic values but they think social problems should be rectified by relatively minor reforms and better regulatory policies. Centrists do not usually see these problems as being endemic to the politico-economic system. They sometimes disapprove of the violent overseas interventionist policies of the United States but they see such actions as irrational mistakes and not as rational functions in the service of a global capitalist order. They support those interventions in the Third World that appear to uphold democracy, and do not allow themselves to consider that most such ventures uphold corporate investments and often suppress democratic forces.

Centrists generally support some government intervention in the economy and see a need for spending more money on public services and environmental protections and a little less on the military. But they also support subsidies and tax breaks for business, although not as singlemindedly as the rightists. They advocate protection of individual rights against government surveillance and suppression. But many moderate and liberal centrists in Congress (mostly affiliated with the Democratic party) vote for huge mili-

---

14. Jon Murray in *American Atheist,* May 1987, p. 4; Sara Diamond, *Spiritual Warfare: The Politics of the Christian Right* (Boston: South End Press, 1989); Flo Conway and Jim Siegelman, *Holy Terror,* updated edition (New York: Dell, 1989).

15. Although GOP leaders rejected him, Duke maintained correctly that his program (large military budget, cutbacks in welfare, abolition of racial job quotas, and support for big business) was no different from a mainstream Republican one. On the GOP's ties with Hitler collaborators, see Russ Bellant, *Old Nazis, the New Right and the Reagan Administration* (Cambridge, Mass.: Political Research Associates, 1988). On right-wing extremist groups, see Scott Anderson and Jon Lee Anderson, *Inside the League* (New York: Dodd, Mead, 1986).

tary budgets, support security and intelligence agencies, and have gone along with cuts in human services for the needy.

On the political Left are the progressives and socialists. They want to replace the capitalist system with a system of public and communal ownership, or at least modify it drastically so that it becomes more of a social democracy, with strong labor unions and effective controls on the powers and privileges of big business. Leftists argue that untrammeled free-market capitalism (a) strikes hardest at those who are least able to protect themselves—the disabled, unemployed, aged, and indigent; (b) has given us twenty-seven industrial depressions in 122 years; (c) leaves millions without adequate housing, employment, and food; (d) concentrates economic wealth and political influence in the hands of a privileged few; and (e) organizes the land, labor, resources, and technology of society around no goal other than the accumulation of capital.

Some leftists reject recently defunct communist societies as models for American socialism, pointing out that countries like the Soviet Union come from a different tradition and a history of poverty, foreign hostility, and invasion. Other leftists note that whatever the faults, past crimes, and social problems of communist societies, their citizens did have a guaranteed right to a job; were free from hunger and homelessness; had free medical care and free education to the highest level of their ability; and enjoyed such things as subsidized utilities and transportation, and a guaranteed pension after retirement.

Socialists are distinguished from liberal reformers in their belief that our social problems cannot be solved within the very system that is creating them. Socialists do not believe that every human problem is caused by capitalism but that many of the most important ones are and that capitalism propagates a kind of culture and social organization that guarantees the perpetuation of poverty, racism, sexism, and exploitative social relations at home and abroad.

Socialists believe that American corporate and military expansionism abroad is not the result of "wrong thinking" but the natural outgrowth of profit-oriented capitalism. To the socialist, American foreign policy is not beset by folly and irrationality but has been quite successful in maintaining the status quo and the interests of multinational corporations, crushing social change in many countries and establishing an American financial and military presence throughout much of the world.

U.S. PUBLIC OPINION: WHICH DIRECTION?

Throughout the 1970s and 1980s the media portrayed the public as going through a "conservative mood." In fact, during those decades most Americans had—and still have—serious questions about our institutions and public policies. Surveys show that public confidence in corporate, religious, military, and other establishment elites has declined significantly. A majority of Americans believe that both the Democratic and Republican parties favor big business over the average worker. Eighty-three percent feel that the gap between rich and poor is growing and that the economic system is "inherently unfair." By lopsided majorities, Americans (a) oppose reductions in government safety and environmental regulations, wanting more—not less—activist government; (b) would like to see less spent on the huge military budget and more on health, education, and other human services; (c) favor a federal job program for the unemployed and aid to the needy (as long as it is not termed a "welfare handout"); (d) believe the tax system favors the rich at the expense of the average person; and (e) have a favorable view of the women's movement and having more women in Congress. In recent times, 90 percent of Americans have felt that fundamental changes were needed in the health insurance system. Smaller but growing majorities approved of labor unions and legalized abortion, and supported racial equality, gay rights, and the rights of atheists to hold political office.[16]

In sum, on almost every important issue, a majority seems to hold positions contrary to those maintained by conservative politico-economic elites—hardly the portrait of a conservative public. Opinion polls are only part of the picture. There is the whole history of progressive democratic struggle—continuing to this day and remaining largely untaught in the schools and unreported in the media—of people protesting the unjust uses of state power at home and abroad.[17] Across the nation in recent decades, there have been mass demonstrations, strikes, boycotts, civil-disobedience actions, and thousands of arrests—targeting such things as poverty, unemployment, unsafe nuclear reactors, nuclear weapons, Klan rallies, CIA campus recruitment, U.S. wars in Central America and the Middle East, and U.S. investments in South Africa. There have been mass mobilizations in support of legalized abortion and women's equality, gay and lesbian rights, and environmental rights. There have been organized housing takeovers for the homeless, demonstrations and riots against police brutality, and noncompliance with draft registration. The Selective Service System admitted that over the years some 800,000 young men have refused to register (the actual number is probably higher).[18] At the same time, major strikes have

---

16. Surveys reported in *Washington Post,* October 3 and 7, 1989, July 19, 1990, November 3 and December 4, 1991; *Nation,* March 23, 1992, p. 381; *Z Magazine,* November 1992, p. 11; *Economic Notes,* September/October 1988; *New York Times,* November 9, 1989; *Insider's Newsletter* (Austin, Tex.), September 1987, p. 6; Herbert McClosky and John Zaller, *The American Ethos* (Cambridge, Mass.: Harvard University Press, 1984), passim.

17. See the discussion in chapter 9.

18. Tony Vellela, *New Voices, Student Political Activism in the '80s and '90s* (Boston: South End Press, 1988); Mike Davis and Michael Sprinker, *Reshaping the U.S. Left* (London:

occurred in a wide range of industries, showing that labor militancy is not a thing of the past.[19]

This is not to deny that there remain millions of Americans who are racist, sexist, and homophobic; who dislike labor unions and look down on the poor; and who support conservative, repressive, authoritarian, and militaristic policies at home and abroad. It is ironic that people of modest means sometimes become conservative out of a scarcity fear bred by the very capitalist system they support.

Nor can it be denied that hate crimes against African Americans, Asians, Latinos, recent immigrants, Jews, and gays have increased over the last decade, and that advocates of compulsory pregnancy have committed acts of violence against abortion clinics. The portion of first-year college students who identify with the "far-right" has reached an all-time high of 22 percent. (A slightly larger number, however, consider themselves "far-left.") And millions are readily whipped into jingoistic fervor when their leaders go to war against vastly weaker adversaries.[20] But these are not the only kind of Americans around, and on many issues they are outnumbered.

This society does not produce large numbers of conservative activists. There are no mass demonstrations on behalf of tax cuts for big business or for more war and more privileges for the rich. But the system does produce millions who are uninformed and turned off toward politics, who have been made apolitical by the insipid nature of much of public life and the seemingly insuperable obstacles to change. Socialization in the United States is largely an apolitical one and this itself is a significant political fact.

Yet despite the endless distractions of a mind-numbing mass culture, despite news media and political commentators who give more attention to superficial questions and image manipulation than to substantive policies, and despite all the propaganda and indoctrination by plutocratic institu-

Verso, 1988); *Washington Post,* October 18, 1988; *Guardian,* March 29, 1989; Alex Vitale, "Homes Not Jails," Z *Magazine,* February 1933, pp. 53–56; Stephen Kohn, *The History of American Draft Law Violations 1658–1985* (Westport, Conn.: Greenwood Press, 1986).

19. The best coverage of labor's struggles can be found in *Economic Notes* and *People's Weekly World.* For further comments on organized labor, see chapter 11.

20. See surveys in *Washington Post,* January 9, February 26, and December 24, 1991; Kevin Flynn and Gary Gerhardt, *The Silent Brotherhood, Inside America's Racist Underground* (New York: Free Press, 1989); Jack Levin and Jack McDevitt, *Hate Crimes, The Rising Tide of Bigotry and Bloodshed* (New York: Plenum Publishing, 1993); "American Survey, But to Be Young," *Economist,* January 14, 1989. The strongest supporters of the U.S. massacre of Iraqis in the 1990–91 Gulf War were White, affluent, male college graduates, ages 26 to 44. Opposition was strongest among women, African Americans, the less affluent and less educated: *Washington Post,* December 23, 1990. Most Americans initially opposed military intervention, preferring a course of negotiations. But once the war started, a large majority rallied "in support of our troops."

tions, Americans still have some real concerns about the conditions of their lives. The disparities between what the ruling interests profess and what they practice remains apparent to large numbers of people. There is a limit to how effectively the sugar-coated orthodoxies of capitalist culture can keep our citizens from tasting the bitter realities of economic life.

In addition, political socialization often produces contradictory and unexpected spin-offs. When opinion makers indoctrinate us with the notion that we are a free and prosperous people, we, in fact, begin to demand the right to be free and prosperous. The old trick of using democratic rhetoric to cloak an undemocratic class order will backfire if people begin to take the rhetoric seriously and translate it into democratic economic demands. Also, there are people who love justice more than they love money or a narrow professional success, and who long not for more things for themselves but for a better quality of life for all. It is not that they are without self-interests, but that they define their interests in a way that conflicts with the interests of the privileged and the powerful. In general, if Americans were given more truthful information and if they could see a way to change things, they would be more likely to move in a progressive direction on most economic policies—and, indeed, they show signs of wanting to do just that. A conservative newspaper, the *Brooklyn Tablet,* ran an editorial on a senior-citizens conference that serves as a good description of working Americans of all ages.

> They all are concerned about the economy. They had worked hard all their lives and felt themselves entitled to freedom from money worries at this stage of their lives. They felt betrayed by inflation, government promises and the general lack of fairness in the way they were treated by society. . . .
>
> Yet once they began to articulate what they wanted from society it was also obvious that they were demanding deep social changes in our economic system.
>
> They wanted their income protected from inflation. They wanted their decreased income sheltered from taxation, and taxes shifted to those who had greater ability to pay them. They wanted corporate profits limited in order that adequate pensions could be paid workers. Yet it was a federalized program of income maintenance, social security, that they most trusted and respected. They felt that medical services and housing were rights they were entitled to and at government expense.
>
> They were not trying to write a socialistic charter. They would deny that they were anything but conservative Americans. . . . Yet when they looked carefully at the social problems that they understood and wanted to help solve, they came up with some very radical solutions.[21]

---

21. *Tablet* editorial quoted in Gus Hall, "The New Political Reality," *Political Affairs,* January 1981, pp. 2–3.

DEMOCRACY: FORM AND SUBSTANCE

People on the left, right, and center profess a dedication to "democracy" but tend to mean different things by the term. In this book, democracy refers to a system of governance that represents both in *form* and *content* the interests of the ruled. Decision makers are to govern for the benefit of the many, not for the advantages of the privileged few. The people hold their representatives accountable by subjecting them to open criticism, the periodic check of elections, and, if necessary, recall and removal from office. Democratic government is limited government, the antithesis of despotic absolutism.

Besides living without fear of state tyranny, a democratic people should be able to enjoy freedom from economic, as well as political, oppression. In a real democracy, the material conditions of people's lives should be humane and not grossly unequal. Many conservatives and even some liberals would disagree, arguing that democracy is simply a system of rules for playing the political game, allowing for some measure of mass participation and elec-toral accountability, and that the Constitution and the laws are a kind of rule book. We should not try to impose particular class relations, economic philosophies, or other substantive arrangements on this open-ended game, they argue. This approach certainly does reduce democracy to a game. It presumes that formal rules can exist in a meaningful way independently of substantive realities. But whether one is treated by the law as pariah or prince depends largely on material realities that extend beyond a written constitution or other formal guarantees of law.

The law in its majestic equality, Anatole France once observed, prohib-its rich and poor alike from stealing bread and begging in the streets. And in so doing the law becomes something of a farce, a fiction that allows us to speak of "the rights of all" divorced from the class conditions that often place the rich above the law and the poor below it. In the absence of certain substantive conditions, formal rights are of little value to millions who lack the time, money, and opportunity to make a reality of their rights. Take the "right of every citizen to be heard." In its majestic equality, the law allows both the rich and the poor to raise high their political voices: both are free to hire the best-placed lobbyists and Washington lawyers to pressure public officeholders; both are free to shape public opinion by owning a newspaper or television station; and both rich and poor have the right to engage in multimillion-dollar election campaigns in order to pick the right persons for office or win office themselves. But again, this formal political equality is something of a fiction, as we shall see in the pages ahead. Of what good are the rules for those millions who are excluded from the game?

For conservatives, liberals, and most others on the right and center, capitalism and democracy go together. The free market supposedly creates a society of diverse and pluralistic groups that act independently of the state and provide the basis for political freedom. In fact, most capitalist societies—from Nazi Germany to today's Third World autocracies—have private enterprise systems but no political freedom. In such systems, economic freedom means the freedom to exploit the labor of the poor and get endlessly rich, and little more than that. Capitalism is no guarantee of political democracy.

Progressives, socialists, and other leftists argue further that serious contradictions exist between capitalism and democracy. Capitalism is concerned with maximizing private profits for the benefit of relatively few, with many of the diseconomies shifted onto the shoulders of the people. Thus, unemployment, poverty, pollution, occupational injuries, and harmful commodities are all by-products of the private economy—yet government is expected to take care of these problems at public cost.

Capitalism propagates a reward system that encourages individuals to amass as much wealth as possible. It hails the free market as the most efficient and even fairest mechanism for the distribution of rewards. In contrast—when it works with any efficacy—democracy is dedicated to protecting the material well-being of the many and limiting or eliminating the economic oppressions that serve the few. Democracy attributes roughly equal value to all individuals and seeks to ensure that even those who are not advantaged by wealth or special talent can earn a decent livelihood. It gives majorities the right to override market mechanisms in order to deal with socioeconomic distress. Such is the contradictory nature of a "capitalist democracy": it professes egalitarian political principles while generating enormous disparities in economic well-being and political influence.

Some people think that if you are free to say what you like, you are living in a democracy. But freedom of speech is not the sum total of democracy, only one of its necessary conditions. Too often we are free to say what we want, while those of wealth and power are free to do what they want regardless of what we say. Democracy is not a seminar but a system of power, like any other form of governance. Freedom of speech, like freedom of assembly and freedom of political organization, is meaningful only if it keeps those in power responsible to those over whom power is exercised.

Nor are elections and party competitions a sure test of democracy. Some two-party or multiparty systems are so thoroughly controlled by like-minded elites that they discourage broad participation and offer policies that serve establishment interests no matter who is elected. In the chapters ahead, we will take a critical look at our own political system and measure it not by its undoubted ability to hold elections but by its ability to serve democratic ends. It will be argued that whether a political system is democratic or not depends not only on its procedures but on the *substantive* outputs—that is, the actual material benefits and costs of policy and the kind of social justice or injustice it propagates. By this view, a government that pursues policies that by design or neglect are so inequitable as to deny people the very conditions of life is not democratic no matter how many elections it holds.

Again, it should be emphasized that when we criticize the lack of democratic substance in the United States, we are not attacking or being disloyal to our nation itself. A democratic citizenry should not succumb to uncritical state idolatry but should remain critical of the powers that work against our democratic interests.

4

A Constitution for the Few

To understand the U.S. political system, we need to investigate its origins, fundamental structure, and the interests it represents, beginning with the Constitution and the individuals who wrote it. It is commonly taught that in the early days of the Republic, economic leaders preferred a laissez-faire government that did not intrude upon matters of trade and commerce. But not for a moment did they desire a weak, inactive government. They strove to erect a civil authority that worked vigorously for the interests of the propertied class. They advocated an extension rather than a diminution of state power, agreeing with Adam Smith that government was "instituted for the defense of the rich against the poor" and "grows up with the acquisition of valuable property."[1]

CLASS POWER IN EARLY AMERICA

In the first twelve years of the United States's existence, 1776–87, the period from the American Revolution to the Constitutional Convention, the "rich and the wellborn," the merchants, bankers, and big landowners, exercised a strong influence over political and economic life. They "often dominated the local newspapers which voiced the ideas and interests of commerce" and they identified such interests with the good of the whole people.[2]

The United States of that day has been described as an egalitarian society free from the extremes of want and wealth that characterized Europe.

---

1. For citation and fuller quotation, see chapter 1.
2. Merrill Jensen, *The New Nation* (New York: Random House, 1950), p. 178.

In fact, from early colonial times onward, men of influence received vast land grants from the crown and presided over estates and mansions that bespoke an impressive munificence. By 1700, three-fourths of the acreage in New York belonged to fewer than a dozen persons. In the interior of Virginia, seven individuals owned over 1.7 million acres. By 1760, fewer than five hundred men in five colonial cities controlled most of the commerce, shipping, banking, mining, and manufacturing on the eastern seaboard.[3] Some years later, James Madison himself would write that he had "nothing to brag of as to the state and liberty of my country. Poverty and luxury prevail among all sorts."[4]

In twelve of the thirteen states (Pennsylvania excepted), only property-owning White males could vote or hold office. Excluded were all Native American Indians, persons of African descent, women, indentured servants, and White males without sufficient property. Property qualifications for holding office were so steep as to exclude even most of the White males who could vote. A member of the New Jersey legislature had to be worth at least 1,000 pounds. South Carolina state senators had to possess estates worth at least 7,000 pounds clear of debt (equivalent to about a million dollars today). In Maryland, a candidate for governor had to own at least 5,000 pounds of property. In addition, the absence of a secret ballot and of a real choice among candidates and programs led to widespread apathy.[5]

Not long before the Constitutional Convention, the French chargé d'affaires wrote to his government:

> Although there are no nobles in America, there is a class of men denominated "gentlemen." . . . Almost all of them dread the efforts of the people to despoil them of their possessions, and, moreover, they are creditors, and therefore interested in strengthening the government and watching over the execution of the law. . . . The majority of them being merchants, it is for their interest to establish the credit of the United States in Europe on a solid foundation by the exact payment of debts, and to grant to Congress powers extensive enough to compel the people to contribute for this purpose.[6]

In 1787, it was just such wealthy and powerful "gentlemen," many linked by kinship, marriage, and business dealings, who congregated in Philadel-

---

3. Sidney Aronson, *Status and Kinship in the Higher Civil Service* (Cambridge, Mass.: Harvard University Press, 1964), p. 35.

4. Letter to William Bradford Jr., January 24, 1774, in Marvin Meyers (ed.), *The Mind of the Founder* (New York: Bobbs-Merrill, 1973), p. 6.

5. Aronson, *Status and Kinship*, p. 49; A. E. McKinley, *The Suffrage Franchise in the Thirteen English Colonies in America* (Philadelphia: B. Franklin, 1969, originally published 1905); Arthur Ekrich Jr., *The American Democratic Tradition* (New York: Macmillan, 1963).

6. Quoted in Herbert Aptheker, *Early Years of the Republic* (New York: International Publishers, 1976), p. 41.

phia for the professed purpose of revising the Articles of Confederation and strengthening the central government.[7] Under the Articles, "the United States in Congress" wielded a broad range of exclusive and binding powers over treaties, trade, currency, disputes among the various states, war, and national defense. But these and other actions, including those relating to borrowing money and making appropriations, required the assent of at least nine states.[8] The Congress also had no power to tax, which left it dependent upon levies agreed to by the states. And without the power to tax, it could not compel the people to contribute to the full payment of the public debt, most of which was owed to rich private creditors.

The delegates to Philadelphia wanted a stronger central power that would (a) resolve problems among the thirteen states regarding trade and duties, (b) protect overseas commercial and diplomatic interests, (c) effectively propagate the financial and commercial interests of the affluent class, and (d) defend the wealthy from the competing claims of other classes within the society. It is (c) and (d) that are usually ignored or denied by most historians.[9]

Most troublesome to the framers of the Constitution was the increasingly insurgent spirit evidenced among the people. Even plutocrats like Gouverneur Morris, who shortly before were inclined to avoid strong federation, now "realizing that a political alliance with conservatives from other states would be a safeguard if the radicals should capture the state government . . . gave up 'state rights' for 'nationalism' without hesitation."[10] Their newly found nationalist conviction did not possess them as a sudden inspiration, a "dream of nation-building." As their private and public communications show, it was a practical response to material conditions affecting them in the most immediate way, born of a common class interest.

The working populace of that day has been portrayed as parochial spendthrifts who never paid their debts and who believed in nothing more than timid state governments and inflated paper money. Most historians say little about the actual plight of the common people, the great bulk of whom lived at a subsistence level. Most of the agrarian population consisted of

---

7. On the class interests of the framers, see Charles Beard, *An Economic Interpretation of the United States* (New York: Macmillan, 1936). Even Forrest McDonald, a conservative critic of Beard's interpretation, documents the opulent background of fifty-three of the fifty-five delegates; see his *We, the People: The Economic Origins of the Constitution* (Chicago: University of Chicago Press, 1958), chapter 2.

8. Articles of Confederation, in *National Documents* (New York: Unit Book Publishing, 1905), pp. 59–71.

9. For instance, see most of the articles in Robert Goldwin and William Schambra (eds.), *How Democratic Is the Constitution?* (Washington, D.C.: American Enterprise Institute, 1980).

10. Merrill Jensen, *The Articles of Confederation* (Madison: University of Wisconsin Press, 1948), p. 30.

poor freeholders, tenants, and indentured hands (the latter lived in conditions of servitude). Small farmers were burdened by heavy rents, ruinous taxes, and low incomes. To survive, they frequently had to borrow money at high interest rates. To meet their debts, they mortgaged their future crops and went still deeper into debt. Large numbers were caught in that cycle of rural indebtedness which is today still the common fate of agrarian peoples in this and other countries.[11]

Throughout this period, newspapers complained of the increasing numbers of young beggars in the streets. Economic prisoners crowded the jails, incarcerated for debts or nonpayment of taxes.[12] Among the people there grew the feeling that the revolution against the English crown had been fought for naught. Angry armed crowds in several states began blocking foreclosures and forcibly freeing debtors from jail. In the winter of 1787, debtor farmers in western Massachusetts led by Daniel Shays took up arms. But their rebellion was forcibly put down by the state militia after several skirmishes that left eleven men dead and scores wounded.[13]

CONTAINING THE SPREAD OF DEMOCRACY

The specter of Shays's Rebellion hovered over the delegates who gathered in Philadelphia three months later, confirming their worst fears. They were determined that persons of birth and fortune should control the affairs of the nation and check the "leveling impulses" of the propertyless multitude that composed "the majority faction." "To secure the public good and private rights against the danger of such a faction," wrote James Madison in *Federalist* No. 10, "and at the same time preserve the spirit and form of popular government is then the great object to which our inquiries are directed." Here Madison touched the heart of the matter: how to keep the "spirit and form" of popular government with only a minimum of the substance; how to construct a government that would win some popular sup-

---

11. Ibid., pp. 9–10; also Beard, *An Economic Interpretation*, p. 28. The historian Richard Morris writes, "Unable to pay for seed and stock and tools, farmers were thrown into jail or sold out to service [to work off their debts to creditors]. Except for the clothes on the debtor's back, no property was exempt from seizure or execution": quoted in Aptheker, *Early Years of the Republic*, p. 33. Interest rates on debts ranged from 25 to 40 percent and taxation systems discriminated against those of modest means: Aptheker, p. 36. Historians like Robert Brown, who attack Beard's interpretation, assert that little poverty existed in post-Revolutionary America. They ignore the large debtor class, poorhouses, and debtor jails. They also ignore studies like Clifford Lindsey Alderman, *Colonists For Sale, The Story of Indentured Servants in America* (New York: Macmillan, 1975).

12. Aptheker, *Early Years of the Republic*, pp. 137, 144–145.

13. David Szatmary, *Shays' Rebellion: The Making of an Agrarian Insurrection* (Amherst: University of Massachusetts Press, 1980).

port but would not tamper with the existing class structure, a government strong enough to service the growing needs of an entrepreneurial class while withstanding the democratic egalitarian demands of the popular class.

The framers of the Constitution could agree with Madison when he wrote in *Federalist* No. 10 that "the most common and durable source of faction has been the various and unequal distribution of property. Those who hold and those who are without property have ever formed distinct interests in society" and "the first object of government" is "the protection of different and unequal faculties of acquiring property." The framers were of the opinion that democracy was "the worst of all political evils," as Elbridge Gerry put it. For Edmund Randolph, the country's problems were caused by "the turbulence and follies of democracy." Roger Sherman concurred, "The people should have as little to do as may be about the Government." According to Alexander Hamilton, "All communities divide themselves into the few and the many. The first are the rich and the well-born, the other the mass of the people. . . . The people are turbulent and changing; they seldom judge or determine right." He recommended a strong state power to "check the imprudence of democracy." And George Washington, the presiding officer at the Philadelphia Convention, urged the delegates not to produce a document merely to "please the people."[14]

There was not much danger of that. The delegates spent many weeks debating and defending their interests, but these were the differences of merchants, slave owners, and manufacturers, a debate of haves versus haves in which each group sought safeguards in the new Constitution for its particular concerns. Added to this were disagreements about constitutional structure. How might the legislature be organized? How much representation should the large and small states have? How should the executive be selected? What length of tenure should exist for the different officeholders?[15] Other questions of major significance, relating to the new government's ability to protect the interests of property, were agreed upon with surprisingly little debate. On these issues, there were no poor farmers or artisans attending the convention to proffer an opposing viewpoint. Ordinary working people could not take off four months to go to Philadelphia and write a constitution. The debate between haves and have-nots never occurred.

---

14. For these and other unflattering comments by the delegates regarding the common people and democracy, see Max Farrand (ed.) *Records of the Federal Convention of 1787* (New Haven: Yale University Press, 1937, 1966), volumes 1–3, passim.

15. As most American students should know, the founders decided on two houses, a Senate with six-year staggered terms (a third of the Senate to be elected every two years) and a House of Representatives with two-year terms. It was decided that seats in the House of Representatives should be allocated among the states according to population, while each state, regardless of population, would have two seats in the Senate.

Not surprisingly, Article I, Section 8 of the Constitution, which gives the federal government the power to support commerce and protect the interests of property, was adopted within a few days with little debate.[16] Congress was to regulate commerce among the states and with foreign nations and Indian tribes; lay and collect taxes, imposts, and excises; impose duties and tariffs on imports but not on commercial exports; "Pay the Debts and provide for the common Defence and general Welfare of the United States"; establish a national currency and regulate its value; borrow money; fix the standard of weights and measures necessary for trade; protect the value of securities and currency against counterfeiting; establish uniform bankruptcy laws throughout the country; and raise and support an army and navy.[17] Most of these measures were primarily of concern to investors, merchants, and creditors.

---

16. Once the small states were given equal representation in the Senate, much of the work for building a strong national government "was purely formal": Max Farrand, *The Framing of the Constitution of the United States* (New Haven: Yale University Press, 1913), pp. 134–135; also John Bach McMaster, *The Political Depravity of the Founding Fathers* (New York: Farrar, Straus, 1964), p. 137.

17. Congress was limited to powers delegated by the Constitution or implied as "necessary and proper" for the performance of the delegated powers. Under this "implied power" clause, federal intervention in the economy has grown dramatically.

Some of the delegates were land speculators who expressed a concern about western holdings. Accordingly, Congress was given the "Power to dispose of and make all needful Rules and Regulations respecting the Territory or other Property belonging to the United States." Most of the delegates speculated in highly inflated and nearly worthless Confederation securities. Under Article VI, all debts incurred by the Confederation were valid against the new government, a provision that allowed affluent speculators to make enormous profits when their securities, bought for a trifling, were honored at face value.[18]

By assuming this debt, the federal government—under the policies of the first Secretary of the Treasury, Alexander Hamilton—used the public treasury to create a vast amount of credit for a propertied class that then could invest further in commerce and industry. Hamilton thereby bolstered not only the speculators and creditors but the overall interests of an emerging capitalist class, helping to finance the early process of capital formation. Financing this assumed debt consumed nearly 80 percent of the annual federal revenue during the 1790s.[19] The payment of the debt came out of the pockets of the general public. This process of using the taxing power to gather money from the working populace in order to subsidize private investment continues to this day.

In the interest of merchants and creditors, the states were prohibited from issuing paper money or imposing duties on imports and exports or interfering with the payment of debts by passing any "Law impairing the Obligation of Contracts." The Constitution guaranteed "Full Faith and Credit" in each state "to the Acts, Records, and judicial Proceedings" of other states, thus allowing creditors to pursue their debtors across state lines.

Slavery—another form of property—was afforded special accommodation in the Constitution. Three-fifths of the slave population in each state were to be counted when calculating representation in the lower house. The importation of slaves was given constitutional protection for another twenty years. And slaves who escaped from one state to another had to be delivered up to the original owner upon claim, a provision that was unanimously adopted at the Convention.

The framers believed the states acted with insufficient force against popular uprisings, so Congress was given the task of "organizing, arming, and disciplining the Militia" and calling it forth, among other reasons, to "suppress Insurrections." The federal government was empowered to protect the states "against domestic Violence." Provision was made for "the

---

18. Beard, *An Economic Interpretation,* passim. The profits that accrued to holders of public securities were in the millions.

19. Aptheker, *Early Years of the Republic,* p. 114.

Erection of Forts, Magazines, Arsenals, dock-Yards and other needful Buildings" and for the maintenance of an army and navy for both national defense and to establish an armed federal presence within the potentially insurrectionary states—a provision that was to prove a godsend to the industrial barons a century later when the army was used repeatedly to break strikes by miners and railroad and factory workers.

In keeping with their desire to contain the majority, the founders inserted "auxiliary precautions" designed to fragment power without democratizing it. By separating the executive, legislative, and judicial functions and then providing a system of checks and balances among the various branches, including staggered elections, executive veto, Senate confirmation of appointments and ratification of treaties, and a bicameral legislature, they hoped to dilute the impact of popular sentiments. They contrived an elaborate and difficult process for amending the Constitution, requiring proposal by two-thirds of both the Senate and the House, and ratification by three-fourths of the state legislatures.[20] (Such strictures operate with anti-majoritarian effect to this day. Thus, although national polls show a substantial majority of Americans supports the Equal Rights Amendment for women, the proposal failed to make its way through the constitutional labyrinth.) To the extent that it existed at all, the majoritarian principle was tightly locked into a system of minority vetoes, making swift and sweeping popular action less likely.

The propertyless majority, as Madison pointed out in *Federalist* No. 10, must not be allowed to concert in common cause against the propertied class and its established social order.[21] First, it was necessary to prevent a unity of public sentiment by enlarging the polity and then compartmentalizing it into geographically insulated political communities. The larger the nation, the greater the "variety of parties and interests" and the more difficult it would be for a majority to act in unison. As Madison argued, "A rage for paper money, for an abolition of debts, for an equal division of property, or for any other wicked project will be less apt to pervade the whole body of the Union than a particular member of it." An uprising of impoverished farmers may threaten Massachusetts at one time and Rhode Island at another, but a national government will be large and varied enough to contain each of these and insulate the rest of the nation from the contamination of rebellion.

---

20. Amendments could also be proposed through a constitutional convention called by Congress on application of two-thirds of the state legislatures and ratified by conventions in three-fourths of the states. This method has yet to be tried.

21. *Federalist* No. 10 can be found in any of the editions of the *Federalist Papers*. It is one of the most significant essays on American politics. With clarity and economy of language it explains how government may preserve the existing undemocratic class structure under the legitimating cloak of democratic forms.

Second, not only must the majority be prevented from finding horizontal cohesion, but its vertical force, its upward thrust upon government, should be blunted by interjecting indirect forms of representation. Thus, the senators from each state were to be elected by their respective state legislatures rather than directly by their constituents. The chief executive was to be selected by an electoral college voted by the people but, as anticipated by the framers, composed of political leaders and men of substance who months later would gather in their various states and choose a president of their own liking. It was believed that they would usually be unable to muster a majority for any one candidate, and that the final selection would be left to the House, with each state delegation therein having only one vote. In time, of course, the electoral college became something of a rubber stamp. Its main function has been to create artificial majorities out of slim pluralities. Thirteen times since 1838, a candidate with a plurality (the largest vote of all the various candidates but still short of a majority) was elected president with a substantial majority of the electoral college.[22]

The Supreme Court was to be elected by no one, its justices being appointed to life tenure by the president, with confirmation by the Senate. The Seventeenth Amendment, adopted in 1913, provided for direct popular election of the Senate—demonstrating that the Constitution is sometimes modifiable in democratic directions.

The only portion of government directly elected by the people was the House of Representatives. Many of the delegates would have preferred excluding the public entirely from direct representation. John Mercer observed that he found nothing in the proposed Constitution more objectionable than "the mode of election by the people. The people cannot know and judge of the characters of Candidates. The worst possible choice will be made." Others were concerned that demagogues would ride into office on a populist tide only to pillage the treasury and wreak havoc on the wealthy class. "The time is not distant," warned Gouverneur Morris, "when this Country will abound with mechanics [artisans] and manufacturers [industrial workers] who will receive their bread from their employers. Will such men be the secure and faithful Guardians of liberty? . . . Children do not vote. Why? Because they want prudence, because they have no will of their own. The ignorant and dependent can be as little trusted with the public interest."[23]

---

22. This happens because a candidate might have, say, 45 percent of the vote in a particular state (with the other 55 percent divided among several other candidates), but wins 100 percent of the winner-take-all electoral college vote, thus greatly inflating the winning vote.

23. Farrand, *Records of the Federal Convention,* vol. 2, p. 200ff.

When the delegates finally agreed to having "the people" elect the lower house, as noted earlier, they were referring to a select portion of the population that excluded propertyless White males, all females, Native Americans, and indentured servants. Also excluded were slaves—who constituted almost one-fourth of the entire population. Even among those African Americans who had gained their freedom, in both the North and South, few were allowed to vote until the passage of the Fourteenth Amendment after the Civil War.

PLOTTERS OR PATRIOTS?

In *An Economic Interpretation of the Constitution,* first published in 1913, Charles Beard argued that the framers were guided by the interests of their class. Disputing Beard are those who say that the framers were concerned with higher things than just lining their purses. True, they were moneyed men who profited directly from policies initiated under the new Constitution, but they were motivated by a concern for nation building that went beyond their particular class interests, the argument goes. To quote Justice Holmes, "High-mindedness is not impossible to man." That is exactly the point: high-mindedness is a common attribute among people even when, or especially when, they are pursuing their personal and class interests. The fallacy is to presume that there is a dichotomy between the desire to build a strong nation and the desire to protect wealth and that the framers could not have been motivated by both. In fact, like most other people, they believed that what was good for themselves was ultimately good for their country. Their nation-building values and class interests went hand in hand, and to discover the existence of the "higher" sentiment does not eliminate the self-interested one.

Most persons believe in their own virtue. The founders never doubted the nobility of their effort and its importance for the generations to come. Just as many of them could feel dedicated to the principle of "liberty for all" and at the same time own slaves, so could they serve both their nation and their estates. The point is not that they were devoid of the grander sentiments of nation building but that there was nothing in their concept of nation that worked against their class interest and a great deal that worked for it.

People tend to perceive issues in accordance with the position they occupy in the social structure; that position is largely—although not exclusively—determined by their class status. Even if we deny that the framers were motivated by the desire for personal gain that moves others, we cannot dismiss the existence of their class interest. They may not have been solely concerned with getting their own hands in the till, although enough of them did, but they were admittedly preoccupied with defending the interests of the wealthy few from the laboring many. "The Constitution," as Staughton Lynd noted, "was the settlement of a revolution. What was at stake for Hamilton, Livingston, and their opponents, was more than speculative windfalls in securities; it was the question, what kind of society would emerge from the revolution when the dust had settled, and on which class the political center of gravity would come to rest."[24]

The small farmers and debtors, who opposed a central government that was even farther beyond their reach than the local and state governments, have been described as motivated by self-serving, parochial interests—unlike the supposedly higher-minded statesmen who journeyed to Philadelphia.[25] How and why the wealthy became visionary nation-builders is never explained. Not too long before, many of them had been proponents of laissez-faire and had opposed a strong central government. In truth, it was not their minds that were so much broader but their economic interests. Their motives were no higher than those of any other social group struggling for place and power in the United States of 1787. But possessing more time, money, information, and organization, they enjoyed superior results. For the founders to have ignored the conditions of governance necessary for the maintenance of the social order that meant everything to them would have amounted to committing class suicide—and they were not about to do that.

Those who argue that the founders were motivated primarily by high-minded objectives consistently overlook the fact that the delegates repeatedly stated their intention to erect a government strong enough to protect the haves from the have-nots. They gave voice to the crassest class prejudices and never found it necessary to disguise the fact—as have latter-day apologists—that their concern was to diminish popular control and resist all tendencies toward class equalization (or "leveling," as it was called). Their opposition to democracy and their dedication to their class interests were unabashedly avowed and so pronounced that one delegate, James Wilson of Pennsylvania, did finally complain of hearing too much about how the sole or primary object of government was property. The cultivation and improvement of the human mind, he maintained, was the most noble object—a fine

---

24. Staughton Lynd, *Class Conflict, Slavery and the United States Constitution* (Indianapolis: Bobbs-Merrill, 1967). For discussions of the class interests behind the American Revolution, see Alfred Young (ed.), *The American Revolution: Explorations in the History of American Radicalism* (DeKalb, Ill.: Northern Illinois University Press, 1977); and Edward Countryman, *A People in Revolution* (Baltimore: Johns Hopkins Press, 1982).

25. For examples of those who confuse the founders' broad class interests with the national interest, see several of the essays in Goldwin and Schambra (eds.), *How Democratic Is the Constitution?*; also David G. Smith, *The Convention and the Constitution* (New York: St. Martin's Press, 1965).

sentiment that evoked no opposition from his colleagues as they continued about their business.

If the founders sought to "check power with power," they seemed chiefly concerned with restraining mass power, while assuring the perpetuation of their own class power. They supposedly had a "realistic" opinion of the rapacious nature of human beings—readily evidenced when they talked about the common people—yet they held a remarkably sanguine view of the self-interested impulses of their own class, which they saw as inhabited largely by virtuous men of "principle and property." According to Madison, wealthy men (the "minority faction") would be unable to sacrifice "the rights of other citizens" or mask their "violence under the forms of the Constitution."[26] They would never jeopardize the institution of property and wealth and the untrammeled uses thereof, which in the eyes of the framers constituted the essence of "liberty."

In sum, the Constitution was consciously designed as a conservative document, elaborately equipped with a system of minority checks in order to resist the pressure of popular tides. It provided ample power to build the state services and protections needed by a growing capitalist class but made difficult the transition of rule to a different class.

For the founders, liberty meant something different from and antithetical to democracy. It meant liberty to invest, speculate, trade, and accumulate wealth and to secure its possession without encroachment by sovereign or populace. The civil liberties designed to give all individuals the right to engage in public affairs won little support from the delegates. When Colonel Mason recommended that a committee be formed to draft "a Bill of Rights," a task he said could be accomplished "in a few hours," the other convention members offered little discussion on the motion and voted almost unanimously against it.

If the Constitution was so blatantly elitist, how did it manage to win ratification? Actually, it did not have a wide backing, initially being opposed in most of the states. But the same superiority of wealth, organization, and control of political office and the press that allowed the rich to monopolize the Philadelphia Convention enabled them to orchestrate a successful ratification campaign. The Federalists also used bribes, intimidation, and fraud against opponents of the Constitution. What's more, the Constitution never was submitted to a popular vote. Ratification was by state convention composed of delegates drawn mostly from the same affluent strata as the framers. Those who voted for these delegates were themselves usually subjected to property qualifications.[27]

---

26. *Federalist* No. 10.
27. Jackson Turner Main, *The Antifederalists* (Chapel Hill: University of North Carolina Press, 1961). For a state-by-state account see Michael Gillespie and Michael Lienesch (eds.)

DEMOCRATIC CONCESSIONS

For all its undemocratic aspects, the Constitution was not without its historically progressive features. Consider the following:[28]

1. The very existence of a written constitution with specifically limited powers represented an advance over more autocratic forms of government.

2. No property qualifications were required for any federal officeholder, unlike in England and most of the states. And salaries were provided for all officials, thus rejecting the common practice of treating public office as a voluntary service, which only the rich could afford.

3. The president and legislators were elected for limited terms. No one could claim a life tenure on any elective office.

4. Article VI reads: "no religious Test shall ever be required as a Qualification to any Office or public Trust under the United States," a feature that represented a distinct advance over a number of state constitutions that banned Catholics, Jews, and nonbelievers from holding office.

5. Bills of attainder, the practice of declaring by legislative fiat a specific person or group of people guilty of an offense, without benefit of a trial, were made unconstitutional. Also outlawed were ex post facto laws, the practice of declaring an act a crime and punishing those who had committed it before it had been unlawful.

6. Supporters of the new Constitution recognized their tactical error in failing to include a Bill of Rights and pledged the swift adoption of such a bill as a condition for ratification. So, in the first session of Congress, the first ten amendments were swiftly passed and then adopted by the states; these rights included freedom of speech and religion; freedom to assemble peaceably and to petition for redress of grievances; the right to keep arms; freedom from unreasonable searches and seizures, self-incrimination, double jeopardy, cruel and unusual punishment, and excessive bail and fines; the right to a fair and impartial trial; and other forms of due process. The Bill of Rights also prohibited Congress from giving state support to any religion. Religion was to be some-

---

Ratifying the Constitution (Lawrence: University Press of Kansas, 1989). Probably not more than 20 percent of the adult White males voted for delegates to the ratifying conventions. Even the Federalist leader John Marshall allowed that in some states a majority of the people were against ratification: Beard, *An Economic Interpretation of the Constitution,* pp. 250, 299. Even a conservative like Forrest McDonald agrees with the low turn-out estimates, see his *We, the People.*

28. This section on the Constitution's progressive features is drawn mostly from Aptheker, *Early Years of the Republic,* p. 71ff. and passim.

thing apart from government, supported only by its own constituents and not by the taxpayer—a stricture that often has been violated in practice.

7. The Constitution represented a consolidation of national independence, a victory of Republicanism over British imperialism. It guaranteed a republican form of government and explicitly repudiated monarchy and aristocracy; hence, Article I, Section 9 states: "No title of Nobility shall be granted by the United States." According to James McHenry, a delegate from Maryland, at least twenty-one of the fifty-five delegates favored some form of monarchy. Yet few dared venture in that direction out of fear of popular opposition. Furthermore, delegates like Madison believed that stability for their class order was best assured by a republican form of government. The time had come for the bourgeoisie to rule directly without the baneful intrusions of kings and nobles.

Time and again during the Philadelphia Convention, this assemblage of men who feared and loathed democracy found it necessary to show some regard for popular sentiment (as with the direct election of the lower house). If the Constitution was going to be accepted by the states and if the new government was to have any stability, it had to gain some measure of popular acceptance. While the delegates and their class dominated the events of 1787–89, they were far from omnipotent. The class system they sought to preserve was itself the cause of marked restiveness among the people.

Land seizures by the poor, food riots, and other violent disturbances occurred throughout the eighteenth century in just about every state and erstwhile colony.[29] This popular ferment spurred the framers in their effort to erect a strong central government but it also set a limit on what they could do. The delegates "gave" nothing to popular interests, rather—as with the Bill of Rights—they reluctantly made concessions under the threat of democratic rebellion. They kept what they could and grudgingly relinquished what they felt they had to, driven not by a love of democracy but by a fear of it, not by a love of the people but by a prudent desire to avoid popular uprisings. The Constitution, then, was a product not only of class privilege but of class struggle—a struggle that continued and intensified as the corporate economy and the government grew.

---

29. Howard Zinn, *A People's History of the United States* (New York: Harper & Row, 1980), chapter 3.

5

The Rise of the Corporate State

Although the decisions of government are made in the name of the entire society, they rarely benefit everyone. Some portion of the populace, frequently a majority, loses out. What is considered national policy is usually the policy of dominant groups strategically located within the political system. Standard American government textbooks seldom, if ever, refer to the class biases of public policy. The political system supposedly involves a give-and-take among "a plurality of interests," with government acting as a regulator of interest-group conflict. I will argue for a different notion: the existing political system enjoys no immunity from the way economic resources are distributed in society. Thus, the rise of corporate society brought the rise of the corporate state.

SERVING BUSINESS: THE EARLY YEARS

The upper-class dominance of public life so characteristic of the founding fathers' generation continued throughout the nineteenth century. As early as 1816, Thomas Jefferson complained of an "aristocracy of our monied corporations which . . . bid defiance to the laws of our country."[1] In the 1830s, the period of "Jacksonian democracy," supposedly the "era of the common man," a financial aristocracy controlled the economic life of the major northeastern cities and exercised a vast influence over the nation, while "the common man appears to have gotten very little of whatever it

---

1. Andrew Lipscomb (ed.), *The Writings of Thomas Jefferson* (New York: G. P. Putnam's, 1897), vol. 15, p. 112.

was that counted for much."[2] President Andrew Jackson's key appointments were drawn overwhelmingly from the ranks of the rich, and his policies regarding trade, finances, and the use of government lands reflected the interests of that class.[3]

The destitute comprised upwards of a third of the population, even more in the South and the immigrant-congested cities. Poverty and overcrowding brought the cholera and typhoid epidemics of 1832, 1837, and 1842, during which the wealthy fled the cities, while the poor stayed and died.[4] In 1845 in New York, Baltimore, New Orleans, St. Louis, and other urban centers, the richest 1 percent owned 40 to 50 percent of the wealth, and the upper 10 percent owned 80 percent.[5] Adolescent girls labored from six in the morning until midnight for three dollars a week. Women fainted beside their looms. Children as young as nine and ten toiled 14-hour shifts, falling asleep beside the machines they tended, suffering from malnutrition, sickness, and stunted growth. In an address before "the Mechanics and Working Classes" in 1827, a worker lamented: "We find ourselves oppressed on every hand—we labor hard in producing all the comforts of life for the enjoyment of others, while we ourselves obtain but a scanty portion."[6] As early as 1805, when eight shoemakers were indicted in Philadelphia for "a combination and conspiracy to raise wages," employers used the courts to brand labor unions as conspiracies against property and the Constitution. Similar charges were brought against workers throughout the first half of the nineteenth century.[7]

Contrary to the view that the nation was free of class conflict, class struggles in nineteenth-century America "were as fierce as any known in the industrial world."[8] After the sporadic uprisings and strikes of the early

---

2. Edward Pessen, *Riches, Class and Power Before the Civil War* (Lexington, Mass.: D.C. Heath, 1973), pp. 278 and 304.

3. Howard Zinn, *A People's History of the United States* (New York: Harper & Row, 1980), pp. 125–129 and passim.

4. Ibid., p. 213.

5. Edward Pessen, *The Many Faceted Jacksonian Era* (Westport, Conn.: Greenwood Press, 1977), pp. 7–31.

6. Zinn, *A People's History*, p. 216; also Richard Boyer and Herbert Morais, *Labor's Untold Story* (New York: United Electrical, Radio and Machine Workers, 1971), p. 25 and passim; also John Spargo, *The Bitter Cry of the Children* (Chicago: Quadrangle, 1968, originally published 1906).

7. Boyer and Morais, *Labor's Untold Story*, p. 216.

8. Historian David Montgomery quoted in ibid., p. 221. A comprehensive study is Philip Foner, *History of the Labor Movement in the United States*, vols. 1–6 (New York: International Publishers, 1947, 1955, 1964, 1965, 1980, 1981). While industrial struggles were waged, the slaughter of Native American Indians and the expropriation of their lands, a process begun with the earliest seventeenth-century settlements, continued full force until the final massacre of Sioux in 1890: Dee Brown, *Bury My Heart at Wounded Knee* (New York: Holt, Rinehart & Winston, 1970).

decades, there came the railroad strikes of the 1870s, followed by the farmers' rebellions and the industrial strikes of the 1880s and 1890s. Involving hundreds of thousands of people, these struggles were highly developed in organization and sometimes even revolutionary in tone.

Part of the struggle between labor and capital was an attempt to define the role of the state. Would it move toward a social democracy responsive to the needs of the working populace? Or would the financial and industrial class succeed in using the state as an instrument to expand their wealth and power? In fact, civil authorities intervened almost invariably on the side of the wealthy, using police, state militia, and later federal troops to crush strikes. Scores of workers were killed, hundreds wounded and maimed, thousands beaten and jailed.[9] "The industrial barons made a habit of calling soldiers to their assistance; and armories were erected in the principal cities as measures of convenience."[10] Short of having the regular army permanently garrisoned in industrial areas, as was the desire of some owners, government officials took steps "to establish an effective antiradical National Guard."[11]

High-ranking officials who applied force against workers often were themselves men of wealth. President Cleveland's attorney general, Richard Olney, a millionaire owner of railroad securities, used antitrust laws, mass arrests, labor spies, and federal troops against workers and their unions. From the local sheriff and magistrate to the president and Supreme Court, the forces of "law and order" were utilized to suppress unions. Statutes declared to be unworkable against the well-known monopolistic and collusive practices of business were now effectively invoked against "labor conspiracies."[12]

The same federal government that remained immobilized while violence was perpetrated against abolitionists, and while slaves were imported into the United States in violation of the Constitution right until the Civil War, was able to comb the land with bands of federal marshals and troops to capture fugitive slaves and return them to their masters. The same government that could not find the constitutional means to prevent the distribution of contaminated foods and befouled water supplies could use federal troops to break strikes, shoot hundreds of workers, and slaughter thousands of Indians. The same government that had not a dollar for the indigent (poverty being a matter best left to private charity) gave 21 million

---

9. Foner, *History of the Labor Movement,* passim; and Boyer and Morais, *Labor's Untold Story,* passim.

10. Matthew Josephson, *The Robber Barons* (New York: Harcourt, Brace, 1934), p. 365.

11. William Preston Jr., *Aliens and Dissenters* (Cambridge, Mass.: Harvard University Press, 1963), p. 24.

12. For instance, the Sherman Antitrust Act of 1890, intended to outlaw monopolies and conspiracies in restraint of trade, was rarely used in its first dozen years except against labor unions.

acres of land and $51 million in government bonds to the few railroad financiers.

While insisting that the free market worked for all, most businesspeople showed little inclination to deliver their own interests to the stern judgments of an untrammeled, competitive economy; instead they resorted to such things as tariffs, public subsidies, land grants, government loans, contracts, and other services provided by civil authority.

Well before the Civil War, the common law was redone to favor the financial and industrial interests at the expense of the general public. Through the law of "eminent domain" the government took land from farmers and gave it to canal and railroad companies. The idea of a fair price was replaced in the courts with the doctrine of *caveat emptor* (let the buyer beware). Contract law was used to deny compensation to injured employees and withhold back pay from workers who wished to quit undesirable jobs. Workers were killed or maimed because of inadequate safety measures, without employers being held liable. By these and other measures, the law promoted a state-supported redistribution of wealth against the weakest groups in the society.[13] Such were the blessings of the "free market."

In the late nineteenth century, the millions of dollars collected by the government "from the consuming population, and above all from the . . . poor wage earners and farmers," constituting an enormous budget surplus, was paid out to big investors in high-premium government bonds.[14] Likewise, a billion acres of land in the public domain, almost half of the present area of the United States, was given over to private hands. Matthew Josephson describes the government's endeavors to transform the common wealth into private wealth:

> This benevolent government handed over to its friends or to astute first comers, . . . all those treasures of coal and oil, of copper and gold and iron, the land grants, the terminal sites, the perpetual rights of way—an act of largesse which is still one of the wonders of history. The Tariff Act of 1864 was in itself a sheltering wall of subsidies; and to aid further the new heavy industries and manufactures, an Immigration Act allowing contract labor to be imported freely was quickly enacted; a national banking system was perfected.[15]

Though strenuously active on behalf of business, the government remained laissez-faire in regard to the needs of the common people, giving little attention to poverty, unemployment, unsafe work conditions, child labor, and the spoliation of natural resources.

---

13. Morton Horowitz, *The Transformation of American Law 1780–1860* (Cambridge, Mass.: Harvard University Press, 1977).

14. Josephson, *The Robber Barons*, p. 395.

15. Ibid., p. 52.

Despite the largely one-sided role played by government, democratic struggle persisted throughout the nineteenth century. A women's suffrage movement gathered strength. Labor unions repeatedly regrouped their shattered ranks to fight pitched battles against the industrial moguls. One important victory that came with the Civil War was the defeat of the Southern slavocracy and the abolition of slavery. The Reconstruction period that followed was one of the few times the power of the federal government— backed by troops and the participation of poor Whites and former slaves organized into leagues and self-defense militias—was used to decree equal rights, enfranchisement for all males, popular assemblies, fairer taxes, schools for the poor, and some very limited land reform. But once the Northern capitalists put an end to Reconstruction and allied themselves with the Southern oligarchs, better to face their struggles against labor and western farmers, most of the democratic gains in the former Confederate states were rolled back, not to be regained until well into the next century—if then.[16]

THE NOT-SO-PROGRESSIVE ERA

In the twentieth century, as in the centuries before, people of wealth looked to the central government to do for them what they could not do for themselves: repress democratic forces, limit economic competition, and in other ways bolster the process of capital accumulation. In 1900, price competition with smaller companies was vigorous enough to cut into the profits of major firms.[17] Unable to regulate prices, expand profits, and free themselves from the "vexatious" reformist laws of state and local governments, big business began demanding action by the national government. As the utilities magnate Samuel Insull said, it was better to "help shape the right kind of regulation than to have the wrong kind forced upon [us]."[18] During the 1900–1916 period, known as the Progressive Era, federal price and market regulations in meat packing, food and drugs, banking, timber, and mining were initiated at the insistence of the strongest companies within these industries. The overall effect was to raise profits for the larger producers, tighten their control over markets, and weed out smaller competitors.

The individuals who occupied the presidency during the Progressive Era were faithful collaborators of big business. Teddy Roosevelt, for one,

---

16. James S. Allen, *Reconstruction: The Battle for Democracy, 1865–1876* (New York: International Publishers, 1937); Eric Foner, *Reconstruction* (New York: Harper & Row, 1988).

17. Gabriel Kolko, *The Triumph of Conservatism* (Chicago: Quadrangle, 1967), chapters 1 and 2.

18. James Weinstein, *The Corporate Ideal in the Liberal State* (Boston: Beacon Press, 1968), p. 87.

was hailed as a "trust-buster" because of his occasional verbal attacks against the "malefactors of great wealth," yet his major proposals reflected corporate desires. He was hostile toward unionists and reformers, derisively dubbing the latter "muckrakers," and enjoyed close relations with business magnates, inviting them into his administration. Similarly, neither William Howard Taft nor Woodrow Wilson, the other two White House occupants of that period, saw any "fundamental conflict between their political goals and those of business."[19] Wilson railed against corrupt political machines and big trusts, but his campaign funds came from a few rich contributors, and he worked closely with associates of Morgan and Rockefeller, showing himself as responsive to business as any Republican. "Progressivism was not the triumph of small business over the trusts, as has often been suggested, but the victory of big businesses in achieving the rationalization of the economy that only the federal government could provide."[20]

The period is called the Progressive Era because of the much publicized but largely ineffectual legislation to control monopolies; the Sixteenth Amendment, which allowed for a graduated income tax; the Seventeenth Amendment, which provided for the direct popular election of United States Senators; and such dubious electoral reforms as the long ballot and the nonpartisan election. By 1915, many states had passed laws limiting the length of the workday and providing worker's compensation for industrial accidents. Several states had passed minimum wage laws and thirty-eight states had enacted child labor laws restricting the age children could be employed and the hours they could work. In a few industries, workers won an eight-hour day and time-and-a-half overtime pay.[21]

These enactments represented longstanding demands by American workers, in some cases going back over a century. They were wrested from a fiercely resistant owning class by democratic forces after bitter and sometimes bloody struggle. Even with these victories, the conditions of labor remained far from good. The American workers' "real wages—that is, their ability to buy back the goods and services they produced—were lower in 1914 than during the 1890s."[22] Millions worked 12- and 14-hour days, usually six or seven days a week, and 2 million children, according to government figures, were still forced to work in order to supplement the family income. As is the case today, much of the reform legislation went unenforced.

World War I brought industry and government even closer. Sectors of the economy were converted to war production along lines proposed by

---

19. Kolko, *The Triumph of Conservatism*, p. 281.
20. Ibid., pp. 283–284; also Frank Harris Blighton, *Woodrow Wilson and Co.* (New York: Fox Printing House, 1916).
21. Boyer and Morais, *Labor's Untold Story*, p. 180.
22. Ibid., p. 181.

business leaders—many of whom now headed government agencies in charge of defense mobilization.[23] As of 1916, millions worked for wages that could not adequately feed a family. Each year 35,000 were killed on the job, mostly because of unsafe work conditions, while 700,000 suffered injury, illness, blindness, and other work-related disabilities.[24] The war helped quell class conflict at home by focusing people's attention on the menace of the "barbarian Huns" of Germany, who supposedly threatened Anglo-American civilization. Americans were exhorted to make sacrifices for the war effort. Strikes were now treated as seditious interference with war production. Federal troops raided and ransacked IWW (Industrial Workers of the World) headquarters and imprisoned large numbers of workers suspected of socialist sympathies.

During the postwar "Red scare" of 1919–21, executive state power continued to violate individual rights by suppressing radical publications, issuing injunctions against strikes, and violently mistreating strikers. Radical dissidents endured mass arrests, deportations, political trials, and congressional investigations. All these repressive measures were designed to suppress labor unrest and anticapitalist ideas. The public was treated to lurid stories of how the Russian Communists ("Bolsheviks") were about to invade the United States, and how they were murdering anyone in their own country who could read or write or who wore a white collar.[25] The capitalist leaders of the world greeted the Russian Revolution of 1917 as a nightmare come true: the workers and peasants had overthrown not only the autocratic Czar but the capitalist class that owned the factories, mineral resources, and most of the lands of the Czarist empire. As Secretary of State Robert Lansing noted, this revolution was a bad example to the common people in other nations, including the United States.[26] Along with England, France, and eleven other capitalist nations, the United States invaded Soviet Russia in 1917 in a bloody but unsuccessful three-year attempt to overthrow the revolutionary government.

The "Jazz Age " of the 1920s (the "roaring twenties") was supposedly a prosperous era. Stock speculations and other get-rich-quick schemes abounded. Not since the Gilded Age of the robber barons in the 1890s had the more vulgar manifestations of capitalist culture enjoyed such an un-

---

23. Paul Koistinen, "The 'Industrial-Military Complex' in Historical Perspective," *Journal of American History*, 56, March 1970, reprinted in Irwin Unger (ed.), *Beyond Liberalism* (Waltham, Mass.: Xerox College Publishing, 1971), pp. 228–229.

24. Boyer and Morais, *Labor's Untold Story*, p. 184 and passim.

25. Preston, *Aliens and Dissenters,* passim; Robert Murray, *Red Scare* (New York: McGraw-Hill, 1955), pp. 95–98; Christopher May, *In the Name of War* (Cambridge, Mass.: Harvard University Press, 1989).

26. William Appleman Williams, "American Intervention in Russia: 1917–1920," in David Horowitz (ed.), *Containment and Revolution* (Boston: Beacon Press, 1967), p. 38.

critical reception. But the bulk of the population still suffered severe want. In 1928, Congressman Fiorello La Guardia reported on his tour of the poorer districts of New York: "I confess I was not prepared for what I actually saw. It seemed almost incredible that such conditions of poverty could really exist."[27] According to one study, in the late 1920s almost 60 percent of U.S. families did not receive enough income to provide for basic necessities.[28] On top of this, the stock market crash of 1929 signaled a major collapse of productive forces, issuing in the Great Depression.

THE NEW DEAL: HARD TIMES AND TOUGH REFORMS

The Great Depression of the 1930s brought an increase in hunger, destitution, and unemployment. Those lucky enough to have jobs faced a worsening of already poor working conditions:

> Speed-up, reduced work hours, reduced salaries, the firing of high-salaried employees and the employing of those willing to work for much less, exposure to deteriorated and dangerous machinery and a general reduction of safety standards, thought and speech control so intense in some plants that workers never spoke except to ask or give instructions, inability to question deductions from paychecks, beatings by strikebreaking Pinkertons and thugs, and compelled acquiescence to the searches of their homes by company men looking for stolen articles.[29]

Speaking of the depression, banker Frank Vanderlip admitted: "Capital kept too much and labor did not have enough to buy its share of things."[30] Such candor was not characteristic of most members of the plutocracy, who treated economic misery as if it were a natural disaster, a product of "hard times." Others blamed the depression on its victims. Millionaire Henry Ford said the crisis came because "the average man won't really do a day's work. . . . There is plenty of work to do if people would do it." A few weeks later Ford laid off 75,000 workers.[31]

---

27. Zinn, *A People's History*, p. 376.
28. Boyer and Morais, *Labor's Untold Story*, p. 237, citing a Brookings Institution study.
29. Charles Eckert, "Shirley Temple and the House of Rockefeller," in Donald Lazare (ed.), *American Media and Mass Culture* (Berkeley: University of California Press, 1987), p. 174.
30. Boyer and Morais, *Labor's Untold Story*, p. 249. Senator Hugo Black (D-Ala.) observed in 1932: "Labor has been underpaid and capital overpaid. This is one of the chief contributing causes of the present depression. We need a return of purchasing power. You cannot starve men employed in industry and depend upon them to purchase": Rhonda Levine, *Class Struggle and the New Deal* (Lawrence: University Press of Kansas, 1988), p. 70.
31. Zinn, *A People's History*, p. 378.

With a third of the nation ill-fed, ill-clothed, and ill-housed, and at least another third just managing to get by, a torrent of strikes swept the nation, involving hundreds of thousands of workers. Between 1936 and 1940, the newly formed Congress of Industrial Organizations (CIO) organized millions of workers and won significant gains in wages and work conditions. These victories were achieved only after protracted struggles in which many thousands went on strike, demonstrated, or occupied factories in sitdowns; thousands were locked out, fired, blacklisted, beaten, and arrested; and hundreds were wounded or killed by police, soldiers, and company thugs.[32] The gains were real but they came at a high cost.

The first two terms of President Franklin D. Roosevelt's administration have been called the New Deal, an era commonly believed to have brought great transformations on behalf of "the forgotten man." Actually, the New Deal's central dedication was to business recovery rather than social reform. First came the National Recovery Administration (NRA), which set up "code authorities," usually composed of the leading corporate representatives in each industry, to restrict production and set minimum price requirements—with results that were more beneficial to big corporations than to smaller competitors.[33] In attempting to spur production, the government funneled large sums from the public treasury into the hands of the moneyed few. In nine years the Reconstruction Finance Corporation alone lent $15 billion to big business.

The federal housing program stimulated private construction, with subsidies to construction firms and protection for mortgage bankers through the loan insurance program—all of little benefit to the many millions of ill-housed. Likewise, the New Deal's efforts in agriculture primarily benefited the large producers through a series of price supports and production cutbacks, while many tenant farmers and sharecroppers were evicted when federal acreage rental programs took land out of cultivation.[34]

Faced with mass unrest, the federal government created a relief program that eased some of the privation and—more importantly from the perspective of business—limited the instances of violent protest and radicalization. But as the New Deal moved toward measures that threatened to compete with private enterprises and undermine low wage structures, business withdrew its support and became openly hostile. While infuriating

32. Irving Bernstein, *Turbulent Years, A History of the American Worker 1933–1941* (Boston: Houghton Mifflin, 1970); Boyer and Morais, *Labor's Untold Story,* passim.

33. Barton Bernstein, "The New Deal," in Barton Bernstein (ed.), *Toward a New Past* (New York: Pantheon, 1963), p. 269; Levine, *Class Struggle and the New Deal,* p. 3 and chapter 4.

34. Frances Fox Piven and Richard Cloward, *Regulating the Poor* (New York: Pantheon, 1971), p. 76; also Bernstein, "The New Deal," pp. 269–270.

"We're out of soup, but you'll be glad to hear that our city balanced its budget."

New Masses
May 29, 1934

Roosevelt, who saw himself as trying to rescue the capitalist system, business opposition enhanced his reformist image in the public mind.

The disparity between the New Deal's popular image and its actual accomplishments remains one of the unappreciated aspects of the Roosevelt era. To cite specifics: the Civilian Conservation Corps provided jobs at subsistence wages for 250,000 out of 15 million unemployed persons. At its peak, the Works Progress Administration (WPA) employed almost nine million people but often with work of unstable duration and wages below the already inadequate ones of private industry. Of 12 million workers who were earning less than forty cents an hour, only about a half-million were reached by the minimum wage law. The Social Security Act of 1935 covered but half the population and provided no medical insurance and no protection against illness before retirement. Similarly, old-age and unemployment insurance applied solely to those who had enjoyed sustained employment in select occupations. Implementation was left to the states, which were free to set whatever restrictive conditions they chose. Welfare programs were regressively funded through payroll deductions and sales taxes.[35]

Government programs were markedly inadequate for the needs of the destitute, but they achieved a high visibility and did much to dilute public discontent. Once the threat of political unrest subsided, federal relief was drastically slashed, as in 1936–37, reducing many families to a destitution worse than any they had known since the 1929 crash. "Large numbers of people were put off the rolls and thrust into a labor market still glutted with unemployed. But with stability restored, the continued suffering of these millions had little political force."[36]

The Roosevelt administration's tax policies provide another instance of the disparity between image and performance. New Deal taxation was virtually a continuation of the Hoover administration's program, with its generous loopholes for business. When taxes were increased to pay for military spending in World War II, the major burden was taken up by those of more modest means, who had never before been subjected to income taxes. "Thus, the ironic fact is that the extension of the income tax to middle- and low-income classes was the only original aspect of the New Deal tax policy."[37]

All this is not to deny that, in response to enormous popular agitation and the threat of widespread radicalization, the Roosevelt administration produced real democratic gains, including some long overdue social welfare legislation, a number of worthwhile conservation and public-works projects, a rural electrification program for many impoverished areas, a reduction in unemployment from 25 to 19 percent, a program to finance middle-class home buyers, and a Federal Deposit Insurance statute to protect small bank savings.

Before the 1930s, workers who were fired for organizing unions or going on strike had no legal recourse. Unions were readily destroyed by court injunctions, heavy fines, and violent repression. "In all too many cases, employers with their private police forces (or public ones that followed their directives) would arrest, beat, and murder militant workers with impunity."[38] The New Deal produced a series of laws to strengthen labor's ability to organize and bargain collectively. The Norris-La Guardia Act greatly lim-

---

35. Piven and Cloward, *Regulating the Poor*, chapters 2 and 3; Paul Conkin, *The New Deal* (New York: Crowell, 1967).

36. Piven and Cloward, *Regulating the Poor*, p. 46.

37. Gabriel Kolko, *Wealth and Power in America* (New York: Praeger, 1962), p. 31; also Conkin, *The New Deal*, p. 67.

38. Michael Goldfield, "Worker Insurgency, Radical Organization, and New Deal Labor Legislation," *American Political Science Review*, 83, December 1989, p. 1258. For evidence of this repression, see Art Preis, *Labor's Giant Step* (New York: Pioneer, 1964); Roger Keeran, *The Communist Party and the Auto Workers' Union* (New York: International Publishers, 1981); Boyer and Morais, *Labor's Untold Story*.

ited the use of injunctions and made unenforceable the hated yellow-dog contract (which forced workers to swear they would never join a union). Other legislation banned management-controlled company unions. Probably the most important New Deal legislation was the National Labor Relations Act (1935), which set up the National Labor Relations Board (NLRB) with broad powers to oversee the certification of unions and penalize employers who violated the organizing rights of workers. Such legislation was both a response and a stimulus to labor's growing organization and militancy.[39]

Yet the New Deal era hardly adds up to a triumph for the people. They were ready to go a lot further than Roosevelt did, and probably would have accepted a nationalized banking system, a less begrudging and more massive job program, and a national health-care system. Of the New Deal's "three Rs"—relief, recovery, and reform—it can be said that *relief* was markedly insufficient for meeting the suffering of the times and, in any case, was rather harshly curtailed after the 1936 electoral victory; *recovery* focused on business and achieved little until the advent of war spending; and *reform*, of the kind that might have ended the maldistribution and class abuses of the capitalist political economy, was attempted in only a few important ways.

In regard to school desegregation, open housing, fair employment practices, voting rights for Blacks, and antilynch laws, the New Deal did nothing. Blacks were excluded from jobs in the Civilian Conservation Corps, received less than their proportional share of public assistance, and under the NRA were frequently paid wages below the legal minimum.[40] By 1940, the last year of peace, unemployment and poverty continued as major problems.

> The New Deal failed to solve the problem of depression, it failed to raise the impoverished, it failed to redistribute income, it failed to extend equality and generally countenanced racial discrimination and segregation. It failed generally to make business more responsible to the social welfare or to threaten business's pre-eminent political power. In this sense, the New Deal, despite the shifts in tone and spirit from the earlier decade, was profoundly conservative and continuous with the 1920s.[41]

Only by entering the war and *remaining thereafter on a permanent war economy* was the United States able to maintain a shaky "prosperity" and significantly lower the Depression era unemployment.

In sum, it is commonly taught that the United States government has been a neutral arbiter presiding over an American polity free of the class

---

39. Goldfield, "Worker Insurgency, Radical Organization . . ." p. 1258.
40. Bernstein, "The New Deal . . ." pp. 278–279.
41. Ibid., pp. 264–265.

antagonisms that beset other societies. The truth is, our history has been marked by intense and often violent class struggles, and government has played a partisan, repressive role in these conflicts, mostly on the side of the business interests. When divisions have arisen *within* the business class, as between large and small competitors, not surprisingly, government usually has resolved matters to the satisfaction of the more powerful.

Government's growing involvement in economic affairs was not at the contrivance of meddling Washington bureaucrats, but was a response to the increasing concentration of production and wealth. Along with the many small labor conflicts, handled by local government, there developed large-scale class struggle—which had to be contained by a large state. The centralization and growth of the powers of the federal government, a process initiated by the framers of the Constitution to secure the class interests of property, continued at an accelerated pace through the nineteenth and twentieth centuries. Government provided the regulations, protections, subsidies, and services that business could not provide for itself. The corporate society needed a corporate state.

While the populace won formal rights to participate as voters, the state with its judges, courts, police, army, and officialdom remained mostly at the disposal of the wealthy class. The law was rewritten and reinterpreted to better serve capital and limit the ability of labor to fight back. However, working people were not without resources of their own, specifically the ability to disrupt and threaten the process of capital accumulation by withholding their labor through strikes, and by engaging in other acts of protest and resistance. Such agitation wrested concessions from the owning class and the state, including rural electrification, the minimum-wage law, the eight-hour workday, the right to organize unions, Social Security, unemployment compensation, and restrictions on child labor. These victories fell far short of any all-out attack on capitalism but they represented important democratic gains for working people.

6

Politics: Who Gets What?

With the advent of World War II, business and government became ever more entwined. Occupying top government posts, business leaders were able to set the terms of war production. They froze wages and allowed profits to soar.[1] The big corporations picked up the lion's share of war contracts, accelerating the trend toward still greater capital concentration. The war demonstrated that the government's immense power to borrow, tax, and spend could be used to sustain demand and avoid the kind of breakdown in the business system experienced during the Great Depression.

From the 1950s to today, successive Democratic and Republican administrations have dedicated themselves to underpinning the corporate system by (a) offering an array of subsidies and services to business, (b) imposing a taxation system that shifted costs and diseconomies onto the general public, and (c) launching military spending programs that transformed the United States into a permanent war economy. Rather than a laissez-faire government that does little, we have a corporate state that plays an increasingly active role in sustaining the process of capital accumulation.

WELFARE FOR THE RICH

In the 1950s, the Eisenhower administration sought to undo what conservatives called the "creeping socialism" of the New Deal by handing over to private corporations some $50 billion worth of offshore oil reserves,

---

1. Richard Boyer and Herbert Morais, *Labor's Untold Story* (New York: United Electrical, Radio and Machine Workers, 1972), pp. 331–332, 339.

government-owned synthetic rubber factories, public lands, and public power and atomic installations.² The federal government built a multibillion dollar interstate highway system that provided the infrastructure for the trucking and automotive industries and a national network of urban airports and air traffic control systems that subsidized the operational costs of the airline industry.³

The pattern of using the public's money to bolster the profits of private enterprise continues to this day. The federal government leases or sells—at a mere fraction of market value—billions of dollars worth of oil, coal, mineral reserves, and grazing and timber lands.⁴ In any given year, the government hands out billions to big business in tax exclusions, tax credits, price supports, loan guarantees, payments in kind, export subsidies, subsidized insurance rates, marketing services, irrigation and reclamation programs, and research and development grants.⁵ The government pays out billions of dollars in unnecessarily high interest rates, permits public funds to remain on deposit in banks without collecting interest, tolerates overcharging by firms with whom it does business, and provides long-term credits, tariff protections, and reduced tax assessments to large companies.

Over $26 billion a year in federal crop subsidies benefit mostly agribusiness and affluent farmers, with relatively little going to small producers.⁶ The government directly subsidizes the railroad, airline, and shipping

---

2. Ibid. The $50 billion value would be about $200 billion today.

3. The aircraft industry itself was built almost entirely by federal funds. Of the $3.7 billion invested in expansion from 1940 to 1944, private industry provided only $293 million; federal support amounted to $3.4 billion, or 92 percent of the total: Frank Kofsky, *Harry S Truman and the War Scare of 1948* (New York: St. Martin's Press, 1994).

4. As of 1993, the federal government was losing up to $52 million a year by charging ranchers below-cost grazing rates on public lands. At least $97 billion in public subsidies have gone to the nuclear industry and another $76 billion worth of federally funded research and development has passed straight into corporate hands without the government collecting a cent in royalties on sales. Under the Mining Act of 1872, companies mine valuable minerals and metals from federal lands without paying royalties. One company is mining a gold deposit in Nevada with an estimated value of over $7 billion without paying a royalty fee, and with a right under the law to purchase the land for $5 an acre. The U.S. Forest Service continues to open national forests to timber companies—at below the cost of running the program—for an average yearly governmental loss of $31.1 million. See *Washington Post,* January 12, 1990 and April 30, 1992; Jonathan Dushoff, "Gold Plated Giveaways," *Multinational Monitor,* January/February 1993, pp. 16–20; Randal O'Toole, "Last Stand—Selling Out the National Forests," ibid., pp. 25–29.

5. Congressional Budget Office, *Federal Support of U.S. Business* (Washington, D.C.: Government Printing Office, 1984); Chris Lewis, "Public Assets, Private Profits," *Multinational Monitor,* January/February 1993, pp. 8–11; *New York Times,* February 26 and November 17, 1985. Likewise, state and local governments provide business with low-interest loans, tax-free investment opportunities, special zoning privileges, below-market land sales, and other such favors.

6. The General Accounting Office (GAO) estimates that farmers and agriculture investors, who use legal loopholes to circumvent subsidy limits, collect more than $2 billion in un-

industries, and exporters of iron, steel, textiles, tobacco, paper, and other products. Energy companies have received huge amounts in grants and tax "incentives" to encourage oil exploration.[7] Billions of dollars go to bail out such giant companies as Chrysler and Lockheed, while small businesses are left to sink or swim on their own. When one of the nation's largest banks, Continental Illinois, was on the brink of failure, it received $7.5 billion in federal aid. Another $8 billion went to the International Monetary Fund to offset the losses incurred by U.S. banks in bad loans to Third World nations.[8]

Under corporate-state capitalism the ordinary citizen pays twice for most things: first, as a taxpayer who provides the subsidies and supports, then as a consumer who buys the high-priced commodities and services. Whole new technologies are developed at public expense—nuclear energy, electronics, aeronautics, space communications, mineral exploration, computer systems, biomedical genetics, and others—only to be handed over to industry for private gain. Thus, AT&T managed to have the entire satellite communications system put under its control in 1962 after U.S. taxpayers had put up the initial $20 billion to develop it.[9]

The U.S. government, through its Agency of International Development (AID), spent $1 billion in taxpayer money over the past decade to help U.S. companies move U.S. jobs to cheaper labor markets abroad. AID provided low-interest loans, tax exemptions, travel and training funds, ad-

---

justified farm program payments. In one year, big producers in feed grain and wheat collected $4.45 billion in federal subsidies; cotton, $675 million; rice, $475 million; and dairy, $677 million. Other big subsides go to wool, honey, tobacco, and peanut producers. In one year, the California wine industry received $175 million in federal subsidies, with Gallo, the largest and wealthiest wine producer, raking in over $5 million. See *Washington Post,* April 2, 1987, July 16 and August 2, 1990; *San Francisco Chronicle,* November 16, 1992.

7. Congressional Budget Office, *Federal Support of Business.* Several major petroleum companies leased acreage in Alaska for oil exploration, paying $900 million for lands that were expected to yield $50 *billion:* Barry Weisburg, "Ecology of Oil," in Editors of *Ramparts* (eds.), *Eco-Catastrophe* (San Francisco: Canfield Press, 1970), pp. 107, 109.

8. *New York Times,* May 18, 1984. David Yallop, *In God's Name* (New York: Bantam Books, 1984), pp. 15–55, 169–170, reports that Franklin Bank senior executives were eventually arrested and charged with conspiring to misapply funds in foreign speculations. Probably the most outrageous case of compensation involved Du Pont, Ford, GM, and ITT. During World War II, these firms owned factories in Germany that produced tanks, bombers, and synthetic fuels for the Nazi war machine. After the war, rather than being prosecuted for aiding and abetting the enemy, ITT collected $27 million from the U.S. government for war damages inflicted on its German plants by Allied bombings. General Motors received over $33 million for damages to its enemy war plants: Charles Higham, *Trading with the Enemy* (New York: Dell, 1983).

9. *Z Magazine,* July/August 1992, pp. 18–19; Leonard Minsky and David Noble, "Corporate Takeover on Campus," *Nation,* October 30, 1989, pp. 477, 494–495. On the AT&T deal, see Steve Babson and Nancy Brigham, "Why Do We Spend So Much Money?" *Liberation,* September/October 1973, p. 19.

vertising, and blacklists to weed out union sympathizers and organizers in the various countries.[10]

In the late 1980s and early 1990s, the government poured over $500 billion into bailing out the savings and loan (S&L) associations. Under the deregulated thrift market adopted during the Reagan years, S&Ls could take any investment risk they wanted with depositors' money, often at great profit to themselves, with the understanding that failures and bad debts

10. *Paying to Lose Our Jobs,* report by the National Labor Committee Education Fund, September 1992; also Jonathan Tasini, "The Great American Job Giveaway," *Union* (publication of Service Employees International Union) Winter 1993, pp. 20–24. In October 1992 Congress passed an act prohibiting use of U.S. monies to assist businesses in relocating abroad. It remains to be seen how well enforced the law will be.

would be picked up by the government. In many instances, thrift industry heads funneled deposits directly into family accounts, executive salaries, or fraudulent deals—sometimes involving organized crime and the CIA. When hundreds of thrifts failed, the government had to compensate depositors, 90 percent of whom held accounts of $100,000 or more. The Federal Savings and Loan Corporation (FSLC) issued promissory notes to new investors who took over the failed S&Ls. Without Congress's approval, the FSLC guaranteed the principal and interest on all loans, including many that had been written off as worthless, in what amounted to the biggest bailout and financial scandal in human history. The people who have benefited the least from deregulation are the ones most burdened by the S&L cleanup, the ordinary taxpayers.[11]

The corporate state strives for optimal investment conditions at home and abroad. The General Agreement on Tariffs and Trade (GATT) facilitates international investment—mostly in ways desired by the multinational corporations—undermining environmental and consumer protections and labor standards. So with the North American Free Trade Agreement (NAFTA), which gives a free hand to big corporations in Canada, Mexico, and the United States, in effect enabling multinational capital to invest where wages are at their lowest, while paying little or no taxes, and undermining labor gains and health, safety, consumer, and environmental protections.[12]

In sum, free-market advocates, who constantly admonish the poor to lift themselves by their own bootstraps, are the first to turn to the government for handouts, bailouts, special services, and privileged protections.

TAXES: HELPING THE RICH IN THEIR TIME OF GREED

The capitalist state uses taxation as well as public spending to redistribute income in an upward direction. Taking into account all taxes on sales, services, and income at the federal, state, and local levels, as well as Social Security payments, we find that lower-income people pay a higher percentage of their earnings than do upper-income people, while generally getting much less in return.[13]

---

11. Peter Brewton, *The Mafia, CIA & George Bush* (New York: Shapolsky, 1992); *New York Times*, August 13, 1989; *Washington Post*, September 2, 1988 and May 27, 1990. For more on the S&L scandal, see chapter 8.

12. Charles Lewis and Margaret Ebrahim, "Can Mexico and Big Business USA Buy NAFTA?" *Nation*, June 14, 1993, pp. 826–839; John Cavanagh, "We Will Regret a Rush to Free Trade," *New York Times*, October 6, 1991; Daniel Brook, "Toxic Trade," *Z Magazine*, September 1992, pp. 55–58.

13. *Washington Post*, February 18, 1990. The wealthiest 3 percent of the population earn 33 percent of income (as reported) but pay only 15 percent of taxes. The rest of us together

Over the last decade the trend has worsened. The wealthiest 1 percent increased their income by 85.4 percent, while paying 23.2 percent less in taxes. In 1992 alone, they raked in more than $71 billion from tax breaks. The rich have grown richer, but their tax rate has declined. The poor have grown poorer, but their taxes have increased. Income from property ownership (dividends, interest, rents) has risen three times faster than income from work—and the inequality is greater after taxes than before.[14]

The proportion of federal revenues coming from corporate taxes has dropped dramatically from 50 percent in 1945 to 8 percent by 1994. The resultant revenue loss was made up for by an increase in taxes on middle and working-class earnings and greater government borrowing. In 1983, a working mother with three children and a salary of $10,500 paid more federal taxes than Boeing, General Electric, Du Pont, Texaco, Mobil, and AT&T combined. These companies paid nothing, though they enjoyed combined profits of $13.7 billion. After the Tax Reform Act of 1986, which was supposed to abolish such corporate freeloading, sixteen major firms, including General Motors, IBM, Hewlett-Packard, and Greyhound, still paid no taxes—despite combined profits of $9.6 billion. Instead, they received tax rebates totaling $1.1 billion.[15]

Not without cause did the multimillionaire Leona Helmsley say, "We don't pay taxes. Only the little people pay taxes."[16] The federal tax code is written to allow the wealthiest interests to enjoy lightly taxed or tax-free income, including tax-free bonds and tailor-made write-offs and exclusions.[17] Companies can deduct for production costs, wages, marketing ex-

---

earn only 67 percent of the nation's income but pay 85 percent of the taxes: Citizens for Tax Justice report summarized in *People's Weekly World,* April 13, 1991.

14. The Chairman's Report: Joint Economic Committee of the Congress, Washington, D.C., December 28, 1989; U.S. House of Representatives, Ways and Means Committee, *Background Material on Federal Budget and Tax Policy for Fiscal Year 1991 and Beyond,* Committee print 101–121, Washington, D.C., February 6, 1990; Lawrence Mishel and Jacqueline Simon, *The State of Working America* (Washington, D.C.: Economic Policy Institute, 1988); *Washington Post,* February 18, 1990; *New York Times,* March 25, 1990; Holly Sklar, "The Truly Greedy," *Z Magazine,* June 1991, pp. 10–12; Report by Citizens for Tax Justice: *Nation,* March 1, 1993.

15. *The Corporate Tax Comeback,* study by Citizens for Tax Justice (Washington, D.C., September 1988); *Washington Post,* May 13, 1985. William Simon, former Secretary of the Treasury under Richard Nixon, paid no federal income taxes in the seven years that his net worth ballooned from $2.5 million to $200 million. Real estate developer and media tycoon Mortimer Zuckerman, with a net worth of $250 million, paid no taxes through most of the 1980s: see Robert Lekachman, "A Mystery Readily Solved," *New Leader,* October 5, 1987, p. 19. In 1991, billionaire presidential contender Ross Perot pocketed $285 million from his investments and paid $15 million in federal taxes, about 6 percent (a lower rate than what a janitor or school teacher is taxed): NBC-TV evening news, October 16, 1992.

16. Quoted in *New York Times,* July 12, 1989.

17. Members of tax-writing committees in Congress often slip obscure provisions into tax legislation to benefit a specific individual or firm: *Washington Post,* June 13, 1989.

penses, advertising, business meals, travel and entertainment, investment incentives, operational losses, bankruptcy, interest payments, and depreciation. American-owned shipping companies incorporated in foreign countries are exempted from U.S. income taxes. By manipulating the prices charged among their own subsidiaries, multinational companies can concentrate profits in countries with lower tax rates and pay almost nothing to the U.S. treasury. Overseas earnings that are not repatriated are tax-exempted. And oil and mineral royalties that firms pay abroad can be treated as tax credits at home.[18]

Every year, over one hundred of the largest private utilities collect taxes on their monthly billings to customers, but by taking advantage of write-offs, they are able to pocket most of what they collect. In addition, some 338,000 companies are illegally pocketing almost $4 billion a year in Social Security and withholding taxes from their employees paychecks. Relatively few of these delinquent firms have been prosecuted.[19]

Tax cuts are supposed to spur new investments, but studies show that firms enjoying reduced taxes actually have cut back on jobs. The rate of investment today, now that the rich pay less taxes, is no better and, if anything, more sluggish than in earlier years because of the decline in consumer buying. The additional billions in tax cuts that the rich won under the Reagan administration, do not go into new investment but into higher dividend payments to stockholders and bigger executive salaries, and into luxury consumption and quick-profit speculation.[20]

Creating a super-rich class does not bring prosperity. Numerous Third World nations have extremely wealthy classes that live lavishly off the backs of the common people. In contrast, social democracies like Sweden and Denmark tax their rich companies and wealthy individuals heavily, enabling their citizens to enjoy a higher and more equitable standard of living than do Americans.

It has been argued that taxing the wealthy more heavily would make no appreciable difference in federal revenue since they are relatively few in number. In fact, if rich individuals and top corporations paid a graduated progressive tax of 70 percent, with no loopholes, shelters, or major deductions, hundreds of billions of dollars would be collected yearly and there

---

18. *The Corporate Tax Comeback*, report by Citizens for Tax Justice; Donald Barlett and James Steele, *American: What Went Wrong?* (Kansas City: Andrews & McMeel, 1992). A tax credit is even better than a tax deduction. A $5,000 deduction means that $5,000 of your income can be treated as nontaxable, saving you $1,550 (at a 31 percent tax rate). But a $5000 tax *credit* means you can subtract that amount from the taxes you have to pay, saving you $5,000. The royalties that Exxon and Mobil give to Saudi Arabia for the oil they extract from that country are treated as a "tax credit," directly subtracted from the taxes the companies might have paid to the U.S. government.

19. *Washington Post*, March 3, 1988.

20. Citizens for Tax Justice report: *Washington Post*, January 28 and May 14, 1985.

would be no federal deficit. Just the deductions that corporations claim for the interest on their business loans costs the government nearly $100 billion a year in lost revenue. In the early 1980s, a 39 percent reduction in the top tax rate, benefiting the richest 1 percent, caused an annual revenue loss of at least $70 billion.[21] These are not trifling sums.

There are several ways people can be taxed. A *progressive* income tax imposes a substantially higher effective tax rate on the rich than the poor. Thus, in 1980 the very richest paid 70 percent in income tax and the poorest only 18 percent.[22] The assumption is that the burden should fall most heavily on those who live the most privileged lives, who have an abundance of surplus funds beyond what is needed for necessities.

A *proportionate* income tax, or "flat tax," imposes the same rate on everyone, regardless of ability to pay. Thus if both rich and poor pay, say, 20 percent of their income, then a person who earns $10,000 pays $2,000 in taxes and has only $8,000 to live on, while one who receives $1 million pays $200,000 but still has $800,000 to spend. Those who advocate a progressive tax consider the flat tax to be unfair, for while everyone is paying the same rate, and the richer person is paying more dollars, the poorer person will have a harder time of it. A dollar taken from someone of modest means has a greater deprivation impact than a dollar taken from the very affluent.

A *regressive* tax is even more unfair than a flat tax, for it imposes a higher effective rate upon those who have the least. Instead of paying the same *rate* as in a flat tax, rich and poor pay the same *amount* in actual dollars as with a sales tax. When both a janitor and a top executive pay the exact same amount of sales tax on a gallon of gas, the janitor is sacrificing a far greater portion of income than the executive. Sales, excise, and Social Security taxes are regressive.

Given the many tax loopholes that have been available to rich persons and corporations, the progressive income tax has proved to be not all that progressive. Under the Reagan administration, the progressive income tax was practically abolished. Today, the federal income tax is close to a flat tax in its rates—and a regressive tax in its effect, because it still allows many write-offs for business and big earners, taking proportionately less from the very rich than from the rest of us.

The unjustly regressive nature of our tax system is even more evident at the state and local levels. In forty-five of fifty states, the poorest 20 percent of the population pay higher state and local taxes than the richest 1 percent.

---

21. *Washington Post,* June 3, 1991. During the Reagan years, inheritance taxes on the wealthiest estates were reduced to almost nothing, causing an average yearly revenue loss of about $5 billion. The sixty-four richest persons in the U.S. are worth $207 billion: *Connections,* June 1993, reprinted in *Gray Panther Newsletter,* July–August 1993, p. 7.

22. The 70 percent tax rate was not quite as severe as it sounds. It did not apply to the entire income. The tax was graduated so that the very rich paid the highest rates only on those portions of their income that went above the middle brackets.

These taxes average 13.8 percent for the poorest quintile and only 7.6 percent for the most affluent quintile. In recent years, numerous states have raised taxes on the general public while cutting taxes for the highest bracket.[23]

Taking all the above into consideration, it is no wonder a retired Internal Revenue Service employee wrote that he and his colleagues were convinced that the nation's tax laws "are largely legalized deceptions that encourage wealthy individuals and corporations to escape with little or no tax payment, while the middle class and the poor pay punitive taxes to make up the deficiency."[24]

DEFICIT SPENDING AND THE NATIONAL DEBT

When government expends more than it collects in revenues, this is known as "deficit spending." To meet its yearly deficits, the government borrows from wealthy individuals and financial institutions in the United States and abroad, borrowing on the future earnings of the U.S. people. The yearly accumulation of these budget deficits is what is known as the national debt.

By 1940, given the deficit spending of the New Deal, the national debt had grown to $43 billion. The cost of World War II brought it to $259 billion. By 1981, it had climbed to $908 billion. Conservative leaders who sing hymns to a balanced budget have been among the wildest deficit spenders. Most notably, the Reagan administration in eight years (1981–88) tripled the national debt to $2.7 trillion. Its successor, the Bush administration, during the next four years brought the debt to $4.5 trillion. In the 1950s, the national debt grew an average of less than $1 billion a year. In 1994, the debt was increasing at a rate of $1 billion every two days. Conservatives usually blame the runaway debt on liberal "tax and spend" Democrats in Congress, who supposedly vote profligate sums for welfare and human services. In fact, during the Reagan-Bush years, Congress's yearly budgets generally were about the same size as the ones proposed by Reagan and Bush.[25] The growth in deficit spending has several causes:

---

23. In Washington State, the tax difference between poor and rich is 17.4 to 3.4 percent; in Texas, 17.1 to 3.1 percent; in South Dakota, 10.8 to 2.2 percent; in Connecticut, 11.9 to 4.2 percent: *A Far Cry from Fair,* report by Citizens for Tax Justice, Washington, D.C., April 1991; *The Sorry State of State Taxes,* report by Citizens for Tax Justice, January 1987; and Alan Finder and Richard Levine, "When Wealthy Pay Less Tax Than the Other Homeowners," *New York Times,* special report, May 29, 1990.

24. Emil Poggi, letter to *New York Times,* September 25, 1988; see also David Burnham, *A Law Unto Itself, the IRS and the Abuse of Power* (New York: Vintage, 1989).

25. The accumulated budget outlays from 1982 to 1993 were $12,699 billions from Congress and $12,692 billions from the White House, not an appreciable difference: Jerome Grossman, "Blame Game," *Nation,* October 26, 1992, p. 457.

First, there are the billions in lost revenue because of tax cuts to wealthy individuals and corporations. The government is now borrowing furiously from the moneyed interests it should be taxing.[26]

Second, in eight years, Reagan spent almost $2.5 trillion on the military, allocations that have had a budget-busting impact.

Third, the national debt itself contributes to debt accumulation, growing at an increasing rate, so that the interest paid on the national debt has been expanding faster than the economy and twice as fast as the budget. Every year, a higher portion of debt payment is for interest alone, with less and less for retirement of the principle. By 1990, over 80 percent of all government borrowing went to pay for interest on money previously borrowed. Thus, the debt becomes its own self-feeding force. The interest paid on the federal debt each year is the second largest item in the discretionary budget (after military spending).[27]

To borrow money, the government sells treasury bonds. These bonds are promissory notes that are repaid in full after a period of years. Who gets the hundreds of billions in yearly interest on these bonds? The individuals, investment firms, banks, and foreign investors with money enough to buy them. Who pays the interest? Ordinary working people who contribute most of the taxes. Interest payments on the federal debt constitute an upward redistribution of wealth from those who work to those who live off personal wealth. Moneyed creditors lend their surplus capital to the U.S. government and watch it grow risk-free at public expense, backed by the "full faith and credit" of the U.S. government, just as the framers of the Constitution intended. We and our children will be paying increasingly larger sums to service this astronomical debt. As Karl Marx wrote, "The only part of the so-called national wealth that actually enters into collective possessions of modern peoples—is their national debt."[28]

Often left unmentioned is the "off-budget" deficit, an accounting gimmick that allows the government to borrow additional billions outside the regular budget. A government-created (but nominally "private") corporation is set up to borrow money in its own name. For instance, monies to subsidize agricultural loans are raised by the Farm Credit System, a network of off-budget banks, instead of being provided by the Agriculture Department through the regular budget. Congress also created an off-budget

---

26. Citizens for Tax Justice, *Inequality and the Federal Budget Deficit*, 1990 edition, Washington, D.C.

27. Lawrence Malkin, *The National Debt* (New York: Henry Holt, 1987); Joe Kahn, "The National Debt," *Economic Notes*, May–June 1985. In 1993, the interest on the national debt came to $210 billion. By the end of this decade, interest payments are likely to climb to at least $350 billion: *San Francisco Chronicle*, February 18, 1993.

28. Karl Marx, *Capital*, vol. 1 (Harmondsworth, Middlesex, England: Penguin Books, 1976), p. 919.

agency known as the Financing Corporation to borrow the hundreds of billions needed for the savings-and-loan bailout, instead of using the Treasury Department. Sooner or later, these sums have to be paid back by U.S. taxpayers.[29] So the actual yearly deficits are much larger than the publicized figures.

Social Security also is used to disguise the real deficit. The Social Security payroll deduction—a regressive tax—soared during the Reagan years, enough to produce a yearly surplus of over $70 billion by 1990 and it is still growing. By 1991, 38 percent of U.S. taxpayers were paying more in Social Security tax than in federal income tax. Many Americans willingly accept these payroll deductions because they think the monies are being saved for their retirement. In fact, Social Security taxes are used to offset deficits in the regular budget, paying for White House limousines, FBI agents, jet bombers, and corporate subsidies. The Social Security reserve fund of $330 billion (by 1993) exists only on paper; it has already been spent by the government. The fund is nothing but a gigantic bundle of IOUs that will have to be made good by the future earnings of U.S. taxpayers.[30]

Conservatives insist that the deficit can be eliminated by cutting out bureaucracy and "nonessential" spending. But even if the *entire* nondefense apparatus of the federal government were eliminated, the deficit would still approach $190 billion.[31] Both the Clinton administration and its opposition have assiduously ignored the surest remedies for reducing the deficit: (a) sharply reduce individual and corporate tax credits and deductions, (b) reintroduce a progressive income tax that would impose appropriately high rates on high incomes; and (c) greatly reduce the bloated military budget and redirect spending toward more productive and socially useful sectors of the economy.

MILITARY SPENDING: BUTTERING THE GUNS

Military spending is another way to accumulate capital for the few while shifting most of the financial burden onto the many. In the twelve years of the Reagan and Bush administrations (1981–1992), the Department of

29. Robert Samuelson, "Backdoor Government," *Washington Post,* October 12, 1988. Another hidden deficit is in trade. As we consume more than we produce and import and borrow from abroad more than is exported, the U.S. debt to foreign creditors increases. Interest payments on these hundreds of billions borrowed from abroad have to be met by U.S. taxpayers.

30. Henry Aaron, Barry Bosworth, and Gary Burtless, *Can America Afford to Grow Old* (Washington, D.C.: Brookings Institution, 1989); Robert Kuttner, "Stop Raiding Social Security," *Washington Post,* December 26, 1988; *AARP Bulletin,* March 1990, pp. 11–12; Peter Kilborn, "The Temptations of the Social Security Surplus," *New York Times,* November 27, 1988; "Harper's Index," *Harper's Magazine,* February 1991.

31. Senator Ernest Hollings, "The Great Budget Hoax," *Washington Post,* March 11, 1991.

Defense (also known as the Pentagon) spent an astronomical $3.7 trillion. Defense production grew at three times the pace of U.S. industry as a whole.[32] During this period, the United States maintained upwards of a million military personnel and civilian employees and dependents at over 350 major bases and hundreds of minor installations in thirty-five foreign countries, and deployed nearly 4,500 nuclear weapons abroad.[33]

This global military apparatus was supposedly needed to protect us from an increasingly powerful Soviet Union—although evidence indicates that the Soviets were never as strong nor as eager to pursue the arms race as our cold-war policymakers would have had us believe.[34] Despite the collapse of the Soviet Union and other Eastern European communist nations in 1990–91, U.S. military allocations remained at around the $290 billion level for several years. President Clinton's proposed military budget of $277 billion for 1994 was still much higher than the cold-war budgets of the 1970s (even after adjusting for inflation).[35] In his 1994 State of the Union message Clinton announced, "Defense spending will not be cut."

Taking into account veterans benefits, the military's share of federal debt payments, the 60 percent of all federal research and development funds that go to the military, and other overlooked defense expenses picked up by agencies outside the Pentagon, actual annual military spending has averaged over $400 billion in recent years.[36]

Waste and Fraud

The Pentagon procurement program is rife with waste, fraud, and profiteering. President Reagan's own director of the Office of Management and Budget, David Stockman, described the Department of Defense as a "swamp of waste." The Pentagon itself admits it loses or misplaces more

---

32. Center for Defense Information, *The Defense Monitor*, vol. 15, nos. 1 & 2, 1986; Tom Gervasi, *Arsenal of Democracy* (New York: Grove, rev. ed. 1981); Georgi Tsagolov, *War Is Their Business* (Chicago: Progress Publishers, 1985). About 70 percent of federal research and development funds are for military purposes.

33. Center for Defense Information, *The Defense Monitor*, vol. 18, no. 2, 1989.

34. For a detailed discussion of this, see Michael Parenti, *The Sword and the Dollar: Imperialism, Revolution, and the Arms Race* (New York: St. Martin's Press, 1989).

35. "President Clinton and the Military," *Defense Monitor*, vol. 22, no. 2, 1993. Clinton's 1994 budget fails to cancel any of the major new weapons systems begun during the Cold War. Even the Strategic Defense Initiative, the "Star Wars" system of space-based missiles and X-ray lasers, a hairbrained scheme of the Reagan era that consumed nearly $30 billion, was not really abolished so much as renamed and redone as a ground-based antimissile system: *New York Times*, May 14, 1993.

36. Center for Defense Information, *The Defense Monitor*, vol. 20, no. 2, 1991, and vol. 22, no. 2, 1993; *Washington Post*, December 10, 1991. Military research and development funds do not include monies budgeted to the Energy Department, space research, and "general science" that also have military functions.

than $1 billion of weaponry each year. The General Accounting Office (GAO), an investigative arm of Congress, found that the military budget was regularly padded by billions of dollars to ensure against congressional cuts. Corporate contractors have been known to make out duplicate bills to different military agencies, in effect getting paid twice for the same service.[37]

A Senate investigation ascertained that military warehouses were glutted with $30 billion of unneeded supplies and equipment gathering dust or rusting away. Another $50 billion worth of new orders were in the pipeline or waiting to be spent. Military agencies continued to buy items after they had been identified as unneeded. On over a thousand items, the Pentagon has accumulated inventories that will last more than a half-century. In one instance, the U.S. Navy acquired 53,268 duplicates of a certain machine tool needed for F-14 airplanes, a tool with a replacement rate of about four a year, leaving a stock that should last 13,317 years. When it comes to defense, it's important to plan ahead.[38]

The Defense Department is unable to spend its money as fast as it gets it. But this backlog of funds, estimated at $244 billion in 1985, is not a result of thrift, for no one can throw money around like the Pentagon. The following is a small sampling.

Item: the army allocated $1.5 billion to develop a heavy-lift helicopter, even though it already had such helicopters and the navy was building an almost identical one.[39]

Item: the navy built a $30 million pier in Honolulu for the USS *Missouri*—after the battleship and other such ships had been mothballed.[40]

Item: a GAO three-year audit discovered that the air force had understated the costs of fighter and bomber fleets by more than $27 billion, and had bought $18 billion in unneeded equipment, making "unsupported and arbitrary adjustments" to hide mismanagement and fraud.[41]

Item: a review of thirty-nine major projects supervised by the military found serious defects in thirty-two; contractors repeatedly were allowed

---

37. General Accounting Office, *Managing the Cost of Government,* Washington, D.C., October 1989; Harvey Rosenfeld, "Fraudulent Billing Costs," *Public Citizen,* February 1986, p. 20; *New York Times,* September 29, 1985.

38. U.S. Senate Budget Committee, *Department of Defense Spare Parts Management Report,* prepared by Majority Staff, Committee on the Budget, Washington, D.C., February 4, 1990; General Accounting Office, *Financial Integrity Act Report,* Washington, D.C., January 1990; *Los Angeles Times,* February 5, 1990.

39. Kai Bird and Max Holland, "Pentagon Bulimia," *Nation,* June 21, 1986.

40. CBS-TV *Hard Copy* report, May 11, 1993.

41. General Accounting Office, *Financial Management: Billion Dollar Decisions Made Using Inaccurate and Unreliable Air Force Data* (Washington, D.C.: Government Printing Office, February 1990); also Justice Department investigation of overcharging and mismanagement on the B-2 "stealth" bomber: *Washington Post,* July 19, 1990.

to pocket millions of dollars for shoddy work, without having to make repairs.[42]

Item: the air force spent almost $2 billion on electronic equipment that did not work and $1.1 billion to correct flaws on the B-1 bomber and make other costly repairs for shoddy work.[43] Many of the B-1s had to be grounded indefinitely.[44]

Item: the nation's largest military contractors routinely charge the Pentagon hundreds of millions of dollars in unjustified consultation fees.[45]

Item: millions of dollars have been expended improperly on military golf courses, restaurants, and officers' clubs—complete with gold-plated chandeliers, oak paneling, and marble fixtures.[46]

For years the military services have rigged tests and falsified data to make weapons appear more effective than they actually were. Many of the top defense contractors have been under criminal investigation for fraud or other such charges. But most fraud goes unpunished.[47]

Virtually all large military contracts have cost overruns of 100 to 700 percent. The C-5A transport plane had a $4 billion cost overrun (and its wings kept falling off). The navy contracted a San Diego firm to build four advanced supply ships for $863 million but the cost overrun threatens to reach $600 million.[48] Defense contractors pilfer the public purse on small items too. The military paid $511 for light bulbs that cost ninety cents and $640 for toilet seats that cost $12. After paying Boeing Aircraft $5,096 for two pliers, the tough Pentagon procurers renegotiated the price down to $1,496—a real bargain. Five years after the Pentagon set up a Defense Management Review that was supposed to abolish such abuses, the military was paying $1,868 for a toilet cover, $999 for a pair of pliers, and $668,000 for a fax machine.[49]

---

42. *Washington Post,* March 15, 1985.

43. GAO investigation reported in *Washington Post,* July 17, 1990. When the equipment *did* work, it was sometimes with disastrous effect. The Aegis, a high-tech radar system costing $500 million each, consistently performed poorly in every test. Installed aboard a U.S. cruiser, the Aegis mistook an Iranian civilian airliner for a fighter plane, determined that it was descending in an attack when it was actually ascending in a take-off, and shot the plane down, resulting in the death of 290 passengers: *Harper's Magazine,* September 1988, pp. 64–65.

44. Nick Kotz, *Wild Blue Yonder: Money, Politics and the B-1 Bomber* (Princeton, N.J.: Princeton University Press, 1989); *Washington Post,* October 24, 1988.

45. *New York Times,* November 4, 1988.

46. *New York Times,* August 6, 1990.

47. *Washington Post,* March 27, 1987 and August 29, 1990; *San Francisco Chronicle,* June 30, 1993; *Guardian,* July 6, 1988.

48. *San Francisco Chronicle,* June 16, 1992.

49. *New York Times,* November 20, 1983; *Washington Post,* February 24, March 30, and July 11, 1985, and July 13, 1990. The air force ordered 174 of the fax machines for a cost of over $116 million.

There are additional costs to the environment and human life. The armed services use millions of acres of land at home and abroad in bombing runs and maneuvers, causing long-lasting damage to vegetation and wildlife. The military is the single biggest polluter of the environment, contaminating the air, soil, and groundwater with plutonium, tritium, lead, fuel, solvents, lubricants, and other toxic wastes, while creating over 90 percent of our radioactive waste and amassing a stockpile of tens of thousands of tons of lethal chemical and biological agents. There are some 21,000 contaminated sites on military bases and at nuclear weapons plants. In 1990, the military used sixteen million tons of ozone-depleting materials and had 9,600 military specifications calling for ozone-destroying chemicals.[50] In sum, one of the greatest dangers to the security and well-being of the U.S. public and to the planet itself is the U.S. military.

The military is also a danger to its own ranks. Enlisted personnel are regularly killed in firing exercises, practice flights, maneuvers, and other readiness preparations—resulting in an astonishing 20,269 *noncombat* deaths from 1979 to 1988, or 2,027 a year.[51] Tens of thousands of veterans have been sickened or have died from exposure to atomic testing during the 1950s or from toxic herbicides used in the Vietnam War. Growing numbers of Gulf War veterans suffer an array of health disorders due to untested vaccines and exposure to radiation and toxic chemicals.[52]

Wonderful Profits

From the taxpayer's point of view, much of defense spending is wasteful. But for the financial and industrial plutocrats, defense spending is wonderful. First, there are almost no risks. Unlike automobile manufacturers, who must worry about selling the cars they produce, the weapons dealer has a contracted market, complete with cost-overrun guarantees.

---

50. Center for Defense Information, *Defense Monitor,* vol. 18, nos. 3 and 6, 1989 and vol. 20, no. 6, 1991; Martin Calhoun, "Nuclear Weapons Production Poisons the Environment," *Disarmament Times,* June 1991, p. 4; *Ozone: The Hole Story,* PBS-TV special November 9, 1992; Reto Pieth, "Toxic Military," *Nation,* June 8, 1992, p. 773; Seth Shulman, *The Threat at Home: Confronting the Toxic Legacy of the U.S. Military* (Boston: Beacon Press, 1992).

51. Department of Defense, *Worldwide U.S. Military Active Duty Military Personnel Casualties, October 1979 through September 30, 1988,* Directorate for Information Operations and Reports booklet M07.

52. Michael Uhl and Tod Ensign, *GI Guinea Pigs* (New York: Playboy Press, 1980); Tod Ensign, "Guinea Pigs & Disposable GIs," *CovertAction Quarterly,* Winter 1992–1993, pp. 19–28. Those who suffer death and disability in military service are disproportionately working-class Whites and persons of color. During the Vietnam War, certain Army Reserve and National Guard units were reserved for White persons of privileged background like former Vice-President Dan Quayle and some famous professional ballplayers: Adam Hochschild, "Me and Quayle at War," *Washington Post,* August 28, 1988.

Second, the government picks up most of the costs of production, including research technology, buildings, and public lands, making for astronomical profits. Companies like Boeing, Litton, Tenneco, and RCA enjoy a return on their military contracts that is easily two or three times higher than on their nonmilitary investments.[53]

Third, almost all contracts are awarded at about whatever price a corporation sets, ensuring high costs and fat profits.

Fourth, in a capitalist economy the overproduction of consumer products leads to a glutted market and a falling rate of profit. But the arms market provides an area of demand and investment that does not compete with the consumer market and is virtually limitless.

Military spending is preferred by the business community to other forms of federal spending. Government funds invested in public works, schools, scholarships, fire fighting, environmental protection, drug rehabilitation, and other human services expand the nonprofit public sector of the economy and sometimes redistribute income in a way favorable to ordinary citizens, shifting demand away from the private-profit market. But for a business firm, a weapons order is just like an order from a private customer; it pumps public money right back into the private-profit sector, and redistributes income in an upward direction at an unusually high rate of profit.

U.S. leaders acknowledge that the arms budget is dictated in part by the needs of the corporate economy rather than by defense imperatives. Military spending, they say, creates jobs. So do pornography and prostitution, but there are more worthwhile things that might command our labor and resources. In any case, arms spending provides proportionately fewer jobs than any other government expenditure except the space program. One study found that an annual shift of $30 billion from military to urban programs would generate a net yearly gain of 298,000 jobs.[54] A congressional study concluded that shifting funds from the Pentagon to state and local governments could create two new jobs for every one eliminated.[55]

---

53. Richard Kaufman, *The War Profiteers* (Garden City, N.Y.: Doubleday, 1972); James Cypher, "The Basic Economics of 'Rearming America,'" *Monthly Review*, November 1981, pp. 11–27.

54. *A Shift in Military Spending to American Cities* (Washington, D.C.: Employment Research Association/U.S. Conference of Mayors, 1988). In another report, Employment Research Association notes that three out of four congressional districts pays more in taxes to the military than is returned to them in military contracts and wages: *Bankrupting America* (Washington, D.C., 1989). Major cities are also cheated, paying far more in taxes for the Pentagon than they receive in military spending: *New York Times*, May 12, 1992. On the impact that military spending has on agriculture, see the report by James Anderson, *Plowing Under the Farmers* (Washington, D.C.: Employment Research Association, 1986).

55. *San Francisco Examiner*, January 25, 1993. The study was undertaken at the behest of Representative John Conyers (D-MI). Military spending is more capital intensive and less labor intensive than much-needed services at the state and local level.

To get a better idea of how much is spent on the military, keep in mind that total annual expenses of the legislative and judiciary branches and all the regulatory commissions combined constitute little more than one-half of 1 percent of what the Pentagon spends. The $300 million that President Reagan saved by denying aid to 700,000 undernourished infants, children, and pregnant women was equivalent to what the Pentagon spent in ten hours. The cost of only one B-1 bomber is more than the entire budget for the homeless and enough to build 424 new elementary schools. The $114 billion for F-22 fighters could finance the construction of modern mass-transit systems for most of our major cities. What the people of Cleveland spend in a few weeks in taxes to the Pentagon would be enough to wipe out Cleveland's debt and end its financial crisis. The same holds for most other municipalities. Pensions for the top military brass amounts to more than the total costs of federal welfare, the school lunch program, and all other child nutrition expenditures combined.[56]

As the leading beneficiaries of defense spending, the giant corporations propagate the military's cause with campaign contributions, lobbying, and mass advertising—stressing the importance of keeping America on its arms-spending binge. The Department of Defense spends over $2 billion a year on recruitment drives and hundreds of millions more on exhibitions, films, publications, and a flood of press releases that are planted as "news reports" in the media to advance the military's view of a world full of lethal adversaries who threaten our national security. The Pentagon finances military-related research projects in the sciences and social sciences at more than 230 institutions of higher learning, both public and private, religious and secular. In hundreds of conferences and thousands of brochures, articles, and books written by "independent scholars" in the pay of the government, military propaganda is lent an aura of academic objectivity. Casting a shadow on their own professional integrity, such intellectuals transmit to an unsuspecting public the military's agenda and the Pentagon's sense of its own indispensability.[57]

The United States is said to be a constitutional democracy and not a dictatorship, yet it is a military state, the biggest in history. The political

---

56. *Washington Post,* March 21, 1985 and May 28, 1989; Seymour Melman in *New York Times,* April 22, 1985; *San Francisco Chronicle,* July 8, 1992. The bulk of military pensions goes to senior officers "who are comfortably ensconced in the wealthiest one-fifth of our society": *Washington Post,* March 10, 1985. Top military and civilian officials who dine at the Pentagon enjoy a $14 subsidy per meal. The school lunch program for poor children gets by on $1.20 a meal: *Parade,* November 7, 1982.

57. William Fulbright, *The Pentagon Propaganda Machine* (New York: Vintage, 1971); NARMIC report (American Friends Service Committee) in *The Witness,* April 1986; Jonathan Feldman, *Universities in the Business of Repression* (Boston: South End Press, 1989); John Trumpbour, *How Harvard Rules, Reason in the Service of Empire* (Boston: South End Press, 1989).

system of a nation is of less importance in determining its military capacity than is the need to bolster and protect corporate profits at home and abroad.

ECONOMIC IMPERIALISM

In recent decades, U.S. industries and banks have invested heavily in the Third World (Asia, Africa, and Latin America), attracted by the high return that comes with underpaid labor and the near absence of taxes, environmental regulations, and safety and consumer protections. Rather than discouraging the overseas flight of capital and jobs, the U.S. government offers the multinational corporations tax concessions and compensations for losses due to war or confiscation by a foreign government.[58]

U.S. corporate investments do little to improve the lot of Third World people. The multinationals push out local businesses and buy up the best land for cash export crops, leaving less acreage for homegrown foods to feed the indigenous populations. Thus, poor countries support the corporate interests of rich countries, exporting meats, fish, fruits, vegetables, coffee, cocoa, sugar, tin, timber, and a vast array of other products, while their own peoples are increasingly undernourished and ill-housed.[59]

The U.S. government expends over $23 billion yearly on foreign aid and billions more on loans. Most of these funds go directly to cooperative oligarchs in Asia, Africa, and Latin America, enabling them to live in the manner to which they are accustomed and helping them maintain the security forces needed to keep their restive populations in line. Aid money also pays for the infrastructure—ports, highways, security, and the like—needed by private corporate investors. Such U.S. "assistance" comes with strings attached. The recipient nations must give the multinationals tax breaks, guarantee low wages, and make no attempt to protect local businesses. They must make efforts to fully privatize their economies, transferring their publicly owned mines, railroads, and utilities into corporate hands. To qualify for loans, the poor nations usually must agree to cut back on health, education, and food subsidies to their people, consuming less and exporting more in order to earn more and meet the payments on their growing foreign debt.[60]

As corporate investments and government aid in the Third World have grown over the years, so have poverty and destitution. Through much of the

---

58. As a matter of policy, the federal government refuses aid to any country that nationalizes, without compensation, assets owned by U.S. firms.

59. For a fuller exposition of imperialism see Parenti, *The Sword and the Dollar;* also Michael Parenti, *Against Imperialism* (San Francisco: City Lights Press, 1995).

60. Ibid. and the sources cited therein.

Third World, real wages have declined, unemployment is higher than ever, and national debts have soared to the point where debt payments to U.S. financial institutions absorb almost all of the poorer countries' export earnings. Their land, labor, and resource development increasingly are made to fit the profit interests of rich foreign investors rather than the needs of the populace.[61]

To make the world safe for the capitalist global economy, the U.S. government has engaged in a global counterrevolutionary strategy, suppressing insurgent peasant and worker movements and even reformist governments throughout Asia, Africa, and Latin America. But the interests of the big investors never stand naked; rather they are wrapped in the flag and coated with patriotic appearances. Knowing that the American people would never agree to sending their sons and daughters to fight wars in far-off lands in order to protect the profits of Mobil Oil and General Motors, the corporate elites and their political spokespersons play upon popular fears, telling us that our "national security" necessitates U.S. intervention wherever the socioeconomic status quo is threatened.

For decades every popular insurgency against reactionary dictatorships, from Africa to Central America, was depicted as Soviet inspired—as if the indigenous peoples of these countries fought not for their own interests but because the Kremlin commanded them to do so. This view of the world was instrumental in winning ever fatter military budgets at home and further U.S. intervention to protect corporate interests abroad. With the collapse of

---

61. Susan George, *A Fate Worse Than Debt* (New York: Grove Press, 1988); Michael Barratt Brown, *The Economics of Imperialism* (Baltimore: Penguin, 1974).

the Soviet Union and the transformation of communist states into right-wing capitalist countries, U.S. leaders now warn that there are "other" adversaries, who apparently were not perceived a few years before. So the immense military apparatus that was supposedly necessary to protect us against the Soviet threat remains in place only slightly diminished—to continue performing its real function of making the global economy and capitalist world order safe from reform, revolution, or any of the other competing economic demands of dispossessed peoples.

To justify U.S. interventionism in other countries, our policymakers long claimed they were defending democracy from communism. But closer examination shows they have been defending the capitalist world from social change—even if the change be peaceful and democratic. Iran in 1953, Guatemala in 1954, the Dominican Republic in 1962, Brazil in 1964, and Chile and Uruguay in 1973 are cases in point. In all these countries popularly elected governments began instituting progressive changes for the benefit of the destitute classes and began to nationalize or threatened to nationalize U.S. corporate holdings. And in each instance, the United States was instrumental in overthrowing these governments and instituting right-wing regimes that accommodated U.S. investors and ruthlessly repressed the peasants and workers. Similarly, in Greece, the Philippines, Indonesia, East Timor, and at least ten Latin American nations, popular governments were overthrown by military oligarchs—largely trained and financed by the Pentagon and the CIA— who prove themselves friendly to capitalism.[62]

For all their talk about "human rights," U.S. government leaders have propped up regimes throughout the world that have used assassination squads, torture, and terror to support the allies of the corporate world order. In many U.S.-supported states, strikes have been outlawed, unions destroyed, wages cut, and dissidents murdered.[63]

If the U.S. government lost the war in Indochina, it was not for want of trying. Both Democratic and Republican administrations spent $150 billion and more than ten years prosecuting that war, dropping almost 8 million tons of bombs, 18 million gallons of chemical defoliants, and nearly 400,000 tons of napalm. Over 40 percent of Vietnam's plantations and orchards were destroyed by chemical herbicides, as were over 40 percent of its forest lands and much of its fish and sea resources. Several million Vietnamese, Laotians, and Cambodians were killed, maimed, wounded, or left contami-

62. See Stephen Schlesinger and Stephen Kinzer, *Bitter Fruit, The Untold Story of the American Coup in Guatemala* (Garden City, N.Y.: Doubleday, 1982); James Petras and Morris Morely, *The United States and Chile: Imperialism and the Overthrow of the Allende Government* (New York: Monthly Review Press, 1975); Edward Herman, *The Real Terror Network* (Boston: South End Press, 1982).

63. Parenti, *The Sword and the Dollar,* and the studies cited therein.

nated by Agent Orange and other toxic chemicals, and almost 10 million were left homeless. Some 57,000 Americans lost their lives and hundreds of thousands more were wounded or permanently disabled. But the war did bring enormous benefits to a tiny segment of the American population: corporate defense contractors like Du Pont, ITT, and Dow Chemical.[64]

Throughout the 1980s and early 1990s, the United States continued to support bloody interventions against popular reformist governments in Nicaragua, Angola, Mozambique, and East Timor. In Nicaragua, the U.S.-backed mercenary force killed over 30,000 people, orphaned more than 9,000 children and caused over $3 billion destruction of homes, schools, health clinics, crops, and other facilities. In Angola, a war of attrition waged by CIA-backed forces has left 200,000 killed, more than 20,000 children orphaned, and 50,000 seriously maimed—giving Angola the highest amputee rate in the world.[65]

In addition, the United States invaded Grenada to overthrow a revolutionary government and Panama to overthrow a populist reformist government, replacing both with free-market client-state regimes propped up by U.S. bayonets. What Nicaragua, Angola, Mozambique, East Timor, Grenada, and Panama had in common were governments that were redirecting some portion of their countries' labor and resources toward the needs of the people and away from the profitable exploitation of the multinationals. They were developing a different kind of class order, one that ultimately might pose a threat to the capitalist global economy and the existing class order within the United States itself.

Then there was the destructive war waged against Iraq by President George Bush—after that country refused to go along with oil quotas and pricing that was favorable to the giant petroleum companies. In retaliation for the slant drilling of its oil fields by the feudal rulers of Kuwait, Iraqi dictator Saddam Hussein (a former CIA client) invaded Kuwait, providing the excuse needed by Bush to pulverize Iraq, killing an estimated 200,000 people in the process—under the guise of fighting aggression. The war gave Bush a temporary boost in the opinion polls but its effects and the

---

64. William Hoffman, "Vietnam: The Bloody Get-Rich-Quick Business of War," *Gallery,* November 1978, p. 42. Hoffman notes that the top ten military contractors grossed $11.6 billion from the Vietnam War. Also Marvin Gettleman et al. (eds.) *Vietnam and America* (New York: Grove Press, 1985), which despite its sloppy editing contains some pertinent data.

65. Parenti, *The Sword and the Dollar,* chapters 4, 5, 10, and passim; United Church of Christ Commission for Racial Justice, "Why is the U.S. Prolonging War in Angola?" *Washington Post,* October 5, 1989; Reed Brody, *Contra Terror in Nicaragua* (Boston: South End Press, 1985); Holly Sklar, *Washington's War on Nicaragua* (Boston: South End Press, 1985). In Cambodia, the U.S. supported the genocidal, maniacal Khmer Rouge in order to destabilize the socialist-leaning government of that country: Jack Colhoun, "U.S. Supports Khmer Rouge," *CovertAction Information Bulletin,* Summer 1990, pp. 37–40.

subsequent United Nations blockade continued to take a horrendous toll on the Iraqi people.[66]

If we define "imperialism" as that relationship in which one country dominates, through use of economic and military power, the land, labor, resources, finances, and politics of another country, then the United States is the greatest imperialist power in history. The American empire is of a magnitude never before seen, with military bases that ring the entire globe, a nuclear overkill capacity of over 8,000 strategic weapons and 22,000 tactical ones, and a fleet larger in total tonnage and firepower than all the other navies of the world combined, consisting of missile cruisers, nuclear submarines, nuclear aircraft carriers, destroyers, and spy ships, that sail every ocean and make port on every continent.

With only 5 percent of the earth's population, the United States expends one-third of the world's military funds. Since World War II, more than $200 billion in U.S. military aid has been given to some eighty nations. The U.S. has trained and equipped over two million troops and police in foreign lands, the purpose being not to defend these countries from outside invasion but to protect capital investments and the ruling oligarchs from the dangers of domestic insurgency.[67]

This U.S. global expansionism is designed to prevent the emergence of social orders that are revolutionary—or even populist or conservative nationalist (as in Iraq), ones that might utilize their wealth and labor in ways that cut into the profits or challenge the hegemony of a corporate global economic empire. The profits of this empire flow into corporate hands, while the growing costs are largely borne by the American taxpayer and the common people of the various client states. What passes for the "national interest" are policies that favor the interests of a privileged and powerful class, making the world safe for plutocracy at the expense of democracy.

To summarize the main points of this chapter: this ostensibly democratic political system operates mostly for the benefit of those who own the wealth of the nation, at the expense of the working populace at home and abroad. In almost every enterprise, government has provided business with opportunities for private gain at public expense. Government nurtures private capital accumulation through a process of subsidies, supports, and

---

66. Ramsey Clark et al., *War Crimes: A Report on U.S. War Crimes Against Iraq* (Washington, D.C.: Maison Neuve Press, 1992); United Nations, *The Impact of War on Iraq,* Report to the Secretary-General on Humanitarian Needs in Iraq in the Immediate Post-Crisis Environment by a Mission to the Area, March 20, 1991; Joe Stork and Ann Lesch, "Why War?" *Middle East Report,* November/December 1990. Pentagon officials estimate that 200,000 Iraqis may have been killed in the Gulf War: *London Times,* March 3, 1991.

67. Center for Defense Information, "We Arm the World," *Defense Monitor,* vol. 20, no. 3, 1991.

deficit spending and an inequitable taxation system; offers a huge market in the defense industry; and sustains the economic imperialism of the multinational corporations through an often brutal global military apparatus, the costs of which are absorbed by the working public. From ranchers to resort owners, from brokers to bankers, from automakers to missile makers, there prevails a welfarism for the rich of such stupendous magnitude as to make us marvel at the big businessperson's audacity in preaching the virtues of self-reliance whenever lesser forms of public assistance threaten to reach hands other than his or her own.

How to limit and reverse the economic injustice of the corporate state? Some vital steps would be:

1. Do away with the huge subsidies and welfare handouts to rich corporations and agribusinesses.

2. Pass a progressive tax law that also eliminates loopholes and special favors to the wealthy class.

3. Initiate a wealth tax or capital accumulation tax. Even a 1 percent tax on assets, most of which would be paid by the 840,000 super-rich families, would generate $100 billion annually and cut the deficit in half.[68]

4. Drastically cut the bloated and wasteful military budget; stop all nuclear tests and wage a diplomatic offensive for a nuclear-free world.

5. End the costly and murderous interventions into other nations. Stop supporting brutal oligarchs and repressive police states. Allow other countries to develop in accordance with the needs of their own peoples.

6. Embark upon a massive conversion of our war economy to a peace economy, putting the many billions of dollars saved from the military budget into socially useful services such as environmental protection, conservation, housing, transportation, education, urban rehabilitation, and the like.[69]

As we shall see in the chapters ahead, there are reasons why the political system does not produce such policies.

---

68. Arthur Carter, "How About a Capital Accumulation Tax?" *New York Times,* September 23, 1986.

69. Seymour Melman, *The Demilitarized Society: Disarmament and Conversion* (Montreal: Harvest House, 1988); Ann Markusen and Joel Yudken, *Dismantling the Cold War Economy* (New York: Basic Books, 1992).

7

Health, Environment, and Human Services: Sacrificial Lambs

The plutocracy rules but not always in the way it would like. From time to time, those of wealth and power must make concessions to popular resistance, giving a little in order to keep a lot, taking care that the worst abuses of capitalism do not cause people to agitate against the system itself. Concessions thus extracted by the democratic forces of society become the base from which to launch further struggles. The class struggles that brought important gains during the Great Depression of the 1930s did not end there. In the half-century that followed, labor unions, minorities, the poor, environmental groups, peace groups, women's-rights groups, public-interest organizations, and other progressive-minded people continued to press their fight against economic and social injustice. In response to this popular pressure, the federal government initiated a series of human services programs that bettered the lot of many although failing to reach millions, including many of the people most in need. In recent years even these inadequate gains have come under attack.

THE POOR GET LESS (AND LESS)

Government assistance programs often do not reach the neediest constituencies. Thus, in the 1960s, as part of a "war on poverty" $7 billion was invested by federal, state, and local governments in the impoverished Appalachia region, yet the bulk of the poor remained "largely untouched" by a program that was "chiefly a boon for the rich and for the entrenched

99

political interests," the merchants, bankers, coal companies, and contractors.[1] Generally the federal government expends more money in affluent counties than in poor ones. Federal transfer payments such as Social Security, workers' compensation, and unemployment and disability benefits distribute much more money to people earning middle incomes than to those in the lowest brackets.[2]

Federal programs frequently reach only a minority of those in need, as with school lunches, Medicaid (medical payments for the poor), food stamps, subsidized housing, and unemployment benefits.[3] In 1990, the $2.1 billion that went into the Special Supplemental Food Program for Women, Infants, and Children (WIC) assisted only half of those eligible.[4] Worse still, between 1981 and 1991, low-income programs to the needy were subjected to heartless cuts: 14.7 percent from maternal and child health care (after inflation), 69 percent from training and employment programs, and over 94 percent from both rural and urban community service grants.[5] Billions of dollars were eliminated from food stamp programs, college scholarships, legal services for the poor, remedial education, school breakfast programs, and welfare for the aged, blind, and disabled. Programs employing hundreds of thousands of people—mostly women—to staff day-care centers and libraries and offer services to the disabled and aged were entirely abolished.[6] The Reagan administration also cut Supplemental Security Income (SSI), supposedly the "safety net" for low-income aged, blind, or disabled persons. At least 33 percent of those needing SSI are no longer being reached.[7] In its first two years the Clinton administration did relatively little to undo these slashes.

Translated from abstract figures into human experience, the reductions in federal services have meant more hunger and malnutrition; more iso-

1. Officials in the Office of Economic Opportunity, quoted in *New York Times,* November 29, 1970.

2. Gordon Tullock, *Economics of Income Distribution* (Hingham, Mass.: Kluwer, 1983); *New York Times,* May 11, 1992.

3. *New York Times,* November 15, 1988; *People's Weekly World,* December 8, 1990.

4. *New York Times,* May 29, 1990. Studies show that WIC saves lives, prevents illness, and saves money for Medicaid.

5. Reported by Center for Budget and Policy Priorities in *Dollars and Sense,* May 1990, p. 13. *Forbes* (October 1987) announced that the number of billionaires had doubled in the past year. That same month Shasta County, California, closed its entire ten-branch library system for lack of money: *Washington Spectator,* January 1, 1988.

6. *Washington Post,* July 20 and September 26, 1986: Anthony Champagne and Edward Harpham, *The Attack on the Welfare State* (Prospect Heights, Ill.: Waveland Press, 1984). Among the programs abolished were the Comprehensive Employment and Training Administration (CETA) and Volunteers in Service to America (VISTA). Also cut was the Summer Feeding Program that provided meals for one million poor children, who depended on school lunches and went without that midday meal during summers.

7. *New York Times,* March 14, 1985.

lation and unattended illness; more homelessness, and suffering among those with the fewest economic resources and the least political clout.[8]

The picture is no brighter at other levels of government. Municipal, county, and state programs suffer from a multiple squeeze. As the federal government reduced its public assistance programs to the needy, the burden fell more heavily upon the states and cities. Federal grants to states and cities have been slashed by as much as 40 to 60 percent. A prolonged recession has increased the numbers of hardship cases and shrunk the tax base. And state revenues have dropped because of the reduction in upper-income tax rates. In addition, corporations have substantially increased prices for the foods, infant formula, and other commodities and services they sell to states.[9]

Class inequality extends into the field of education. Low-income school districts get far less revenues than well-off ones. Today, cutbacks in federal, state, and municipal funding put the entire public education system at risk. Likewise, aid to higher education tends to favor the elite universities rather than the community colleges and commuter schools that serve more students of modest means. During the fiscal crisis of the early-to-mid 1990s, public institutions of higher education suffered serious budget cuts and fee increases, none more severely than the community colleges—leading to overcrowded classrooms and insufficient course offerings and making it more difficult for low-income persons to get a higher education.[10]

Reductions in human services have been defended as a way of getting "welfare chiselers" off the dole. But of the fourteen million recipients of Aid to Families with Dependent Children (AFDC or "welfare") consisting of five million families or 2.8 persons per family, almost all are single mothers and children with no other means of support. Less than 1 percent are able-bodied men. While there are occasional instances of fraud, AFDC is among the most strictly supervised federal programs. And contrary to conservative myths:

1. Most welfare recipients are White (although poor Blacks and Hispanics are disproportionately represented).
2. Most recipients stay on welfare for not more than two years.

---

8. For some real-life cases, see Theresa Funicello, *Tyranny of Kindness* (New York: Atlantic Monthly Press, 1993); Camille Colatosti, "Governor Shreds Michigan Safety Net," *Guardian*, December 4, 1991, p. 3.

9. On that last point see Gideon Forman, "Cutting WIC," *Nation*, July 9, 1990, p. 57.

10. Jonathan Kozol, *Savage Inequalities* (New York: Crown, 1991); Peter Mathews et al., "Rescue Education," newsletter of Rescue Education, Long Beach Calif., April 1993; *New York Times*, December 26, 1992. Family income is a more decisive determinant of who goes to college than high-school performance. Every year hundreds of thousands of academically qualified high-school graduates do not continue their education because they cannot afford it: see correspondence *New York Times*, October 18, 1986.

3. Welfare mothers do not have lots of children in order to collect more money. Over 60 percent of AFDC families consist of a mother with only one or two offspring.

4. Recipients do not live in luxury. Their combined food, rent, and clothing allotments are far below the poverty level. With inflation, cutbacks, and tightened eligibility, real welfare benefits have fallen nearly 40 percent in the past twenty years.

5. The federal government spends $23 billion on AFDC, about 1.5 percent of the U.S. budget.[11] As already explained, interest payments on the national debt, military spending, and big tax cuts for the rich are the culprits behind the huge federal deficit—not welfare spending.

The swelling welfare rolls have not been due to an epidemic of laziness but to chronic poverty, unemployment, and cutbacks in subsidized day-care services for children of single mothers. Putting welfare recipients to work is a fine idea but, contrary to another myth, there are not "jobs for everyone who wants to work." The New York City region alone lost 500,000 jobs from 1989 to mid-1992. Real income among lower paid working-class families dropped 14 percent in the past decade.[12] Welfare is hardly an adequate solution to the problems inflicted upon the poor by a capitalist economy, but eliminating it without providing other economic opportunities is an even worse solution.[13]

"URBAN REMOVAL" AND "MESS TRANSIT"

Housing is another policy area that reflects the class inequities of "free-market" society. Every year, homeowners with upper and upper-middle incomes, the richest 20 percent of the population, receive nearly 60 percent of federal housing subsidies in the form of property-tax exemptions, interest deductions, and capital gains deferral on housing sales. Over half of all federally subsidized mortgages go to affluent families that could have bought

---

11. On these various points, see Funicello, *Tyranny of Kindness;* Bureau of the Census, *Money Income and Poverty Status in the United States 1988,* series P-60, no. 166 (Department of Commerce, Washington, D.C., 1989); Ohio Children's Defense Fund, *Building on Promises* (Cleveland, Ohio, 1989); House Ways and Means report on how inflation has eroded welfare benefits: *Washington Post,* May 14, 1991; Jamie Sanbonmatsu, "Class Warfare," *Z Magazine,* April 1990, pp. 63–66; *New York Times,* December 14, 1993, and March 10, 1994.

12. Christopher Meade, "The Myth of Welfare," *Z Magazine,* September 1992, pp. 34–36.

13. Frances Fox Piven and Richard Cloward, *The New Class War* (New York: Pantheon, 1982), p. 4.

homes without help.[14] Upper-income people who own beachfront homes—that no private insurance company would insure because of hurricanes and shoreline erosion—receive federally subsidized insurance, leaving the government (taxpayers) liable for billions of dollars in insurance claims.[15]

Private housing developments built with federal assistance are often rented to low-income people for a year or two to qualify for federal funds, then sold to other private owners who, not held to the original contract, evict the tenants and turn the units into high-priced rentals or condominiums. Many soundly built houses are unnecessarily rehabilitated with federal funds so that landlords can drive out the poorer occupants and make a greater return on their investment. Ever year, half a million low-income housing units are lost to demolition, arson, gentrification, and sales to private investors.[16] In Virginia, for example, more than half of the federally subsidized low-income homes "have gone to high-income investors and rents charged to tenants have doubled and tripled over their previous mortgage payments."[17]

Most of the billions spent by the Department of Housing and Urban Development (HUD) have been channeled into the private sector in response to the profit interests of developers, banks, and speculators, producing relatively few homes for persons of modest income. As the real estate market has declined during the 1990s, luxury apartment building owners who received federal subsidies, tax-free bonds, and government insured loans, have defaulted on their mortgages, creating almost $12 billion in losses to be borne by the taxpayers.[18]

---

14. Report by National Coalition for the Homeless: *San Francisco Examiner,* December 14, 1990; Benjamin DeMott, op-ed, *New York Times,* October 10, 1990; Peter Dreier and John Atlas, "Reforming the Mansion Subsidy," *Nation,* May 2, 1994, pp. 592–595. During the Reagan–Bush years, aid to low-income public housing was phased out in favor of "moderate-income" housing, including federal cash and tax subsidies to complexes that rented apartments at $3,000 a month: *Washington Post,* July 20, 1986.

15. Molly Ivins, "On the Beach: Subsidized Stupidity," *Washington Post,* May 29, 1992. One of the beneficiaries has been a multimillionaire conservative U.S. president, George Bush, who regularly preached free-market self-reliance. Most of the $300,000 to $400,000 storm damage to his Maine vacation estate was covered by federal insurance: *Los Angeles Times,* April 18, 1992.

16. Peter Dreier, "Communities, Not Carpetbaggers," *Nation,* August 21/28, 1989, pp. 198–200; *New York Times,* April 14, 1987; *Washington Post,* July 7, 1989.

17. Ward Sinclair, "U.S. Accused of Taking Homes from Poor and Selling to Rich," *Washington Post,* October 29, 1983. Rents went up 18 percent faster than general inflation in the 1980s, rising faster among the poor: *People's Weekly World,* December 25, 1993.

18. *New York Times,* June 20, 1993. Finding itself the owner of thousands of defaulted units, the government sells them off at half the market value, more often to profit-oriented corporate giants like General Electric than to nonprofit organizations whose mission is to help provide affordable housing for the poor: *New York Times,* June 27, 1991.

Only one-quarter of poor households receive any kind of housing subsidy—the lowest level of any industrialized nation. During the Reagan–Bush years, funds for public housing were slashed by 81 percent.[19] The Clinton administration has restored little of those sums. As the supply of affordable housing shrank, rents rushed far ahead of income, and millions of Americans not classified as homeless doubled up, paying more than they could comfortably afford for cramped, substandard quarters. Generally, poor families pay a larger share of their income for housing than better-income households. A million or so low-income households receive rent vouchers, intended to help them pay rent for apartments in the private market. About half of them return the vouchers unused because affordable apartments are so scarce.[20]

Urban renewal might be better described as "urban removal." Such are the irrationalities and expenses of government subsidized "free-market" housing: thousands of luxury units and condominiums that cost billions of taxpayer dollars lie vacant, while hundreds of thousands of people are homeless. The reduction in federal housing budgets during the 1980s was the major cause of homelessness.[21] Homeless people and street beggars, a relatively rare problem in previous decades, are now a common sight, accepted as part of the urban landscape by a whole generation of young Americans who have no idea that such things were once considered a social outrage.[22]

The transportation system provides another example of how private profit takes precedence over public need. Earlier in this century the transporting of passengers and goods was done mostly by electric car and railroad. One mass-transit railway car can do the work of fifty automobiles, and railroads consume one-sixth the energy of trucks to transport goods. But these very efficiencies are what make railroads so *un*desirable to the oil and auto industries. For over a half-century their response has been to undermine the nation's rail and electric-bus systems.

Consider the fate of Los Angeles. In 1935 a once beautiful Los Angeles was served by one of the largest interurban railway systems in the world,

---

19. Ernest Hollings in *Minneapolis Star Tribune*, May 2, 1989.

20. Dreier, "Communities, Not Carpetbaggers," p. 199; Paul Leonard and Edward Lazere, *A Place to Call Home: The Low Income Housing Crisis in 44 Major Metropolitan Areas* (Washington, D.C.: Center on Budget and Policy Priorities, November 1992): this study found that 47 percent of the poor are paying 70 percent of their income for housing.

21. According to a U.S. House of Representatives task force: *Washington Post*, December 26, 1987.

22. About half the homeless are White; the other half Black or Latino; the fastest growing group of homeless are families: Joel Blau, *The Visible Poor, Homelessness in the United States* (New York: Oxford University Press, 1992); Lilia Reyes and Laura Waxman, *A Status Report on Hunger and Homelessness in America's Cities* (Washington, D.C.: U.S. Conference of Mayors, 1989). For a personal account of the cruelty, pain, and dangers of homelessness, see Joe Homeless, *My Life on the Street* (Far Hills, N.J.: New Horizon Press, 1992).

covering a 75-mile radius with 3,000 quiet, pollution-free electric trains that carried 80 million people a year. But General Motors and Standard Oil, using dummy corporations as fronts, purchased the system, scrapped its electric cars, tore down its transmission lines, and placed GM buses fueled by Standard Oil on Los Angeles's streets. By 1955, 88 percent of the nation's electric-streetcar network had been eliminated by collaborators like GM, Standard Oil, Greyhound, and Firestone. In short time, they cut back city and suburban bus services, forcing people to rely increasingly on private cars. In 1949, General Motors was found guilty of conspiracy in these activities and fined the devastating sum of $5,000.[23]

Given the absence of alternative modes of transportation, people become dependent on the automobile as a way of life so that their need for cars is often as real as their need for jobs—and mass transit devolves into "mess transit." The social costs are staggering. Each year in the United States about 46,000 people are killed in motor vehicle accidents and two million are injured or maimed. As of 1994, an estimated three million will have perished on the roads, more than twice the accumulated number of Americans killed in all the wars ever fought by the United States.[24] The automobile is also the single greatest cause of air pollution in urban areas throughout the world. Almost a half-billion motor vehicles clog the world's roads—a tenfold increase since 1950—constituting a major menace to the planet's survival.[25]

Over 60 percent of the land in most U.S. cities is taken up by the movement, storage, and servicing of vehicles. Whole neighborhoods are razed to make way for highways. But building more highways to ease traffic congestion only attracts more vehicles and creates more congestion. The automobile requires communities to spread out to make room for it, causing (a) premature obsolescence of streetcar neighborhoods whose compactness cannot accommodate vast numbers of cars; (b) higher per capita costs for sewage construction, road maintenance, and other services; and (c) higher food transportation costs as farms on the metropolitan fringe are displaced by suburban sprawl.[26] But as worldwide car usage grows so do the profits of the oil, auto, trucking, tire, cement, construction, and motel businesses.

---

23. Jonathan Kwitny, "The Great Transportation Conspiracy," in Cargan and Ballantine (eds.), *Sociological Footprints,* 2nd ed. (Belmont, Calif.: Wadsworth, 1982).

24. Bureau of the Census, *Statistical Abstract of the United States 1992* (Washington, D.C.: Government Printing Office, 1992); Andrew Kimbrell, "Car Culture: Driving Ourselves Crazy," *Washington Post,* September 3, 1989. Kimbrell notes that fatality statistics may be too low since they do not include deaths that occur several days after accidents or off-road. He points out that motor vehicles kill easily one million animals *each day,* making road kills second only to the meat industry. More deer are killed by cars than by hunters.

25. Kimbrell, "Car Culture."

26. An item of food consumed in the USA travels an average of 1,200 miles before it is eaten: "Harper's Index," *Harper's,* February 1991.

In this country, tens of billions are spent each year to produce, advertise, and sell motor vehicles. In addition, federal, state, and local governments spend $300 billion annually to subsidize automotive use through road construction and maintenance, highway patrols, tax losses from land lost to highways, and ambulance and hospital services. At the same time, the federal government has slashed railroad service and has done relatively little for mass transit—the most efficient, cleanest, and safest form of transporting goods and people.

Municipal transit systems are funded by deficit spending, with tax-free bonds sold to wealthy individuals and banks. These bondholders receive millions of dollars in interest payments, causing transit systems to cut services, raise fares, and go deeper into debt, spending more money for less service. Meanwhile, the monies expended by the government on urban mass transit are used mostly to build metrorails that benefit the few rather than the many, the affluent suburbanites who commute to legal, financial, and business centers, rather than the working poor, the elderly, and other transit-dependents.[27]

HEALTH AND SAFETY FOR NOBODY

Consumer safety is another area in which government serves the interests of profit-oriented producers, allowing them to flood the market with adulterated and unsafe products. The Food and Drug Administration (FDA) tests only about 1 percent of the drugs and foods marketed. Of the drugs approved by the FDA, half of them cause serious adverse reactions. Some drug companies have concealed data and misrepresented the potential dangers of their products.[28] With standards so poorly enforced, says one federal inspector, the government label on meat and poultry products should be changed from "USDA Inspected and Approved" to "Eat at Your Own Risk."[29] In 1993, an outbreak of fatal food poisonings caused by contaminated beef served by a chain of fastfood restaurants brought the point home.

Drugs are often drastically overpriced. In the case of medicines, drug companies claim they need high prices to support innovative research. But

---

27. *New York Times,* March 9, 1987. Metrorail systems work when combined with land-use planning, good bus services (to give working populations access to the rails), and limits on downtown parking—as Portland, Oregon, and a number of other cities have demonstrated. The result is thousands of more jobs downtown, less auto traffic, and better air quality: Jessica Mathews, "The Costs of Unplanned Urban Sprawl," *Washington Post,* January 13, 1991.

28. General Accounting Office, *FDA Drug Review Disapproval Risk* (Washington, D.C.: Government Printing Office, May 1990); "Free-Market Medicine," *Progressive,* March 1992, p. 11. On how doctors continue to prescribe unsafe drugs, see Ellen Ruppel Shell, "Health: First Do No Harm," *Atlantic Monthly,* May 1988, pp. 83–84.

29. *Washington Post,* May 16, 1987.

they spend three times more on sales promotions than on research. In just six years, top prescription drug prices rose 80 percent and company profits 145 percent.[30]

A government report showed that the health gap between economic classes has widened greatly over several decades, with low-income individuals having a death rate more than three times that of affluent persons.[31] Millions of Americans live in areas where medical treatment is unavailable except at high fees, and public hospitals are closing down for lack of funds. Medical bills in for-profit private hospitals are substantially higher than in hospitals that are not investor-owned.[32] Though patients are often turned away, a surplus of beds exist in many private hospitals. These for-profit hospitals are interested only in insured, *paying* customers. Many people of modest means have discovered that an oversupply of hospital beds does not guarantee access to medical care.[33]

Too often the first examination patients receive in an emergency room is of their wallets. An estimated one million are refused emergency care each year because they cannot show proof of ability to pay. Others are ejected from hospitals in the midst of an illness because they run out of funds. Others are bankrupted by medical bills despite supposedly "comprehensive" insurance coverage.[34] For the sake of profit, hospital staffs are cut and downgraded in skills; hospital personnel are often poorly trained, inadequately supervised, and overburdened with speedups. The end result is high turnover, absenteeism, and poor and often injurious treatment.[35]

Some conservatives maintain that health costs are high because so many people are self-indulgent hypochondriacs. In fact, in an average year nearly one in four Americans put off medical treatment for fear they cannot afford it.[36] As of 1992, almost 39 million Americans lacked any kind of health insurance.[37]

---

30. *Solidarity* (publication of the United Auto Workers), January–February 1993, p. 18.

31. National Center for Health Statistics report: *New York Times*, July 8, 1993.

32. Stanley Wohl, M.D., *The Medical Industrial Complex* (New York: Harmony Books, 1984): *Washington Post*, August 27, 1991.

33. Rosemary Stevens, *In Sickness and in Wealth* (New York: Basic Books, 1989).

34. Howard Waitzkin, *The Second Sickness: Contradictions of Capitalist Health Care* (New York: Free Press, 1983); J. Weissman and A. M. Epstein, "Case Mix and Resource Utilization by Uninsured Hospital Patients in the Boston Metropolitan Area," *Journal of the American Medical Association*, 261, June 23–30, 1989, pp. 3572–3576.

35. Vicente Navarro, *Dangerous to Your Health: Capitalism and Health Care* (New York: Monthly Review Press, 1993); Walt Bogdanich, *The Great White Lie, How America's Hospitals Betray Our Trust and Endanger Our Lives* (New York: Simon & Schuster, 1991). About one in 400 patients, or 100,000 a year, die from iatrogenic illness, injuries incurred from treatment itself: *Washington Post*, February 18, 1992, also December 3, 1989.

36. *Los Angeles Times*, February 5, 1990; *People's Weekly World*, January 23, 1993.

37. *New York Times*, April 13, 1994. It was recently discovered that the number lacking health insurance in California is one-third higher than previously estimated: *San Francisco Examiner*, April 8, 1993. If the same is true for the entire country then the number of uninsured is more like forty-nine million.

Millions who *are* insured pay monthly premiums that place a crushing burden on family finances. Health insurance is a benefit earned by workers just as money wages are. Yet most employees have no ownership rights over their insurance. Management can reduce benefits, increase deductibles, and sometimes even cancel coverage for an employee who gets seriously ill.[38] Health costs have soared, yet the care people are receiving is not getting better, only more expensive. Treatment is provided for the poor through Medicaid and to the elderly through Medicare. But the greatest beneficiaries of these programs have been the doctors and hospitals that overcharge, give unnecessary treatment, rush patients through as quickly as possible, and fraudulently bill the government for over $10 billion a year.[39]

Major beneficiaries of the private-care system are the big insurance companies and Health Maintenance Organizations (HMOs).[40] While countries such as Canada and Germany have a single national plan for their entire population, the United States has 1,500 different health insurance programs. Of the vast sums the health insurance companies gouge out of the American public, over $100 billion is wasted on billing costs and duplicated promotional and administrative costs. That sum is enough to insure every uninsured person, provide long-term care, and cover most prescription drugs.[41] U.S. private health insurance companies spend 12 percent of premiums on overhead costs, compared to 3.2 percent for Medicaid and Medicare, or 0.9 percent for Canada's single-payer system—which got rid of health insurance companies over two decades ago.[42] To maximize profits, U.S. health insurance companies and HMOs try to exclude people most likely to need expensive care, thereby undermining the very notion of insurance as a strategy for spreading risk.[43]

By 1993, the health-care system cost Americans $800 billion a year—yet left millions without coverage and millions more overburdened with pay-

---

38. Statement by National Center for Policy Analysis: *New York Times,* February 3, 1993.

39. In regard to overbilling and unnecessary billing of Medicare patients, see *The Secret Benefits. The Failure to Provide Buy-In to Poor Seniors,* Report by the Family USA Foundation, Washington, D.C., 1991; Al Cole, "The $10 Billion Dollar Blank Check," *Modern Maturity,* April–May 1990, pp. 38–44; and *USA Today,* April 8, 1992. Medicaid is having a problem attracting a sufficient number of physicians: *Washington Post,* June 10, 1991. In 1941, U.S. doctors earned 3.5 times as much as average workers. Today they earn six times more: Dave Elsila, "The Pressure Builds for Health Care Reform," *Solidarity* (publication of United Auto Workers), July 1993, pp. 9–11.

40. An HMO is a group of physicians, or an insurance company contracting with a group of physicians, who accept a monthly payment per individual for providing comprehensive health-care needs. They best serve those who can afford them.

41. See Neighbor to Neighbor Action Fund statement: *New York Times,* June 8, 1993; also *Washington Post,* May 2, 1991.

42. "The U.S. Health Care Crisis," United Food and Commercial Workers Newsletter, November 1991.

43. *New York Times,* April 28, 1991.

ments. On a per capita basis, we spent 41 percent more than Canada, 49 percent more than Germany, and 85 percent more than France. Yet these nations (and a number of other countries) provide medical care to all their citizens. The Canadian and Western European systems have more physicians and hospital beds per person, lower infant mortality rates, and higher life expectancies.[44]

Rather than adopting a national health plan that would eliminate the profiteering and administrative duplication of the private insurance system, the Clinton administration supported a "managed competition" plan, a private-market approach that provides minimum care through the larger insurance companies and super-HMOs. Patients with money enough could buy more elaborate plans. Managed competition would subsidize the enormous overhead and duplication of the private insurance system, while rationing health care and generating still greater profits at greater public expense.[45] What Dr. Bernard Winter said about the U.S. health-care system in 1977 remains true today: "It is a costly, wasteful mechanism for funneling money to a sprawling medical industry that encompasses not only physicians and hospitals but equipment manufacturers, pharmaceutical corporations, banks and insurance companies. The impulse that drives this industry is the same that drives every industry—the maximization of profit."[46]

One cannot talk about the health of America without mentioning occupational safety. Every year over 11,000 die from injuries sustained at work and another 50,000 from occupationally related diseases. In addition, there are about 1.8 million job injuries annually; 60,000 workers sustain permanent disability; and millions more suffer cumulative disabilities and other work-related illnesses.[47] Industrial work always carries some risk, but the present carnage is mostly due to inadequate safety standards and lax enforcement of codes. Every dollar a company spends on safety for work-

44. *Premiums Without Benefits,* report by Citizens Fund, Washington, D.C., October 1990; Colin Gordon, "Health Care the Corporate Way," *Nation,* March 25, 1991, p. 376; Elsila, "The Pressure Builds for Health Care Reform," p. 9; "The Canadian Health Care System," *Economic Notes,* July–August 1991, pp. 6–7; Craig Whitney, "Medical Care in Germany," *New York Times,* January 23, 1993; *Washington Post,* December 18, 1989.

45. Robert Dreyfuss, "The Big Idea," *Mother Jones,* May–June 1993, pp. 18–22; "Managed Competition versus Single-Payer Health Insurance Reform," report by Local 250 Hospital and Health Care Workers Union, SEIU/AFL-CIO, March 1993; also the entire issue of *1199 News* (publication of Local 1199 Drug, Hospital, and Health Care Employees Union), January/February 1993.

46. Bernard Winter, M.D., "Health Care: The Problem Is Profits," *Progressive,* October 1977, p. 16.

47. Joseph Kinney, project director, *Ending Legalized Workplace Homicide* (Chicago: National Safe Workplace Institute, 1988) and Kinney, *Failed Opportunity: The Decline of U.S. Job Safety in the 1980s* (Chicago: National Safe Workplace Institute, 1988); also Environmental Protection Agency, *Acute Hazardous Data Base* (Washington, D.C.: Government Printing Office, 1989).

ers (and consumers) is one less dollar in profits. As one farm worker testified:

> I began to see how everything was so wrong. When growers can have an intricate watering system to irrigate their crops but they can't have running water inside the houses of workers. Veterinarians tend to the needs of domestic animals but they can't have medical care for the workers. They can have land subsidies for the growers but they can't have adequate unemployment compensation for the workers. They treat [them] like a farm implement. In fact, they treat their implements better and their domestic animals better.[48]

For years organized labor has fought for safe work conditions. In 1970 Congress finally created the Occupational Safety and Health Administration (OSHA). In the chemical industry alone, OSHA regulations brought a 23 percent drop in accidents and sickness.[49] Yet OSHA's resources have proven vastly insufficient. The agency had only about 1,200 inspectors to cover some five million private-sector workplaces, an average of one inspection per workplace every eighty years. During the Reagan-Bush era (1981–92), the number of inspectors was cut to 800, OSHA's safety standards were weakened, and its records often falsified. There was deliberate underreporting of injuries and fatalities by companies. When caught with violations, corporations like Union Carbide, Shell, and Chrysler found it less expensive to pay the relatively light fines—often renegotiated and greatly reduced—than to sustain the production costs that would bring better safety conditions. The end result has been a marked increase in occupational injuries, illnesses, and fatalities.[50]

Workers' compensation laws usually place the burden of proof on the injured worker, provide no penalties when industry withholds or destroys evidence, and impose a statute of limitation that makes it difficult to collect on diseases that have a long latency period. Only about 10 percent of the millions of workers injured actually win any benefits. And those who receive compensation forfeit their right to sue a negligent employer. Thus, the government compensation program actually shields industry from liability.[51]

Conservative interests have waged extended campaigns against human services and public assistance. Less public assistance, more cuts in disability and unemployment insurance, and a freezing of minimum wages deprive

---

48. Quoted in Studs Terkel, *Working* (New York: Pantheon, 1972), p. 12.

49. Ruth Ruttenberg and Randell Hudgins, *Occupational Safety and Health in the Chemical Industry*, 2nd ed., (New York: Council on Economic Priorities, 1981).

50. Joan Claybrook, *Retreat from Safety: Reagan's Attack on America's Health* (New York: Pantheon, 1984); Kinney, *Failed Opportunities.*

51. Mark Reutter, "Workmen's Compensation Doesn't Work or Compensate," *Business and Society*, Fall 1980, pp. 39–44.

millions of people of alternative sources of income, forcing many back into the job market and intensifying the competition for employment.[52] This, in turn, deflates the price of labor and helps keep wages from cutting into profits—which partly explains why profits remain so high even during times of stagnation. Though the pie is not growing, those at the top manage to get a larger slice through the upward redistribution of income.

ECOLOGICAL DISASTER

Like sin, environmental pollution is regularly denounced but vigorously practiced. Great quantities of sulfur dioxide, nitrogen dioxide, carbon dioxide, carbon monoxide, selenium, mercury, lead, and hundreds of other substances continue to be dumped into our environment. Industry introduces about a thousand new chemicals into the marketplace annually, often with insufficient or fraudulent information about their effects.[53] Each year some 10,000 spills from pipelines and tankers spread millions of gallons of oil over our lands and coastal waters, destroying wildlife habitats and taking a dreadful toll on birds, mammals, and marine life as the oil works its way through fish-spawning and animal-breeding cycles.[54]

Large quantities of heavy metals and other poisons leach from mines to contaminate surrounding areas. Strip mining and deforestation by coal and timber companies continue to bring ruination to forests and watersheds.[55] Rain forests throughout the world, with their precious stock of flora and fauna, are being turned into wastelands. Floods and sediments pour from millions of acres of denuded watersheds into waterways and irrigation systems, ruining food production and fisheries.[56] The Department of Agricul-

---

52. Bereft of public assistance, low-income people presumably would be forced to range more widely to compete for jobs, more effectively deflating wages by adding to the labor surplus in areas where unemployment is relatively low.

53. Michael Brown, *Laying Waste: The Poisoning of America by Toxic Chemicals* (New York: Pantheon, 1980). Just one Procter & Gamble factory in Florida dumps fifty million gallons of waste water into the Fenholloway River every day—and it is legal: Sheila O'Donnell, "Targeting Environmentalists," *CovertAction Information Bulletin*, Summer 1992, p. 43.

54. *New York Times*, April 18, 1992. In March 1989, an Exxon oil tanker spilled eleven million gallons of oil over eight hundred miles of Alaskan shoreline causing major ruination to hundreds of miles of coast and to the fishing industry. Exxon's clean-up efforts amounted to little more than a $2 billion public relations campaign; it had no cleanup technology or plan worth the name: John Keeble, *Out of the Channel, The Exxon Valdez Oil Spill in Prince William Sound* (New York: HarperCollins, 1991).

55. On toxic leaks in mining, see the report by a coalition of environmental groups: *New York Times*, April 12, 1993.

56. Adrian Cowell, *The Decade of Destruction* (Garden City, N.Y.: Doubleday, 1992); Susanna Hecht and Alexander Cockburn, *The Fate of the Forest* (New York: Verso, 1989).

ture estimates that every year up to 400,000 acres of wetlands in the United States are obliterated by commercial farming and developers.[57]

Six million acres of topsoil are eroded yearly by chemical farming. The use of toxic herbicides and pesticides has increased dramatically, approaching three billion pounds a year, causing high rates of birth defects, liver and kidney diseases, and cancer.[58] To "protect" against pests such as the gypsy moth and Mediterranian fruit fly, authorities have imposed aerial spraying over large areas in California, Maryland, and Virginia, for example, with little regard for health hazards.[59] Homeowners drench their yards and lawns with three to six times more herbicides and insecticides per acre than even farmers use, causing serious harm to groundwater and residents, while killing many useful insects that aerate the soil and pollinate plants.[60]

Chemicalization generates the conditions for further environmental degradation. For example, forest and lawn pesticides kill the songbirds that eat bugs, thereby removing a natural pest control and causing greater insect infestation—which in turn creates a greater reliance on pesticides. Pesticides produce generations of insects more resistant to chemical controls—which calls for still more potent chemicals. The result is that over a thirty-five year period, pesticide use has increased tenfold, yet crop losses to insects and other pests have almost doubled.[61]

Excess lead levels have been found in the drinking water of one of every five Americans, contributing to hypertension, strokes, heart ailments, and learning disabilities. Toxic waste dumps and incinerators are situated predominantly in or near low-income African American, Latino, and Native American Indian communities.[62] Particle pollution, or soot, causes an estimated 60,000 deaths in the United States each year. Between 1980 and

57. Jim Schwab, "The Attraction is Chemical," *Nation,* October 16, 1989, p. 415.

58. Rick Hind and Eliza Evans, *Pesticides in Ground Water* (Washington, D.C.: U.S. Public Interest Research Group, Summer 1988): Al Meyerhoff, "No More Pesticides for Dinner," *New York Times,* March 9, 1993.

59. Jay Feldman, Kevin Thorpe, correspondence in *Washington Post,* May 7, 1988. We have little idea what is done to our health by the inactive ingredients in pesticides (sometimes 75 percent of the product and more toxic than the active ingredients).

60. John Skow, "Can Lawns Be Justified?" *Time,* June 3, 1991, p. 63. Toxifying lawns and gardens is a $1.5 billion business and growing.

61. Robert Van Den Bosch, *The Pesticide Conspiracy* (Garden City, N.Y.: Doubleday, 1978). The loss of tropical rain forests has brought a dramatic decline in the populations of many species of migratory birds, including North American songbirds: *Washington Post,* July 26, 1989.

62. *Washington Post,* November 6, 1986. Low-income people suffer disproportionate exposure to industrial effluent, hazardous waste dumps, and vehicular pollution, while benefiting least from cleanup programs: David Perez, *Destruction of the Environment* (New York: World View Forum, 1993); *New York Times,* January 11, 1992. The lower the income, the higher the lead content in children's blood; race is also a factor: *Washington Post,* January 16, 1992. On the social and psychological impact of residential toxic exposure, see Michael Edelstein, *Contaminated Communities* (Boulder, Colo.: Westview Press, 1988).

1989, the nation's death rate from asthma increased by more than 30 percent as air quality deteriorated.[63] Not without cause do some ecologists conclude that the air we breathe, the water we drink, and the food we eat are the leading causes of death in the United States.

Nuclear power is another major menace. Serious mishaps have occurred at Three Mile Island in Pennsylvania and at reactors in a dozen other states. In the area around Three Mile Island, livestock have aborted and died prematurely, and households have been experiencing what amounts to an epidemic of cancer, birth defects, and premature deaths.[64] Malfunctions have plagued almost every one of the nuclear plants in the United States. These plants are so hazardous that insurance companies refuse to cover them.[65]

Laboratories and factories used for making nuclear weapons have repeatedly released radioactive wastes and poisonous chemicals into the air and waterways, including millions of gallons dumped illegally into makeshift evaporation ponds, pits, and seepage basins, causing a contamination that will require tens of billions of dollars in cleanup costs—if ever cleaned up.[66] Residents in Utah, Nevada, and other parts of the USA, exposed to atmospheric nuclear tests and the contaminating clouds vented from underground tests, have suffered a variety of tragic illnesses.[67]

---

63. *New York Times*, July 19, 1993; *Los Angeles Times*, April 3, 1990; *Washington Post*, June 4, 1989. Factory workers who produce DDT suffer almost twice the national rate of pancreatic cancer deaths: *Miami Herald*, July 27, 1990.

64. Jane Lee, a resident of the Three Mile Island area, claims, "I've been finding cancers at every other house. We have raging cancer. . . . All people talk about is cancer, leukemia, breast cancer, prostate, muscle cancer. You name it, people got it": Karl Grossman, "Three Mile Island: They Say Nothing Happened," *Extra!*, July/August 1993, pp. 6–7. Three Mile Island has been the biggest media cover-up of an industrial accident in U.S. history. The mainstream media has had almost nothing to say about it except to claim that all is well.

65. Richard Webb, *The Accident Hazards of Nuclear Power Plants* (Amherst: University of Massachusetts Press, 1976) John Fuller, *We Almost Lost Detroit* (New York: Crowell, 1976); Ralph Nader and John Abbotts, *The Menace of Atomic Energy*, rev. ed., (New York: Norton, 1979); Ian Gilbert and Elliot Negin, "America's Chernobyls," *Public Citizen*, August 1986, pp. 12–14.

66. *New York Times*, June 7, 1988; October 15, 1988; May 4, August 2, and December 10, 1989. At the Hanford Nuclear Reservation in Washington State, the Department of Energy allowed General Electric to dump 200 billion gallons, contaminating the earth and ground water: John Glenn, "The Mini-Hiroshima," *New York Times*, January 24, 1989; and the documentary film *Deadly Deception: General Electric, Nuclear Weapons and Our Environment* (INFACT, Oakland Calif., 1991). Included among serious offenders are the plants in Fernald, Ohio, and Rocky Flats, Colorado, and the Savannah River plant in South Carolina: *Washington Post*, September 6, 1989 and September 22, 1991.

67. Philip Fradkin, *Fallout: An American Nuclear Tragedy* (Tucson: University of Arizona Press, 1989); Richard L. Miller, *Under the Cloud: The Decade of Nuclear Testing* (New York: Free Press, 1986); Harvey Wasserman and Norman Solomon, *Killing Our Own: The Disaster of America's Experience with Atomic Radiation* (New York: Dell, 1982); Carole Gallagher, *American Ground Zero* (Cambridge, Mass.: MIT Press, 1993); Jay M. Gould and Benjamin

"GOOD NEWS – WE'VE REDUCED THE NUCLEAR THREAT FROM ABROAD"

It was promised that nuclear power would be clean and inexpensive. In fact, the construction of nuclear plants has involved cost overruns of 400 to 1000 percent, bringing higher rather than lower electric rates. And the nuclear industry has no long-term technology for safe waste disposal nor for the entombment or decontamination of old nuclear plant sites.[68]

A. Goldman, *Deadly Deceit: Low-Level Radiation, High-Level Cover-Up* (New York: Four Walls Eight Windows, 1990). For a personal testimony by a "downwinder" victim, see Tom Bailie, "Growing Up as a Nuclear Guinea Pig," *New York Times,* July 22, 1990.

68. See the series by Matthew Wald in the *New York Times,* February 26–28, 1984; also *New York Times,* May 27 and September 11, 1986. A typical example of nuclear cost overrun is the New York Shoreham plant. Originally priced at $261 million, it ended up costing $4.1 billion.

Profits are higher when corporations can plunder our natural resources at will, dump their diseconomies onto the public, and get us to consume at unusually high and wasteful levels. The costs of disposing of industrial effluents (which compose 40 to 60 percent of the loads treated by municipal sewage plants), of developing new water sources (while industry and agribusiness consume 80 percent of the nation's daily water supply), of cleaning up radioactive sites, and tending to the sickness and disease caused by pollution, are passed on to the public. So with the costs of floods and droughts, inefficient and wasteful energy usage, and the loss of top soil, farmlands, wetlands, fisheries, and aquifers. Those who worship at the altar of "profitable growth" take no account of these losses.

We are told we must choose between economic growth and environmental protection.[69] But without environmental protection there eventually will be no economic growth—and no economy to speak of. Fast-buck exploitation of the planet's resources, along with population explosion, have brought an annual extinction rate of 17,500 plants and animals.[70] Per capital food production is dropping in many parts of the world. Chemical fertilizers, used so abundantly in the United States and elsewhere, now do little to raise output. Since 1984, world grain production has been falling behind population growth.[71]

The life support systems of the entire ecosphere—the planet's thin skin of air, water, and soil—are threatened by global warming, ozone depletion, and overpopulation. Global warming is caused by tropical deforestation, motor vehicle exhaust, and other fossil fuel emissions that create a "greenhouse effect," trapping heat close to the earth's surface.[72] Carbon dioxide, the most common of greenhouse gases, has increased by about 25 percent since the mid-1800s. This massed heat is altering the chemical composition, atmospheric currents, and climatic patterns on which we depend for our rainfall—resulting in meteorological aberrations across much of the planet. In northern climes as well as warmer ones, rising temperatures have caused more droughts and forest fires and less soil moisture, thereby disrupting

---

69. Note President Bush's repeated statements that environmental protections have to be "consistent with economic growth and free market principles": *Los Angeles Times,* February 6, 1990. Polls show that a majority of Americans want the government to take serious action against polluters even if it means slower economic growth and closing down some factories in their own communities: Golin/Harris Communications poll reported in *Greenpeace,* October/November/December 1991, p. 4.

70. That figure refers to the entire planet. In the United States, 300 kinds of plants and animals have vanished over the last two decades: *Greenpeace,* October/November/December, 1991, p. 7; *Washington Post,* September 8, 1987.

71. Lester Brown, "Natural Limits," *New York Times,* July 24, 1993; Zero Population Growth newsletter, Washington, D.C., June 1993.

72. Tropical deforestation now accounts for an estimated 25 percent of the greenhouse effect: Bob Munga, "Torching God's Pharmacy," *Longevity,* August 1989, pp. 65–69.

the ability of forests to renew themselves. Today, serious water shortages exist in approximately eighty nations.[73] Eventually, chronic drought brings mass famine.

Another potential catastrophe is the shrinkage of the ozone layer that shields us from the sun's deadliest rays. About 2.6 billion pounds of ozone-depleting chemicals, chiefly chlorofluorocarbons (CFCs), are emitted into the earth's atmosphere every year. (The top five dischargers in the United States are corporate military contractors.) The worst batches of CFCs, released over the last two decades, have yet to reach the ozone. So the dangers will increase in the years ahead. Already, excessive ultraviolet radiation has begun to damage trees, crops, and coral reefs and destroy the ocean's phytoplankton—source of about half this planet's oxygen. Ultraviolet radiation also depresses the human immune system (regardless of skin pigmentation or the use of most sunscreen lotions) and greatly increases the likelihood of numerous illnesses.[74]

Capitalism's modus operandi is to produce and sell an ever expanding supply of goods and services for ever greater profits. But the earth is finite. So is its ability to absorb wastes and toxins. While food yields shrink, the world's population grows 90 million a year and the planet's life support systems move closer to catastrophe. An ever expanding capitalism and a fragile, finite ecology appear to be on a calamitous collision course.

With the fate of the planet at stake, the U.S. government's response has been dismal—even with a Democratic president in the White House, who professes a concern for these things. The Safe Drinking Water Act remains largely unenforced; the Clean Air Act became a multibillion dollar bailout for coal producers; and the Endangered Species Act, one of the world's toughest wildlife preservation laws, has proven ineffectual over the last two decades, with the failures mounting faster than the successes.[75]

Polluters are more often rewarded than punished. The Defense Department has paid private defense contractors upwards of $1 billion to

---

73. Michael Oppenheimer and Robert Boyle, *Dead Heat* (New York: Basic Books, 1990); Barry Commoner, *Making Peace with the Planet* (New York: Pantheon, 1990); Editors, "Global Warming" *Nucleus* (publication of Union of Concerned Scientists), Winter 1992–1993, pp. 1–4, 12.

74. Julia May, Michael Belliveau, and Jim Jenal, *Deadly Rays: Fragile Shield* (San Francisco: Citizens for a Better Environment, 1990); Al Gore, *Earth in the Balance* (New York: Houghton Mifflin, 1992); *Washington Post*, November 16, 1991. U.S. space shuttles have significantly damaging effects on the ozone layer: Christian Parenti, "NASA's Assault on the Ozone Layer," *Lies of Our Times*, September 1993, pp. 22–23. CFCs are used as solvents and insulators. One-fourth of the world's CFC is produced by Du Pont corporation, who is doing little about the problem other than partly converting to hydrochlorofluorocarbons (HCFCs) which are only marginally less destructive than CFCs: see "Ozone Shock," full-page Greenpeace statement in *New York Times*, October 5, 1992.

75. Bruce Ackerman and William Hassler, *Clean Coal/Dirty Air* (New Haven, Conn.: Yale University Press, 1981); *Washington Post*, September 8, 1987.

clean up pollution from their own operations.[76] When the Energy Department fines contractors who violate its safety rules, the companies are allowed to bill the government for the fines.[77] Private contractors virtually took over the Superfund toxic waste cleanup program, raking in profits as high as 940 percent for sloppy work. In Superfund's first eight years only a handful of the thousands of toxic sites were cleaned up—for a runaway cost of $8.5 billion.[78]

The federal government's Environmental Protection Agency (EPA) has conducted almost no basic research on long-term environmental processes and health effects. It has completed tests on only a small number of the hundreds of new contaminants and chemicals, including many known carcinogens, released into the environment each year.[79] An estimated thirty million people are exposed to potentially contaminated water systems, yet most violations go unreported by the EPA. State and federal officials take action in less than 2 percent of the thousands of annual complaints.[80]

The government not only fails to stop environmental damage, it actively contributes to it. For example, the U.S. Forest Service is the largest road-building agency in the world, having constructed 358,000 miles of logging roads within our national forests, eight times the size of the entire federal interstate highway system.[81] In 1992, the Interior Department announced it would open millions of acres of national parks and forests to strip mining.[82] The Army Corps of Engineers recently opened 60 million acres of wetlands to developers.[83] The Corps has spent $25 billion in this century building dams, levees, and diversion channels that destroy habitats containing some of the country's richest biological resources. Levees and channels also prevent the surrounding wetlands and other floodplains from performing one of their most important natural functions: controlling floods by absorbing overflow. Containing rivers in narrowly corseted waterways only intensifies the velocity and height of the flood.[84]

There are some 20,000 radioactive and toxic chemical sites on military bases and at nuclear weapons plants spread across the United States, contaminating air, land, and urban water supplies. Cleanup costs are estimated to be in the hundreds of billions of dollars. Some sites are so contami-

---

76. *Los Angeles Times,* July 7, 1992.
77. *New York Times,* September 26, 1989.
78. *Washington Post,* January 30, 1989.
79. *New York Times,* March 20, 1992; *Washington Post,* August 11, 1989.
80. *People's Weekly World,* October 13, 1990; *Washington Post,* December 24, 1987.
81. *Seattle Post-Intelligencer,* January 13, 1989. Almost all these roads are subsidies to the timber industry.
82. *New York Times,* September 28, 1992.
83. *Washington Post,* September 29, 1990.
84. William Stevens, "The High Risk of Denying Rivers Their Flood Plains," *New York Times,* July 20, 1993; *San Francisco Chronicle,* July 13, 1993. The great Midwest floods of 1993 were due largely to levee construction.

nated they are considered "sacrifice zones," to be sealed off from humanity for the foreseeable future. The Department of Energy has no known safe method of disposing of radioactive waste. For decades the government repeatedly suppressed findings by its own scientists and investigators that demonstrated the dangers of nuclear energy. The government knowingly let uranium and other lethal substances leak into the underground water supplies and drinking wells near various nuclear weapons sites. And it has allowed private industry and the military to deposit radioactive nuclear wastes into ocean dumps and prime fishing beds along the east and west coasts of the United States.[85]

In the midst of this disheartening record, there are hopeful developments, if not within official circles, then among growing sectors of the public, especially those who have been developing organic agriculture and environmentally sustainable fuel sources such as solar, geothermal, and tidal energies. More effective than cleaning up pollution is preventing it before it occurs. Today there are hundreds of thousands of people in this country and around the world already relying on solar heating devices. Wind and solar power plants in California provide power for nearly a million people. They can be built faster and cheaper than nuclear or fossil fuel plants and have no toxic emissions. Renewable nonpolluting energy provides about 7.5 percent of this country's energy production. Twelve states in the Great Plains have a wind energy potential greater than the electric use of our entire nation.[86] However, recent administrations (including Clinton's) have done next to nothing to develop these alternative sources and much to keep them in the unfriendly grip of corporate interests.[87]

It is argued that alternative renewable energy is not cost efficient. But if one takes into account all the hidden costs of fossil fuels, including global

---

85. U.S. Senate, Committee on Government Affairs, *Early Health Problems of the U.S. Nuclear Weapons Industry and Their Implications for Today* (Washington, D.C.: Government Printing Office, 1989); Lennie Seigel, Barry Cohen, and Ben Goldman, *U.S. Military Toxic Legacy* (Washington, D.C.: National Toxic Campaign Fund, March 1991); Seth Shulman, *The Threat at Home: Confronting the Toxic Legacy of the U.S. Military* (Boston: Beacon Press, 1992); Gallagher, *American Ground Zero;* Center for Defense Information, *Defense Monitor,* vol. 20, no. 6, 1991; *Deadly Defense,* report by the Radioactive Waste Campaign, New York, 1988; *New York Times,* September 27, 1992. The military and the National Aeronautics and Space Administration (NASA) are exempt from federal environmental regulations. By 1991, the Department of Energy could more accurately have been called the Department of Nuclear Weaponry; 63 percent of its budget went to nuclear weapons.

86. Tom Lent, Greenpeace representative, correspondence in *San Francisco Chronicle,* November 20, 1992; *Building Economic Alternatives* (publication of Co-Op America), Winter 1990, p. 13; *Cool Energy, The Renewable Solution to Global Warming,* (publication of the Union of Concerned Scientists), Cambridge, Mass., 1990.

87. Ray Reece, *The Sun Betrayed, A Report on the Corporate Seizure of U.S. Solar Energy Development* (Boston: South End Press, 1979).

warming, acid rain, erosion, oil spills, pollution, and damage to our health and property, renewable energy sources are far less costly. Cheap and efficient solar and wind sources would be readily accessible if the government devoted more resources to their technological development and distribution. But this would undercut the immense profits of the oil, coal, natural gas, and nuclear industries—and this is what is so undesirable about alternative energy.

The same with organic farming. Thousands of farmers have abandoned chemical farming and have turned to organic farming (now called "low-input" farming). They are achieving larger yields for less cost by using crop rotation, natural pest control, and nonchemical fertilizers, at the same time revitalizing the soil and improving the health of their livestock. But this means no profits for chemical companies. Alternative agriculture has developed without government assistance and against the opposition of the Department of Agriculture.[88]

In sum, serious contradictions exist between our human needs and our economic system, a system whose primary goal is to maximize profits regardless of the waste, cost, and hazards. We see that government is an insufficient bulwark against the baneful effects of giant corporate capitalism and often a willing handmaiden. Why that is so will be explained in the chapters ahead.

---

88. *Washington Post,* March 1 and November 23, 1987, September 30, 1989; National Public Radio news report, June 16, 1993.

8

Unequal before the Law

Some government programs are designed to take the edge off popular discontent and blunt any challenge to the politico-economic system. But government also relies on sterner measures. Besides the carrot, there is the stick. Behind the welfare bureaucracy, there stand the police, courts, prisons, and the various agencies of the national security state.

CRIMINAL LAW: A DOUBLE STANDARD

Since we have been taught to think of the law as a neutral instrument serving the entire community, it is discomforting to discover that laws are often written and enforced in the most tawdry class-biased ways, favoring the rich over the rest of us. Even when the letter of the law is on their side, working people seldom have the time or money to seek redress through the courts. When they find themselves embroiled in the legal system, it is almost always at the initiative of bill collectors, merchants, or landlords.

In a capitalist system, those who invest money have a legal claim over corporate property not granted to those who invest their labor and lives in the productive process. The protection of corporate holdings is deemed tantamount to the protection of society itself, so that the interests of the investor class are misleadingly equated with the general interest. The very definition of what is or is not lawful contains a class bias. The theft of merchandise from a neighborhood store is unlawful, but the theft of the store itself and the entire surrounding neighborhood in an urban "renewal" program instigated by speculators, bankers, and public officials is hailed as an act of civic development.

People fear street crime more than the white-collar variety because of the immediacy of its violence and its vivid portrayal in movies and television shows—but white-collar crime inflicts far greater monetary, environmental, and human costs.[1] The National Association of Attorneys General estimates that white-collar fraud costs the nation $100 billion a year, a figure that excludes antitrust violations like price-fixing, which may amount to as much as another $160 billion.[2] In addition, corporations have looted worker pension funds of billions of dollars. In 1989, the Labor Department found violations in one-third of all private pension plans.[3]

White-collar crime is not a rarity but a regularity. Many companies are repeat offenders. The Justice Department found that 60 percent of the 582 largest U.S. companies were guilty of one or more criminal actions, be it tax evasion, price-fixing, illegal kickbacks, bribes to public officials, consumer fraud, or violations of labor codes, workplace safety, and environmental laws.[4] In recent years, General Electric was convicted of 282 counts of contract fraud and fined $20 million; GTE, Boeing, RCA, and Hughes Aircraft all pleaded guilty to felony charges of trafficking in stolen Pentagon budget documents; Dale Electronics was fined $3.7 million for deliberately concealing flaws in military electronic equipment; Eastern Airlines pleaded guilty to criminal charges of falsifying aircraft maintenance records. Prudential Securities agreed to pay $90 million in restitutions and fines because of widespread fraud. Ashland Oil was fined $2.2 million for dumping massive amounts of diesel fuel into the Ohio River and contaminating the water supplies of several cities. U.S. Steel pleaded no contest to charges of illegally dumping toxic wastes. Litton Industries agreed to pay $3.9 million in fines and civil claims in a federal fraud case.[5] Not one of the executives involved in these crimes went to jail.

---

1. Mark Green and John Berry, "White Collar Crime as Big Business," *Nation*, June 8, 1985, p. 704; also Robert Elias, *The Politics of Victimization* (New York: Oxford University Press, 1985).

2. Russell Mokhiber, correspondence, *Washington Post*, July 31, 1989.

3. *Newsday*, November 4, 1985; U.S. Department of Labor, Office of the Inspector General, *Changes Are Needed in the ERISA Audit Process to Increase Protections for Employee Benefit Plan Participants*, Report no. 09-90-001-12001, Washington, D.C., November 9, 1989. Private pension plans in the United States contain a total of $2 trillion.

4. Ben Bagdikian, *The Media Monopoly*, 3rd ed. (Boston: Beacon Press, 1990); Marshall Clinard and Peter Yeager, *Corporate Crime* (New York: Free Press, 1986). Among the biggest firms "the rate of documented misbehavior has been even higher," according to *U.S. News and World Report*, as quoted in Green and Berry, "White Collar Crime . . .", p. 704.

5. *Miami Herald*, July 27, 1990; *Los Angeles Times*, March 10, 1990; *Washington Post*, September 22, 1990 and March 2, 1991; Joan Claybrook, "White Collar Crime Boom," *Public Citizen*, July/August 1985, p. 5; *New York Times*, May 14, 1985, February 24, 1988, October 22, 1993, and January 22, 1994. Space does not allow for a more comprehensive list of corporate crimes.

The 2,729 people on death rows in the United States (as of the end of 1993) killed only a few more than their own number, using knives, guns, and the like. Had they used lethal industrial chemicals, mislabeled pharmaceutical drugs, manufactured defective automobiles, produced dangerous consumer devices, illegally dumped toxic wastes, and maintained unsafe work conditions, they could have killed and crippled tens of thousands more without ever going to prison.[6] For example, Honeywell ignored defects in gas heaters resulting in twenty-two deaths and seventy-seven crippling injuries, for which it was fined $800,000. Johns-Manville Corporation suppressed information about the asbestos poisoning of its workers; when ordered to pay damages in civil court it declared bankruptcy to avoid payment.[7] SmithKline Beckman failed to tell the Food and Drug Administration that hundreds of users of one of its drugs had suffered kidney and liver damages and thirty-six had died.[8] General Motors produced a pickup truck with a dangerously faulty gas tank design. The Center for Auto Safety reported that three hundred people have died in GM pickup fires since 1973.[9] In none of these cases did those responsible for the deaths and disabilities go to jail.

Corporate executives almost never are incarcerated for the felonies they commit. An executive of Eli Lilly pleaded no contest for failing to inform the government about the effects of Oraflex, a drug suspected of causing forty-nine deaths in the USA and several hundred abroad. He was fined $15,000.[10] When a worker was killed because of unsafe standards at the

6. Russell Mokhiber, *Corporate Crime and Violence* (San Francisco: Sierra Club Books, 1988); Robert Sherrill, "Murder Inc.—What Happens to Corporate Criminals?" *Utne Reader,* March/April 1987, p. 48.

7. *New York Times,* September 12, 1985 and November 9, 1986.

8. *Washington Post,* October 23, 1988.

9. *America's Censored Newsletter,* March 1993, p. 1.

10. *New York Times,* September 12, 1985 and November 9, 1986; *Newsday,* November 4, 1985; Paul Brodeur, *Outrageous Misconduct: The Asbestos Industry on Trial* (New York: Pantheon, 1985); Sherrill, "Murder Inc. . . ."

Philips Petroleum plant in Pasadena, Texas, the company was fined $720.[11] W. R. Grace pleaded guilty to having lied to the Environmental Protection Agency about dumping toxic chemicals into well water subsequently linked to eight leukemia deaths. Grace was fined $10,000.[12] In child-labor violations involving death or permanent injury the average fine is $750—and no one goes to jail.[13] After being charged with unlawfully burning toxic wastes into the atmosphere for twenty years, Potomac Electric Power Co. of Washington, D.C., was fined $500.[14] When Firestone pleaded guilty to filing false tax returns concealing $12.6 million in income and conspiring to obstruct legal audits of its accounts, it was fined the grand sum of $10,000 and no one went to jail.[15] In 1990, the average fine of ninety-seven major corporate offenders was $183,588.[16] Even when the fine is substantially more, it usually represents a fraction of company profits and fails to compensate for the damage wreaked. Rockwell International agreed to pay a seemingly hefty $18.5 million after pleading guilty to five felonies for radioactive and chemical contamination at the Rocky Flats nuclear bomb plant—but the actual cleanup will cost the government billions of dollars.[17] Over several years Food Lion cheated its employees of at least $200 million by forcing them to work "off the clock," but in a court settlement the company paid back only $13 million.[18]

Penalties often go uncollected. Protex Industries was fined $7.5 million for endangering workers at a hazardous-waste site, but the fine was later suspended.[19] The GAO discovered that the Justice Department had not collected some $7 billion in fines and restitutions from corporations and individuals convicted of felonies.[20] More than one hundred savings and loan (S&L) plea-bargainers, who escaped long prison terms by promising to

---

11. Later on, a massive explosion at the Philips plant killed twenty-three and injured 314: David Moberg, "Putting Out the Fire" *In These Times,* December 12–18, 1990, pp 12–13.

12. *Washington Post,* June 1, 1988.

13. Judy Mann, "The Grisly Child Labor Picture," *Washington Post,* March 6, 1991.

14. *Utility Notes,* Bulletin from the Office of the People's Counsel, Washington, D.C., December 30, 1988. When two Wall Street investors were fined $75,000 and $25,000 for illegal bidding in a Treasury auction, one writer noted, "Because of the men's wealth, the fines are about the equivalent of a parking ticket for most people": Kurt Eichenwald in *New York Times,* December 4, 1992.

15. *Nation,* August 11–18, 1979, p. 101. Over 700 people a year go to jail for tax evasion, almost all of them for sums that were smaller than the amount Firestone tried to conceal.

16. *Greenville News,* April 11, 1990.

17. *New York Times,* June 2, 1992.

18. *People's Weekly World,* August 14, 1993.

19. *Washington Post,* December 28, 1989.

20. General Accounting Office, *Financial Integrity Act Report,* (Washington, D.C.: Government Printing Office, January 1990); More than 37,000 convicted white-collar criminals have paid back little or nothing, even after many years: *Washington Post,* September 18, 1989.

make penalty repayments of $133.8 million, repaid less than 1 percent of that amount.[21] Former deputy chief of staff to President Reagan, Michael Deaver, found guilty of lying under oath about his influence peddling, was sentenced to three years in prison—but the entire sentence was then suspended. Deaver was also fined $100,000, but a year later had paid not a cent.[22]

As the Deaver case suggests, on the relatively rare occasions that white-collar criminals are given prison terms, the sentence is usually light and sometimes not even served. The S&L defendants who actually went to prison "spent fewer months behind bars on average than car thieves"—and at relatively comfortable minimum security prisons.[23] Sentenced to five years for her role in a $165-million financial swindle in California, Beverly Haines spent only sixty-seven days behind bars.[24] Wall Street investor Michael Milken pleaded guilty to six securities violations and was sentenced to ten years—reduced to twenty-two months, most of which was spent doing community service. Milken had to pay back $1.1 billion to settle criminal and civil charges but retained a vast fortune of $1.2 billion from his dealings.[25] Likewise, after paying his fine for insider trading and doing a brief spell behind bars, Ivan Boesky was left with $25 million. "Every major participant in these [Wall Street investment] crimes emerged from the experience as a wealthy man."[26] Who says crime doesn't pay?

Many major white-collar crimes are not even prosecuted. All three of President George Bush's sons were implicated in shady deals but none was indicted.[27] Claiming it did not have enough lawyers and investigators, the government failed to pursue more than one thousand fraud and embezzlement cases involving S&L associations and banks, amounting to billions of dollars in losses to U.S. taxpayers.[28]

---

21. *San Francisco Examiner,* February 25, 1993.

22. *City Paper* (Washington, D.C.), September 15, 1989. Instead of prison, Deaver was given probation and 1,500 hours of community service. White-collar criminals who are sentenced to community service seldom do but a small portion of it, if any. For other examples of leniency toward major white-collar felons, see *Washington Post,* February 21, 1987 and April 7, 1990; and *Wall Street Journal,* February 23, 1987.

23. *San Francisco Examiner,* February 25, 1993.

24. *Press Democrat* (Santa Rosa, Calif.), March 14, 1991.

25. Benjamin J. Stein, *A License to Steal: The Untold Story of Michael Milken and the Conspiracy to Bilk the Nation* (New York: Simon & Schuster, 1992); *New York Times,* January 30, 1993.

26. James Stewart, *Den of Thieves* (New York: Touchstone, 1992), p. 527.

27. Stephen Pizzo, "Family Value$" *Mother Jones,* September/October 1992; *Dollars and Sense,* January/February 1991; *Los Angeles Times,* May 23 and 24, 1990; *Washington Post,* April 19, 1991. Neil Bush used taxpayer-backed funds to purchase a property lease for himself, drew a salary from the funds, and awarded conflict-of-interest loans to business partners that cost the taxpayers about $1 billion.

28. *Los Angeles Times,* March 15, 1990; Michael Waldman, *Who Robbed America* (New York: Random House, 1990); *Washington Post,* February 4, 1989. The government supposedly does not have enough investigators and lawyers to prosecute all the S&L frauds.

VICTIMS OF THE LAW

Who you are may be more important than what offense you commit. A public defense attorney who specializes in juvenile cases notes that young-sters from well-to-do families, who get into minor scrapes with the law, are turned over to their parents with a warning to stay out of trouble. "But when the same incidents happen in the less affluent neighborhoods, chil-dren are arrested and charged and brought to court."[29] Arrest situations often have enough ambiguity to allow authorities some discretion in deter-mining charges. Whether a situation is treated as "disorderly conduct" or "assault" may depend on how the law enforcers feel about the suspect's social status or race.

Supreme Court Justice Hugo Black once noted that there "can be no equal justice where the kind of trial a man gets depends on the amount of money he has."[30] Legal service in our society best serves those who can buy it. The corporate executive with a team of high-powered attorneys experi-ences a different treatment from the law than the poor person with an under-paid and understaffed court-appointed lawyer who is granted only minimal investigative funds and who sees the defendent for the first time on the day of the trial.[31] Numerous states grant little or no funds for appeals. This means a penniless individual will have a difficult time appealing a harsh sentence or unfair trial.[32]

In many states, prospective jurors are chosen from voter registration rolls, county tax lists, or residency lists that underrepresent racial minorities, women, young people, laborers, and the poor. The rich person's lawyers check the backgrounds of prospective jurors to make informed challenges against those who might prove unsympathetic. The poor person's court-appointed lawyer usually has neither the time nor the resources for such investigations.

At arraignment judges have the option of doing anything from releasing the accused on their own recognizance to imposing a bail high enough to keep them in jail until the trial date, which might not come for many months. Studies show that judges are far more likely to deny pretrial release to indigent people than to "respectable," middle-class persons, and more in-

---

29. *Washington Post*, November 30, 1986; also Robert Lecourt (ed.), *Law Against the People* (New York: Random House, 1971). A Black teenager arrested on drug charges is four times more likely to be transferred to an adult court than a White teenager.

30. *Griffin* v. *Illinois* (1956).

31. Stephen Gillers, "Poor Man, Poor Lawyer," *New York Times*, February 28, 1986. One criminal lawyer observes that most people in federal prisons are indigent: *New York Times*, April 8, 1900.

32. Federal and state courts reverse 40 percent of all death sentences on important procedural or constitutional grounds: *New York Times*, June 4, 1993.

"You have a pretty good case, Mr. Pitkin. How much justice can you afford?"

clined to persuade a poor person to waive the right to counsel and plead guilty.[33] Judges more often incarcerate poorly educated, low-income persons and less often give them suspended sentences or probation than better educated, higher-income persons convicted of the same or more serious crimes.[34] Consider these instances of racial and class bias. A judge imposed a small fine on a stockbroker who made $20 million in illegal market manipulations and, on the same day, sentenced an unemployed African-American man to one year in jail for stealing a $100 television set from a truck shipment.[35] And a man in Houston, Texas, convicted of tamper-

33. Jeffrey Reiman, *The Rich Get Richer and the Poor Get Prison* (New York: Macmillan, 1990); Stuart Nagel, "Disparities in Criminal Procedure," *UCLA Law Review* 14, August 1967, pp. 1272–1305.

34. Reiman, *The Rich Get Richer* . . .

35. Leonard Downie Jr., *Justice Denied* (New York: Praeger, 1971). On the inequities of the criminal justice system, New York Governor Mario Cuomo commented, "If you're a kid from [a poor neighborhood] and you get caught stealing a loaf of bread, they'll send you to Rikers Island [prison] and you'll be sodomized the first night you're there. But if you're a

ing with his electric meter (costing the power company $1,000 in lost revenues and slightly damaging the meter), was sentenced to forty years in prison.[36]

The trick is to steal big. Two wealthy contractors, who pocketed $1.2 million in government contracts for work they never did, were ordered to pay $5,000 in fines and do 200 hours of community service. But a Norfolk, Virginia man got ten years for stealing 87 cents; a youth in Louisiana received fifty years for selling a few ounces of marijuana; a Houston youth was sentenced to fifty years for robbing two people of $1 as they left a restaurant; a five-time petty offender in Dallas was sentenced to *one thousand* years in prison for stealing $73. A man caught trying to break into a house in Florida, thus violating his probation for shoplifting a pair of shoes, was sentenced to life in prison.[37]

Such instances should remind us that this society is not "soft on crime" as some conservatives claim. Nor do offenders go free in undue numbers. In New York City, considered one of the more lenient criminal justice systems, about nine of every ten suspects arrested for robbery are convicted, and most are incarcerated.[38] Recent studies find that criminals are getting sentences averaging twice as long as in earlier years.[39] As noted in chapter 2, the United States has the highest incarceration rate in the world, with some 1.2 million people in jail (and more than twice that number on probation). In the last twenty years, the number of inmates has tripled.[40]

Prisons are anything but "correctional institutions." Most of them remain overcrowded breeding grounds for disease, rape, murder, and suicide. Prisoners often endure terrorization and physical torture from guards and other prisoners and protracted confinement in filthy, lightless cells. Some are forced by authorities to take powerful body-racking, mind-altering

---

businessman ripping us off for billions, they'll go out and play golf with you": *Washington Post,* May 27, 1990.

36. *City Paper* (Washington, D.C.), January 19, 1990.

37. *New York Times,* August 5, 1984; Gary Cartwright, "The Tin-Star State," *Esquire,* February 1971, p. 100; *Daily World,* June 9, 1984; *City Paper* (Washington, D.C.), April 21, 1989. Consider this case: An unemployed farm worker, Thomas Boronson, and his family were eating one meager meal a day from money earned by selling their blood. One of his children was a sick infant who had been denied medical care because the family could not pay. Boronson and a friend, Lonnie Davis, took over a welfare office in an attempt to get the several hundred dollars owed by the state to the Boronsons. Arrested and convicted of kidnapping and robbery, even though the welfare workers refused to press charges, Boronson and Davis were sentenced to nine and seven years respectively: *Guardian,* May 26, 1976.

38. Charles Silberman, "What You Didn't Know About Criminal Justice," *American Heritage,* June 1982, p. 84.

39. Study by Judge Gerald Heaney, reported in *Washington Post,* August 23, 1991.

40. *San Francisco Chronicle,* February 20, 1992. President Clinton called for a $23 billion crime bill to establish a national police force, build more prisons, and provide severer sentences including life without parole for three-time felony offenders.

drugs. Prisoners who protest such treatment risk being subjected to harsh retribution.[41]

There now exist super-maximum security prisons designed to minimize human contact and maximize sensory deprivation. These "high-tech dungeons" have increased rather than reduced the level of violence and abuse. Prisoners in such special control units never see daylight nor breathe fresh air. They live under constant electronic monitoring, isolated in bare concrete cells. They may not decorate their white cell walls; are denied classes, books, counseling, religious services, communal activities, and hobbies; must eat in their cells; and are not allowed to speak to anyone who passes by. And they are repeatedly harassed, taunted, and severely beaten for infractions of trivial and inconsistent rules. Consequently, some suffer serious physical or psychological deterioration and retreat into madness. Delusional prisoners are put on psychiatric medication and subjected to a still greater frequency of abuse.[42]

The criminal enforcement system is not only unjust, it is highly fallible. Too frequently the guilty go free while the innocent are incarcerated. In hundreds of documented cases, the wrong person is arrested and convicted.[43] A compelling argument against capital punishment is that it assumes the infallibility of a very fallible enforcement process, tainted by coerced confessions, mistaken identification, perjurious testimony, overzealous law officers, suppression of troublesome evidence and fabrication of false evidence, incompetent defense, and rampant class and racial prejudices of judges and juries.[44]

---

41. Jack Henry Abbott, *In the Belly of the Beast, Letters from Prison* (New York: Random House, 1981); Jessica Mitford, *Kind and Usual Punishment: The Prison Business* (New York: Vintage, 1974); Peter Applebome, "Mississippi Jail Deaths Prompt Call for Inquiry," *New York Times,* March 18, 1993. A 1985 study estimated that 26,000 male adult prisoners and additional thousands of incarcerated boys are raped each day in U.S. correctional institutions; the figure is doubtless higher today and is ten times the number of women raped inside and outside of prison: *Press Democrat* (Santa Rosa, Calif.), March 14, 1991. Stephen Donaldson, president of Stop Prisoner Rape, estimates there are 45,000 male prison rapes a day: *New York Times,* August 24, 1993. In a two-year period in the Birmingham, Alabama, jail there were fifty-seven suicide attempts; four were successful: *Pelican Bay Prison Express,* April 1993, p. 10.

42. *Pelican Bay Prison Express,* various issues, 1992 and 1993; Corey Weinstein and Eric Cummins, "The Crime of Punishment at Pelican Bay Maximum Security Prison," *CovertAction Quarterly,* Summer 1993, pp. 38–45. Amnesty International charged that Marion Federal Penitentiary in Illinois violated the United Nations rules for humane treatment of prisoners with a total control environment including permanent lock-down, leg irons, and physical and psychic assaults: NPR news report, December 16, 1987.

43. Martin Yant, *Presumed Guilty: When Innocent People are Wrongly Convicted* (Amherst, N.Y.: Prometheus Books, 1991); Michael Radelet, Hugo Adam Bedau, and Constance Putnam, *In Spite of Innocence: The Ordeal of 400 Americans Wrongly Convicted of Crimes Punishable by Death* (Boston: Northeastern University Press, 1992).

44. Yant, *Presumed Guilty;* Radelet, Bedau, and Putnam, *In Spite of Innocence; New York Times,* April 22, 1994.

Of the people on death row, some are mentally ill or retarded; 10 percent are without counsel and almost all the rest have court-appointed lawyers; a disproportionate number are African Americans charged with killing Whites. Prosecutors are far more likely to seek the death penalty if the victim is White. And White murderers are significantly more likely to have their death sentences commuted than are Black murderers.[45] Almost all death-row inmates are low-income and working class. As Justice William Douglas noted, the death penalty is selectively applied against those who are poor and politically powerless.[46]

Scores of demonstrably innocent persons have been executed in the United States since 1900 and hundreds have been wrongly convicted of capital crimes. In one part of New Jersey alone, a clergyman managed to get authorities to release three men wrongly convicted of capital crimes who had served many years behind bars. If they and hundreds like them had been executed instead of given prison terms, there would have been no opportunity to reopen their cases and demonstrate their innocence.[47]

In brief, poor and working-class persons, the uneducated, and racial minorities are more likely to be arrested, denied bail, induced to plead guilty, and do without a pretrial hearing or adequate representation. They are less likely to have a jury trial if tried; more likely to be convicted and receive a harsh sentence—including the death penalty; and less likely to receive probation or a suspended sentence than are mobsters, businesspeople, and upper- and middle-class Caucasians in general. As has been said, the rich have little reason to fear the legal system and the poor have little reason to respect it.

NONENFORCEMENT: WHEN THE LAW FAILS US

All this is not to suggest that we should be "soft" on crime. It is no crime to be against crime. Effective law enforcement is needed to protect the public from corporate felons, organized mobsters, murderers, muggers, child abusers, spouse batterers, racists, hate-crime perpetrators, and others. But the law frequently fails those most in need of its protection.

---

45. Jeffrey Trachtman, "Why Execute the Retarded?" *Washington Post*, November 17, 1988; Barry Nakell and Kenneth Hardy, *The Arbitrariness of the Death Penalty* (Philadelphia: Temple University Press, 1987); Coleman McCarthy's column in *Washington Post*, December 14, 1986; *New York Times*, August 10, 1989 and May 26, 1993. As of August 1993, 50.6 percent of the prisoners on death row were White; 39.3 percent were African American; the rest were Latino or Native American Indian: *New York Times*, August 20, 1993.

46. *Furman v. Georgia* (1972).

47. *New York Times*, November 9, 1986. On the execution of innocent individuals, see Radelet, Bedau, and Putnam, *In Spite of Innocence*. See also Lake Headley and William Hoffman, *Loud and Clear* (New York: Henry Holt, 1990); *New York Times*, March 15, 1984, November 1, 1987, and December 14, 1989; *Washington Post*, July 17, 1989 and February 13, 1991. An alternative to the death penalty is life in prison without parole.

Women

For instance, every year an estimated two to four million women are beaten by their husbands, ex-husbands, or boy friends. Domestic violence is the single largest cause of injury and second largest cause of death to women in the United States. Women who leave their batterers run an even greater risk of being killed by them than those who stay in the abusive relationship. The law offers little protection. Only a small percentage of male batterers are ever incarcerated. Likewise, only a tiny fraction of rapists are ever prosecuted or incarcerated for any appreciable time.[48] But women who kill their abusers usually receive severe sentences even if the battering has been life threatening and has gone on for many years.

The courts are often a generator of sexism rather than a safeguard against it. Studies show that female lawyers are routinely demeaned by male judges and attorneys. Female witnesses are treated as less credible than males. Child support and alimony are set unfairly low. Female victims of domestic violence find their complaints trivialized by unsympathetic judges.[49] Most women in prison (and many out of prison) have histories of rape, molestations, or beatings by their fathers, husbands, or other men. Incarcerated women are subjected to sexual assault and abuse by male guards.[50] Women who have agitated for equal pay, prison reform, day care, lesbian rights, and legalized abortion have been the object of government surveillance.[51]

Women often earn less for doing the same work as men and are more likely to be relegated to lower-paying, dead-end jobs. The law has been less than energetic in protecting women from sexual harassment on the job or from discriminatory employment practices.[52] Yet, after years of struggle, working women have made important gains, organizing themselves into

---

48. Howard Kurtz, "Battered Women, Reluctant Police," *Washington Post*, February 28, 1988; Jane Caputi and Diana Russell, "'Femicide': Speaking the Unspeakable," *Ms.*, September/October 1990, pp. 34–37; Michael Parenti, *Land of Idols: Political Mythology in America* (New York: St. Martin's Press, 1994), chapter 11, "The Victimization of Women"; East Bay National Organization for Women (California), *News Now* July/August 1993, p. 2.

49. *Washington Post*, May 4, 1989; *Los Angeles Times*, March 24, 1990; *New York Times*, April 20, 1986.

50. *Workers World*, November 26, 1992; Ann Jones, "Sex Exploitation Behind Bars," *Nation*, April 17, 1982, pp. 456–459; *Pelican Bay Prison Express*, April 1993, p. 11. The number of women in prison has quadrupled over the last decade and was 47,691 by the end of 1991.

51. Letty Cottin Pogrebin, "The FBI Was Watching You," *Ms.*, June 1977, pp. 37–44.

52. Title VII of the Civil Rights Act of 1964 offers little protection or remedy from sexual and racist harassments on the job: *Washington Post*, October 22, 1991. As of 1993, women's wages were only 78 percent of men's: *San Francisco Chronicle*, August 20, 1993; Michael Horrigan and James Markey, "Recent Gains in Women's Earnings, Better Pay or Longer Hours," *Monthly Labor Review* (publication of Bureau of Labor Statistics, U.S. Department of Labor), July 1990, pp. 11–17.

unions as nurses, clerical workers, domestics, and factory employees. In noticeable numbers women are moving into professions and occupations previously deemed "unsuitable" for them. Women have won access to safe and legal abortion, although the struggle to retain that right—as with all rights—remains an ongoing one. Feminist organizations also have had some limited success in getting law officials to take more active measures against rapists, batterers, and child molesters.

The agencies of law have been noticeably lax in protecting a woman's right to safe and legal abortion. Advocates of compulsory pregnancy—who believe that a fertilized ovum is a human being with rights that take precedence over its human carrier—have perpetrated scores of bombings and arson attacks against community clinics that provide abortion services, along with hundreds of bomb threats, death threats, acts of vandalism and intimidation, numerous assaults and burglaries, two kidnappings, two attempted murders, and two shootings (one of them fatal) of doctors who performed legal abortions. Police have been openly sympathetic toward the compulsory-pregnancy terrorists who call themselves "pro-life" and remarkably lax about deterring and arresting them.[53]

Gays and Lesbians

Homosexuals are another group who have been the target of legal and social oppression. The U.S. Supreme Court ruled that a teacher could be fired for no other reason than being gay and that the Constitution does not protect homosexual relations between consenting adults even in the privacy of their own homes.[54] Thousands of lesbians and gays have been hounded out of the armed forces because of their sexual orientation.[55] Mothers have been denied custody of their children on the grounds that their lesbian preferences made them unfit parents.[56] In recent years, gays and lesbians have been subjected to a dramatic increase in violent crimes, ranging from physical harassment to murder. The perpetrators frequently get off with lenient

---

53. "Pro-Life?" *In These Times,* April 5, 1993; John Roemer, "Reign of Terror," *San Francisco Weekly,* March 17, 1993, pp. 10–12; *New York Times,* March 11, 1993. Erstwhile FBI director William Webster would not take action against a group of antiabortionists called "Warriors of God," who perpetrated more than twenty bombings and burnings of family planning clinics; Webster claimed they did not constitute "a definable group": *New York Times* editorial, December 7, 1984.

54. *Gish* v. *Board of Education of Paramus, N.J.* (1976); *Bowers* v. *Hardwick* (1986).

55. *New York Times,* August 10, 1989 and September 2, 1990. In 1993, the Clinton administration abolished the policy of trying to screen out gays at the recruitment level and weeding them out once they were in uniform. But they were required to refrain from any public profession and private practice of their sexual preferences while in the military.

56. Mary Jo Risher, *By Her Own Admission* (Garden City, N.Y.: Doubleday, 1977).

sentences or acquittals.[57] The organized struggles launched by homosexuals against antigay housing and employment practices and homophobia in general have met with some success. But homophobic attitudes and actions remain a widespread problem—including among law enforcers themselves.[58]

Children

Children are another seriously oppressed group. Studies suggest that about 25 percent of all women and over 10 percent of all men have been sexually victimized as children, most often between the ages of nine and twelve, usually by close relatives or family acquaintances—criminal offenses that leave lifelong emotional scars on the victims. Yet, only a minute percentage of molesters are ever convicted, and four of every ten convicted are released on probation, with many others receiving only light sentences. Frequently, judges grant custody or unsupervised visitation rights to the sexually abusive parent. Women who try to protect their offspring from abusive mates often face more vigorously punitive court action than the molesters.[59]

More than a million children are kept in orphanages, reformatories, and adult prisons. Most have been arrested for minor transgressions or have committed no crime at all and are jailed without due process. Almost all incarcerated children are from impoverished backgrounds, a majority are African American, Latino, or of some other ethnic minority. Parents who dislike their children's life-style, friends, or "bad attitude" can have them confined indefinitely in psychiatric institutions almost as a matter of course. Minors usually have no standing in court and few legal protections. Incarcerated children are subjected to beatings, sexual assault, prolonged solitary confinement, psychoactive drugs, and, in some cases, psychosurgery.[60]

---

57. *Anti-Gay Violence, Victimization and Defamation,* project director: Kevin Berrill (Washington, D.C.: National Gay and Lesbian Task Force, annual reports 1985 through 1991); Donna Minkowitz, "It's Still Open Season on Gays," *Nation,* March 23, 1992, pp. 368–370; *New York Times,* March 20, 1992. A similar leniency is shown toward hate crimes against ethnic minorities. Thus, in Fort Worth, Texas, a 17-year-old White supremist convicted of participating in the murder of a 32-year-old African American man was let off with probation: *New York Times,* March 25, 1993.

58. In 1992, voters in Colorado passed a measure that denied gays legal protection against discrimination. If the law stands, gays could be fired from their jobs, evicted from their apartments, and denied access to public accomodations without recourse under the law.

59. For personal testimonials regarding incest abuse, see "Childhood Sexual Abuse," *Central Park* (New York), no. 22, Spring 1993; also "Incest Statistics," *Witness,* April 1988, p. 21. In California, incarcerated sex offenders average only thirty-eight months behind bars; nor is it much different in other states: *San Francisco Chronicle,* June 28, 1993; see series on judicial leniency toward sex offenders in *Oakland Tribune,* December 6, 7, and 8, 1992; and Eleanor Bader, "Family Court Fails Abused Children," *Guardian,* March 22, 1989.

60. Louise Armstrong, *And They Call It Help, The Psychiatric Policing of America's Children* (Reading, Mass.: Addison-Wesley, 1993); Bruce Mirken, "Fighting Back" *San Francisco Bay Guardian,* August 19, 1993; Thomas Cottle, *Children in Jail* (Boston: Beacon

War on Drugs?

Even in the much vaunted "war on drugs" one might wish that the law moved more vigorously and in the right direction. The growing prison population consists mostly of petty drug offenders not violent felons and organized mobsters. The federal prison population has tripled since 1980; three-quarters of the new arrivals are drug offenders. They face harsh mandatory sentencing. To illustrate: a California teenager on his way to a rock concert was arrested and sentenced to fifteen years without parole for possession of three grams of LSD, an hallucinogen. (If he had been carrying his LSD in sugar cubes or orange juice, thereby increasing its weight, he would have received life without parole.) In Texas, a young man with less than a gram of LSD got twenty years without parole in federal prison. In Michigan, possession of cocaine has sent first offenders to jail for life without parole. First offenders in nonviolent drug cases average more jail time than murderers and other violent criminals with long records.[61]

The "war on drugs" is principally a war on drug victims, leaving the well-connected, big-time narcotic cartels largely untouched. Little has been done to stop the laundering of drug money through established financial institutions or to prevent U.S. companies from selling the precursor chemicals used in cocaine production. Legislation exists in both instances but it remains virtually unenforced. The Reagan and Bush administrations talked a tough line but drastically cut the Drug Enforcement Agency's investigative staff and halted law enforcement efforts to keep narcotics out of the United States. Profits from the drug trade were being used to fund the right-wing mercenary war against a progressive government in Nicaragua.[62]

Press, 1977); Kenneth Wooden, *Weeping in the Playtime of Others* (New York: McGraw-Hill, 1976). The number of children on Ritalin, a mind-control drug, has doubled every five years and is now about one million a year: Daniel Safer and John Krager, "A Survey of Medication Treatments for Hyperactive Inattentive Students," *Journal of the American Medical Association,* 260, October 21, 1988, pp. 2256–2258.

61. "Notes and Comments" *New Yorker,* April 13, 1992, p. 27; Jim Newton, "Long LSD Prison Terms" *Los Angeles Times,* July 27, 1992; *Wall Street Journal,* December 17, 1991; *Famm-Gram,* nos. 1–7, 1991–1992, newsletter of Families Against Mandatory Minimums. Be it cocaine, marijuana, crack, or alcohol, drug use is significantly higher among White male high-school seniors than among Black male high-school seniors, according to the National High School Senior Surveys, released by the U.S. Department of Health and Human Services, Washington, D.C., 1992. But Black and Latino drug users run a greater risk of arrest partly because law enforcement efforts focus more on low-income urban areas than on affluent White suburbs: *Washington Post,* August 4, 1993.

62. Senate Committee on Foreign Relations, Subcommittee on Terrorism, Narcotics, and International Operations, *Drugs, Law Enforcement and Foreign Policy* (Washington, D.C.: Government Printing Office, 1989); Dan Moldea, *Dark Victory* (New York: Penguin, 1987), pp. 317–324; Coletta Younger in *Christian Science Monitor,* September 11, 1989. Richard Held resigned as head of the FBI's San Francisco office, commenting: "There's never been any war on drugs" just much manipulation of appearances "to give the public the impression something is being done": *San Francisco Examiner,* May 24, 1993.

Racist Law Enforcement

The narcotics infestation also served the function of keeping inner-city populations under siege, leaving them little energy and organization to mobilize against impoverished conditions. For all the talk about favored treatment and quotas, African Americans still confront serious racism in job recruitment, housing, medical care, education, and at the hands of the law.[63] The class and racial biases of the judicial system, along with the higher crime rates in poverty areas, explain why this nation's prison population is disproportionately African American, Latino, low-income, and underemployed. African Americans are less often allowed to plea-bargain their way out of tough mandatory prison sentences and more likely to get longer prison terms than Whites convicted of the same crimes, even when they are first offenders and the Whites are second- or third-offenders.[64]

Police work in the inner cities concentrates on small-time drug dealers, gambling, and larceny. Investigations of police departments in Los Angeles, Las Vegas, Detroit, Chicago, Philadelphia, Baltimore, New York, Houston, and numerous other cities and towns reveal that racism and brutality are widespread and often tolerated by department commanders. The victims of police crimes are most often African American or Latino, and the officers almost always are White.[65]

Here is a very incomplete list of recent instances: Marcus Wiggins, age thirteen, no previous record, beaten and tortured with electric shock by Chicago police; Rodney King, clubbed over fifty times by four Los Angeles officers as he lay on the ground after a car chase; Malice Green, beaten to death by Detroit police officers who dragged him out of his car; Tracy May-

---

63. Mike Davis, *City of Quartz* (New York: Vintage, 1992), pp. 126–127, 159–165, 271–277, 284–296, and passim; Holly Sklar, "Young and Guilty by Stereotype," *Z Magazine*, July/August 1993, pp. 52–61; Jose Suarez, "Survey Reveals Housing Bias in East Bay," *Bay Guardian* (San Francisco), August 19, 1992; *New York Times*, August 26, 1993.

64. *Special Report to the Congress: Mandatory Minimal Penalties in the Federal Criminal Justice System* (Washington, D.C.: U.S. Sentencing Commission, August 1991); Frank Morris, "Black Political Consciousness in Northern State Prisons," paper presented at the National Conference of Black Political Scientists, New Orleans, May 1973; Haywood Burns, "Can a Black Man Get a Fair Trial in This Country?" *New York Times Magazine*, July 12, 1970, pp. 5, 38–46. African-American males are 44 percent of all prison inmates. "Poverty is the key factor in higher Black homicide rates. . . . About 90 percent of victims and killers are of the same race.": Holly Sklar, "Young and Guilty by Stereotype," *Z Magazine*, July/August 1993, pp. 52–61.

65. Christian Parenti, "Law and Order: Torture in Chicago," *Z Magazine*, May 1993, pp. 43–45; Kim Lersch, *Current Trends in Police Brutality: An Analysis of Newspaper Accounts*, Master of Arts Thesis, Sociology Department, University of Florida, 1993; *New York Times*, March 21, 1991; Edward Escobar, "The Dialectics of Repression: The Los Angeles Police Department and the Chicano Movement, 1968–1971," *Journal of American History*, March 1993, pp. 1483–1514; Dan Nicolai, "City Police Get Away with Murder," *Guardian*, April 26, 1989.

berry, age thirty-one, died after a police beating in Hollywood; Annie Rae Dixon, age eighty-four, shot to death by police in Tyler, Texas as she lay in bed; Alex Rivera, a mechanic, shot to death by New York police who believed he had a gun in a paper bag (actually a soda can); Federico Pereira, choked to death by New York police as they removed him from a car; Charles Bush, killed by Las Vegas police who entered his home without a warrant as he slept; Phillip Pannell, age sixteen, fatally shot in the back by police in Teaneck, N.J., as he ran away from officers who were frisking youth in a school yard. Few of the police involved in such cases have been indicted, convicted, or sentenced.[66]

---

66. Parenti, "Torture in Chicago," p. 43; "Public Presses to Stop Police Crimes," *Organizer* (publication of National Alliance Against Racist and Political Repression), January–March 1993, p. 5; *New York Times,* March 21, 1991, and August 5 and August 24,

About twenty U.S. inner cities are being transformed into military occupation zones in what is called "Operation Weed and Seed," a program that targets specific areas for saturation by federal agents, the National Guard, and local police. Criminals are supposedly then "weeded" out with massive paramilitary "antigang" and "antidrug" sweeps, aerial and video surveillance, and special ID requirements for all residents. What actually gets weeded out are the civil liberties of the residents. In addition, under Weed and Seed the Justice Department controls funds previously allocated to human services, thereby preventing monies from going to community activists who might be critical of the status quo.

> Operation Weed and Seed is classic counterinsurgency, and racist to the core. It portrays Black and Latino youth as the enemy. . . . Ultimately there is no plan to eradicate crime in the U.S.—merely a strategy to contain and manage it. Though crime has a somewhat destabilizing and delegitimating effect on the social order, it also functions to keep oppressed people in their place by keeping them terrorized and in disarray. . . . Weed and Seed . . . will help turn large parts of the inner city into crime preserves where the "structurally unemployed" are kept out of sight, confused about the real source of oppression.[67]

Workers

Working people in general have much reason to complain about how the law is enforced. Through most of the history of labor struggle, law officers have been on the side of corporate owners. Police have either looked the other way or actively cooperated when company goons and vigilantes attacked union organizers and picketers. In recent years, in various parts of the country, police have attacked striking farm laborers, truckers, miners, meatpackers, janitors, and factory and construction workers, arresting and injuring hundreds. Many workers have been imprisoned for resisting court injunctions against strikes and pickets, and even for shouting at scab workers or daring to talk back to police while on picket lines. In Elmwood, Indiana, seven strikers were shot by company goons. A striking coal miner in Harlan County, Kentucky, was shot to death by a gun thug, as was another miner in McDowell County, West Virginia, and a farm worker in

1993. For other instances see, Andy Stapp, "24 Lynchings Feared in Mississippi," *Workers World*, November 12, 1992; and Howard Smead, *Blood Justice* (New York: Oxford Univ. Press, 1986). Police crimes also include torture of prisoners: see correspondence from the Center for Constitutional Rights in *Nation*, July 29/August 5, 1991, p. 142.

67. Christian Parenti, "Weed and Seed: The Fortress Culture," *CrossRoads*, September 1993, p. 18.

Texas. In none of these cases did police apprehend anyone—despite eye-witness evidence of the identity of the killers.[68]

The law and its enforcement agents do many worthwhile things. Many laws enhance public safety and individual security. The police sometimes protect life and limb, direct traffic, administer first aid, assist in times of community emergency, and perform other services with commendable dedication and courage. But aside from this desirable *social-service* function, the police serve a *class-control* function—that is, they must protect those who rule from those who are ruled. And they protect the interests of capital from those who would challenge the inequities of the system. The profiteering corporate managers, plundering slumlords, swindling merchants, racist school boards, special-interest legislators, and others who contribute so much to the scarcity, misery, and anger that lead to individual crimes or mass riots leave the dirty work of subduing these outbursts to the police. When the police charge picket lines—beating, gassing, and occasionally shooting workers—they usually are operating with a court injunction that allows them to exert force in order to protect the interests of the corporate owners.

The police confront dangers and social miseries of a kind most of us can only imagine. They deal with the waste products of a competitive corporate society: the ill-fed, the ill-housed, the desperate, and the defeated. The slums are not the problem, they are the solution; they are the way capitalism deals with the surplus people of a market economy. And for all they cost the taxpayer in crime, police, and welfare, the slums remain a source of profit for certain speculators, arsonists, realtors, big merchants, and others. But they do present problems of violence and social pathology that need to be contained. And that is the job of the police: to sweep protest and poverty under the rug—even if it takes a club or gun. Repressive acts by police are not the aberrant behavior of a few psychotics in uniform but the outgrowth of the kind of class-control function that law officers perform and rulers insist upon—which explains why the police are able to get away with murder.

Some police are aware of the class function they serve. Former Boston Police Commissioner Robert DiGrazia summed it up:

> [T]hose who commit the crime which worries citizens most—violent street crime—are, for the most part, the products of poverty, unemployment, broken homes, rotten education, drug addiction and alcoholism, and other social and economic ills about which the police can do little, if anything.

---

68. *Los Angeles Times*, June 16, 1990; *People's Daily World*, June 14, 1989; *People's Weekly World*, January 23, 1990; documentary film, *Harlan County, USA* (1976). On labor's struggle, see Richard Boyer and Herbert Morais, *Labor's Untold Story*, 3rd ed. (New York: United Electrical, Radio, and Machine Workers, 1972).

Rather than speaking up, most of us stand silent and let politicians get away with law and order rhetoric that reinforces the mistaken notion that police—in ever greater numbers and with more gadgetry—can alone control crime. The politicians, of course, end up perpetuating a system by which the rich get richer, the poor get poorer, and crime continues.[69]

A final word about white-collar crime and street crime. We should also be aware of how they are interrelated. The poor get poorer because the rich get richer. The white-collar corporate plunderers take a terrible toll on society, especially upon those who are least able to defend themselves. They help create the very want, scarcity, injustice, and maldistributions that contribute so much to street crime. If it is true that we need more law and order, more respect for other people's rights, then we should start at the top, vigorously applying the law to those who try to grab everything for themselves regardless of the social costs, the illegalities, and the ruinous effects on others.

---

69. Quoted in *Parade*, August 22, 1976. However, even in the best of social circumstances there are ruthlessly self-interested people who resort to violent and unlawful means to get what they want. Not all crime is a reaction to deprivation and class inequity.

9

Political Repression and National Insecurity

Among those whom the state treats repressively are persons who advocate a more egalitarian economic system. According to the established ideology, free-market capitalism is an essential component of Americanism and democracy. If so, then anticapitalists are antidemocratic, un-American, and a threat to national security. Hence, repression is directed against anticapitalists and eventually against anyone who shows an active interest in progressive causes that challenge privileged interests. Under the guise of defending democracy, security agencies regularly violate our democratic rights.

THE REPRESSION OF DISSENT

When directed toward social reforms that benefit the many, the law often appears ineffective. But when mobilized against political dissenters, the resources of the law appear boundless, and enforcement is pursued with a punitive vigor that itself becomes lawless. Dissenters have been spied on, raided, threatened, maligned, beaten, murdered, arrested on trumped-up charges, held on exorbitant bail, and subjected to costly, time-consuming trials that, whether won or lost, paralyze their organizations, exhaust their funds, and destroy their leadership. So people learn that they are not as free as they might think. If they engage in progressive causes that challenge privileged interests, they risk being targeted for repression.

One mechanism of repression is the grand jury. Supposedly intended to weigh the state's evidence and protect the innocent from unjustifiable prosecution, the grand jury usually ends up doing whatever the prosecution wants. Grand juries have been used to conduct "fishing expeditions" against persons with unconventional political views. Required to appear without benefit of counsel and without being told the nature of the investigation, dissidents have been forced to answer questions about their political ideas and personal associations or face imprisonment for refusing. The upshot is to turn them into involuntary informers regarding any conversation or activity to which they have been privy.[1]

Another political-control agency is the Internal Revenue Service (IRS), which has gone after dissidents for purposes having little to do with tax collection. A General Accounting Office study found that some twenty-eight civil rights leaders were audited repeatedly. The Communist Party had its assets seized and was illegally denied tax exemption for years—while the two major pro-capitalist parties enjoyed uninterrupted tax exemption. The IRS audited the National Council of Churches, a liberal organization, and various antiwar groups in order to uncover the sources of their support. Prodded by the White House or conservatives in Congress or even by the CIA, or sometimes acting on its own, the IRS has investigated the Black Panther Party, Students for a Democratic Society, gay rights advocates, environmental groups, journalists, liberal politicians, and many other politically oriented individuals, organizations, and publications.[2]

Disagreement with official policy is often treated as disloyalty. In 1990, when a group of activists and church groups ran a newspaper advertisement calling for a suspension of U.S. aid to the oppressive Salvadoran government, the Justice Department's criminal division demanded that the organization reveal its sources of support and register as a foreign agent—because its advertisement had lent support to anticapitalist guerrillas in El Salvador.[3]

The government often decides which ideas we may be exposed to from abroad. Laws passed during the McCarthy era permit the State Department and the Immigration and Naturalization Service (INS) to exclude anyone who might be affiliated with communist, anarchist, or "terrorist" groups, or engaged in activities "prejudicial to the public interest" and harmful to "national security." Every year under these sweeping provisos, dozens of prominent authors, artists, performers, journalists, scientists, and

---

1. Marvin Frankel and Gary Naftalis, *The Grand Jury* (New York: Hill & Wang, 1977). The Fifth Amendment gives us the right to refuse to testify against ourselves so as to avoid self-incrimination. But if granted immunity from prosecution, a witness no longer has any self-protective grounds for claiming the Fifth and must answer all questions or be jailed for contempt—as happened recently to supporters of a Puerto Rican liberation movement: *Guardian*, December 26, 1984; *New York Times*, June 9, 1988.

2. David Burnham, *A Law Unto Itself, The IRS and the Abuse of Power* (New York: Vintage, 1989), pp. 255–290.

3. See David Corn's report in *Nation*, August 13/20, 1990, p. 156.

labor-union leaders from other countries have been denied the right to visit and address audiences in the United States. Under a 1990 change in the law, supposedly no one can be denied a visa because of ideology, but the State Department and the INS still maintain an ideological "lookout list" of some 345,000 individuals.[4]

Officials and operatives of repressive right-wing governments and almost any emigre departing from a communist country—including persons who just want to pursue more lucrative careers in the USA—have gained easy entry as visitors or permanent residents.[5] In contrast, the *victims* of rightist pro-capitalist regimes—refugees fleeing political repression in El Salvador, Haiti, Chile, and other U.S.-sponsored client states—have been denied entry and deported back to their countries, often to face jail and death.[6] This seeming inconsistency has an underlying logic: rightists are allowed into the country and leftists are not because the left generally opposes the capitalist class order, while the right supports it. In fact, that is the major differentiation between right and left.

Though the U.S. government signed the Helsinki accords (the international agreement not to restrict freedom of movement), it continues to impose travel restrictions on its own citizens. Critics of U.S. policy have been denied passports because the State Department decided that their activities were "contrary to the interests of the United States." Thousands of Americans have been prevented from traveling to Cuba and other communist countries. But there are no restrictions on travel to autocratic dictatorships that are capitalist.[7]

"Loyalty and security" checks have been used by government agencies to deny public employment to people of left persuasion. Private sector em-

---

4. *Washington Post,* July 9, 1990. Persons can be removed from the list if they recant and demonstrate five years of active opposition to communism. For instance, Canadians who have been associated with left groups must formally denounce their past political beliefs, file their fingerprints with the FBI and the Royal Canadian Mounted Police, make pro-American vows, provide proof that they are actively engaged in opposing communism, and provide letters of reference from five persons who are themselves then investigated: Merrily Weisbord, *The Strangest Dream, Canadian Communists, the Spy Trials, and the Cold War* (Toronto: Lester and Orpen Dennys, 1983), p. 7.

5. These include Vietnamese, Salvadoran, Nicaraguan, Cuban, and Afghan right-wingers and erstwhile terrorists.

6. Gil Loescher and John Scanlan, *Calculated Kindness, Refugees and America's Half-Open Door* (New York: Free Press, 1985); United States Committee for Refugees, *Bias and Restrictionism Towards Central American Asylum Seekers in North America* (Washington, D.C.: October 1988); *New York Times,* May 8 and November 12, 1986; *Washington Post,* July 9, 1987.

7. *Cuba Update,* Winter/Spring 1991 and various other issues; *Washington Post,* July 9, 1990. Journalist William Worthy, artist Rockwell Kent, peace advocate Corliss Lamont, and ex-CIA agent (cum-CIA critic) Philip Agee are among the many U.S. citizens who have been denied passports: Corliss Lamont, "Humanism and Civil Liberties," *Humanist,* January/February 1991, p. 7; Philip Agee, *On the Run* (Secaucus, N.J.: Lyle Stuart, 1987).

ployees have no First Amendment protection from employers who might fire them for their views. The courts have ruled that the Constitution prohibits the government but not private businesses or institutions from suppressing speech.[8] People with affiliations to anticapitalist groups have been hounded out of jobs in labor unions, academia, entertainment, and various other fields by both private employers and government investigators.[9]

During the Vietnam War, protestors were attacked by police on dozens of campuses throughout the country and in major demonstrations in Chicago, New York, Los Angeles, and elsewhere.[10] In Orangeburg, South Carolina, police fired into a peaceful campus demonstration, killing three Black students and wounding twenty-seven others. In 1970, Ohio National Guardsmen killed four students and maimed two others who were participating in an antiwar protest at Kent State University. Ten days later, at the all-Black Jackson State College in Mississippi, police opened fire into a women's dormitory where protesting students had congregated, killing two and wounding a dozen others.[11] In these and other such incidents, law-enforcers whose lives were never in danger used lethal weapons against protestors, none of whom were armed. "Impartial investigations" by the very authorities responsible for the killings exonerated the uniformed murderers and their administrative chiefs.

From 1968 to 1971, police attacked the headquarters of the Black Panther Party (a Marxist revolutionary organization) in more than ten cities, wrecking offices, stealing thousands of dollars in funds, and arresting, beating, and shooting occupants in planned, unprovoked attacks, coordinated with the FBI. More than forty Panthers were murdered by police in that period, including Chicago leader Fred Hampton, who was shot while asleep in his bed.[12]

---

8. *Lloyd Corporation* v. *Tanner* (1972); also Max Gordon, "Can Business Fire at Will?" *Nation*, July 14–21, 1979, pp. 42–44.

9. David Caute, *The Great Fear* (New York: Simon & Schuster, 1978); Stanley Kutler, *The American Inquisition* (New York: Hill & Wang, 1982); Philip Meranto et al., *Guarding the Ivory Tower, Repression and Rebellion in Higher Education* (Denver, Colo.: Lucha Publications, 1985); Sigmund Diamond, *Compromised Campus, The Collaboration of Universities with the Intelligence Community, 1945–1955* (New York: Oxford University Press, 1992); Richard Curry (ed.), *Freedom at Risk: Secrecy, Censorship and Repression in the 1980s* (Philadelphia: Temple University Press, 1988).

10. Meranto, *Guarding the Ivory Tower;* Michael Parenti, "Repression in Academia: A Report from the Field," *Politics and Society*, 1, August 1971, pp. 527–537.

11. Jack Nelson and Jack Bass, *The Orangeburg Massacre* (New York: World, 1969); I. F. Stone, "Fabricated Evidence in the Kent State Killings," *New York Review of Books*, December 3, 1970, p. 28; Tim Spofford, *Lynch Street: The May 1970 Slayings at Jackson State College* (Kent, Ohio: Kent State University Press, 1988).

12. Ward Churchill and Jim Vander Wall, *Agents of Repression: The FBI's Secret Wars Against the Blank Panther Party and the American Indian Movement* (Boston: South End Press, 1988).

Through much of the 1970s, a paramilitary "peacekeeping" force, established by the U.S. Bureau of Indian Affairs under FBI direction, carried out a terrorist campaign on the Pine Ridge Reservation that was directly responsible for the deaths of more than sixty supporters of the American Indian Movement and for hundreds of assaults.[13]

The suppression of community activists is a form of counterinsurgency, a way of keeping people victimized. A Chicago community worker observed:

> I remember the police harassment, assisted by the FBI. If it were not for their cruel and unjust campaign, there would probably be a top-notch democratic community organization here, lead by citizens groups and the Panthers. The leaders instead are all dead or in Marion prison, Puerto Rican and Black, and the near west side is still a disaster in spirit and physically. . . . The despair that followed paved the way for [drug] traffickers to stake out the territory— and the Feds helped them. . . . To this day kids are threatened from a very young age, and the family unit is fragmented by deplorable employment and housing policies.[14]

From a class-control perspective, a demoralized, disorganized community is far more easily subjugated than a community operating with democratic unity and strength.

POLITICAL PRISONERS, USA

While we are taught that the United States has no political prisoners, in truth, we have endured a long history of politically motivated jailings. The great American labor leader Eugene Debs and some 6,000 other socialists, pacifists, and radical labor organizers were imprisoned or deported during the First World War or immediately afterward in the Palmer Raids. The anarchists Sacco and Vanzetti were arrested and eventually executed for a crime most investigators and historians say they never committed. Numerous war resisters were arrested during World War II and the Korean War. During the Vietnam War, several thousand youths were jailed for refusing to serve in what they felt was an unjust conflict; thousands more chose exile. Almost every antiwar activist who occupied a position of national or even local leadership was arrested at one time or another; many were jailed or went underground.[15]

---

13. Churchill and Wall, *Agents of Repression;* Peter Mathiessen, *In the Spirit of Crazy Horse* (New York: Viking Press, 1983).

14. Katherine Warpeha, letter to me, December 3, 1992.

15. American Civil Liberties Report edited by Norman Dorsen, *Our Endangered Rights* (New York: Pantheon, 1984).

The Smith Act of 1940 prohibited the mere advocacy of revolutionary ideas and was used to jail scores of Communist Party leaders and other anti-capitalists. Many spent time in jail for refusing to cooperate with congressional witch-hunts during the McCarthy era. Two communists, Julius and Ethel Rosenberg, were convicted of having stolen "atomic secrets" and executed, on what many critics believe was flimsy or nonexistent evidence.[16]

Hundreds of political dissenters have been given astronomical jail sentences—many on relatively minor or vague charges such as illegal possession of weapons, illegal interstate travel, "sedition," and "seditious conspiracy."[17] Aside from the small numbers of radicals who committed acts of violence (bombings, bank robberies, and the like), almost all dissenters have been persecuted primarily for their beliefs and their lawful political activities.

Numerous African American leaders, involved in progressive community causes and struggles against drug pushers, were railroaded into prison on trumped-up charges. There was Martin Sostre, long an opponent of heroin traffic, sentenced to thirty years for dealing in heroin—convicted on the sole testimony of a convict who later admitted that his testimony had been fabricated. Sostre served nine years, mostly in solitary confinement. After much pressure from progressive groups, the governor of New York granted him amnesty.[18]

There was the Reverend Ben Chavis, now president of the NAACP, arrested over a three-year period on seventy-eight trumped-up charges, and acquitted on all in Wilmington, North Carolina. When a White mob invaded the Black community in Wilmington, setting fire to several buildings, the police did nothing to stop them. But a year later, in connection with these same fires, Chavis and nine other community activists were arrested and convicted on the testimony of three persons, including two who were themselves facing long jail terms for an unrelated crime. All three subsequently recanted. Chavis and the nine others received sentences of twenty-nine to thirty-four years.[19]

16. Robert J. Goldstein, *Political Repression in Modern America, From 1870 to the Present* (Boston: Schenkman/Hall, 1978); Bud and Ruth Schultz, *It Did Happen Here, Recollections of Political Repression in America* (Berkeley, Calif.: University of California Press, 1989); Gil Green, *Cold War Fugitive* (New York: International Publishers, 1985); William Schneiderman, *Dissent on Trial* (Minneapolis: Marxist Educational Press, 1983). On the Rosenbergs, see Walter and Miriam Schneir, *Invitation to an Inquest* (New York: Penguin, 1973).

17. *Can't Jail the Spirit, Political Prisoners in the U.S.* (Chicago, Ill.: Editorial El Coqui, c.1990). Webster's dictionary defines "sedition" as "the stirring up of discontent, resistance, or rebellion against the government in power."

18. *Martin Sostre v. Nelson Rockefeller [et al]*, U.S. District Court, New York, May 1970, reprinted in Theodore Becker and Vernon Murray (eds.), *Government Lawlessness in America* (New York: Oxford University Press, 1971), pp. 153–157; *New York Times*, December 25, 1975.

19. Buffy Spencer, "North Carolina: Laboratory for Racism and Repression," *Outfront*, August 1976, p. 9. Chavis served five years before winning release.

Frank Shuford, an African American activist and anticapitalist in Santa Ana, California, developed a number of community programs and helped people organize against drug dealers and their corrupt police allies. He was arrested for the shooting of two store clerks. Neither clerk identified him as the gunman and no material evidence was presented against him. At his trial, Shuford was branded a "revolutionary troublemaker" by the prosecution. His own lawyer conducted a strangely lackadaisical defense, then was himself appointed a district attorney immediately after Shuford was found guilty by an all-White jury and sentenced to thirty years. In prison, Shuford was drugged, beaten, denied medical care, and scheduled for a lobotomy. Only community pressure on his behalf prevented the operation from taking place.[20]

Police seem curiously protective of drug dealers. Leaders of Black Men's Movement Against Crack in New York were spied on, harassed, arrested, and convicted of "illegal possession of weapons, attempted escape, and assault," charges they repeatedly denied.[21] Native American Indian activists Timothy Jacobs and Eddie Hatcher took over a Robeson County, North Carolina, newspaper office one day to bring attention to rampant police corruption, drug dealing, racism, and murder by officials. Tried in federal court for kidnapping, they were acquitted. Tried for the same action in state court, they were sentenced to prison for long terms.[22]

Of the many "legal lynchings" of African American leaders, consider the case of Eddie Carthan. The first African American mayor in Tchula, Mississippi, since Reconstruction and the first to buck the local plutocracy, Carthan refused to appoint cronies of the big planters, declined bribes, and investigated the corruption of previous administrations. He started doing things for the poor who composed the majority in Tchula: a nutrition program, a health clinic, day-care centers, and a housing rehabilitation program. The Board of Aldermen, dominated by planter interests, cut his salary from $600 to $60 a month and barred him from his city hall office. The governor had all federal funds to Tchula cut off, ending most of the mayor's programs. When Carthan retook his office with five auxiliary police, he was charged with assault, convicted on the testimony of a witness who later recanted, and sentenced to three years. The FBI then conducted an exhaustive investigation that led to an additional four-year sentence for fraud (authorizing an assistant to sign his name to a delivery receipt for day-care equipment). Then, after a Black alderman was robbed and murdered and the murderer caught and convicted, Carthan was charged with having

---

20. *Guardian,* September 24, 1975; Shuford Defense Committee Newsletter, January 1978. Shuford served over ten years.

21. *Guardian,* August 3, 1988.

22. *Guardian,* April 5, 1989; *Can't Jail the Spirit,* pp. 37–38.

plotted the murder.[23] He served two years in prison and was released only after protest campaigns were launched around the country. The low-income Black voters of Tchula got a lesson in what happens to democracy when it intrudes upon the interests of entrenched wealth.

Prison inmates who propagate anticapitalist or Black nationalist views or who engage in prison protests have been singled out for mind-control programs. Prisoners like the socialist Stephen Kessler, charged with disrupting a federal penitentiary by "promoting racial unity, collectivizing the inmate population, attempting to secure legislative inquiries . . . into prison conditions and being involved with outside radical groups," are placed in "behavior modification" units to be subjected to mind-altering drugs, beatings, forced rectal searches, prolonged shackling, isolation, and other tortures.[24] In the words of one Oklahoma prisoner: "As long as prisoners confine themselves to gambling, shooting dope, running loan rackets and killing each other, everything is fine. Let them pick up a book on Marx's theory of dialectical materialism and they are immediately branded a communist agitator and locked in solitary confinement."[25] In a class-action suit, Warden Ralph Aaron testified that the special control unit in Marion Federal Penitentiary was used "to control prisoners with revolutionary attitudes and tactics."[26]

The prison uprising at Attica State Penitentiary against inhumane conditions was denounced by Governor Nelson Rockefeller as the work of "revolutionaries." On Rockefeller's orders, state troopers blasted their way into the prison yard. The troopers killed thirty-four inmates and nine prison

---

23. John Wojcik, "The Incredible Frameup of Mayor Eddie Carthan," *World Magazine*, May 6, 1982, pp. 10–11.

24. *Guardian*, January 21, 1976. With its brain-and-body-destroying arsenal of electroshock, psychosurgery, and phenothiazines, psychiatry becomes a weapon of social control, used mostly against recalcitrant women and children, low-income people, the unemployed, and political and cultural dissidents: Bruce Ennis, *Prisoners of Psychiatry* (New York: Avon, 1972); Elliot Valenstein, *Great and Desperate Cures* (New York: Basic Books, 1986); Lenny Lapon, *Mass Murderers in White Coats* (Springfield, Mass.: Psychiatric Genocide Research Institute, 1986); William Arnold, *Frances Farmer, Shadowland* (New York: McGraw-Hill, 1978). At least 5,000 psychiatric patients are killed each year by mind-control drug treatments: Morton Silverman and Phillip Lee, *Pills, Profits and Politics* (Berkeley, Calif.: University of California Press, 1974). An estimated thirty-five million people in the USA are regular users of some form of psychotropic drug; it is a billion-dollar industry: Jenny Miller, "Psychiatry As a Tool of Repression," *Science for the People*, March/April 1983, pp. 14–34.

25. Letter from Chuck Stots, inmate in Oklahoma State Prison, *Liberation*, February 1975, p. 5. Inmates frequently are not allowed to receive political literature and cannot correspond with the editor of any publication that is not on an approved list: *Guardian*, January 17, 1990.

26. Aaron quoted in Phyllis Roa, correspondence in *New York Review of Books*, March 9, 1978. For the horrifying story of how a spirited, politically dissident actress was railroaded into an asylum, tormented, raped, drugged, and finally lobotomized into submission, see Arnold, *Frances Farmer: Shadowland*.

guards who were being held hostage and wounded more than one hundred other inmates. Not a single gun was found among the prisoners. A Special Commission declared the assault to be "the bloodiest attack by Americans on Americans" since the 1890 U.S. Army massacre of Sioux at Wounded Knee.[27]

In the late 1960s and early 1970s, over three hundred members of the Black Panther Party were arrested, many held without bail or trial for long durations. At least fifteen former Panthers, convicted on fabricated evidence and testimony that was subsequently recanted, are still in prison, some for over twenty years, including Panther leader Geronimo Pratt, who has spent eight of his twenty-three years of imprisonment in solitary confinement. Pratt was charged with murdering a woman when he was a twenty-one-year-old UCLA student and Panther leader in Los Angeles. He was convicted on the testimony of a witness who was identified years later as a paid FBI informant. The FBI conveniently lost their surveillance records showing that Pratt was 400 miles away attending a Panther meeting in Oakland at the time of the murder.[28]

An ex-Panther facing the death penalty is Mumia Abu-Jamal, a radio journalist and former president of the Association of Black Journalists. After repeated harassment from law officers, he was shot when trying to stop police from beating his brother. An officer was killed by one of the bullets fired. Abu-Jamal was charged with the death, even though no weapon or ballistic evidence was ever produced linking him to the shooting.[29]

In prison, as of 1994, along with the Black Panthers, were members or former members of the American Indian Movement, (including Leonard Peltier, who has been incarcerated for over seventeen years), the Black Liberation Army, the Republic of New Afrika (a Black separatist movement), Puerto Rican liberation advocates, Irish nationalists, Chicano and North American anticapitalist revolutionaries, community radical organiz-

---

27. Annette Rubinstein, "Attica Now," *Monthly Review,* January 1976, pp. 12–20. A still bloodier attack came in 1993 in Waco, Texas, when FBI and Bureau of Alcohol, Firearms, and Tobacco agents attacked with heavy armor the residence of a Branch Davidian religious group—instead of just arresting its leaders when they were shopping at the mall. The action was initiated supposedly because of illegal possession of firearms. More than eighty members perished in the attack, including at least seventeen children: *New York Times,* October 1, 1993. For an exposé video documentary, see *Waco, the Big Lie* (WACO, P.O. Box 14, Beech Grove, IN 46107).

28. In an earlier armed attack on Panther headquarters, the police attempted to kill Pratt. For Pratt's case and other trumped-up Panther cases, see Nelson Blackstock, COINTEL-PRO (New York: Anchor Foundation, 1988); Ward Churchill and Jim Vander Wall, "The Case of Geronimo Pratt," *CovertAction Information Bulletin,* Winter 1989, pp. 35–39. *Framing the Panthers in Black and White* (documentary film by Chris Bratton and Annie Goldson, WNET-TV, New York, June 26, 1990); *Guardian,* April 4, 1990 and April 3, 1991.

29. Heike Kleffner, "Ex-Panther on Death Row Leads Strike," *Guardian,* November 15, 1989.

ers, and peace activists.[30] The Puerto Rican nationalists, who claim prisoner-of-war status, were given an average sentence of sixty-seven years for seditious conspiracy.[31] One of them, Carmen Vallentin, a housing activist, teacher, and organizer against police brutality, is serving a ninety-eight-year sentence for seditious conspiracy. Like his recent Republican predecessors, President Clinton has done nothing about any of these cases.

Among U.S. political prisoners were the members of Plowshares, a peace group, who jackhammered the concrete around a Minuteman missile silo in Kansas in 1984. For this protest action against nuclear weapons, eleven of them were sentenced to eighteen years in prison.[32] Still in prison is Barbara Curzi-Laaman, a White working-class woman once active in anti-racist organizing and in an "underground anti-imperialist movement." She was given fifteen years for "seditious conspiracy" and has been threatened with additional sentences of 265 years.[33] Another White woman, Linda Evans, organized so effectively against racism that the Louisiana Ku Klux Klan put her on their death list. To protect herself, she purchased guns using a false identification. For this and for harboring a fugitive, Evans was arrested and sentenced to forty-five years.[34] Susan Rosenberg, a revolutionary advocate and former acupuncturist, was arrested along with anticapitalist associate Tim Blunk for weapons possession and false identification. Both were convicted and given fifty-eight years each.[35]

Silvia Baraldini, an Italian citizen, was an antiwar activist and sympathizer of Puerto Rican independence and Black liberation. Refusing to testify before a grand jury, she was tried for conspiracy and criminal contempt and sentenced to forty-three years. Along with Susan Rosenberg and Puerto Rican nationalist Alejandrina Torres, Baraldini was held for two years in the high security unit at Lexington, Kentucky, enduring windowless, unadorned cells, deprived of fresh air and human contact, and sub-

---

30. For a partial listing, see *Can't Jail the Spirit*. One could argue that all prisoners are in some way the victims of capitalism or racism and therefore "political prisoners." But I define political prisoners as only those who are incarcerated because of politically related activities and beliefs, or who suffered extended sentences and mistreatment for becoming politically aware while in prison.

31. *Guardian*, May 30, 1990. Political prisoners like Geronimo Pratt, Puerto Rican nationalist Oscar Lopez-Rivera, and anti-imperialist physician Alan Berkman have been denied medical attention for illnesses contracted or seriously aggravated while in prison. Berkman has been denied treatment for cancer: ibid.

32. *Witness*, March 1986, pp. 14–15 and May 1990, p. 3.

33. *Can't Jail the Spirit*, pp. 170–171.

34. The same Louisiana district court that sentenced Evans also sentenced Don Black, a KKK member who transported illegal weapons and attempted to set up a drug cartel, to three years. He was out in two: Susie Day, "Resistance Conspiracy Trial," *Z Magazine*, September 1989, p. 85.

35. William Reuben and Carlos Norman, "The Women of Lexington Prison," *Nation*, June 27, 1987, pp. 881–883; Day, " Resistance Conspiracy Trial," p. 86.

jected to constant surveillance by a battery of cameras and hostile male guards. In time, their eyesight and health deteriorated.[36]

Neither Curzi-Laaman, Evans, Rosenberg, Blunt, Baraldini, Torres, nor many others like them were ever convicted of assaulting or injuring anyone.

Mark Curtis, packinghouse worker, labor unionist, and a leader in the Socialist Workers Party, was arrested in Des Moines, Iowa, and charged with having sexually assaulted a fifteen-year old. He was severely beaten and knocked unconscious by police. The alleged victim said her attacker was five-feet six-inches tall, had smoke on his breath, and broke into her house. Curtis is over six-feet tall, does not smoke, and was in a restaurant with a dozen other people at the specified time of the rape. After Curtis was convicted on the testimony of one police officer, a juror presented an affidavit indicating that she believed Mark Curtis was not guilty and that she was one of four who voted for conviction even though they had grave doubts about the case. Curtis was sentenced to twenty-five years for "sexual abuse" and "burglary."[37]

During the Gulf War, some 2,000 military personnel were denied their requests for conscientious-objector status and forced to go to war. At least two dozen other service personnel refused on moral grounds to participate and were sentenced to military prison, some for as long as six years. A number of them were worked twelve-hour days and fed starvation diets while incarcerated.[38] In sum, political prisoners receive grossly disproportionate sentences, are routinely denied parole even when qualifying for it, and are subjected to isolation, behavior modification, brutality, and other punitive treatments.

TOWARD A POLICE STATE

Over the years, local and state police have worked closely with federal authorities to suppress anticapitalist and other protest movements. The FBI devoted more effort to investigating the civil rights movement than to the violence perpetrated against it. Those who engaged in the struggle

---

36. Reuben and Norman, "The Women of Lexington Prison," p. 881; Mary O'Melveny, "Lexington Prison High Security Unit," *CovertAction Information Bulletin*, Winter 1989, pp. 49–54. Inmates in the special unit suffer from acute depression, chronic rage reaction, claustrophobia, visual disturbances, vertigo, weight loss, heart palpitations, general malaise, and exacerbation of previous medical problems. Baraldini underwent two operations for cancer. Torres suffered a heart attack.

37. *Guardian*, June 1, 1988; *Des Moines Register*, February 1, 1992; Report from Mark Curtis Defense Committee, Des Moines, Iowa, n.d. As I write this six years later, Curtis is still in jail, having been repeatedly denied parole.

38. Jim Genova and Tim Wheeler, "Two Years after Desert Shield: COs Still in Jail," *People's Weekly World*, August 1, 1992, pp. 12–13.

against racial segregation in the South during the 1960s sometimes suffered physical assault and even death at the hands of White vigilantes, while police and FBI informants either looked the other way or actually assisted.[39]

Nowadays police utilize billions of dollars worth of surveillance hardware—provided by federal authorities—against anticapitalist groups. In 1970, one police official declared that there were more law officers throughout the country "on political intelligence assignments than are engaged in fighting organized crime."[40] A Rand Corporation engineer has speculated that "we could easily end up with the most effective, oppressive police state ever created."[41] In various cities, secret police units, commonly known as "Red squads," spy on and harass lawful advocacy groups, sometimes poking into the private lives of public figures to embarrass or pressure them.[42] In places like Detroit, Los Angeles, Chicago, and New York, Red squads have monitored hundreds of thousands of individuals and organizations.[43] Perhaps one reason authorities cannot win the "war on crime" and the "war on drugs" is that they are too busy fighting the war on political heterodoxy.

As part of that war, the Federal Bureau of Investigation launched—with White House authorization—a counterintelligence program (Cointelpro) designed to expose, disrupt, and misdirect members of progressive groups of any stripe.[44] Working closely with local police Red squads and private

39. Anthony Summers, *Official and Confidential, The Secret Life of J. Edgar Hoover* (New York: G. P. Putnam's Sons, 1993), p. 351. Kenneth O'Reilly, *Racial Matters, The FBI's Secret File on Black America, 1960–1972* (New York: Free Press, 1989). Only after national protests did a reluctant FBI investigate the killing of civil rights advocates James Chaney, Michael Schwerner, and Andrew Goodman: Seth Cagin and Philip Dray, *We Are Not Afraid* (New York: Macmillan, 1988).

40. Quoted in Frank Donner, "The Theory and Practice of American Political Intelligence," *New York Review of Books*, April 22, 1971, p. 28; see also Frank Donner, *The Age of Surveillance* (New York: Knopf, 1980).

41. Quoted in Robert Barkan, "New Police Technology," *Guardian*, February 2, 1972; Les Gapay, "Pork Barrel for Police," *Progressive*, March 1972, pp. 33–36.

42. Mike Rothmiller and Ivan Goldman, *L.A. Secret Police* (New York: Pocket Books, 1992); Frank Donner, *Protectors of Privilege, Red Squads and Police Repression in Urban America* (Berkeley, Calif.: University of California Press, 1991); Steve Burkholder, "Red Squads on the Prowl," *Progressive*, October 1988, pp. 18–23; John Ross, "The Salvador–SF Spy Connection," *Bay Guardian* (San Francisco), May 19, 1993, p. 20.

43. Donner, *Protectors of Privilege;* Rothmiller and Goldman, *L.A. Secret Police;* see also Morris Gleicher, "Detroit's Red Squad Files Open 'Sins of the Past,'" *Guardian*, May 15, 1991, p. 9; Brochure from the Committee Opposed to Police Spying (New York), May 1987. Of the one million police in the United States, half are employed by private corporations to harass and spy on workers, union organizers, and "cause" groups that might prove troublesome to business. These private police firms regularly collaborate with federal and local police: George O'Toole, *The Private Sector: Rent-a-Cops, Private Spies and the Police-Industrial Complex* (New York: Norton, 1978); Jim Hougan, *Spooks* (New York, Murrow, 1978).

44. Quoted in *Village Voice*, September 9–15, 1981, p. 25; see also Nelson Blackstock, *COINTELPRO* (New York: Pathfinder, 1988); Ward Churchill and Jim Vander Wall,

right-wing organizations, the FBI used forged documents, illegal break-ins, intercepted mailings, telephone taps, undercover provocateurs and informants, and false charges.[45] The bureau has infiltrated various labor unions in attempts to brand them "communist controlled" and has cooperated with management in the surveillance of strikers.[46]

As director of the FBI for almost a half-century, J. Edgar Hoover kept elaborate dossiers on the private lives of labor leaders, noted authors, Hollywood stars, and high-placed officials—including presidents and their cabinet members, liberal Supreme Court justices, and members of Congress—often wielding the threat of political blackmail over them. Hoover planted witch-hunting stories in the press, and leaked prejudicial materials to favored columnists. He collaborated with segregationists and harassed civil rights leaders like Martin Luther King Jr. He used FBI funds for his private profit and pleasure and accepted lavish gifts from wealthy friends whom he then protected from criminal investigation. He also cultivated close and corrupt relations with organized crime figures, making no serious effort to move against the mob for more than thirty years.[47]

While much of the FBI's power has been attributed to the unscrupulous resourcefulness of its erstwhile director, Hoover also greatly benefited from the anticommunism that permeated the entire political mainstream. Liberal leaders, fearful of being called "soft on communism," cooperated in extending the FBI's authority.[48] The limitations of law seldom deterred the bureau. Thus it has kept a "security index" of some 15,000 persons, mostly members of anticapitalist groups, who are slated for arrest and detention in case of a "national emergency"—even though the law authorizing this practice was declared unconstitutional.[49]

COINTELPRO Papers: Documents from the FBI's Secret Wars Against Dissent in the United States (Boston: South End Press, 1990).

45. As the *New York Times* belatedly noted, November 24, 1974, "Radical groups in the United States have complained for years that they were being harassed by the Federal Bureau of Investigation and it now turns out that they were right."

46. *Guardian,* July 5, 1978. I found evidence of FBI surveillance of labor disputes in my own FBI dossier, which I received under the Freedom of Information Act. It consisted of reports of my picket-line and boycott work for the United Farm Workers and a report, accidentally placed in my file, of a striking worker in Albany, N.Y., who happened to have the same name as mine.

47. Summers, *Official and Confidential;* Athan Theoharis and John Stuart Cox, *The Boss: J. Edgar Hoover and the Great American Inquisition* (Philadelphia: Temple University Press, 1988); Herbert Mitgang, *Dangerous Dossiers* (New York: Donald Fine, 1988); Hank Messick, *John Edgar Hoover: A Critical Examination of the Director and of the Continuing Alliance Between Crime, Business, and Politics* (New York: David McKay, 1972).

48. William Keller, *The Liberals and J. Edgar Hoover* (Princeton, N.J.: Princeton University Press, 1989).

49. *New York Times,* August 3 and October 25, 1975; Brian Glick, *War at Home* (Boston: South End Press, 1989).

©1976 HERBLOCK

Executive Order 12333, issued by President Ronald Reagan, authorized intelligence agencies to infiltrate and "influence the activities" of organizations—even in the absence of any suspected lawbreaking. The order virtually legalized many illegal Cointelpro tactics used in earlier years. During this period, under the flimsy pretext of fighting "terrorism," the FBI conducted a three-year surveillance of the Committee in Solidarity with the People of El Salvador, resulting in hundreds of organizations and thousands of individuals being placed on its security index.[50] In 1989, it was disclosed

50. General Accounting Office, *International Terrorism: FBI Investigates Domestic Activities to Identify Terrorists* (Washington, D.C.: GAO/GGD-90-112, September 7, 1990); *Washington Post*, November 5, 1989 and February 10, 1991. In 1986, in different parts of the country, more than twenty-five break-ins occurred at homes and offices of opponents of

that the National Lawyers Guild (composed mostly of progressive-minded attorneys) had been repeatedly burglarized and that the FBI had kept that organization under surveillance for fifty years without turning up a bit of illegal activity. During the Gulf War of 1990–91, the bureau questioned some two hundred persons whose only "suspicious" trait was that they had Arab ancestry.[51]

Following the Gulf War, the FBI continued with its break-ins, disruptive infiltrations, and grand jury fishing expeditions. The targeted groups included anticapitalist parties, antiwar organizations, environmental groups, lesbian/gay activists, militant feminists, and supporters of Native American, Central American, Puerto Rican, and political prisoner solidarity groups.[52]

In contrast to the way they treat the left, federal agents have done little to discourage violent right-wing extremist groups and sometimes have supported their activities. In San Diego, the FBI financed a crypto-fascist outfit called the Secret Army Organization, whose operations ranged from burglary and arson to kidnapping and attempted murder.[53] The Senate Intelligence Committee revealed that the FBI organized forty-one Ku Klux Klan chapters in North Carolina. Paid FBI informants in the Klan did nothing to stop Klan members and Nazis who committed murder and other acts of violence. In some instances they assisted the murderers by procuring weapons for them and directing them to the right location.[54]

From 1969 to 1972, U.S. Military Intelligence and the Chicago police Red squad jointly operated an organization called the Legion of Justice. Its

---

Reagan's interventions in Central America; no property ever was stolen. Then-FBI director William Webster claimed these were just individual cases with no links between them: *Washington Post*, December 5, 1986.

51. General Accounting Office, *International Terrorism;* Ann-Mari Buitrago, "The FBI Before Congress: Sessions' Confessions," *CovertAction Information Bulletin,* Winter 1989, pp. 17–19. Ann Talamus, "FBI Targets Arab-Americans," *CovertAction Information Bulletin,* Spring 1991, pp. 4–6.

52. Heather Rhoads, "FBI Ups Psychological Warfare Against Activists," *Guardian,* August 28, 1991, p. 3. As noted earlier, the bureau also has been involved in armed, homicidal attacks—as against the Black Panthers and the American Indian Movement: Churchill and Vander Wall, *Agents of Repression.*

53. *San Francisco Examiner,* January 11, 1976. The FBI provided the Secret Army Organization with $10,000 worth of weapons and explosives and hid a gun used in the group's assassination attempt against a leftist professor: Donner, *The Age of Surveillance,* pp. 444–445.

54. Earl Caldwell's report in *Rights* (National Emergency Civil Liberties Committee) March–April 1983, pp. 3–4; *New York Times,* May 12, 1985; *Guardian,* February 23, 1983; Michael Parenti and Carolyn Kazdin, "The Untold Story of the Greensboro Massacre," *Monthly Review,* November 1981, pp. 42–50. Just before dying, a Klan member and FBI informer confessed to his wife his role in the killing of an African-American man thirty-six years earlier. This has prompted an inquiry into whether or not the bureau tried to protect him from prosecution: *San Francisco Chronicle,* September 11, 1993.

members clubbed and maced protestors and antiwar demonstrators, broke into their headquarters, stole files, vandalized a progressive bookstore, and committed other acts of disruption and violence.[55]

In Chicago, after repeated death threats, Rudy Luzano, a Chicano union organizer and communist, who worked effectively to unite Latinos, African Americans, and Whites around working-class causes, was shot dead in his home by someone who came to his door on the pretense of asking for a drink of water and who stole nothing. According to family members, paramedics who arrived at the scene thought they could save Lozano's life, but police blocked them from getting near him, because "evidence might be destroyed."[56]

In instances of right-wing violence against the left, police rarely manage to catch the perpetrators. Political violence as such seldom bothers the authorities; it depends on who is using it against whom. Thus, when asked what they intended to do about the fifteen or so right-wing paramilitary terrorist camps within the United States, a Reagan-appointed Justice Department official said the camps did not appear to be in violation of any federal statute.[57] When two Chicano socialists were killed by bombs planted in their cars, the FBI made no arrests. When a powerful bomb wrecked the offices of several progressive and civil-liberties groups in New York, injuring three people, the police made only a perfunctory investigation. After a series of threats, an antinuclear organizer was shot dead in Houston and an assistant was seriously wounded; police came up with not a clue.[58]

When agents of the Philippine dictator Ferdinand Marcos conducted operations against Filipino dissidents in the United States, the FBI cooperated with them. One known FBI informant admitted to having witnessed the murder of two Filipino union leaders who were prominent in the anti-Marcos movement in this country.[59]

The FBI also cooperated with El Salvador's security forces, supplying them with the names of Salvadoran refugees who were about to be deported from the United States—so that the security police could apprehend them upon their return. Many of these refugees had fled here in the hope of escaping death and torture.[60] Salvadoran activists in this country have endured assaults, kidnappings, and numerous car smashings and apart-

---

55. Ken Lawrence, "Klansmen, Nazis, and Skinheads: Vigilante Repression," *Covert-Action Information Bulletin,* Winter 1989, p. 31.

56. *Daily World,* June 10, 1983.

57. James Ridgeway, "Looney Tune Terrorists," *Village Voice,* July 23, 1985, p. 23.

58. *Guardian,* February 4, 1981; *New Age,* July 1979, p. 10.

59. The FBI refuses to release hundreds of documents relating to the case: Tony Harrah, "FBI Helped Finger Marcos Foes in U.S.," *Guardian,* June 14, 1989.

60. Vince Bielski, Cindy Forster, and Dennis Bernstein, "The Death Squads Hit Home," *Progressive,* October 1987, p. 18.

ment break-ins (with threatening notes left against them and relatives in El Salvador). The police hardly bestirred themselves, making no attempts to question right-wing suspects.[61]

Individuals in the Cuban American community who have advocated a more conciliatory policy toward the Cuban communist government have been subjected to threats and attacks. An antisocialist Cuban-exile terrorist group claimed credit for some twenty-one bombings between 1975 and 1980 and for the murder of a Cuban diplomat in New York; the group escaped arrest in all but two instances. A car bombing in Miami that cost a Cuban radio news director both his legs also remains unsolved.[62] Likewise, three Haitian talk-show hosts in Miami, who aired critical commentaries about military repression in Haiti, were shot dead between 1991 and 1993.[63]

In the United States, between 1981 and 1987, there were eleven fatal shootings of Vietnamese publishers, journalists, and activists who had advocated normalized relations with the communist government of Vietnam. In each instance, the U.S.-based "Vietnamese Organization to Exterminate Communists and Restore the Nation" (VOECRN) claimed responsibility. One of VOECRN's victims, a publisher of a Vietnamese-language weekly, survived his shooting and identified the gunman, a leader of a Vietnamese extortion gang. The assailant was convicted but the conviction was reversed at the prosecutor's request because "he had no prior criminal record in this country."[64] The police repeatedly claimed that such attacks were unrelated and devoid of a political motive—despite VOECRN's communiqués claiming responsibility. Asserting there was no pattern and no political motive, the FBI refused to get involved.[65]

There is the strange case of Professor Edward Cooperman, an American, who was shot dead while working in his office at California State University, Fullerton. As founder of an organization advocating scientific cooperation with Vietnam, Cooperman had received death threats. Lam

61. Bielski et al., "The Death Squads Hit Home," pp. 15–19.

62. Jeff Stein, "Inside Omega 7," *Village Voice,* March 10, 1980, pp. 1, 11–14; *Cuba Update* (Center for Cuban Studies, New York), October 1980, p. 3; Peter Katel, "A Rash of Media Murders," *Newsweek,* July 5, 1993, p. 50. The Center for Cuban Studies was itself destroyed by a bomb in March 1973; its director Sandra Levinson miraculously escaped serious injury. Police hardly bestirred themselves.

63. Their names were Jean-Claude Olivier, Fritz Dor, and Dona St. Plite: Committee to Protect Journalists, report, *Silenced by Death: Journalists Killed in the United States (1976–1993)* (New York, 1993); *New York Times,* October 26, 1993.

64. Steve Grossman, "Vietnamese Death Squads in America?" *Asia Insights* (Asia Resource Center, Summer 1986), pp. 1–8; Steve Grossman, "Vietnamese Death Squads: Is This the End?" *Indochina Newsletter* (Asia Resource Center), May–June 1988, pp. 1–7.

65. Grossman, "Vietnamese Death Squads in America?" and his "Vietnamese Death Squads: Is This the End?"

Van Minh, a Vietnamese émigré and Cooperman's former student, admitted witnessing the professor's death and was arrested. As he tells it, Cooperman produced a gun that accidentally discharged and killed him. Minh left in a panic, taking the gun with him. He then took a female friend to a movie, after which, he returned to the office and placed the gun in Cooperman's hand. The office had the appearance of a struggle which, Minh's attorney argued, resulted merely from the professor's attempts to get up after being left for dead. The prosecution introduced little to dispute Minh's improbable story. He was convicted only of involuntary manslaughter, sentenced to three years and served one.[66]

In 1987, after a bombing that killed a Vietnamese-language publisher in Garden Grove, California, police finally acknowledged the existence of right-wing Vietnamese terrorism and officially requested FBI assistance. The bureau launched an investigation to determine whether "a pattern is emerging."[67]

Other political murders (or suspicious deaths) in the United States include Manuel De Dios, a reporter and editor who frequently pointed the finger at drug dealers and money launderers; Alan Berg, a popular Denver talk-show host who engaged in impassioned arguments with anti-Semitic and racist callers and who was shot by members of a White supremist group; Don Bolles who, at the time of his murder, was involved in an investigation of a far-reaching financial scandal said to implicate some of Arizona's most powerful political and business leaders; Karen Silkwood, who was investigating radiation safety negligence at Kerr-McGee corporation; and Danny Casolaro, whose investigation of government and business corruption might have implicated high-ranking U.S. officials.[68] None of these murders has been thoroughly investigated.

The FBI was quick to make arrests when environmentalists Judi Bari and Darryl Cherney were seriously injured by a car bomb in 1990. They arrested the victims, Bari and Cherney, calling them "radical activists," charging that the bomb must have belonged to them. Bari is an outspoken

---

66. Grossman, "Vietnamese Death Squads in America," pp. 3–4. Minh had been previously arrested for possession of stolen property, at which time police found guns and ammunition in his car and home. Minh's lawyer was procured by Tran Minh Cong, spokesman for the right-wing "National United Front for the Liberation of Vietnam": ibid.

67. Grossman, "Vietnamese Death Squads: Is this the End?" pp. 3–4; Committee to Protect Journalists, *Silenced by Death.* Occasionally the FBI acts as it should. When Henry Liu, who wrote critically of the Taiwan government, was murdered in 1984, the FBI made a vigorous investigation leading to the conviction of a Taiwanese émigré in this country and several officials in Taiwan: Katel, "A Rash of Media Murders," p. 50.

68. Committee to Protect Journalists, *Silenced by Death;* Richard Rashke, *The Killing of Karen Silkwood* (New York: Penguin, 1981); David MacMichael, "The Mysterious Death of Danny Casolaro," *CovertAction Quarterly* (Winter 1991–92), pp. 53–57; on Don Bolles, see Max Dunlap and William Hofman, *Loud and Clear* (New York: Henry Holt, 1990).

advocate of nonviolence. The charges were eventually dropped for lack of evidence. The FBI named no other suspects.[69]

That neo-Nazis, skinheads, and other rightist terrorists repeatedly have been able to commit acts of violence and even publicly claim responsibility without getting caught, means law enforcers have made little effort to monitor and deter their actions, unlike the way they monitor legal, peaceful groups on the Left.[70] Again, there is nothing inconsistent about this position. Left groups—no matter how nonviolent and lawful—challenge the capitalist system or some aspect of its privileges and abuses, while rightist groups—no matter how violent and unlawful—do the dirty work for that system. Thus there is a community of interest between the rightists and the law agencies and often a community of methods.

THE NATIONAL SECURITY AUTOCRACY

Within the government there exists what some have called "the national security state," consisting of the president, the secretaries of state and defense, the National Security Council, the Joint Chiefs of Staff, and numerous intelligence agencies. The national security state often operates like an unaccountable sovereign power of its own. Its primary function is to defeat political forces that seek alternatives to capitalism at home or abroad or that try to introduce any economically redistributive politics, even within the existing capitalist framework.[71]

Making the world safe for free-market capitalism is a massive enterprise. Security agencies expend an estimated $28 billion to $30 billion yearly on operations at home and abroad, probably more.[72] Congress has no exact idea how much it allocates for intelligence operations because the total figure is hidden in other budget items—in violation of the U.S. Constitution.[73]

---

69. *Guardian,* July 3, 1991, p. 5; Judi Bari, "The Return of COINTELPRO," *Lies of Our Times,* September 1993, pp. 3–5.

70. *SPLC Report* (publication of the Southern Poverty Law Center), October 1993, p. 1. However, when right-wing extremists engage in counterfeiting and bank robberies, and plan attacks against police and military bases as part of a war against the government, then law enforcers move against them: Lawrence, "Klansmen, Nazis, and Skinheads . . ." pp. 32–33.

71. See Michael Parenti, *The Sword and the Dollar: Imperialism, Revolution, and the Arms Race* (New York: St. Martin's Press, 1989); Darrell Garwood, *Under Cover: Thirty-Five Years of CIA Deception* (New York: Grove Press, 1985); William Blum, *The CIA, A Forgotten History* (London: Zed Press, 1986); Victor Marchetti and John Marks, *The CIA and the Cult of Intelligence* (New York: Dell Books, 1980).

72. *Washington Post,* July 21, 1990.

73. Article I, section 9 of the Constitution reads: "No Money shall be drawn from the Treasury, but in Consequence of Appropriations made by Law; and a regular Statement and

Of the various agencies of the national security state, the Central Intelligence Agency (CIA) is the most widely known, probably because of its extensive covert actions throughout the world.[74] In addition, there is the Pentagon's National Security Agency (NSA). Created in 1952 by President Truman in an executive order that has remained secret to this day, NSA's mission is to break codes and monitor nearly all telephone calls and telegrams between the United States and other countries and a great deal of domestic telephone traffic. There is the Pentagon's Defense Intelligence Agency, which deals with military espionage and counterintelligence around the world; the State Department's Bureau of Intelligence and Research, and the FBI's counterintelligence program. Within the Pentagon itself, every echelon—be it the Office of the Secretary of Defense, the Army, Navy, or Air Force, or the regional commands around the globe—has its own intelligence service with its own security, communications, and support services.[75]

While supposedly protecting us from foreign threats, the various intelligence agencies spend a good deal of time policing and propagating views among the U.S. public. They have admitted to maintaining surveillance on members of Congress, the White House, the Treasury and Commerce departments, and on vast numbers of private citizens. They have planted stories in the U.S. media to support their cold-war and counterinsurgency view of the world, secretly enlisting the cooperation of newspaper owners, media network bosses, and hundreds of journalists and editors.[76] The CIA alone has subsidized the publication of hundreds of books and has owned outright "more than 200 wire services, newspapers, magazines, and book publishing complexes," according to a Senate Intelligence Committee report.[77] The agency has recruited some 5,000 academicians from across

---

Account of the Receipts and Expenditures of all public Money shall be published from time to time." In 1993, by a 264–164 vote, the House of Representatives again violated the Constitution, defeating an amendment that would have required public disclosure of expenditures for intelligence agencies: *Pittsburgh Post-Gazette,* August 5, 1993.

74. See Philip Agee and Louis Wolf (eds.), *Dirty Work, The CIA in Western Europe* (Secaucus, N.J.: Lyle Stuart, 1978); Philip Agee and Louis Wolf (eds.), *Dirty Work II, The CIA in Africa* (Secaucus, N.J.: Lyle Stuart, 1979); John Ranelagh, *The Agency* (New York: Simon & Schuster, 1985); Marchetti and Marks, *The CIA and the Cult of Intelligence.*

75. *Final Report of the Select Committee to Study Governmental Operations With Respect to Intelligence Activities,* Senate Report 755, 94th Congress, 2nd Session, 1976; James Bamford, *The Puzzle Palace: A Report on America's Most Secret Agency* (Boston: Houghton Mifflin, 1982); *Washington Post,* October 9, 1990.

76. Ralph McGehee, *Deadly Deceits* (New York: Sheridan Square Publications, 1983); Stuart Loory, "The CIA's Use of the Press," *Columbia Journalism Review,* September/October 1974, pp. 9–18; Deborah Davis, *Katherine the Great: Katherine Graham and the Washington Post* (Bethesda, Md.: National Press, 1987), pp. 176–189.

77. Melvin Beck, *Secret Contenders: The Myth of Cold War Counterintelligence* (New York: Sheridan Square Press, 1984); *New York Times,* December 25, 26, and 27, 1977.

the country as spies and researchers, secretly financing and censoring their work. CIA agents participate in academic conferences and the agency conducts its own resident-scholar programs. It offers internships and tuition assistance to undergraduate and graduate students while they are still attending school.[78]

Intelligence agencies have infiltrated and financed student, labor, scientific, and peace groups. The CIA has financed research on mind-control drugs, sometimes on unsuspecting persons, and was responsible for the death of at least one government employee.[79] In violation of the National Security Act of 1947, which states that the CIA "shall have no police, subpoena, law enforcement or internal security functions," the agency has

---

78. Robert Witanek, "Students, Scholars and Spies: The CIA on Campus," *CovertAction Information Bulletin* (Winter 1989), pp. 25–28; *New York Times*, February 27, 1980. Among the many academics recruited by the CIA was Harvard professor Samuel Huntington.

79. John Marks, *The Search for the Manchurian Candidate* (New York: Times Books, 1979). The CIA gave Georgetown University $375,000 to subsidize CIA experiments on humans. Erstwhile CIA director Stansfield Turner said 149 mind-control projects were carried out at over eighty institutions over twenty-five years: *First Principles,* September 1977, pp. 8–9.

equipped and trained local police forces in the United States.[80] Under President Reagan's Executive Order 12333, the CIA was authorized to conduct domestic surveillance and covert operations against U.S. citizens both in the United States and abroad. The order (still in effect as of 1994) also authorizes intelligence agencies to train and support local police and enter secret contracts with corporations, academic institutions, other organizations and individuals for the provision of services and goods.[81]

U.S. intelligence agencies have perpetrated terrible crimes against the peoples of other nations. In countries like Guatemala, Greece, Brazil, Chile, Indonesia, Argentina, Zaire, and the Philippines, U.S. national security forces have used military intervention, terror, sabotage, bribery, propaganda, and political disruption to bring down populist or democratically elected governments and install reactionary dictatorships friendly to U.S. corporate interests. Countries that embarked upon popular revolutions, such as Nicaragua, Mozambique, and Angola, found their economies and peoples devastated by the murderous assaults of U.S.-supported mercenary armies. The CIA has sabotaged and stolen elections abroad, waged massive disinformation campaigns, and infiltrated and fractured the trade-union movements of other nations. It has funded and trained secret armies, paramilitary forces, torture squads, and death squads and pursued destabilization and assassination campaigns against labor, peasant, religious, and student organizations in numerous nations.[82]

After World War II, U.S. intelligence agencies put thousands of Nazi war criminals and their collaborators on the U.S. payroll, utilizing them in repressive operations against the Left in Latin America and elsewhere. "Murderers, far from being exempted from such protection, seem to have been among those most likely to obtain it."[83] A network of Eastern Euro-

---

80. *Congress and the Nation, 1945–1964* (Washington, D.C.: Congressional Quarterly Service, 1965) p. 249; Ranelagh, *The Agency*.

81. *New York Times*, December 5, 1981; William Schaap, correspondence in *New York Times*, May 5, 1987.

82. Parenti, *The Sword and the Dollar*; Blum, *The CIA: A Forgotten History*; Agee and Wolf (eds.), *Dirty Work, The CIA in Western Europe* and *Dirty Work II, The CIA in Africa*; Philip Agee, *Inside the Company* (London: Allen Lane, 1975); Garwood, *Undercover: 35 Years of CIA Deception*; Edward Herman, *The Real Terror Network* (Boston: South End Press, 1982); Ralph McGehee, "The Indonesia File," *Nation*, September 24, 1990, pp. 296–297. Jesse Leaf, an ex-CIA agent active in Iran, reported that CIA operatives instructed the Shah's secret police on interrogation "based on German torture techniques from World War II" and that the torture project was "all paid for by the USA": *New York Times*, January 7, 1979.

83. Peter Dale Scott, "How Allen Dulles and the SS Preserved Each Other," *CovertAction Information Bulletin*, Winter 1986, p. 5; also Howard Blum, *Wanted: The Search for Nazis in America* (New York: Quadrangle, 1977); Christopher Simpson, *Blowback: America's Recruitment of Nazis and Its Effects on the Cold War* (New York: Weidenfeld and Nicolson, 1988). The father of General John Shalikashvili, President Clinton's choice as chair of the

pean fascists, anti-Semites, racists, and Nazi collaborators found a home in the ethnic outreach program of the Republican party.[84]

U.S. intelligence agencies have used mobsters, drug dealers, and warlords in their war against those who resist the encroachments of global corporatism. The CIA supplied arms and money to the Italian and Corsican Mafias to beat and murder members of communist-led dockworkers' unions in Italy and France. After these unions were broken, the mobsters were given a freer hand in transporting tons of heroin each year from Asia to Western Europe and North America.[85] The CIA buttressed anticommunist warlords in Southeast Asia and Afghanistan, whose opium production increased tenfold soon after the agency moved into these regions. Likewise, CIA involvement in Central America contributed to the U.S. cocaine epidemic of the 1980s. CIA planes transported guns and supplies down to right-wing mercenary troops in Nicaragua and pro-capitalist military leaders in other countries; the planes then were reloaded with narcotics for the return trip to the United States.[86]

CIA operatives participated with Mafia associates and business and political leaders to profit from the multibillion-dollar savings-and-loan swindles. Monies gained from such deals, along with drug money laundered through various banks and other financial institutions, were illegally used to finance CIA covert activities.[87]

There exists a mountain of evidence suggesting that elements of the intelligence community, assisted by certain mobsters, were involved in the assassination of President John Kennedy in 1963 and in the subsequent massive cover-up. Kennedy was considered a dangerous liability by the intel-

---

Joint Chiefs of Staff, fought in a unit organized by the Nazi SS, yet had no trouble settling in Illinois—despite a law that bans all SS members from entry into this country: *New York Times,* August 28, 1993.

84. Russ Bellant, *Old Nazis, the New Right and the Reagan Administration* (Cambridge, Mass.: Political Research Associates, 1988).

85. Alfred McCoy, *The Politics of Heroin* (Brooklyn, N.Y.: Lawrence Hill, 1991), pp. 61–62.

86. Senate Committee on Foreign Relations, Subcommittee on Terrorism, Narcotics, and International Operations, report, *Drugs, Law Enforcement and Foreign Policy* (Washington, D.C.: U.S. Government Printing Office, 1989); Leslie Cockburn, *Out of Control* (New York: Atlantic Monthly Press, 1987); McCoy, *The Politics of Heroin;* Henrick Kruger, *The Great Heroin Coup* (Boston: South End Press, 1980); Peter Dale Scott and Jonathan Marshall, *Cocaine Politics* (Berkeley: University of California Press, 1991); Jonathan Kwitny, *The Crimes of Patriots* (New York: W. W. Norton, 1987).

87. Senate Committee on Foreign Relations, *Drugs, Law Enforcement and Foreign Policy* and other citations in previous footnote; also Pete Brewton, *The Mafia, CIA & George Bush* (New York: Shapolsky, 1992); Rebecca Sims, "The CIA and Financial Institutions," *CovertAction Information Bulletin,* Fall 1990, pp. 43–48; Joseph Palermo, "CIA Links to the Savings and Loan Scandal," *Monthly Planet,* August 1990, pp. 14–16; Jack Colhoun, "BCCI: The Bank of the CIA," *CovertAction Quarterly,* Spring 1993, pp. 40–45.

ligence community and right-wing groups because of what were perceived to be his "liberal" foreign and domestic policies, including his unwillingness to pursue an all-out ground war in Indochina, and his determination to bring the intelligence community under tighter executive control.[88]

In 1982, at the urging of the Reagan administration, Congress passed a law that made it a crime to publish any information that might lead to the disclosure of the identities of present or former intelligence agents and informers, even if the information came from already published sources. Under the law, some journalistic exposures of illegal covert activities themselves became illegal.

It has been argued that a strong intelligence system is needed to gather information for policymakers. But the CIA and some other agencies have been involved in covert actions that go beyond intelligence gathering and any lawful mandate—including economic and military sabotage, disinformation campaigns directed against the U.S. public itself, drug trafficking, and mercenary wars, assassinations, and other terrorist acts against numerous nations and movements. As one former CIA officer wrote:

> My view, backed by 25 years of experience is, quite simply, that the CIA is the covert action arm of the presidency. Most of its money, manpower and energy go into covert operations that . . . include backing dictators and overthrowing democratically elected governments. . . . The CIA uses disinformation, much of it aimed at the U.S. public, to mold opinion. . . .
>
> But if the Agency actually reported the truth about the third world, what would it say? It would say that the United States installs foreign leaders, arms their armies and empowers their police to help those leaders repress an angry, defiant people; that the CIA-empowered leaders represent only a small fraction who kill, torture and impoverish their own people to maintain their position of privilege. . . .
>
> Instead . . . the Agency plants weapons shipments, forges documents, broadcasts false propaganda, and transforms reality. Thus it creates a new reality that it then believes.[89]

---

88. Here is but a light sampling of the mountain of critical evidence of a national-security state conspiracy in the JFK assassination: Jim Marris, *Crossfire* (New York: Carroll and Graf, 1989); Sylvia Meagher, *Accessories After the Fact* (New York: Vintage, 1992); Jim Garrison, *On the Trail of Assassins* (New York: Sheridan Square Press, 1988); James Di Eugenio, *Destiny Betrayed* (New York: Sheridan Square Press, 1992); Robert Morrow, *First-Hand Knowledge, How I Participated in the CIA–Mafia Murder of President Kennedy* (New York: Shapolsky. 1992); Michael Kurt, *Crime of the Century* (Knoxville: University of Tennessee Press, 1982); Harold Weisberg, *Whitewash II* (privately published, 1966); Mark Lane, *Rush to Judgment* (New York: Holt, Rinehart & Winston, 1966); Mark Lane, *Plausible Denial* (New York: Thunder's Mouth Press, 1991); Alan Weberman and Michael Canfield, *Coup d'Etat in America* (San Francisco: Quick American Archives, 1992).

89. McGehee, *Deadly Deceits,* pp. xi and 194.

Watergate and Iran-contra

In June 1972, a group of ex-CIA agents were caught breaking into the Democratic party headquarters in the Watergate building in Washington, D.C. The burglary was part of an extensive campaign involving electoral sabotage, wiretapping, theft of private records, and illegal use of campaign funds—directed by members of President Nixon's White House staff. It was subsequently revealed that Nixon himself was involved in the Watergate skulduggery and its related cover-up activities. Facing impeachment, he resigned from office. Vice-President Gerald Ford succeeded to the presidency and promptly pardoned Nixon for all crimes relating to Watergate, including any that might come to light at some future time. Members of the administration found guilty in the Watergate affair were given relatively light sentences. Nixon retired on a fat presidential pension.

Congress and the press treated Watergate as a deviant instance of government lawlessness. In fact, for many decades these same practices had been employed against the political left. What shocked the establishment politicians was that this time the crimes were committed against a segment of the establishment itself—specifically the Democratic party and mainstream media people.

In 1986, another scandal, known as "Iran-contra," rocked the White House. It was discovered that the Reagan administration had been sending millions of dollars worth of secret arms shipments to Iran, a country it had repeatedly accused of supporting terrorism. As part of a covert operation to bypass Congress, the law, and the Constitution, the funds had been funneled to the Nicaraguan mercenaries known as the "contras." Funds also may have been diverted to pay for the television campaign expenses of conservative Republican candidates in the 1986 election. President Reagan admitted full knowledge of the arms sales, but claimed that he had no idea what happened to the money earned from the sales. He asked the public to believe that these unusual and unlawful policies were conducted by subordinates, including his own National Security Advisor, without being cleared with him. In subsequent statements, his subordinates said that Reagan had played an active role in the entire Iran-contra affair.[90]

A special prosecutor did manage to get convictions against a number of administration officials involved in Iran-contra. But of the eleven persons convicted of perjury, destroying government documents, obstructing justice, illegally diverting funds, or other such crimes, nine were given pro-

---

90. Jonathan Marshall, Peter Dale Scott, and Jane Hunter, *The Iran-Contra Connection* (Boston: South End Press, 1988); *Report of the Congressional Committee Investigating the Iran-Contra Affair* (Washington, D.C.: Government Printing Office, 1987).

bation and light fines; only one went to jail for a short spell.[91] Some of the people involved in Iran-contra, such as former CIA director and then-Vice President George Bush, were never even called before congressional investigators nor indicted by special prosecutors, despite testimony directly implicating them.[92]

Special prosecutor Lawrence Walsh noted the "lack of concern for applying the rule of law to officials of the intelligence community."[93] As if to confirm his assertion, Senate Republicans managed to kill the legislation that would have renewed the so-called Watergate law, which had assured independent investigations of criminal acts perpetrated by top government officials.[94]

Under the guise of "fighting communism" or "protecting U.S. interests," the purveyors of state power have committed horrendous crimes against the people in this and other countries, violating human rights and the Constitution in order to make the world safe for privilege and profit. The ancient question of political philosophy, *quis custodiet ipsos custodes* (who guards the guardians?), remains with us. The national security state continues to operate like a state within the state, a law unto itself.

---

91. *New York Times,* June 17, 1992; also the correspondence by Garry Emmons on the potentially disqualifying connections and bias of one of the appeals judges in Iran-contra: *New York Times,* August 24, 1990.

92. *New York Times,* July 30, 1990.

93. *People's Daily World,* October 20, 1990.

94. *New York Times,* September 30 and October 1, 1992.

10

The Mass Media: For the Many, by the Few

It is said that a free and independent press is a necessary condition for democracy and that, while the news in autocratic countries is controlled, we Americans supposedly have access to a wide range of competing sources. In reality, we have a press that is far from free. The mass media (newspapers, magazines, radio, films, and television) are owned by the privileged few.[1] How we perceive the politico-economic world is largely determined by those who control the communications world. The issues and events they cover are the ones that win the public's attention; those that are ignored are deprived of visibility and credibility.

HE WHO PAYS THE PIPER

Despite all the talk of a free press, the major media are an inherent component of corporate America, being themselves highly concentrated conglomerates controlled by the top banks and corporations and a handful of conservative tycoons. As of 1989 twenty-three corporations controlled most of the national media—down from fifty in 1982. About 80 percent of the daily-newspaper circulation in the USA belongs to chains like Gannett and Knight-Ridder, and the trend in owner concentration continues unabated. For example, from 1966 to 1990, Gannett grew from 26 dailies to 88 dailies, 23 weeklies, 13 radio stations, 17 TV stations, and numerous cable and sat-

---

1. "Press" and "media" are used interchangeably herein.

ellite operations. Today less than 4 percent of U.S. cities have competing newspapers under separate ownership.[2]

A handful of publishers dominate the magazine business, and six major companies distribute virtually all the magazines sold on newsstands. Eleven publishers control most of the book-sales revenues, and a few bookstore chains enjoy the lion's share of the distribution.[3] A handful of companies and banks control the movie industry. Three giant networks, ABC, CBS, and NBC, still dominate the television industry, and ten corporations command most of the nation's radio audience.[4] The major stockholders of ABC and CBS are banks such as Chase Manhattan, Morgan Guaranty Trust, Citibank, and Bank of America. NBC is owned outright by General Electric. Representatives of the more powerful banks and corporations— including IBM, Ford Motor Corporation, American Express, General Motors, Mobil Oil, Xerox, and many others—sit on the boards of all the major networks and publications.[5]

The corporate media are lucrative investments. Newspapers generally achieve profits of 30 to 35 cents on every dollar of revenue. These bloated margins come mostly out of the labor of those who write and put together the papers. Broadcast revenues are equally lush.[6]

Media owners are not hesitant to exercise an ideological control over news content. As one group of scholars reported: "The owners and managers of the press determine which person, which facts, which version of

---

2. Michael Parenti, *Inventing Reality, The Politics of News Media*, 2nd ed. (New York: St. Martin's Press, 1993), chapters 2, 3, and 7; Ben Bagdikian, *The Media Monopoly*, 3rd ed. (Boston, Beacon Press, 1990); Jean Tepperman, "Sold to the Highest Bidder," *Bay Guardian* (San Francisco), January 6, 1993, pp. 16–19.

3. Major book publishers are now owned by business conglomerates that are not above interfering directly with the publishing process, suppressing books that are critical of the corporate world; for specific instances, see Jon Weiner, "Murdered Ink," *Nation*, May 31, 1993, pp. 743–750; Charlotte Dennett, "Book Industry Refines Old Suppression Tactic," *American Writer*, March 1984, pp. 5–6; Richard Bellman, "Publish or 'Privish,'" ibid., pp. 5, 7.

4. Bagdikian, *The Media Monopoly;* Michael Zagarell, "How the Structural Crisis Affects the Ideological Struggle," *Political Affairs*, August 1987, pp. 7–14; *New York Times*, May 15, 1989.

5. Peter Dreier and Steve Weinberg, "Interlocking Directorates," *Columbia Journalism Review*, November/December 1979, pp. 51–68; Bagdikian, *The Media Monopoly*. Like other businesses, media corporations are diversified and multinational, controlling outlets throughout the world. The U.S. media are global media: Herbert Schiller, *Mass Communication and American Empire*, 2nd ed., (Boulder, Colo.: Westview, 1992).

6. As the conservative *U.S. News and World Report* (May 13, 1985) notes, "The profits are almost unbelievable"; see also *America's Censored Newsletter*, August 1992, p. 3; *Extra!*, January/February 1991, p. 10. Along with stockholders, top media brass get in on the gravy; in 1990 the best paid was Time Warner CEO Steve Ross, who made $78 million in salary and stock profits: *Los Angeles Times*, November 26, 1991.

the facts, and which ideas shall reach the public."[7] In recent times, various media bosses have refused to run ads that advocated single-payer health insurance, criticized U.S. intervention in El Salvador, or opposed the North American Free Trade Agreement (strongly supported by big business). Media heads have suppressed stories critical of corporate and political elites at Bohemian Grove, fired a film reviewer for calling the movie *Patriot Games* a "right-wing cartoon," suppressed a laudatory review of the movie *JFK* and forced its author to resign, fired a writer who admitted to a homosexual orientation in a column dealing with violence against gays, dismissed a reporter for her after-hours advocacy of a ballot proposition that would protect gays and lesbians from workplace discrimination, and suppressed stories and opinion columns criticizing President Bush's pursuit of the Gulf War.[8]

Corporate advertisers also leave their conservative imprint on media content. They might cancel advertising accounts not only when they feel the reporting reflects poorly on their product, but also when they disapprove of what they perceive as "liberal" biases in news reports and commentary. Media bosses are keenly aware of this. As erstwhile president of CBS Frank Stanton said, "Since we are advertiser-supported we must take into account the general objective and desires of advertisers as a whole."[9]

By controlling the journalist's job, the media boss can control the journalist. In addition, newspeople are not immune to the blandishments of moneyed interests. Journalists, who criticize members of Congress for compromising their independence by accepting speaking fees from special interest groups, themselves accept lucrative honoraria from such organizations. How objective can David Broder be about Wall Street corruption after receiving $6,000 for a speech to the American Stock Exchange? How alert can William Safire be to price-gouging among utility companies after pocketing a $15,000 speaker's fee from Southern Electric? Most likely, gratitude will be expressed by toning down opinions regarding the benefac-

---

7. Report by the Commission on Freedom of the Press, quoted in Robert Cirino, *Don't Blame the People* (New York: Vintage, 1972), p. 47. Newspaper owners frequently confer with their editors, kill stories they dislike, and in other ways inject their own preferences, as did Henry Luce, Arthur Ochs Sulzberger, the Duponts, and others: *New York Times,* January 17, 1992; Parenti, *Inventing Reality,* pp. 33–35, 47, 59.

8. *Washington Post,* January 24, 1992; *Workers World,* August 13, 1992; *Bay Guardian* (San Francisco), June 9, 1993; *Extra!,* November/December 1991, pp. 12–13, 16, and October 1993, p. 4. See various other issues of *Extra!* and *Lies of Our Times* for additional examples of suppressed stories, also Parenti, *Inventing Reality,* pp. 46–50.

9. Quoted in Eric Barnouw, *The Sponsor* (New York: Oxford University Press, 1978), p. 57; Parenti, *Inventing Reality,* pp. 35–37; Ronald Collins, *Dictating Content: How Advertising Pressure Can Corrupt a Free Press* (Washington, D.C.: Center for the Study of Commercialism, 1993).

tor's questionable behavior.[10] One might recall how the Shah of Iran, a dictator and torturer detested by most of his people, received a glowing press for twenty-five years. More than five hundred journalists, newscasters, editors, and publishers, including such notables as Marvin Kalb and David Brinkley, were recipients of the Shah's gifts and invited to his lavish parties. Journalists who wrote critically of him did not make the gift list.[11]

THE IDEOLOGICAL MONOPOLY

Our "free and independent press" is largely an ideological monopoly. Across the country, newspapers offer little variety in news perspective and editorial policy, ranging mostly from moderately conservative to ultraconservative, with a smaller number that are tepidly centrist. Most of the "independent" dailies, along with the chains, rely heavily on the Associated Press and other wire services and on big circulation papers for stories, syndicated columns, and special features.[12] Media coverage of public affairs is usually superficial, consisting of a few brief "headline" stories and conservative or simply banal commentaries and editorials.[13]

Reports about State Department or Pentagon policies rely heavily on official releases. Press coverage of the space program uncritically accepts the government's claims and seldom gives exposure to the program's critics. Virtually no positive exposure is afforded anti-imperialist struggles throughout the world or domestic protests against U.S. overseas interventions against Third World peoples. Far from being vigilant critics of government policy, most news organizations share officialdom's counterrevolutionary, pro-capitalist assumptions and vocabulary.[14]

Thus the Vietnam War and Gulf War were portrayed as undertakings arising from noble intentions, with little attention given to the underlying class interests and the horrendous devastation wreaked by U.S. forces upon the Vietnamese and Iraqi peoples. The U.S. press ignored the slaughter of some 500,000 Indonesians by U.S.-supported Indonesian militarists, just as for years it ignored the genocidal campaign waged by those same militarists in East Timor, along with the massive repression of dissident peas-

---

10. Burling Lowrey, "The Media's Honoraria," *Washington Post*, April 26, 1989.

11. William Dorman, "Favors Received," *Nation*, October 11, 1980.

12. Associated Press is owned by Wall Street firm Merrill Lynch and other big companies.

13. Parenti, *Inventing Reality;* Herbert Schiller, *The Mind Managers* (Boston: Beacon Press, 1973).

14. For more detailed discussion and documentation of the various points made in the above paragraph, see Parenti, *Inventing Reality,* passim.

ants, workers, clergy, students, and intellectuals in Uruguay, Guatemala, El Salvador, Zaire, the Philippines, and dozens of other U.S.-supported procapitalist regimes. Ever faithful to the official line, the press repeatedly attacks leftist movements and governments and supports right-wing procapitalist ones, along with the CIA-supported counterrevolutionary mercenary forces, as in Angola, Mozambique, and Nicaragua.[15]

Bombings and sporadic armed attacks carried out by Arab, Irish, Puerto Rican, and Basque nationalists are widely publicized as "terrorism." Left unreported is the widespread U.S.-supported terrorism in scores of countries, utilizing death squads, massacres, and mass detentions. Human rights violations in noncapitalist countries like China, Tibet, and North Korea are given wide play, while long-standing bloody and repressive violations in Turkey, Honduras, Indonesia and dozens of other U.S.-supported, free-market countries receive scant attention.[16]

News reports on business rely almost entirely on business sources. The workings of the capitalist political economy remain virtually uncharted by the press. The tendency toward a falling rate of profit; chronic instability, recession, inflation, and underemployment; dramatic growth of the financial sector and decline of the production sector; the transference of corporate diseconomies onto the public—these and other such problems are treated superficially, if at all, by pundits who have neither the knowledge nor the permission to make critical analyses of our capitalist paradise. Poverty remains an unexplained phenomenon in the media. Whether portraying the poor as unworthy idlers or simple unfortunates, the press seldom if ever gives critical attention to the market forces that help create the conditions that victimize low-income people.[17]

The press has failed to explain the real impact of the national debt and how it has generated an upward redistribution of income. There has been virtually no in-depth media investigation of the corruption behind the savings and loan scandal. Almost nothing has been said in the mainstream media about corporate America's harassment and surveillance of environmental activists and the hunting down of whistleblowing employees; almost

---

15. Parenti, *Inventing Reality*, passim; Michael Parenti, *The Sword and the Dollar: Imperialism, Revolution and the Arms Race* (New York: St. Martin's Press, 1989); also various issues of *Lies of Our Times, Extra!*, and *Propaganda Review*.

16. James Barrett, "'Terrorism' or 'Counter-Terrorism'"? *Lies of Our Times,* October 1993, p. 13; Martin Lee, "Human Rights and the Media," *Extra!*, Summer 1989, pp. 2–11; and citations in the previous footnote. When the press does acknowledge the existence of Third World oppression, it offers not a hint that U.S. policy has some responsibility or culpability, nor does it make any mention of the wealthy interests being defended: Stephen Leiper, "Myths, Lies and Videotape," *Propaganda Review,* no. 8, 1991, pp. 12–13, 45.

17. Renu Nahata, "Persistent Media Myths About Welfare," *Extra!*, July/August 1992, pp. 18–19.

nothing on how the oil, gas, and nuclear interests have stalled the development of solar power.[18]

Much attention is given to crime in the streets, but relatively little to corporate crimes committed against the public. For example, DuPont emits more pollution than any other U.S. company, dumps lethal wastes into oceans, sells toxic pesticides, and is the major producer of the chlorofluorocarbons (CFCs) that destroy the earth's ozone layer. Ozone depletion can cause cancer deaths and serious damage to crops and vegetation. No street criminal could claim such a record of destruction against society, yet the mainstream media says virtually nothing about the human costs of crimes perpetrated by companies like DuPont.[19]

Every evening, network news shows faithfully report stock-exchange averages, but stories deemed important to organized labor are scarcely ever touched upon. Reporters seldom enlist labor's views on national questions. Unions are usually noticed only when they go on strike, but the issues behind the strike, such as occupational safety or loss of benefits, are rarely acknowledged. Unions make "demands" while management makes "offers." The misleading impression is that labor simply turns down "good contracts" because it wants too much for itself. Many newspapers have large staffs for business news but not a single labor reporter. The few labor reporters who do exist are admonished not to be "too proworker."[20]

The "expert" guests appearing on newscasts are predominantly White male Republicans, frequently former government officials, corporate heads, or members of conservative think tanks, along with a sprinkling of centrist Democrats. Likewise, most editorialists, TV pundits, radio talk-show hosts, and syndicated columnists are right wing. A smaller number are moderates or liberals who take care to avoid references to class issues and class power.[21] A few progressive commentators and columnists have occasional access to community radio stations and some small circulation newspapers, which collectively reach no more than a tiny fraction of the population.

18. Carl Jensen (ed.), *America's CENSORED Newsletter,* December 1992, p. 5.

19. Russell Mokhiber, "Corporate Crime and Violence in Review, The Ten Worst Companies of 1991," in Carl Jensen, *Censored* (Chapel Hill, N.C.: Shelburne Press, 1993), p. 118, and "Caution: Environmental Reporting Can Be Hazardous to Your Career," *Extra!,* April/May 1992.

20. International Association of Machinists and Aerospace Workers, *Network News and Documentary Report* (Washington, D.C.), July 30, 1980; Parenti, *Inventing Reality,* chapter 6; William Puette, *Through Jaundiced Eyes: How the Media View Organized Labor* (Ithaca, N.Y.: ILR Press, 1992); Jeff Cohen and Norman Solomon, "Workers Labor in Media Anonymity," *Cleveland Plain Dealer,* September 4, 1993.

21. Marc Cooper and Lawrence Soley, "All the Right Sources," *Mother Jones,* February/March 1990, pp. 20–27, 45–48; David Croteau and William Hoynes, "The Lopsided Worldview of the Nation's Most Syndicated Columnists," *Extra!,* June 1992, pp. 22–25; Janine Jackson, "Talk Radio, Who Gets to Talk?" *Extra!,* April/May 1993, pp. 14–17.

OFFICIAL MANIPULATION

On those occasions when the press takes a critical stance toward official doings, it is most likely to be from a conservative ideological perspective. Thus, the media accorded the right-wing Reagan and Bush administrations twelve years of virtually uncritical coverage. Likewise, the press faulted President Clinton for his few feeble liberal moves and lauded him for his "strong leadership" when he pursued probusiness goals such as NAFTA.

Much has been made of how the military has censored the press during wartime, as during the invasions of Grenada and Panama and the one-sided slaughter in Iraq. But most of the censorship is perpetrated by the press itself. Especially in regard to the national security state, the media kill "sensitive" stories and run favorable ones, and act as cheerleaders when U.S. presidents invade or bomb other countries.[22] The press often chooses to act "responsibly" by not informing the public about U.S. covert actions and other questionable policies abroad and at home. "Journalistic responsibility" should mean the unearthing of true and significant information. But the "responsibility" demanded by government officials and often agreed to by the news media means the opposite—the burying of some troublesome piece of information precisely because it is true.

The Justice Department won a Supreme Court decision requiring newspeople to disclose their sources to grand-jury investigators, in effect reducing the press to an investigative arm of the very officialdom over whom it is supposed to act as a watchdog. Dozens of reporters have been jailed or threatened with prison terms on the basis of that decision.[23] On repeated occasions the government has subpoenaed tapes and other materials used by news media. Such interference imposes a "chilling effect," encouraging the press to censor itself in order to avoid censorship by those in power.

While the government attempts to prevent unauthorized leaks, it continually and deliberately leaks information that serves official purposes. In fact, official "leaks" amount to something of a flood that inundates us daily. The targeted audience is not only some foreign population, whose hearts and minds we supposedly must try to win, but the U.S. public itself. The task is to convince our citizenry that the policies that cost them so much in taxes, exported jobs, and other things are really in their best interest.[24]

---

22. Parenti, *Inventing Reality*, chapters 9 and 10.

23. *United States* v. *Caldwell* (1972); William Porter, *Assault on the Media* (Ann Arbor: University of Michigan Press, 1977).

24. The General Accounting Office, the investigative arm of Congress, found that a diplomatic unit within the State Department illegally planted numerous stories in the media that set the stage for the Reagan administration's interventionist policies in Central America: *Washington Post*, October 11, 1987.

Government manipulation of the press is a constant enterprise. Every day the White House, the Pentagon, and other agencies release thousands of self-serving reports to the media, many of which are then uncritically transmitted to the public as news from independent sources. White House staffers meet regularly with media bosses to discuss or complain about specific stories. Officials give choice leads to sympathetic journalists and withhold information from troublesome ones.

The CIA's disinformation campaigns illustrate how the media have been anything but free and independent. More than four hundred U.S. journalists, including nationally syndicated columnists, editors, and some major publishers, have carried out covert assignments for the CIA over the last four decades, either gathering intelligence abroad or publishing the kind of stories that create a climate of opinion supportive of the CIA's procapitalist objectives. Included among these have been personnel from the *Washington Post*, CBS, NBC, ABC, *Newsweek*, the *Wall Street Journal*, the Associated Press, and United Press International. Among the many prominent press moguls who knowingly cooperated with the CIA were William Paley, erstwhile head of CBS; Henry Luce, late owner of Time Inc.; and Arthur Hays Sulzberger, late publisher of the *New York Times*. The CIA has also conducted surveillance of news reporters to determine their sources and has used its agents to infiltrate news organizations. The CIA has owned more than 240 media operations around the world, including newspapers, magazines, publishing houses, radio and television stations, and wire services. Many Third World countries get more news from the CIA and other such Western sources than from Third World news organizations.[25]

POLITICAL ENTERTAINMENT

As already noted, television networks and the movie industry are controlled by rich conservatives. While these entertainment media supposedly have nothing to do with politics, they in fact undergo a rigorous political censorship. Even the *New York Times* admits that network "production and standards" (censorship) departments have reduced their policing of sexual and other cultural taboos, but "network censors continue to be vigilant when it comes to overseeing the political content of television films."[26] TV shows that treat controversial, antiestablishment subjects often have trou-

---

25. Stuart Loory, "The CIA's Use of the Press," *Columbia Journalism Review*, September/October 1974, pp. 9–18; Carl Bernstein, "The CIA and the Media," *Rolling Stone*, October 20, 1977; Deborah Davis, *Katherine the Great* (Bethesda, Md.: National Press, 1987), pp. 176–189.

26. *New York Times*, November 27, 1988.

ble getting sponsors and network time. Truly radical themes are eschewed by television and Hollywood. On the rare occasions a proworker, anti-imperialist film is produced, it is likely to get no financial backing from the major studios and banks and be consigned to a very limited distribution.[27]

From this we should not conclude that mainstream entertainment is apolitical. In fact, movies and television consistently propagate images and themes that support militarism, imperialism, racism, sexism, authoritarian-ism, and other undemocratic values. In the entertainment world, adversi-ties are caused by ill-willed individuals and cabals, never by the injustices of the socioeconomic system. Problems are solved by individual derring-do rather than by organized collective effort.[28]

In the world of Hollywood and television, conflicts are resolved by gen-erous applications of murder and mayhem. Nefarious violence is met with righteous violence, although it is often difficult to distinguish the two. The concept of due process is lost as television and movie police carry out illegal searches and break-ins, coerce people into confessing, and regularly use homicidal violence against suspected criminals in shoot-'em-up endings. Even though the crime rate has dropped in recent years, the United States has more police per capita than any other nation in the world. Studies indicate that people who watch a lot of television have a higher fear of crime and of urban minorities than those who do not. Crime shows condi-tion viewers into accepting authoritarian solutions and repressive police actions.[29]

In recent years, partly in response to pressures from politically ad-vanced audiences, there have been changes in gender and ethnic portrayals. Women and ethnic minorities now are sometimes portrayed as intelligent and capable persons, occupying positions of authority and empowerment. Despite these advances, gender and ethnic stereotypes still abound in the entertainment media. Women and ethnics appear in leading roles far less often than White males.[30] In daytime TV advertisements women still seem predominantly concerned with being cheery, mindless handmaidens who shampoo a fluffy glow into their hair, wax floors shiny bright, make yummy

---

27. Such was the fate of movies like *1900, Reds, Salvador, Burn, Matwan,* or *Romero.* For a fuller critique of the entertainment media, see Michael Parenti, *Make-Believe Media, The Politics of Entertainment* (New York: St. Martin's Press, 1992). A few exceptions, like Oliver Stone's excellent *JFK,* a dramatization of the John Kennedy assassination, do receive national distribution. But Stone's movie was treated to a relentless battering by a press that refused to consider evidence suggesting an intelligence-community conspiracy to kill the president.
28. Parenti, *Make-Believe Media,* passim.
29. Parenti, *Make-Believe Media,* chapter 7 and studies cited therein.
30. White males predominate disproportionately in the news sector as well as the entertainment sector, up through the entire hierarchy: Nan Robertson, *The Girls in the Balcony* (New York: Random House, 1992); also Junior Bridge's Media Tracking Project, reported in *Guardian,* May 23, 1989.

coffee for hubby, and get Junior's grimy clothes sparkling clean.[31] Worse still are the horror movies and TV shows that offer a glorified blend of sex, terror, and the brutalization of women.[32] African Americans abound in prime-time sitcoms, playing for laughs with put-downs and clowning, but the more serious struggles faced by African Americans in almost every area of life and work are rarely afforded realistic portrayal.[33]

With few exceptions, working people have little representation in the entertainment media except as stock characters. The tribulations of working-class people—their struggle to make ends meet; the dread scourge of unemployment; the lack of decent recreational facilities; the victimization by unscrupulous landlords and realty developers; the loss of pensions and seniority; the bitter strikes and battles for unionization, better wages, and safety conditions; the dirty, noisy, mindless, dangerous quality of industrial work; the lives and families wrecked by work-connected injury and disease— these and other realities are given little if any dramatic treatment in the business-owned entertainment world.[34]

The everyday worker is invisible on public TV as well. While the Public Broadcasting System (PBS) has become more sensitive to race, gender, and multiculturalism in recent years, it virtually ignores working-class concerns out of fear of alienating corporate underwriters.[35] When labor unions have funded documentaries and dramas having a working-class perspective, public television bosses usually have refused to run them, claiming that labor (with its millions of workers) represents a "special interest."[36]

ROOM FOR ALTERNATIVES?

In sum, the media are neither objective nor honest in their portrayal of important issues. While appearing independent, they are really controlled indirectly by government and directly by big business. The news is a prod-

---

31. Paul Farhi, "Welcome to Daytime TV," *This World*, March 14, 1993, pp. 10–11.

32. Kathi Maio, "Hooked on Hate?" *Ms.*, September/October 1990, pp. 42–44.

33. There are some notable exceptions, such as the epic drama *Roots:* Parenti, *Make-Believe Media*, chapter 8.

34. Parenti, *Make-Believe Media*, chapter 5.

35. *PBS and the American Worker*, study by the Committee for Cultural Studies, City University of New York, June 1990. Of course, the same is true of the commercial networks. Jonathan Tasini studied all the reporting on ABC, CBS, and NBC evening news on workers' issues during 1989, including child care, minimum wage, and workplace safety; it came to only 2.3 percent of total news coverage: reported in Cohen and Solomon, "Workers Labor in Media Anonymity."

36. PBS's stance was enough to spark a congressional investigation that mandated public-TV coverage of labor issues: U.S. House of Representatives, 102d Congress, 1st Session, Committee on Energy and Commerce, *Public Telecommunications Act of 1991*, Report 102–363, November 23, 1991, p. 13ff.

uct not only of deliberate manipulation but of the ideological and economic power structure under which journalists operate and into which they are socialized.

The Fairness Law required that unpaid time be given to an opposing viewpoint after a station broadcasts an editorial opinion. But it made no requirement as to the diversity of the opposing viewpoints, so usually the range was between two only slightly different stances. Even this was too much for President Reagan, who vetoed Congress's attempt to extend the life of the "Fairness Doctrine" in 1987.[37] Opponents of the law argue that it is an infringement on the freedom of the press. But the airwaves are the property of the people of the United States and should be open to divergent views, not just those acceptable to network bosses, corporate advertisers, and government officials.

The Public Broadcasting Act of 1967 launched PBS as a public television alternative to commercial TV. Instead of being independently financed by a sales tax on television sets or some other method, PBS was made dependent on annual appropriations from Congress and was run by a board appointed by the president. After running a number of documentaries that revealed the more unsavory aspects of U.S. policy in Vietnam and elsewhere, PBS was reined in by the Nixon administration. It was required to deemphasize public affairs and match federal funds with money from other sources—mostly corporations. PBS and National Public Radio (NPR) are "made possible" by the same corporate sponsors who dominate commercial broadcasting.[38]

With more than 70 percent of its prime-time shows funded wholly or in major part by four giant oil companies, PBS has become known as the "Petroleum Broadcasting System." Both NPR and PBS offer public affairs shows populated by commentators and guest "experts" who are as ideologically conservative and politically safe as any found on the commercial networks—along with nature films, nineteenth-century dramas, concerts and operas, many of which are enjoyable, none of which are likely to disturb the status quo.[39]

---

37. *New York Times*, June 25, 1987. Even in its heyday, the Fairness Doctrine was unfairly applied. The FCC ruled that no broadcast time need by made available to "communists or the communist viewpoint" but only to "controversial issues of public importance on which persons other than communists hold contrasting views": Federal Communications Commission, "Applicability of the Fairness Doctrine in the Handling of Controversial Issues of Public Importance," *Federal Register*, 29, July 25, 1964, p. 10415ff.

38. Martin Lee and Norman Solomon, *Unreliable Sources* (New York: Lyle Stuart, 1990), p. 85.

39. John Weisman, "Why Big Oil Loves Public TV," *TV Guide*, June 20–26, 1981, pp. 5–10; Michael Parenti, "Pack Pluralism," *Lies of Our Times*, May 1990, p. 15; "PBS Tilts Toward Conservatives, Not the Left," *Extra!*, June 1992, pp. 15–16; David Barsamian, "NPR: All the Schmews That's Fit to Soothe," *Audience*, July 4, 1985, p. 3.

Of the many interesting documentaries made by independent producers, dealing critically with racism, women's oppression, labor struggles, corporate environmental abuse, the FBI, and U.S. imperialism in Central America and elsewhere, few if any have ever gained access to mainstream movie houses or major television networks. In 1986, for instance, the documentary, *Faces of War,* revealing the U.S.-supported counterinsurgency destruction visited upon the people of El Salvador, was denied broadcast rights in twenty-two major television markets.[40] The award-winning *Building Bombs* and the exposé documentary on the Iran-contra affair, *Coverup,* were denied access to PBS and all commercial channels. In 1991, *Deadly Deception,* a documentary critical of General Electric and the environmental devastation wreaked by the nuclear weapons industry, won the Academy Award, yet, with a few local exceptions, it was banned from commercial and public television. The feature-length documentary *Panama Deception,* which won the Academy Award in 1992 and offered a critical exposé of the U.S. invasion of Panama, met a similar fate.[41]

Supermarket tabloids are another type of media not considered to be part of the mainstream media. Yet they are among the largest circulation newspapers, reaching millions with their obscurantist, sensationalist notions and often right-wing politics. Likewise, ultraconservatives have poured millions of dollars into building the religious Right's radio network, consisting of 1,300 local stations and its television network, the Christian Broadcasting Network, which has as many affiliates as ABC. Many areas of the country are literally awash in talk shows and news commentary that are outspokenly ultrarightist, procapitalist, militaristic, anticommunist, antiunion, antifeminist, anti-immigrant, homophobic, and racist.

. Denied access to major media, the political Left has attempted to get its message across through little magazines and radical newspapers, publications that suffer chronic financial difficulties and occasional harassment from police, FBI, rightist vigilantes, the IRS, and the U.S. Postal Service.[42] Pacifica network's five radio outlets and other community and listener-sponsored stations sometimes offer alternative political perspectives (along

---

40. Joan Walsh, "Direct Response: The Answer is No," *In These Times,* January 22–28, 1986.

41. *Los Angeles Times,* March 31, 1993; "Press Releases," *Z Magazine,* March 1993; Joan Friedberg, "Promoting a Documentary Cause," *In These Times,* June 24–July 7, 1987, p. 21.

42. Geoffrey Rips, *The Campaign Against the Underground Press* (San Francisco: City Lights Books, 1981) David Armstrong, *A Trumpet to Arms: Alternative Media In America* (Los Angeles: Tarcher, 1981); Angus Mackenzie, "Sabotaging the Dissident Press," *Columbia Journalism Review,* March/April 1981, pp. 57–63; William Preston Jr., "Balancing the News: How the Post Office Controls the Circulation of Information," *World Magazine,* April 3, 1986, p. 14. Skyrocketing postal rates effect a real hardship on small dissident publications. While defending such increases as economy measures, the government continues to subsidize billions of pieces of junk mail sent out every year by business and advertising firms.

with a great deal of cultural esoterica and conventional mainstream views). A growing movement of mostly poor and inner-city individuals and communities across the country have set up "micro-radio" FM stations, which should require no licensing because they have far less than one hundred watts of power and transmit in a limited radius of one to five miles. Micro-radio advocates argue that the airwaves are public space and their broadcasts are too small to interfere with the larger outlets. Yet the FCC has mandated that these stations are illegal and has shut down some of them. The real threat they pose is that low-income people might use the airwaves for community empowerment, voicing grievances that are not heard on the commercial stations.[43]

There are times when a complicit press will report things in a way that is not sufficiently pleasing to conservative interests, the problem being that reality itself is radical. So, there are sometimes limits to how the media can suppress and distort events. The Third World *is* poor and exploited; the U.S. government *does* side with the rich oligarchs; our tax system *is* regressive; real wages *are* declining; corporations *do* plunder and pollute the environment and lay off many workers. To maintain its credibility, the press must occasionally report some of these realities. When it does, the rightists complain bitterly about a liberal bias.

Furthermore, the press is not entirely immune to more democratic and popular pressure. If, despite the media's misrepresentation and neglect, a well-organized and persistent public opinion builds around an issue or set of issues, the press eventually feels compelled to acknowledge its existence. If the opinion is strong and widespread and if it does not attack the capitalist system as a system, it occasionally can break through the media-controlled sound barrier.

There is no such thing as unbiased or objective reporting of news. All reports and analyses are selective and inferential to some inescapable degree—all the more reason to provide a wider ideological spectrum of opinions and not let one bias predominate. If we consider censorship to be a danger to our freedom, then we should not overlook the fact that the media are already heavily censored by those who own or advertise in them. The very process of selection allows the politico-economic interests of the selector to operate as a censor.

There is no mystery as to how the mass media can be made more democratic. Public radio and television should be given back to the public. Representatives of citizens groups of all stripes should appear in greater numbers to give us perspectives that extend beyond the usual conservative

---

43. Luis Rodriguez, "Rebel Radio, Rappin in the 'Hood," *Nation*, August 12/19, 1991, pp. 192, 194–195; Mike Townsend, "Microwatt Revolution," *Lies of Our Times*, January 1991, p. 24; Jesse Drew, "Pirate Radio," *Bay Guardian*, May 13, 1992, pp. 13–14.

think tank experts and public officials. The number and frequency of advertisements should be limited on commercial broadcast media or should be substantially reduced. And public television and radio should be funded by the public rather than by rich corporations and foundations, who get to impose their own ideological preferences while writing off the costs as a tax deduction.

Some measure of ideological heterodoxy could be achieved if public law required all newspapers and broadcasting stations to allot space and time to a diverse array of political opinion, including the most progressive and revolutionary. But given the interests the law serves, this is not a likely development.

Ultimately the only protection against monopoly control of the media is ownership by the people themselves, with legally enforceable provisions allowing for the inclusion of an entire spectrum of conflicting views. This is not as chimerical or radical as it sounds. In the early 1920s, before it was taken over by commercial interests, radio consisted primarily of hundreds of not-for-profit stations run mostly by colleges, universities, labor unions, and community groups.[44] Today more progressive community-supported radio stations and public access cable-TV stations are needed. The micro-radio station should be encouraged rather than discouraged, for it is among the most democratic of media, requiring almost no capital, accessible to the community in which it operates, and responsive to many of the issues that are regularly suppressed by the major media.

Those who own the newspapers and networks will not relinquish their hold over private investments and public information. Ordinary citizens will have no real access to the media until they can gain control over the material resources that could give them such access, an achievement that would take a different kind of economic and social system than the corporate "free market" we have. In the meantime, Americans should have no illusions about the "free press" they are said to enjoy.

---

44. Robert McChesney, *Telecommunications, Mass Media and Democracy: The Battle for the Control of U.S. Broadcasting, 1928–1935* (New York: Oxford University Press, 1993).

11

The Greatest Show On Earth: Elections, Parties, and Voters

As noted earlier, most institutions in America are ruled by self-appointed business elites who are answerable to no one. Presumably the same cannot be said of government, since a necessary condition of our political system is the popular election of those who govern, the purpose being to hold officeholders accountable to the people who elect them. But does it work that way? Not usually.

The American two-party electoral system, with its ballyhoo and hoopla, its impresarios and stunt artists, is the greatest show on earth. Campaign time is show time, a veritable circus brought into our living rooms via television as a form of entertainment. The important thing is that the show must go on—because it is more than just a show. The two-party electoral system performs the essential function of helping to legitimate the existing social order. It channels and limits political expression, and blunts class grievances. It often leaves little time for the real issues because it gives so much attention to the contest per se: who will run? who is ahead? who will win the primaries? who will win the election? It provides the form of republican government with little of the substance. It gives the plutocratic system an appearance of popular participation while being run by and for a select handful of affluent contestants.

But people are tiring of the show. They complain of the quality of the candidates, the lack of real choice, the absence of real issues, the endless primaries, and the vast expenditures of campaign funds. As they watch the parade of clowns and acrobats, elephants and donkeys, they feel something

179

urgent is being trivialized.[1] This public disenchantment is a worrisome development for faithful allies of the existing politico-economic system.[2] They understand it is a serious matter when one of the crucial legitimating institutions of the established order, the two-party electoral system, finds its own legitimacy waning.

THE SOUND AND THE FURY

For generations, the electoral circus was run by professional party politicians who were sufficiently occupied by the pursuit of office and patronage to remain untroubled by questions of social justice. Alan Altshuler describes the machine politicos:

> Though they distributed favors widely, they concentrated power tightly. Though their little favors went to little men, the big favors went to land speculators, public utility franchise holders, government contractors, illicit businessmen, and of course the leading members of the machines themselves. . . . The bosses . . . never questioned the basic distribution of resources in society. Their methods of raising revenue tended toward regressivity. On the whole, the lower classes paid for their own favors. What they got was a *style* of government with which they could feel at home. What the more affluent classes got, though relatively few of them appreciated it, was a form of government which kept the newly enfranchised masses content without threatening the socio-economic status quo.[3]

Old-fashioned political machines can still be found in a number of cities, but they seldom exercise influence beyond the local level. State, local, and national party organizations have declined over the last several decades, for a number of reasons:

First, now that so many states have adopted the direct primary, candidates no longer seek out the party organization for a place on the ticket; instead they can independently pursue the nomination by directly entering the primary.

---

1. A Gallup poll found that voters most disliked the length of campaigns, the amount of mudslinging, the lack of issue discussion, and the high campaign costs, in that order: *Washington Post,* November 23, 1980; see also responses made during the 1988 presidential election: E. J. Dionne Jr., *Why Americans Hate Politics* (New York: Simon & Schuster, 1991), pp. 316–317. One study found that news media devoted more than 57 percent of their campaign stories to the question of who was winning or losing and fewer than 10 percent to the issues: Bruce Buchanan, *Electing A President: The Report of the Markle Commission on the Media and the Electorate* (Austin: University of Texas, 1991).

2. For example, Everett Ladd Jr.'s concerns in his *Where Have All the Voters Gone?* (New York: W. W. Norton, 1978).

3. Alan Altshuler, *Community Control* (New York: Pegasus, 1970), pp. 74–75.

Second, campaign finance laws now allocate federal election funds directly to candidates rather than to parties, further weakening party resources.

Third, since televised political advertisements can reach everyone at home, the precinct captain is less needed to canvas the neighborhood and publicize the candidate.

The outcome is a decline in party organization and an increase in primary contests open to anyone who has the moneyed backers or personal wealth to pay for staffs and costly media campaigns. Rather than relying on a party organization, today's candidate is more likely to bring in a campaign management firm complete with pollsters and media experts, who largely determine electoral strategy and issue selection.[4] Besides making things vastly more costly, this transition to elections-by-television has done little to elevate the quality of political discourse, emphasizing image manipulation and giving little attention to questions of economic and social justice.

Another problem is the limited choice offered by the two major parties. It is not quite accurate to characterize the Republicans and Democrats as Tweedledee and Tweedledum. Were they exactly alike in image and posture, they would have even more difficulty than they do in maintaining the appearances of choice. From the perspective of those who advocate a basic change in national priorities, the question is not, "Are there differences between the parties?" but, "Do the differences make a difference?" On most fundamental economic class issues, the similarities between the parties loom so large as frequently to obscure the differences. Both the Democratic and Republican parties are committed to the preservation of the private corporate economy; huge military budgets; the use of subsidies, deficit spending, and tax allowances to bolster business profits; the funneling of public resources through private conduits, including whole new industries developed at public expense; the use of repression against opponents of the existing class structure; the defense of the multinational corporate empire and intervention against social-revolutionary elements abroad. In short, most Republican and Democrat politicians are dedicated to strikingly similar definitions of the public interest, at great cost to the life chances of underprivileged people at home and abroad.

The lack of real class differences between the major parties is evident to the corporate business elites:

> Top executives may still be Republican, but they are no longer *partisan.*
> . . . Most of them have come to think it does not usually make all that much
> difference which party wins, and indeed that business and the country often
> fare better under the Democrats. Observes Rawleigh Warner, Jr., the chairman

---

4. A. James Reichley, *The Life of the Parties* (New York: Free Press, 1992); and *Washington Post*, January 17, 1989.

of Mobil: "I would have to say that in the last ten to fifteen years, business has fared equally well, if not better, under Democratic administrations as under Republican administrations." Other top executives echo Warner's sentiments.[5]

So, in a different tone, do progressive labor leaders like William Winpisinger, president of the International Association of Machinists: "We don't have a 2-party system in this country. We have the Demopublicans. It's one party of the corporate class, with two wings—the Democrats and Republicans."[6]

Rather than sharpening the partisan differences between the major parties, the accession of Ronald Reagan, an unequivocal right-wing conservative, seemed to blur them still further, as many Democrats retreated from a liberal agenda. None of Reagan's programs, neither the cutbacks in domestic services, nor the massive tax cuts favoring the upper-income brackets, nor the sharp escalation in the cold war and in military spending, could have been enacted without help from a substantial number of Democrats.

From a progressive point of view, the problem with the Democrats is not that they are worse than or as bad as the Republicans, but that they are *perceived* as being far more liberal than they really are. They are seen as the party of labor, the poor, and the minorities, when they have been the party of the business subsidies, tax breaks, and big military budgets almost as much as the GOP.[7]

The similarities between the parties do not prevent them from competing vigorously for the prizes of office, expending huge sums in the doing. The very absence of significant disagreement on fundamentals makes it all the more necessary to stress the personalized features that differentiate oneself from one's opponent. As with industrial producers, the merchants of the political system have preferred to limit their competition to techniques of packaging and brand image. With campaign buttons, bumper stickers, and television and radio spots, with every gimmick devoid of meaningful content, the candidate sells his image as he would a soap product to a public conditioned to such bombardments: his family and his looks; his experience in office and devotion to public service; his sincerity, sagacity, and fighting spirit; his military record, patriotism, and determination to limit taxes, stop inflation, improve wages, and create new jobs; his desire to help the worker, farmer, and businessperson, the young and old, the rich and poor, and especially those in between; his eagerness to end government waste and corruption and make the streets and the world itself safe by strengthening our police and our defenses abroad, bringing us lasting peace and prosperity, and so forth—such are the inevitable appeals that like so

---

5. Ladd, *Where Have All the Voters Gone?* p. 17.

6. *Guardian,* Special Report, Fall 1981.

7. Skipper Canis, "Better a Wolf in Wolf's Clothing," *Progressive,* October 1980, p. 32; also Michael Kinsley, "The Shame of the Democrats," *Washington Post,* July 23, 1981.

many autumn leaves cover the land in November.[8] As someone once said: You can't fool all the people all of the time, but if you can fool them once it's good for four years.

This is not to deny there are differences between—and within—the major parties. Generally, progressives and liberals are more likely to find a home in the Democratic party and conservatives in the GOP. During the New Deal era, Democratic support came predominantly from ethnic minorities, urban workers, Southerners, Catholics, and lower-income groups, while Republican strength rested mostly with White Protestants, middle-class professionals, Midwesterners, New Englanders, rural people, businesspeople, and upper-income strata. For several decades, however, the traditional alignments have been shifting. Republicans are now regularly elected in the South and Democrats in Maine and Vermont, as patterns of one-party regional dominance break down and the parties become more national in scope.[9]

Recent studies show that Democratic strength has gathered increasingly at the lower end of the income scale and Republican strength increasingly in the upper end. In the 1992 election, Democratic presidential candidate Bill Clinton got his strongest support from voters who earned under $15,000, while GOP candidate George Bush's highest vote was among those earning over $70,000. Generally, the Democrats do best among liberals, the poor, union members, Jews, African Americans, Latinos, city dwellers, and to a lesser extent, Catholics. Republicans do best among conservatives, White Protestants, White Southerners, rural and suburban dwellers, born-again Christians, managerial professionals, the upwardly mobile, and the affluent.[10]

THE TWO-PARTY MONOPOLY

Whatever their differences, the two major parties cooperate in various strategems to maintain their monopoly over electoral politics and discourage the growth of progressive third parties. All fifty states have laws, written

---

8. For examples of issueless image manipulation during presidential campaigns see Joe McGinnis, *The Selling of the President 1968* (New York: Simon & Schuster, 1970); and Philip Dougherty, "Advertising: Reagan's Emotional Campaign," *New York Times,* November 8, 1984.

9. William Schneider, "Realignment: The Eternal Question," *PS,* 15, Summer 1982, p. 452.

10. *New York Times* and CBS News survey: *New York Times,* November 5, 1992. Nationwide, 43 percent of voters identify themselves as Democrats, 29 percent as Republicans, and 28 percent as Independents. Democrats hold most of the gubernatorial offices and almost twice as many state legislative seats as Republicans: *Wall Street Journal,* November 10 and 14, 1988.

and enforced by Democratic and Republican officials, regulating and frequently discouraging third-party access to the ballot. In California, independent and minor-party candidates for statewide office must obtain 128,840 signatures of registered voters in order to appear on the ballot. Oklahoma requires 37,640 and Indiana 30,794. In recent times, Alabama went from no petition requirement to 11,000 signatures; Missouri went from zero to 25,000; Maryland from 5,000 to over 50,000. In a national election it takes 750,000 signatures for an independent or minor-party candidate to get on the ballot in all fifty states—but only 25,000 signatures for a Democratic or Republican candidate to do the same.[11]

Minor parties also face limitations on when and where petitions may be circulated, who may circulate them, and who may sign. In some states the time to collect signatures has been cut to one week, virtually an impossible task. In West Virginia, Arizona, Nebraska, New York, and Texas, you cannot vote in the primary if you sign the petition of an independent or third-party candidate. Filing fees discriminate against independent and minor-party candidates. In Florida, an independent or minor presidential candidate must submit 167,000 valid signatures and pay ten cents for each one, meaning a minimum of $16,700 in filing fees. In Louisiana, an independent candidate must pay a $5,000 filing fee just to try to get on the ballot.[12]

In the early 1980s, some of the unfair restrictions against third parties were struck down after court battles in a number of states.[13] In recent sessions of Congress, Representative John Conyers (D-MI) and various co-sponsors have submitted, so far without success, bills that would eliminate discriminatory barriers to ballot access and institute a uniform election law.

It has been argued that restrictive ballot requirements are needed to screen out frivolous candidates. But who decides who is "frivolous"? And what is so deleterious about allegedly frivolous candidates that the electorate must be protected from them by all-knowing major party officials? In any case, the few states that allow an easy access to the ballot—such as Iowa and New Hampshire, where only 1,000 signatures are needed and plenty of time is allowed to collect them—have suffered no invasion of frivolous or kooky candidates.

---

11. Coalition for Free and Open Elections, newsletter, Annapolis MD, March 1988; Jimmie Rex McClellan, *Two-Party Monopoly* (Ph.D. dissertation, Institute for Policy Studies, Washington, D.C., 1984); Simon Gerson, *Does the U.S. Have Free Elections?* (New York: International Publishers, forthcoming). In some states, signatory requirements for a minor-party candidate are even more severe than for an independent.

12. See citations in previous footnote.

13. For instance, *West Virginia Libertarian Party* v. *Manchin* (1982). However, the Supreme Court subsequently upheld a Washington state law that requires minor-party candidates to win at last 1 percent of the total primary election vote in order to run in the general election: *Munro* v. *Socialist Workers Party* (1986), in effect depriving them of ballot access.

The Federal Election Campaign Act provides millions of dollars in public funds to the major parties to finance their national conventions, primaries, and presidential campaigns. But public money goes to third-party candidates only *after* an election and only if they glean 5 percent of the vote (about four million votes), something nearly impossible to achieve without generous funds and regular media access.[14] In sum, they cannot get the money unless they get 5 percent of the vote; but they are not likely to get 5 percent without the money. While receiving nothing from the federal government, minor parties must observe all federal record-keeping and reporting requirements and are subjected to limitations on contribution and expenditure. The Federal Election Commission, designated by law to have three Republican and three Democratic commissioners, spends most of its time looking into the accounts of smaller parties and filing suits against them and other independent candidates. Thus two private political parties have been endowed with public authority to regulate the activities of all other parties.[15]

According to one survey, half the nation's thirteen-year-olds believe it is against the law to start a third party.[16] In a sense they are correct: the electoral law, as written by and for the major parties, accords them something of an official status. We Americans would balk at seeing any particular religious denomination designated the state religion, to be favored by the law over all other religions; indeed, the Constitution forbids it. Yet we have accepted laws that, in effect, make the Democrats and Republicans the official state parties. At a time when they are less popular and less accepted than in a century, this advantaged position serves to sustain them.[17]

Proportional Representation: A Fairer System

The system of representation itself discriminates against third parties. The single-member district, winner-take-all elections used throughout most of the United States tend to magnify the strength of major parties and the weakness of smaller ones, since the party that polls a plurality, be it 40, 50, or 60 percent, wins 100 percent of a district's representation with the election of its candidate, while smaller parties, regardless of their vote, receive zero representation. Since there are few districts in which minor parties

---

14. Richard Walton, "The Two-Party Monopoly," *Nation,* August 30–September 6, 1980, p. 177.

15. McClellan, *Two Party Monopoly.* Lower postal rates for campaign mailings have been granted to Republicans and Democrats but denied to other parties: Walton, "The Two-Party Monopoly."

16. *Progressive,* March 1977, p. 14.

17. Walton, "The Two-Party Monopoly."

have a plurality, they invariably have a higher percentage of wasted or unrepresented votes, that is, they win a lower percentage of seats, if any, than their actual percentage of votes. For a major party, the single-member, winner-take-all system often transforms a slim plurality of votes into an artificially high majority of seats.[18]

This is in contrast to a system of *proportional representation,* which provides a party with legislative seats roughly in accordance with the percentage of votes it wins, so that, in a ten-seat district, a party that gets 50 percent of the vote would get five seats and one that received 20 percent would get two seats. Some political scientists and publicists argue that proportional representation (PR) is an odd, alien, overly complicated system that encourages the proliferation of splinter parties and leads to legislative stalemate, fragmentation, polarization, and instability. They laud the two-party system because it supposedly allows for cohesion, stable majorities, and measured competition.[19]

But why should our two-party system be treated as sacrosanct? In many parts of our country, one party dominates over the other so that the two-party system has been, to some extent, a patchwork of one-party dominances—fortified by the winner-take-all system. The resultant "stability" is often just a code word for "keeping things as they are." And "cohesion" usually means collusion between the major-party leaders on the fundamentals of policy and class interest. (A one-party dictatorship is the most cohesive of all.) Furthermore, we might wonder whether stalemate and fragmentation—supposedly the products of multiparty systems—do not characterize our own two-party system with its lack of coherent agendas and democratically accountable actions.

In any case, there is nothing odd or quirky about proportional representation; it is the most widespread and popular voting system in the world.[20] It usually has produced stable and long-lasting coalition governments that

---

18. Thus, in the 1987 British election, the Tories won 43 percent of the vote and 59 percent of the seats in parliament, while the Alliance, a smaller third party, won 23 percent of the vote but only 3.3 percent of the seats: *Washington Post,* June 13, 1987. In the 1993 Canadian elections, in Manitoba, the Liberals won 93 percent of the seats with only 45 percent of the vote, while the Conservatives and New Democratic Party, respectively with 12 percent and 16.6 percent of the vote, received no seats: Center for Voting and Democracy, newsletter, November 6, 1993. In the recent French elections, the conservative coalition won 80 percent of the parliamentary seats with only about 40 percent of the popular vote.

19. For instance, *New York Times* editorial, "Proportional Representation Flunks," April 24, 1993.

20. Some form of proportional representation is used in Austria, Belgium, Bulgaria, the Czech Republic, Denmark, Finland, Germany, Greece, Hungary, Iberia, Iceland, Ireland, Israel, Italy, Liechtenstein, Luxembourg, Monaco, the Netherlands, Norway, Poland, Portugal, Spain, Sweden, and Switzerland. Single-member, winner-take-all is used in Great Britain, Canada, and the United States. In November 1993, New Zealand adopted proportional representation by a vote of 85 to 15 percent.

are consistently more representative and responsive than winner-take-all systems. PR voting systems are not unmanageably complicated. Citizens are able to cast votes for their preferred candidates and for parties that more closely reflect their interests.[21] Nor is proportional representation alien to the U.S. experience; a few local governments and school districts around the country have used it.[22]

The winner-take-all system deprives the minority parties not only of representation but eventually of voters too, since not many citizens wish to "waste" their ballots on a minor party that seems incapable of achieving a legislative presence. Sometimes it does not even seem worth the effort to vote for one of the two major parties in districts where the other major party so predominates and will be winning the sole representation. If we had PR, however, every vote would be given some representation, and people would be more likely to vote. Indeed, in countries that have PR, there is a broader and more varied choice of parties, a higher rate of participation, and greater representation of ethnic minorities and women than in our two-party system.[23]

The electoral system is rigged in other ways. A common device is *redistricting,* changing the boundaries of a constituency to guarantee a preferred political outcome. Consider this report on Jackson, Mississippi:

> While Blacks make up 47 percent of the population of this Mississippi capital city, no Black has been elected to city office here since 1912. . . . Since 1960, White suburbs have been annexed three times, each time substantially diluting Black voting strength just as it appeared Blacks were about to become a majority. And each election, like this one, has been characterized by racial bloc voting and increasingly apathetic Black voters.

---

21. Douglas Amy, *Real Choice/New Voices: The Case for Proportional Representation Elections in the United States* (New York: Columbia University Press, 1993); Maurice Duverger, *Political Parties* (New York: Wiley and Sons, 1955), pp. 245–255; E. E. Schattschneider, *Party Government* (New York: Holt, Rinehart and Winston, 1960), pp. 74–78. For updated information on PR, contact the Center for Voting and Democracy, Washington, D.C.

22. In 1945, the last proportional representation race for the New York City Council, Democrats won fifteen seats, Republicans three, Liberals and Communists two each, and the American Labor party one. PR was abolished in New York not because it didn't work but because it worked too well, giving representation to a variety of left views. Today under winner-take-all in New York, the Democrats have thirty-four seats and the Republicans have one: Martin Gottlieb, "The 'Golden Age' of the City Council," *New York Times,* August 11, 1991; Leon Weaver and Judith Baum, "Proportional Representation on New York City Community School Boards," in Wilma Rule and Joseph Zimmerman (eds.), *United States Electoral Systems* (New York: Praeger, 1992).

23. On participation rates, see G. Bingham Powell Jr., "Voter Turnout in Thirty Democracies," in Richard Rose (ed.), *Electoral Participation, A Comparative Analysis* (Beverly Hills, Calif.: Sage Publications, 1980), p. 6.

"Many Blacks in Jackson have just given up," [state legislator Henry] Kirksey said.[24]

One form of redistricting is the *gerrymander*. District lines are drawn in elaborately contorted ways so as to maximize the strength of the party that does the drawing.[25] Sometimes the purpose is to weaken the electoral base of progressive members in Congress, state legislatures, or city councils, or to dilute the electoral strength of new or potentially dissident constituencies. In Philadelphia, a Latino community of 63,000 anticipated control of at least one, and possibly two, seats in the Pennsylvania Assembly. Instead, their cohesive community was divided into a number of districts, none of which had more than a 15 percent Latino population. Chicago's Puerto Rican and Mexican-American community suffered a similar plight. And the New York City Council split 50,000 working-class Black voters in Queens into three predominantly White districts, making them a numerical minority in all three.[26]

Sometimes gerrymandering is used not to deny minority representation but to assure it—by creating a district that manages to concentrate enough African American voters so as to assure the election of an African American. Conservative opponents condemn such practices as "racial gerrymandering" and "reverse discrimination." But defendants argue that such districts may look bizarre on a map but are the only way to abridge a White monopoly and ensure some Black representation in states where Whites remain disproportionately overrepresented even after the redistricting; hence, there is no "reverse discrimination."[27]

Proportional representation would be a better way of providing for a more varied ethnic presence at the state, local, and national levels. Under PR, minority votes would be granted some measure of representation in accordance with their number. Hence, parties would be more inclined to include ethnic minority members on their slates. Another alternative would

---

24. *Washington Post*, June 19, 1981. Blacks are nearly 12 percent of the population but compose only slightly more than 1 percent of the elected and appointed officials in the country: Jesse Jackson's commentary in *Washington Post*, June 16, 1986.

25. Named after Governor Elbridge Gerry of Massachusetts, who employed it in 1812, and "salamander," from the odd shape of the district. Congressional districts and state legislative districts are drawn by the state legislatures, subject to veto by the governors. City council districts are drawn by the councils, usually subject to the approval of the mayor.

26. Juan Cartagena, "The Reapportionment Game," *Guild Notes,* March–April 1983, p. 4; also excerpts from Declaration in *Badham* v. *Eu* by Bernard Grofman, Gordon Baker, Bruce Cain, and others, *PS*, 18, Summer 1985, pp. 538–581; and Bruce Shapiro, "D.C. Diary," *Nation*, August 23/30, 1993, p. 198. In Los Angeles county and nine Texas counties, heavy concentrations of Latinos were divided into separate districts to dilute their voting power: *Washington Post*, January 3, 1990.

27. An example is the 12th Congressional district in North Carolina, which has been challenged in the courts: *New York Times*, April 16, 1993.

be *cumulative voting* and *limited voting*, which allow voters to cast multiple votes distributed over several candidates or concentrated on a single candidate. This sometimes enables a nonWhite minority to unite behind a non-White candidate who is then one of the several elected.[28]

Voting fraud is a time-tested way of keeping elections from getting too democratic. Often presumed to have died out with old-time machine politics, crooked vote counts are still very much with us. The computer-based punch-card systems used nowadays in most electoral jurisdictions are at least as susceptible to error, accident, and fraud as paper ballots and mechanical-lever voting machines. Investigations reveal a high instance of tabulation errors and easy opportunities to distort counts. In an election in St. Louis, ballots in working-class African American wards were more than three times less likely to be counted as those in White wards. Computer irregularities were found in locales in at least seven other states.[29]

If, despite rigged rules, dissident groups prove viable, then authorities are likely to resort to more coercive measures. Almost every radical group that has ever managed to gain some grass-roots strength has become the object of official violence. The case of the American Socialist party is instructive. By 1918, the Socialist party held 1,200 offices in 340 cities including seventy-nine mayors in twenty-four different states, thirty-two legislators, and a member of Congress. In 1919, after having increased its vote dramatically in various locales, the Socialists suffered the combined attacks of state, local, and federal authorities. Their headquarters in numerous cities were sacked by police, their funds confiscated, their leaders jailed, their immigrant members deported, their newspapers denied mailing privileges, and their elected candidates denied their seats in various state legislatures and in Congress.[30] Within a few years the party was finished as a viable political force. While confining themselves to legal and peaceful forms of political competition, the Socialists discovered that their opponents were burdened by no similar compunctions. The guiding principle of ruling elites was—and still is: When change threatens to rule, then the rules are changed.

The biggest handicap faced by third-party candidates—and progressive candidates within the major parties—is procuring the growing sums of money needed to win office. Money is the lifeblood of electoral politics,

28. Communities in Alabama, Pennsylvania, Illinois, and various other states have used cumulative voting in local elections: Edward Still, "Cumulative Voting and Limited Voting in Alabama," in Rule and Zimmerman, *United States Electoral Systems;* Peter Applebome, "Where Ideas that Hurt Guinier Thrive," *New York Times,* June 5, 1993.

29. Ronnie Dugger, "Annals of Democracy, Counting Votes," *New Yorker,* November 7, 1988, pp. 40–68, 97–108.

30. James Weinstein, *The Decline of American Socialism* (New York: Monthly Review Press, 1967).

helping to determine the availability of campaign organization, mobility, and most important of all, media visibility. In the 1990 Alabama campaign, gubernatorial candidates spent a total of $16.5 million; in Ohio, they spent $16 million; in Texas, $50.6 million. The bulk of such sums came from rich investors and powerful corporate interests.[31] Advocates of working people are not able to attract that kind of financial backing.

Besides coping with money problems, progressive candidates must try to develop a plausible image among a citizenry conditioned for more than a century to hate socialists, communists, and other leftists. They find themselves dependent for exposure on mass media that are owned by the conservative interests they are attacking. They see that, along with the misrepresentations disseminated by a hostile press, the sheer paucity of information can make meaningful campaign dialogue nearly impossible. The dissenters compete not only against well-financed opponents but also against the media's many frivolous and stupefying distractions. Hoping to educate the public to the issues, they discover that the media allow little or no opportunity for them to make their position understandable to voters who might be willing to listen.

For most voters the campaign has little reality apart from its media version. Since the media do not cover a third party's campaign, most people remain unaware of its existence. During presidential campaigns the television networks give the Democratic and Republican candidates ten to fifteen minutes of prime-time coverage every evening, while minor-party presidential candidates receive but a few minutes' exposure, if that, in their entire campaign. By withholding coverage from minor-party candidates while bestowing it lavishly on major-party ones, the media help perpetuate the two-party monopoly—at the very time more Americans are withdrawing their allegiance from the major parties.

On those infrequent occasions when progressive dissenters win office as mayors, governors, or federal or state legislators, they often find themselves burdened by administrative duties or relegated to obscure legislative tasks. If they attempt changes, they run into the opposition of other elected and bureaucratic officials and of economic interests larger and more powerful than they. Some of them decide that "for now" they must make their peace with the powers that be, holding their fire until some future day when they can attack from higher ground. To get along they decide to go along. Thus begins the insidious process that lets a person believe he or she is still opposing the ongoing arrangements when in fact he or she has become a part of them. There are less subtle instances of cooptation, as when reformers are bought off with favors. Having won election, they may reverse their

---

31. *Common Cause News,* January 28, 1992; *Straight Facts* (Austin, Tex.), April 10, 1992.

stands on fundamental issues and make common cause with established powers, to the dismay of their supporters.

Or they may not. Despite all discouragements and temptations, some dedicated progressives struggle within the constraints of office, attempting to advance the interests of relatively powerless constituencies. Members of Congress such as Adam Clayton Powell and Vito Marcantonio, both from New York, were examples of this. For their pains, both were attacked relentlessly by the press and other members of Congress. Marcantonio offered the only genuinely anticapitalist critique of U.S. foreign policy that could be heard in the U.S. House of Representatives in the late 1940s and early 1950s. So he was mercilessly red-baited and deprived of committee positions. His district was redrawn in order to weaken his electoral base. The FBI collected a huge file on him. And finally, the Democrats, Republicans, and liberals joined together in support of a conservative candidate to defeat him. As one of his biographers notes, "There is something distasteful and disquieting in the amount of power that was amassed to silence the only opposing voice in Congress."[32]

In sum, of the worthwhile functions a political party might serve— (1) selecting candidates and waging election campaigns, (2) articulating and debating major issues, (3) formulating coherent and distinct programs, and (4) implementing a national program when in office—the Republican and Democratic parties fulfill none of these with any distinction. The parties are loose conglomerations organized around one common purpose: the pursuit of office. For this reason, American parties have been characterized as "nonideological." And indeed they are—in the sense that their profound ideological commitment to capitalism at home and abroad and to the ongoing class structure is seldom made an explicit issue. The major parties have a conservative effect on the consciousness of the electorate and on the performance of representative government. They operate from a commonly shared ideological perspective that is best served by the avoidance of iconoclastic politico-economic views and by the suppression or cooptation of dissenters. By evading fundamental issues, the major parties prevent class divisions from sharpening. They maintain a noisy, apolitical politics, narrowing the scope of participation while giving a busy appearance of popular government.

According to democratic theory, electoral competition keeps political leaders accountable to their constituents. Politicians who wish to remain in office must respond to voter preferences in order to avoid being replaced by their rivals in the next election. But do the conditions of electoral com-

---

32. Gerald Meyer, *Vito Marcantonio, Radical Politician 1902–1954* (Albany, N.Y.: State University of New York Press, 1989).

petition actually exist? As noted earlier, legal, political, and moneyed forces so limit the range of alternatives as to raise serious questions about democratic accountability.

About one out of every ten representatives are elected to Congress with no opposition in either the primary or the general election. During the 1980s and 1990s, from 90 to 96 percent of incumbents who sought congressional office were reelected. Death and voluntary retirement seem to be the important factors behind the turnover in representative assemblies. In this respect, legislative bodies bear a closer resemblance to the nonelective judiciary than we would imagine.

THE RIGHT TO VOTE

Supposedly one of the great gifts of our democracy is the right to vote for the candidate of one's choice. But, as we have noted, the "choice" is often narrow and prestructured by a variety of undemocratic features. Furthermore, although two centuries of struggle have brought real gains in extending the franchise, the opportunity to vote is still not available to everyone.

From the early days of the Republic, rich propertied interests sought to limit popular participation. Propertyless White males, indentured servants, women, Blacks (including freed slaves), and Native American Indians had no access to the ballot. In the wake of working-class turbulence during the 1820s and 1830s, formal property qualifications were abolished for White males. And after a century of agitation, women won the right to vote with the adoption of the Nineteenth Amendment in 1920. In 1961, the Twenty-third Amendment allowed District of Columbia residents to vote in presidential elections (but they are still denied full voting representation in Congress). In 1971, the Twenty-sixth Amendment lowered the minimum voting age to eighteen for all elections.

The Fifteenth Amendment, ratified in 1870, written as it were in the blood of civil war, prohibited voter discrimination because of race. But it took another century of struggle to make this right something more than a formality. In 1944, the Supreme Court ruled that all-White party primaries were unconstitutional.[33] Decades of agitation and political pressure (augmented by the growing voting power of African Americans in Northern cities), led to the Civil Rights Acts of 1957 and 1960, the Voting Rights Acts of 1965, 1970, 1975, and 1985, and several crucial Supreme Court decisions.[34] Taken together, these measures (a) gave the federal government

---

33. *Smith* v. *Allwright* (1944).

34. See *Harper* v. *Virginia State Board of Elections* (1966) on poll taxes, and *Dunn* v. *Blumstein* (1972) on residency requirements.

and courts power to act against state officials who were discriminating against nonWhites at the polls, and (b) eliminated state restrictions—such as long-term residency requirements, literacy tests, and poll taxes—that had sharply reduced the electoral participation of the poor and less educated. The result was that in certain parts of the South, African Americans began voting in visible numbers for the first time since Reconstruction.

Yet low-income people, be they Black, Latino, or White, still vote at half the rate of the more affluent. One reason is that while legal restrictions have been removed, administrative barriers remain largely in place. In countries with high voter participation, such as Sweden, governments actively pursue programs to register voters. The U.S. government offers no such encouragement. If anything, federal and state officials—and officials of both major parties—have a history of making it difficult for working people to register and vote. Registration centers are usually open only during working hours. Their locations can be remote and frequently changed. They are likely to be administered by political appointees hostile to people of color and the poor.[35] A change of residence requires a change of registration. Registration forms are frequently unnecessarily complex, acting almost as a kind of literacy test. They are sometimes in short supply, maldistributed, and sluggishly processed. Elections are held on a workday (Tuesday) without enough time for some people to get to the polls. Polling places are sometimes not readily accessible.[36]

During the 1980s, Reagan administration officials threatened to cut off federal aid in order to discourage state and local agencies from assisting in voter registration drives. The threats were partially successful. Federal officials also urged states to prohibit registration drives at food lines; some did. Voting-rights activists who tried to register people in welfare offices were arrested.[37] In 1986, FBI agents streamed into Southern counties and interrogated over 2,000 African Americans about whether their ballots were fraudulently cast. While finding no evidence of fraud, the FBI did cause

---

35. For instance, note how African American voter participation was decreased by such measures in Alabama: *Vote Fraud Trials Threaten Democracy* (Alabama Blackbelt Defense Committee, Gainesville, Ala., February 1986).

36. Frances Fox Piven and Richard Cloward, *Why Americans Don't Vote* (New York: Pantheon, 1988); Warren Mitofsky and Martin Plissner, "Low Voter Turnout? Don't Believe It," *New York Times*, November 10, 1988. In one Texas county, officials closed down all but one of thirteen polling place, and Black and Latino voter turnout plummeted from 2,300 to 300. In Mississippi, a person must sign up both at the town and county courthouses; this can mean driving ninety miles: John Conyers Jr. and Neil Kotler, "The Blacks," *Progressive*, October 1982, p. 40; *Guardian*, February 22, 1984, p. 3. During the 1988 Democratic primary, Flint, Michigan's ninety-one polling places were reduced to nine to discourage a protest vote for Jesse Jackson: *Nation*, April 9, 1988, p. 486.

37. Piven and Cloward, *Why Americans Don't Vote*, pp. 231–234; Jack Anderson, "U.S. Squelches Some Voter Drives," *Washington Post*, October 27, 1985.

11.12

"I'M HAVING SECOND THOUGHTS ABOUT THE
ELECTION... I'M NOT SURE I VOTED AGAINST
THE RIGHT PERSON."

some voters to think twice about ever voting again. Eight voting-rights activists were indicted on 215 criminal charges; five were acquitted; two plea-bargained to misdemeanors and one was convicted of technical violations less serious than those that White registrars had long been committing with impunity.

That same year, the Republican party sent letters to registered voters in heavily Democratic areas in several states. An undeliverable letter would then be used to challenge the addressee's right to vote. The intended effect was to reduce the participation of low-income Democratic (and mostly Black) voters.[38]

In 1992, Congress passed a "motor voter" bill that sought to increase voter turnout among the elderly, the poor, and the infirm, by allowing citizens to register as they renew their driver's licenses, or apply for Social Security, unemployment, welfare, or disability benefits. President Bush vetoed

---

38. *New York Times*, editorial, November 1, 1986.

it. The next year a bill was passed allowing registration at motor vehicle and military recruiting offices but—to avoid a Republican Senate filibuster—the bill made no provision for registration at welfare and unemployment offices.

Administrative barriers exist nationwide, not just in the South, and are directed at the working class as a whole. More than half of the major registration suits filed in recent campaigns were taken against election officials in Northern states.[39] According to the standard view, working-class people and the poor have a low turnout because they are wanting in information, education, and civic awareness. But if they are so naturally inclined to apathy, one wonders why entrenched interests find it necessary to erect such elaborate barriers to discourage their participation.

Other ploys besides administrative ones have been used to discourage low-income voting. In the 1993 New Jersey election, a Republican political consultant claimed that his party paid substantial sums to African American ministers and Democratic campaign workers to refrain from urging their parishioners and constituents to vote on election day. "I think to a certain extent we suppressed the vote," he boasted.[40]

Another ploy is at-large elections, a rarity in Southern towns before 1965, now all but universal, and not unknown in Northern locales where low-income African Americans and Latinos are gathering numerical strength. Instead of election by district, the at-large election gives a winner-take-all victory to a citywide slate, allowing complete White domination and freezing out minority representation.[41] Given all these hindrances it is no wonder that so many poor people are nonvoters.

To worsen matters, nonvoting has a feedback effect. For as fewer among the poor and the ethnic minorities vote, the politicians pay even less attention to them, further convincing the nonparticipants that the realm of politics is inaccessible and that there is no reason to go to the polls. Thus the unresponsiveness of the system discourages the participation and diminishes the influence of the very people who are most in need of making the system responsive to them.

VOTER "APATHY" AND PARTICIPATION

The disappointing performances of politicians are a further discouragement to voting. Many people doubt they have any ability to make govern-

---

39. Piven and Cloward, *Why Americans Don't Vote*, pp. 242–243 and passim.

40. Edward Rollins quoted in *Washington Post*, November 9, 1993.

41. Consider the at-large elections on Maryland's Eastern Shore that prevented African Americans from gaining office and discouraged their voter participation: *New York Times*, August 17, 1988.

ment more responsive to their needs.[42] With good reason they complain: "Politicians tell us one thing to get our votes, then do another thing once they are elected." If many politicians are half-truth artists, it is not necessarily because they are morally flawed. More often, they are caught in the contradiction of having to be both a "candidate of the people" and a servant to the wants of wealthy and powerful contributors and the systemic needs of corporate capitalism.

Many people fail to vote because (1) they do not find anyone who appeals to them, and (2) they have trouble believing that voting makes a difference. Many who do vote do so with little enthusiasm and growing cynicism.[43] In Reagan's "overwhelming" victories in the presidential elections of 1980 and 1984, less than 30 percent of eligible voters actually cast their ballots for him; almost 50 percent stayed home.[44] One nationwide survey found that, for the great majority of citizens interviewed, nonvoting was a result of the anger and frustration they harbored toward the choices available. Some felt there was a dearth of qualified candidates; others complained that candidates did not care about voters. As one forty-four-year-old female factory worker in New Jersey said: "I wasn't interested in any of the candidates. They weren't helping poor people, they were helping the rich."[45]

It has been argued that since nonvoters tend to be among the less educated and more apathetic, then it is just as well they do not exercise their franchise. Since they are likely to be swayed by prejudice and demagogy, their activation would constitute a potential threat to our democratic system.[46] Behind this reasoning lurks the dubious presumption that better-

---

42. Paul Abramson and John Aldrich, "The Decline of Electoral Participation in America," *American Political Science Review,* 76, September 1982, p. 519; Stephen Earl Bennett, "The Uses and Abuses of Registration and Turnout Data," *PS: Political Science and Politics,* June 1990, pp. 167, 170.

43. David Broder, "Massive Survey Finds 'Political Gridlock' of Growing Cynicism," *Washington Post,* September 19, 1990. One news poll found that 66 percent of those who did vote in the 1988 election were unhappy with the choice of candidates: Remarks by Rep. Timothy Penny, *Congressional Record,* 137, February 4, 1991.

44. In the 1988 election slightly over 50 percent of eligible voters stayed home. Voter participation picked up slightly in 1992, climbing to 54 percent, equaling the 1976 turnout. Anger about the recession was a contributing factor as was the presence of an independent presidential candidate Ross Perot, who appealed to some people who felt disfranchised: *New York Times,* November 5, 1992. Unlike most independents or third-party candidates, Perot was given generous media exposure and treated as a serious contender.

45. *Washington Post,* September 23, 1982; also *New York Times,* October 11, 1988.

46. For a typical example of this view, see Seymour Lipset, *Political Man* (Garden City, N.Y.: Doubleday, 1960), pp. 215–219. Occasionally, there is an admission by the well-to-do that voting should be limited not to protect democracy but to protect the well-to-do. A letter to the *New York Times* (December 6, 1971) offered these revealing words: "If everybody voted, I'm afraid we'd be in for a gigantic upheaval of American society—and we comfortable readers of the *Times* would certainly stand to lose much at the hands of the poor, faceless, previously quiet throngs. Wouldn't it be best to let sleeping dogs lie?"

educated, upper-income people who vote are more rational and less compelled by narrow self-interests and racial and class prejudices, an impression that itself is one of those comforting prejudices upper- and middle-class people have of themselves.

Some writers argue that low voter turnout is symptomatic of a "politics of happiness": people are apathetic about voting because they are fairly content with the way things are going.[47] Certainly some people are blithely indifferent to political issues—even issues that seem to affect their lives in important ways. But generally speaking, the many millions of Americans outside the voting universe are not among the more contented but among the less affluent and more alienated, displaying an unusual concentration of socially deprived characteristics.[48] The "politics of happiness" is usually nothing more than a cover for the politics of discouragement. What is seen as apathy may really be antipathy. In any case, apathy is often a psychological defense against powerlessness and frustration. Nonparticipation is not the result of contentment or lack of civic virtue but an understandably negative response to the political frustrations people experience.[49]

About the same number of voters as nonvoters are convinced that government is run "for a few big interests" rather than for the benefit of all the people. This would suggest that many people vote less because of substantive issues than out of a ritualized sense of duty, an exercise more of civic virtue than civic power.[50] This raises the question of who really are the deadwood of democracy: the "apathetic" or the "civic minded," those who see no reason to vote or those who vote with no reason?

Of course, there are other inducements to voting besides a sense of civic obligation. Voters who ascribe undesirable traits to one party are sometimes then inclined to find virtue in the other. Thus, the suspicion that Democrats

---

47. Heinz Eulau, "The Politics of Happiness," *Antioch Review,* 16, 1956, pp. 259–264; Lipset, *Political Man,* pp. 179–219.

48. Voter registration has declined among working-class Democrats, both Black and White, while increasing among high-income Republicans: *New York Times,* November 4, 1988. Persons of little education and presumably lower income have the lowest voting rate of all: U.S. Bureau of the Census, *Statistical Abstract of the United States: 1992* (112th edition) Washington, D.C., 1992, p. 269.

49. Penn Kimball, *The Disconnected* (New York: Columbia University Press, 1972); David Hull and Norman Luttbeg, *Trends in American Electoral Behavior,* 2nd ed. (Itasca, Ill.: F. E. Peacock, 1983), pp. 85–94. One national survey found that nonvoters are not among the more content; they just do not believe their votes would bring any changes for the better: *New York Times,* September 25, 1983.

50. On the attitudes of alienated voters, see *New York Times/*CBS News poll: *New York Times,* November 16, 1976 and November 16, 1980; Angus Campbell et al., *The American Voter* (New York: Wiley and Sons, 1960), pp. 103–106. A *Washington Post/*ABC News poll finds: "To some extent, many people continue to go to the polls because they feel they have to—that their vote is important—and not because they like the choices offered them": *Washington Post,* September 23, 1982.

might favor the urban poor and labor unions leads some middle-class Whites to assume that the Republican party is devoted to their interests, a conclusion that may have no basis in the actual performance of Republican officeholders. Similarly, the identification of Republicans as the party of big business suggests to some working-class voters that, in contrast, the Democrats are not for business but for the "little man," a conclusion that may be equally unfounded in most instances.

When magnified by partisan rhetoric, the differences between the parties appear worrisome enough to induce millions of citizens to vote—if not *for* then *against* someone. Voters who have no great hope that the incumbent will do much for them, might persistently fear that the challenger will make things even worse. Or conversely, they may dislike the challenger but reluctantly vote for him or her only because the incumbent has become unbearable. This lesser-of-two-evils appeal is the single most effective inducement to voter participation and is a marvelous ruling-class device. The people are offered a candidate who violates their interests and who is dedicated to the preservation of capitalism at home and abroad, then they are presented with another candidate who promises to be even worse. Thus, they are not so much offered a choice as forced into one.[51]

On those infrequent occasions when a dedicated candidate emerges who has a chance of winning and who demonstrates his or her commitment to the people, constituents are more inclined to participate, for they begin to perceive that voting can influence public policy and that there is a real—and realistic—choice. In Burlington, Vermont, for instance, six years of rule by the Progressive Coalition (1981–87), led by socialist mayor Bernard Sanders, brought marked improvements in the city government. The condition of Burlington's streets, sidewalks, and sewers noticeably improved. Youth employment programs and cultural activities were implemented. Against the opposition of landlords and business, the Sanders administration attempted to institute a more equitable distribution of the tax burden and reforms in utility rates, while imposing no new property taxes on homeowners. Significantly enough, voter turnout in Burlington—especially in the low-income districts—increased dramatically. City council races no longer went uncontested and thousands of people regularly turned out for public hearings on various issues.[52]

---

51. Surveys indicate that voters cite "the lesser of two evils" as the determining motive in their choice and that they seem most clear on whom they want to vote *against:* "Voters Know What They Don't Like," *Business Week*, June 11, 1984; *Washington Post*, May 27, 1988.

52. My thanks to Bernard Sanders and David Claville, respectively mayor and city constable in Burlington, Vermont, in 1987, for making Burlington's voting records available to me. For an account of the Sanders' administration, see W. J. Conroy, *Challenging the Boundaries of Reform* (Philadelphia: Temple University Press, 1990). In 1990, running on an

When presented with distinct issue-linked choices, voters do respond, in the main, according to their pocketbook interests and other specific preferences. Candidates who stress bread-and-butter issues like jobs, affordable health care, and taxes, along with clearly stated policies relating to peace and the environment, will win votes from constituencies concerned with such matters.[53] Voter turnout in African American communities increases noticeably when candidates are perceived as concerned with the needs of African Americans—even when the prospects for victory are modest. Such was the case with Jesse Jackson's bid for the Democratic presidential nomination in 1988.

The United States has one of the lowest voter participation rates in the world. Some conservatives argue low voter participation is of no great concern since the preferences of nonvoters would be much the same as the preferences of voters.[54] They would have us believe that even though upper-income people vote at almost twice the rate as lower-income people, and vote Republican at almost three times the rate, it would make no difference if low-income citizens voted in greater numbers. One wonders then why Republicans launch registration drives in affluent suburbs and try to discourage voting among inner-city Blacks, blue-collar workers and other traditionally Democratic voters with low turnout rates.

The argument is sometimes made that if deprived groups have been unable to win their demands, it is because they are numerically weak compared to White, middle-class America. In a system that responds to the democratic power of numbers, a minority poor cannot hope to have its way. The deficiency is in the limited numbers of persons advocating change and not in the representative system, which operates according to majoritarian principles. What is curious about this argument is that it is never applied to more select minority interests—for instance, oilmen. Now oilmen are far less numerous than the poor, yet the deficiency of their numbers, or of the numbers of other tiny minorities like bankers, industrialists, and millionaire investors, does not result in any lack of government responsiveness to their

---

explicitly populist ticket, Sanders went on to win election to the U.S. House of Representatives as an Independent.

53. Benjamin Page and Robert Shapiro, *The Rational Public* (Chicago: University of Chicago Press, 1992); John Aldrich, John Sullivan, and Eugene Bordiga, "Foreign Affairs and Issue Voting," *American Political Science Review*, 83, March 1989, pp. 123–141.

54. This curious finding is based on two postelection surveys that indicated if nonvoters had cast ballots in 1988, they would have voted for Bush over Dukakis roughly as did voters: Bennett, "The Uses and Abuses of Registration . . ." pp. 168, 170fn; also *Los Angeles Times*, November 21, 1990. Surveys indicate that after an election people prefer to say they voted for the winner (even if they didn't vote at all). Also, Dukakis was a remarkably inept and ineffectual candidate. It is not surprising that a majority of nonvoters as well as voters did not choose him.

wants. On most important matters, government policy is determined less by the majoritarian principle needs of the working majority and more by the strength of private interests.

DEMOCRATIC INPUT

There are two sweeping propositions that might mistakenly be drawn from what has been said thus far: (1) It does not matter who is elected, and (2) elected officials are indifferent to voter desires and other popular pressures. Both these notions are far from being the whole picture.

Many people reject voting not only because they feel there is no choice but because they see politics itself as something that cannot deliver anything significant even if a dedicated candidate is elected. And given the plutocratic dominance of the two-party monopoly, they are not too far wrong. Yet it should be noted that even within the confines of capitalist public policy, people's lives can be affected for better or worse by what happens within the electoral realm. Having correctly observed that two-party elections are designed to blur real issues, some people incorrectly conclude that what Democrats and Republicans do once elected to office is also inconsequential and farcical. In truth, major-party policies can have an important effect on our well-being—as the previous chapters on what government does in the realm of health, education, the environment, taxation, and foreign and military policy testify.

In Western Europe, benefiting from the more democratic system of proportional representation, left-wing parties have established a viable presence in parliaments, even ruling from time to time, and have helped create labor conditions superior to those found in the United States. Be it disposable income, paid vacations, family allowances, safety conditions, protection from speedups, the right to collective bargaining, or job security, American employees have less protection and fewer benefits than their French, German, Scandinavian, British, and Benelux counterparts. Among industrialized capitalist nations, the United States possesses one of the highest unemployment rates and one of the lowest levels of social services. Lacking any form of organized mass challenge to the existing distribution of wealth and income, and possessing a two-party monopoly that effectively freezes out a left critique, U.S. capitalism is even more successful than European capitalism in shifting onto the working populace the cost of public programs and business subsidies, and the austerities caused by capital flight abroad, foreign competition, and cutbacks in human services.[55]

---

55. "Labor at Home and Abroad," *Economic Notes,* January 1985, pp. 1–15; "Study Shows U.S. Lags in Spending for Welfare," *San Francisco Chronicle,* February 20, 1990; James

Aside from the differences between nations, within the U.S. context itself it can be said that while many electoral contests are meaningless, some reflect real differences between reactionary and progressive forces. Who is elected, then, *can* make a difference within a limited but important range of policy options.

In addition, there is ample evidence indicating that elected representatives are not totally indifferent to voter demands, since—along with money—votes are still the means to office and empowerment.[56] To be sure, officeholders often respond with deceitful assurances. For instance, dozens of members of Congress who pledged to vote *against* draft registration in 1978 voted *for* it in 1980. The heaviest applause line in Jimmy Carter's Inaugural Address was his vow to "move this year a step towards our ultimate goal—the elimination of all nuclear weapons from this Earth." But his administration then went on to build two or three more nuclear bombs a day. In an elaborate publicity campaign President Reagan pledged a war against narcotics—and then went on to cut federal funds for drug rehabilitation and drug enforcement.

Politicians frequently make false assurances and empty promises, but the pressures of democratic opinion and the need to maintain electoral support sometimes force them to place limits on how single-mindedly they will serve the moneyed powers and how unresponsive they will remain to the needs of ordinary people. Thus, in 1993 President Clinton modified his militaristic policy on Somalia because of the public outcry regarding the loss of U.S. lives in that country. However imperfectly and insufficiently, public opinion and voters' preferences sometimes do have an impact on policymakers. Generally speaking, over the long haul just about every life-affirming policy that has come out of government originated not with presidents, cabinet members, congressional leaders, or other policy elites, but with the common people and mass protest. The struggles for women's rights, civil rights, public education, health care, the eight-hour day, workers' benefits, occupational safety, environmental protection, consumer protection, and the abolition of child labor are all examples.

To summarize some points in this chapter: The range of electoral choices are so structured as to raise a serious question about the representative quality of the political system. Being enormously expensive affairs, elections are best utilized by those interests that can meet such expenses. Politics has always been principally "a rich man's game." Ironically, popular elections, the one institutional arrangement ostensibly designed to over-

---

Petras and Morris Morley, *Empire or Republic? American Global Power and Domestic Decay in the 1990s* (New York: Routledge, 1994).

56. Benjamin Page and Robert Shapiro, "Effects of Public Opinion on Policy," *American Political Science Review*, 77, March 1983, pp. 175–190.

come the advantages of wealth and register the will of ordinary people, is itself greatly dependent on wealth. It serves to legitimize the rule of the privileged few while excluding those most in need.

The way people respond to political reality depends on the way that reality is presented to them. If large numbers have become apathetic and cynical, including many who vote, it is at least partly because the electoral system and the two-party monopoly resist the kind of creative involvement that democracy is supposed to nurture. It is one thing to say that people tend to be uninvolved and poorly informed about political life. It is quite another to maintain a system that propagates these tendencies with every known distraction and discouragement. As now practiced in the U.S., elections might better be considered a symbol of democratic governance than a guarantee of it, and voting often seems to be less an exercise than a surrender of sovereignty.

Still, in the face of all discouragements, third-party challenges continue to arise among people who seek a democratic alternative—bringing to mind the observation made years ago by the great American socialist Eugene Debs: "I would rather vote for what I want and not get it than vote for what I don't want and get it." These are not always the only two choices. A third-party vote is not necessarily a wasted vote. Third parties occasionally have an impact on the major parties, forcing them to adopt stances originating outside the two-party ideological monopoly.

Finally, even within the two-party context, elections remain one of the potential soft spots in the capitalist political order, vulnerable to the impact of popular sentiments. When an issue wins broad, well-organized support and receives some attention in the media, then officeholders cannot remain supremely indifferent to it. The grass-roots pressures of demonstrations, civil disobedience, strikes, boycotts, riots, and other forms of popular agitation, along with the mobilization of voters and involvement in electoral campaigns can sometimes have a direct effect on who is elected and how they behave once in office.

12

Who Governs?
Leaders, Lobbyists,
or Labor?

Those who control the wealth of this society have an influence over political life far in excess of their number. They have the inside track on how government must deal with the (capitalist) economy. The owning class has the power to influence policy through the control of jobs and withholding of investments. In addition, since no system automatically maintains and reproduces itself, the capitalists use some portion of their wealth to finance or exercise trusteeship over social and educational institutions, foundations, think tanks, publications, and mass media, thereby greatly influencing society's ideological output, its values and information flow. This power does not result in total ideational domination but it usually gives the plutocracy a preponderate influence in setting the limits of respectable discourse and shaping the nation's political agenda.

Along with these broad powers, the owning class tends to political affairs in a more direct way. The capitalists occupy the most important public offices or see that persons loyal to them do. In that way they can (1) pursue their own particular interests, and (2) safeguard the capitalist social order in its entirety.

THE RULING CLASS

Alexis de Tocqueville once said that the wealthy have little desire to govern the working people, they simply want to use them.[1] Yet, members of the

---

1. Alexis de Tocqueville, *Democracy in America*, vol. 2 (New York: Vintage, 1945), p. 171.

203

owning class seldom have been slow in assuming the burdens of public office. Not every important political leader is rich but many are, and those who are not are usually beholden to moneyed interests. Not all wealthy persons are engaged in ruling; many prefer to concentrate on other pursuits. The ruling class, or plutocracy, consists largely of the politically active members of the owning class.

From the beginning of the Republic to modern times, the top leadership positions—including the presidency, vice-presidency, the cabinet, and Supreme Court—have rested predominantly in the hands of White males from wealthy families, with most of the remainder being of upper-middle class origins (moderately successful businesspeople, commercial farmers, and professionals). Legend has it that many U.S. presidents rose from humble origins. In fact, almost all came from families of a higher socioeconomic status than about 90 percent of the U.S. population.[2]

In recent times, political leaders have been drawn from the directorships of big corporations, prominent law firms, Wall Street banks, and, less frequently, from the military, elite universities, think tanks, foundations, and scientific establishment. More than a third went to elite Ivy League schools.[3] The men who ran the nation's defense establishment in the decades after World War II, "were so like one another in occupation, religion, style and social status that, apart from a few Washington lawyers, Texans and mavericks, it was possible to locate the offices of all of them within fifteen city blocks in New York, Boston and Detroit."[4]

The wealthy carry into public life many of the class interests and values that shape their business careers. Be they of "old families" or newly arrived, liberal or conservative, they do not advocate democratic alternatives to the economic system under which they prosper. The few rich persons who adopt markedly left leanings are not invited into positions of power. Conversely, occasionally persons from relatively modest class background such as Presidents Lyndon Johnson, Ronald Reagan, Bill Clinton, and Richard Nixon, attract the financial backing that enables them to rise to the top by showing themselves to be faithful guardians of privileged circles. For the

---

2. Edward Pressen, *The Social Background of the Presidents* (New Haven, Conn.: Yale University Press, 1984). In the 1992 presidential primaries, the six leading candidates, including President George Bush, all came from families that were wealthier than 95 percent of the voters; all owned investment portfolios, real estate, and bank accounts that earned them substantial sums beyond their six-figure salaries: *San Francisco Chronicle*, February 5, 1992.

3. Sidney Aronson, *Status and Kinship in the Higher Civil Service* (Cambridge, Mass.: Harvard University Press, 1964); Philip Burch Jr., *Elites in American History*, vols. 1–3 (New York: Holmes and Meier, 1980, 1981); G. William Domhoff, *The Powers That Be* (New York: Vintage, 1979); Beth Mintz, "The President's Cabinet," *Insurgent Sociologist* 5, Spring 1975, pp. 131–148; John Schmidhauser, *The Supreme Court* (New York: Holt, Rinehart and Winston, 1960).

4. Richard Barnet, *Roots of War* (New York: Atheneum, 1972), pp. 48–49.

most part, however, the plutocracy recruits its top members from its own social class. The crucial factor is not the class origin of leaders but the class interest they serve. The question is not only who governs, but whose interests and whose agenda are served by who governs, who benefits and who does not—which is why so much attention is given in this book to policy outputs.

Government and business elites are linked by institutional, financial, and social ties and move easily between public and private leadership posts.[5] Policy-advisory groups, with their interlocking network of corporate and political notables, play an unofficial but influential role in shaping U.S. policies and recruiting elites for leadership posts during both Democratic and Republican administrations. One of the more prominent of these is the Council on Foreign Relations (CFR), started in 1918 and consisting primarily of prominent individuals drawn from finance, industry, and statecraft. The CFR has some 1,450 members, almost half of whom are listed in the *Social Register* and came from families of inherited wealth. Over 60 percent are corporate lawyers, executives, or bankers—including representatives from the Rockefeller, Morgan, and Du Pont groups. The private companies that have had the most CFR members are Morgan Guaranty Trust, Chase Manhattan Bank, Citibank, and IBM. In recent decades, CFR members have included U.S. presidents; secretaries of State and Defense and other cabinet members and their top officers; secretaries of the army, navy, and air force; members of the Joint Chiefs of Staff; national security advisors; CIA directors; federal judges; Federal Reserve officers; scores of U.S. ambassadors; officers of the U.S. Agency for International Development and various other agencies; scores of U.S. House and Senate members; executives and directors of almost all the major banks and leading corporations; numerous college and university presidents; and publishers, editors, newscasters, columnists, and media commentators from every major news organization in the United States.[6]

---

5. Regarding their social ties, many elites go to the same schools, work in the same firms, intermarry, and vacation together. For almost a century, the top decision makers in business and government have gathered every summer at Bohemian Grove, a male-only retreat in California: G. William Domhoff, "Politics Among the Redwoods," *Progressive,* January 1981, pp. 32–36; John Roemer, "*People* Writer Kicked Out by Bohemians," *San Francisco Weekly,* August 7, 1991.

6. Council on Foreign Relations, Annual Report 1991–92, Pratt House, New York; Laurence Shoup and William Minter, *Imperial Brain Trust: The Council on Foreign Relations and United States Foreign Policy* (New York: Monthly Review Press, 1977); G. William Domhoff, *Who Rules America Now?* (New York: Simon & Schuster, 1983); Albert Szymanski, *The Logic of Imperialism* (New York: Praeger, 1981). Many of the more influential CFR members have served in top positions of both government and business; for instance, at one time or another John McCone was a director of numerous corporations such as Standard Oil of California and ITT, and undersecretary of the Air Force, deputy to the secretary of defense, chair of the Atomic Energy Commission, and director of the CIA.

The Council on Foreign Relations has played a central role in formulating U.S. foreign policy. It was a major force in creating the Marshall Plan, the International Monetary Fund, and the World Bank. It advocated a strategic nuclear arsenal, U.S. global interventionism after World War II, military action in Guatemala, military escalation in South Vietnam, and eventual diplomatic relations with China. In 1980, the CFR strongly recommended a sharp escalation in military spending and a harder line toward the Soviets. All these positions were eventually adopted by whomever was in the White House.[7]

Some CFR members also belong to the Trilateral Commission, an assemblage of economic and political leaders from the major industrial countries, initiated by David Rockefeller for the purpose of coordinating and protecting international capitalism in a changing world.[8] A similar international organization is the Bilderberg Conference, which each year brings together state leaders, financiers, military commanders, prominent politicians, and a sprinkling of academicians and publicists from around the world. Another ruling-class organization is the Committee for Economic Development (CED), composed of about two hundred U.S. business leaders. The CED produces policy statements on a range of domestic and international issues—a number of which bear a striking similarity to government policies that are subsequently enacted.[9] Then there is the Business Council, composed of representatives from such companies as Chase Manhattan Bank, Morgan Guaranty Trust, General Electric, and General Motors. The Business Council holds regular three-day secret meetings with top government officials in a posh hotel just outside Washington, D.C.[10]

Rather than promoting the interests of particular enterprises, these various ruling-class organizations seek to develop policies to serve the overall system. Instead of being special-interest lobbyists, they are corporate-class policymakers. Their overall influence is drawn from the persuasiveness that inheres in the enormous economic power they wield. Their direct influence is realized in their capacity—unique among social groups—to fill top government posts with persons from their corporate ranks or persons devoted to their interests.

---

7. Shoup and Minter, *Imperial Brain Trust*, passim.

8. Holly Sklar, *Trilateralism* (Boston: South End Press, 1980); Stephen Gill, *American Hegemony and the Trilateral Commission* (New York: Cambridge University Press, 1991).

9. Domhoff, *Who Rules America Now?*, p. 89.

10. The 154 Business Council members listed in *Who's Who in America* together held 730 directorships in 435 banks and corporations, as well as 49 foundation trusteeships, and 125 trusteeships with 84 universities: Domhoff, *Who Rules America Now?*, p. 134. For a detailed listing of the membership and business affiliations of the Business Council (and of the CED and CFR), see Philip Burch Jr., "The American Establishment: Its Historical Development and Major Economic Components," *Research in Political Economy*, vol. 6 (Greenwich, Conn.: JAI Press, 1983), pp. 83–156.

The names of the players change but the game remains much the same. President Ford appointed fourteen CFR members to positions in his administration. Seventeen top members of the Carter administration were Trilateralists, including President Carter himself and Vice-President Mondale. President Reagan's administrators included chief executives of Wall Street investment houses and directors of New York Banks; at least a dozen of them and thirty-one advisors were CFR members. Most of President Bush's cabinet consisted of corporate leaders who were also CFR members and some Trilateralists; Bush himself was a former Trilateralist. President Clinton's administration offered more gender and racial diversity than was usually found but not much class diversity. Clinton's top administrators were drawn from corporate America; many were CFR members. His secretary of the treasury, Lloyd Bentsen, was a Bilderberg member. While still governor of Arkansas, Clinton himself was a member of the Council on Foreign Relations, the Trilateral Commission, and the Bilderberg Conference, having attended the latter in 1991 along with David Rockefeller.[11]

LOBBYISTS: SPECIAL TREATMENT FOR SPECIAL INTERESTS

Lobbyists are persons hired by interest groups to influence legislative and administrative policies. Some political scientists see lobbying as part of the "information process": the officeholder's perception of an issue is influenced primarily by the information provided him or her—and the lobbyist's job is to be the provider. But this process does not occur in a social vacuum. Often the arguments made on behalf of an issue are less important than who is making them and what interests he or she represents. As one congressional committee counsel explains it: "There's the 23-year-old consumer lobbyist and the businessman who gives you $5,000. Whom are you going to listen to?"[12]

Supposedly the techniques of the "modern" lobbyist consist of disseminating data and giving informative testimony before legislative committees rather than the obsolete tactics of secret deals and bribes. In fact, the development of new lobbying techniques have not brought an end to the older, cruder ones. Along with the slick brochures, expert testimony, and technical reports, corporate lobbyists still offer the succulent campaign contri-

---

11. Ron Brownstein and Nina Easton, *Reagan's Ruling Class* (Washington, D.C.: Center for the Study of Responsive Law, 1982); Domhoff, *Who Rules America Now?*, pp. 139–140; At least nine millionaires hold top positions in the Clinton administration, more than either of the previous two administrations: *Workers World*, March 4, 1993.

12. Quoted in "Business Battles Back," *Environmental Action*, December 2, 1978, p. 14.

butions, the "volunteer" campaign workers, the fat lecture fees, the stock awards and insider stock market tips, the easy-term loans, the high-paying corporate directorship upon retirement from office, the lavish parties and accomodating female escorts, the prepaid vacation jaunts, the luxury hotels and private jets, the free housing and meals, and the many other hustling enticements of money. "Many a financial undertaking on Capitol Hill," writes one Washington columnist, "has been consumated in cold cash— that is, with envelopes or briefcases stuffed with greenbacks, a curious medium for honorable transactions."[13]

Summing up the power of lobbyists, former Speaker of the House Tip O'Neill said: "The grab of special interests is staggering. It will destroy the legislative process."[14] It has certainly destroyed much legislative integrity. The case of Claude Wild Jr. is instructive. As a vice-president of Gulf Oil and a lobbyist over a twelve-year period, Wild passed out about $4.1 million of Gulf's money to more than 100 U.S. senators and representatives, eighteen governors, and scores of judges and local politicians. His gift list included Presidents Lyndon Johnson, Richard Nixon, Gerald Ford, and Jimmy Carter (when he was governor of Georgia). Over a ten-year period, four oil companies paid out $8 million in illegal payments to forty-five members of Congress.[15]

"Everyone has a price," Howard Hughes once told an associate who later recalled that the billionaire handed out about $400,000 yearly to "councilmen and county supervisors, tax assessors, sheriffs, state senators and assemblymen, district attorneys, governors, congressmen and senators, judges—yes, and vice-presidents and presidents, too."[16]

The popular reform victories of the late 1960s and early 1970s, which brought gains in human services, occupational safety, consumer protection, environmental law, and a growth in antibusiness sentiment, were not greeted with equanimity by big moneyed interests. Corporations of the Fortune 500 financed conservative think tanks to churn out policy studies and probusiness propaganda. They opened new lobbying offices in Wash-

---

13. Jack Anderson, *Washington Post,* August 7, 1980; *Washington Post,* June 14 and August 28, 1987; Michael Pertschuk and Clifford Douglas, "Internal Documents Detail Aggressive Tobacco Industry Campaign," *Health Letter* (publication of Public Citizen Health Research Group), January 1993, pp. 3–5. A remarkable eyewitness account of the seamy side of lobbying is Robert Winter-Berger, *The Washington Pay-Off* (New York: Dell, 1972); also Lawrence Gilson, *Money and Secrecy* (New York: Praeger, 1972).

14. Quoted in Jack Anderson, "Lobbyists: The Unelected Lawmakers in Washington," *Parade,* March 16, 1980, p. 4.

15. According to SEC investigators: *Washington Post,* March 22, 1976. On Claude Wild and the Gulf payments, see *Wall Street Journal,* November 17, 1975; *Philadelphia Bulletin,* November 12, 1975; *Washington Post,* June 24, 1979.

16. Howard Kohn, "The Hughes-Nixon-Lansky Connection," *Rolling Stone,* May 20, 1976, p. 44.

ington. In 1971, less than two hundred firms had registered lobbyists in the capital. A decade later the number had grown to two thousand.[17] By 1979, the American Petroleum Institute, an organization of oil, gas, and petrochemical companies, was spending $75 million a year in lobbying efforts. The entire oil industry employed over 600 people to pressure Congress and government agencies.[18] Lockheed, a big defense contractor, currently maintains 135 lobbyists in Washington.

Perhaps most influential of all is the Business Roundtable, the "trillion-dollar voice" of big business, composed of 190 chief executives of the nation's blue-chip corporations, one or another of whom are always in contact with key figures in the White House, the cabinet, and Congress. Credited with thwarting or watering down antitrust, environmental, prolabor, pro-consumer, and tax-reform measures, the Roundtable exercises an influence over government eclipsing even that of the National Association of Manufacturers and the U.S. Chamber of Commerce. Many Roundtable members also belong to the Business Council and have immediate access to legislators because they are heads of big corporations.[19]

Some of Washington's top lobbying groups are well funded by foreign governments that are among the world's worst human-rights abusers, including Turkey, Kuwait, Indonesia, Guatemala, Colombia, Saudi Arabia, and the CIA-supported Unita rebel group in Angola. These governments successfully lobby Congress for hundreds of millions of dollars in foreign aid—compliments of the U.S. taxpayer.[20]

The high-powered Washington lobbyists are usually corporate attorneys, businesspeople, ex-legislators, ex-congressional aids, or former government officials with good connections in government. There exists what amounts to a revolving door between government and business lobbying. Officials who are especially responsive to lobbying interests reap rewards as high-paid lobbyists for private business when they leave government service.[21] The most effective resource lobbyists can have at their command is money. Money buys accessibility to the officeholder and, beyond that,

---

17. David Vogel, *Fluctuating Fortunes, The Political Power of Business in America* (New York: Basic Books, 1989).

18. Jack Newfield, "Oil: The Imperial Lobby," *Village Voice,* November 5, 1979; see also *New York Times,* December 10, 1985.

19. "Business Battles Back," p. 13; Mark Green and Andrew Buchsbaum, *The Corporate Lobbies* (Washington, D.C.: Public Citizen, 1980); Philip Burch Jr., "The Business Roundtable," *Research in Political Economy,* vol. 4 (Greenwich, Conn.: JAI Press, 1981), pp. 101–127.

20. *The Torturers' Lobby,* study by the Center for Public Integrity, Washington, D.C., 1992); also Johan Carlisle, "Public Relationships: Hill and Knowlton, Robert Gray, and the CIA," *CovertAction Quarterly,* Spring 1993, pp. 19–25.

21. Attempts to prohibit the revolving door have not been too successful: Douglas Jehl, "Lobbying Rules for Ex-Officials at Issue Again," *New York Times,* December 8, 1993.

the opportunity to shape his or her judgments with arguments of the lobby-ist's own choosing. But access does not guarantee influence. As Woodrow Wilson once pointed out:

> Suppose you go to Washington and try to get at your Government. You will always find that while you are politely listened to, the men really consulted are the men who have the big stake—the big bankers, the big manufacturers, and the big masters of commerce. . . . The masters of the Government of the United States are the combined capitalists and manufacturers of the United States.[22]

It is, then, something more than "information flow" that determines influence, the decisive factor being not just the message but the messenger. The ability to disseminate information to decision makers and propagate one's cause itself presumes organization, expertise, time, and labor—things money can buy. In addition, the mere possession of great wealth and the control of industry and jobs give corporate interests an advantage unknown to ordinary working citizens, for business's claims are paraded as the "needs of the economy" and, as it were, of the nation itself. Having the advantage of pursuing their interests within the framework of a capitalist system, cap-italists can pretty much limit the range of solutions.

Surveying the organized pressure groups in America, E. E. Schatt-schneider notes: *"The system is very small.* The range of organized, identifi-able, known groups is amazingly narrow; there is nothing remotely universal about it."[23] The pressure system, he concludes, is largely dominated by business groups, the majority of citizens belonging to no organization that is effectively engaged in pressure politics.

---

22. Quoted in D. Gilbarg, "United States Imperialism," in Bill Slate (ed.), *Power to the People* (New York: Tower, 1970), p. 67. The biggest political fund-raiser in history was a dinner in Washington attended by President Bush that netted the Republican party $9 million, with individual donations ranging up to $400,000. Presidential press secretary Marlin Fitzwater defended the event: "[The donors] are buying into the political process. . . . That's what the political parties and the political operation is all about." Asked how less wealthy persons could buy into the political process, Fitzwater said, "They have to demand access in other ways": *New York Times,* April 29, 1992.

23. E. E. Schattschneider, *The Semi-Sovereign People* (New York: Holt, Rinehart and Winston, 1960), p. 31; italics in the original. This view is in marked contrast to what might be called "the school of happy pluralism," which sees power as widely and democratically diffused. Thus one political scientist concludes that "nearly every vigorous push in one direction" by a lobbying interest "stimulates an opponent or coalition of opponents to push in the opposite direction. This natural self-balancing factor comes into play so often that it almost amounts to a law": Lester Milbrath, *The Washington Lobbyists* (Chicago: Rand McNally, 1963), p. 345. The evidence presented in this book does not support this cheerful view. Who speaks for the powerless, the homeless, the unemployed? and with how much political clout?

The pressure system is "small" and "narrow" only in that it represents a highly select portion of the public. In relation to government itself, the system is a substantial operation. Over 15,000 lobbyists prowl the Capitol's corridors and lobbies (whence their name). Others seek favorable rulings from agencies within the vast executive bureaucracy. Lobbyists make themselves so helpful that members of Congress sometimes rely on them to perform tasks normally done by congressional staffs. Lobbyists will draft legislation, write speeches, and plant stories in the press on behalf of cooperative lawmakers. Lobbyists "put in millions of hours each year" to make the world a better place for their clients, "and they succeed on a scale that is undreamed of by most ordinary citizens."[24] A favorable adjustment in rates for interstate carriers, a special tax benefit for a family oil trust, a high-interest bond issue for big investors, a special charter for a bank, a tariff protection for auto producers, the leasing of public lands to a private company, emergency funding for a faltering aeronautics plant, a postal subsidy for advertising firms, the easing of safety standards for a food processor, the easing of pollution controls for a chemical company, a special acreage allotment for peanut growers and tobacco growers, an investment guarantee to a housing developer, a lease guarantee to a construction contractor—all these hundreds of bills and their thousands of special amendments and the tens of thousands of administrative rulings, which mean so much to particular business interests and arouse the sympathetic efforts of legislators and bureaucrats, will go largely unnoticed by a public that pays the monetary and human costs and seldom has the means to make its case—or even to discover it has a case.

Attempting to speak for the great unorganized populace, public-interest groups make many proposals for reform but have few of the resources that push officeholders in a reformist direction—especially when their proposals are directed against powerful, entrenched interests in the economy. The relative sparsity of power resources (the most crucial being money) limits the efforts of citizen groups and makes problematic their very survival. Substantial sums are needed just to maintain an office and a tiny staff. Without affluent patrons, many public-interest groups are forced to devote an inordinate amount of their time foraging for funds.[25]

---

24. Richard Harris, "Annals of Politics: A Fundamental Hoax," *New Yorker,* August 7, 1971, p. 56. To draft major legislation on health care, the Clinton administration put together a task force of three hundred experts. But a smaller group composed of representatives from major insurance companies, a hospital owners association, the top pharmaceutical association, and other big corporations like General Electric and Pepsico—the powerful private interests that stood most to gain from the legislation—had "already provided much of the basic blueprint" for "managed competition": *New York Times,* February 28, 1993.

25. Jack Walker, "The Origins and Maintenance of Interest Groups in America," *American Political Science Review,* 77, 1983, pp. 403–440.

Some political scientists have theorized that the diversity of cultural, economic, regional, religious, and ethnic groups in our society creates cross-pressured allegiances that mitigate the strength of any one organized interest. While this may be true of certain broad constituencies, it does not seem to apply to the more powerful and politically active segments of the business community whose interlocking memberships seem to compound rather than dilute their class commitments and power. Certainly the multiplicity of interests within the business community creates problems of cohesion, but these diverse groups are capable of colluding around common class interests, and giving mutual support to each other's special projects. For instance, when defending their depletion allowance, the oil companies mobilized merchant fleet owners, truckers, county highway commissioners, asphalt companies, gas station owners, the National Rifle Association, representatives of military-industrial interests, bankers, and some gamblers.[26] It is not too much to suppose that at least some of these groups, in turn, received support from the oil lobby when pressuring for their interests.

GRASS-ROOTS LOBBYING

Pressure-group efforts are directed not only at officeholders but also at the public, in what has been called "grass-roots lobbying." The goal is to (a) create a general publicity campaign and media blitz to influence the lawmaker's sense of what should be done; (b) get voters to serve as pressure-group advocates by having them directly write or call legislators and other officials; and (c) mobilize corporate members of an industry or trade association to do likewise. Here is one description of grass-roots lobbying:

> The electric companies, organized in the National Electric Light Association, had not only directly influenced [Congress] on a large scale, but had also conducted a massive campaign to control the substance of teaching in the nation's schools. Teachers in high schools and grammar schools were inundated with materials. . . . Each pamphlet included carefully planted disparagement of public ownership of utilities. The Association took very active, if inconspicuous, measures to insure that textbooks that were doctrinally impure on this issue were withdrawn from use and that more favorable substitutes were produced and used. College professors . . . were given supplemental incomes by the Association and, in return, not infrequently taught about the utility industry with greater sympathy than before. . . . Public libraries, ministers, and civic lead-

---

26. Robert Engler, *The Politics of Oil*, 2nd ed. (Chicago: University of Chicago Press, 1976), pp. 390–391; *New York Times*, November 2, 1993.

ers of all kinds were subjected to the propagandistic efforts of the electric companies.[27]

Among the earliest practitioners of grass-roots lobbying were consumer, environmental, and other public-interest groups. Unable to afford high-powered "super-lobbyists" with special access on Capitol Hill, they mobilized their grass-roots networks of members to tell Washington how they felt. Corporations and business associations also adopted this approach, the difference being that they have been able to spend over $1 billion a year, whereas the combined expenditures of environmental, consumer and other public-interest groups comes to less than one percent of that amount.[28] The U.S. Chamber of Commerce alone, with its 215,000 associated businesses and $67 million annual budget, can bring down a snowstorm of mail and a mountain of pressure on lawmakers.[29] In the summer of 1993, the National Association of Manufacturers launched a campaign that inundated Congress with letters and phone calls opposing President Clinton's proposed energy tax, and as a result the plan was squashed.[30]

Using computerized fax machines, a trade association can instruct its member corporations to ask their employees, customers, and others to contact their representatives in Congress. Some trade associations have satellite networks that enable them to appear instantaneously on television monitors in affiliate offices in every state, so better to rally their members to action.[31] Moneyed interests can run TV ads carefully targeted for particular regions and congressional districts. Public interest groups seldom are able to match these efforts. Former President Jimmy Carter wrote that wealthy lobbies can "unleash almost unlimited television and direct-mail assaults on uncooperative legislators. At the same time they can legally reward those who do their bidding. The lobbies are a growing menace to our system of government."[32]

Interest groups sometimes hide behind front organizations that have uplifting, public-service sounding names. The National Wetlands Coalition is a well-financed lobby of giant oil companies, mining companies, and real-estate developers, with the single mission of undoing the regulations

---

27. Grant McConnell, *Private Power and American Democracy* (New York: Knopf, 1966), p. 19.

28. "Business Battles Back," p. 12.

29. Information provided to me by a Chamber of Commerce representative, telephone interview, December 22, 1993; see also Anderson, "Lobbyists: The Unelected Lawmakers . . ."

30. Joel Brinkley, "Cultivating the Grass Roots to Reap Legislative Benefits," *New York Times,* November 1, 1993. On the public relations and lobbying power of the tobacco companies, see Larry White, *Merchants of Death* (New York: Beech Tree/William Morrow, 1988).

31. Brinkley, "Cultivating the Grass Roots . . ."

32. Jimmy Carter, *Keeping Faith* (New York: Bantam, 1982), p. 80.

that protect our endangered wetlands. The Citizens for Sensible Control of Acid Rain is bankrolled by electric utilities and coal companies and has expended more than $3 million mostly for mass mailings urging people to voice their opposition to stricter emission controls on coal-burning facilities. The Coalition for Health Insurance Choices is a front for health insurance companies and their agents, whose goal is to drastically dilute any federal health insurance program.[33]

Some grass-roots lobbying is intended to build a climate of opinion favorable to the corporate giants rather than to push a particular piece of legislation. The steel, oil, and electronics companies do not urge the public to support the latest tax-loophole bill or business handout—if anything, they would prefer that citizens not trouble themselves with such matters—but they do "educate" the public, telling of the many jobs they create, the progress and services they provide, the loving care they supposedly give to the environment, and so on. This kind of "institutional advertising" attempts to place the desires of the giant firms above politics and above controversy—a goal that is itself highly political. Rather than selling their particular products, the corporations sell the business system itself.[34]

Besides working the inside track of influence peddling, business does well in mass campaigns, using the power of money to harness the power of numbers. On occasion, progressive groups in various states are able to place referenda on the ballot supporting reform causes. Polls show that often these referenda are initially backed by large majorities, only to be voted down after public opinion is swayed by multimillion-dollar media assaults launched by affluent interests. Increasingly, the referendum is being successfully employed by well-funded conservative organizations, utilizing newspaper advertisements, radio and TV commercials, and computerized direct-mail appeals.[35]

LABOR BESIEGED

Conservatives tell us that labor unions are corrupt, unpopular, harmful, and too powerful. The truth is something else. In 1935 working people won a major victory when the National Labor Relations Act was passed, giving

---

33. For these several examples, see Newsletter of Natural Resources Defense Council, Washington, D.C., September 1991; *People's Daily World*, August 29, 1987; *New York Times*, October 20, 1993.

34. See Michael Parenti, *Inventing Reality: The Politics of News Media*, 2nd ed., (New York: St. Martin's Press, 1993).

35. On business spending in referenda campaigns, see Martin Espinoza, "Politicians for Sale," *Bay Guardian*, October 14, 1992, pp. 17–18. On issue campaigns waged by industry, see political scientist Tom Konda's correspondence: *New York Times*, November 1, 1993.

them the right to organize and bargain collectively. In the years that followed, union membership increased dramatically. However, in 1947, a Republican controlled Congress passed the Taft-Hartley Act, which imposed restrictions on strikes, boycotts, and labor organizing, resulting in a decline in union membership from 35 percent of the work force in 1950 to 16 percent in 1991.[36]

The number of strikes has dropped drastically as weakened unions have become less able to fight back. Union busting has become a major industry with more than a thousand consulting firms doing a $500 million yearly business, teaching companies how to prevent workers from organizing and how to get rid of existing unions. Industry also uses the threat of plant closings to extract from unions benefit and wage concessions amounting to billions of dollars.[37]

Under federal law, the National Labor Relations Board (NLRB) is an independent federal agency intended to protect labor's right to organize and deal with grievances against management. During the Reagan-Bush administrations, the NLRB was stacked with probusiness appointees who often refused to protect employees from being illegally fired for union activities and imposed only token fines on management for serious violations. They have ruled that middle management could vote in union certification elections—in effect, stacking elections against workers.[38]

During union election drives, management can propagandize workers as a captive audience and ply them with gifts to induce an antiunion vote. In contrast, union organizers are denied access to the work site and are prohibited from giving gifts to workers. Management can threaten to move the plant if a union is voted in. About 10,000 workers a year are illegally fired for their union organizing activities.[39] A company caught threatening a worker with dismissal for union activity suffers the heavy penalty of having to post a notice promising not to do it again.

Bosses can use NLRB procedures to delay the election for months or years. When unions do win elections, management regularly challenges the results. The NLRB will spend months, even years, investigating minor or frivolous management charges. By the time the company is ordered to bar-

36. *Economic Notes*, November/December 1992, p. 15. This 16 percent represents 16.6 million workers. If we don't count public employees and consider only the private sector, union membership is only 12 percent, lower than it was in 1932 before the New Deal: *1199 News*, November 1992, p. 2. On the labor struggle, see Thomas Geoghegan, *Which Side Are You On?* (New York: Farrar, Straus & Giroux, 1991).

37. *New York Times*, March 3, 1991; Peter Ajemian, "Union Busters," *Public Citizen*, April 1986, pp. 14–19.

38. Dennis Schaal, "How Bad Can the NLRB Get?" *Guardian*, January 16, 1985; David Moberg, "Obstacles to Union Organizing," *In These Times*, July 11–24, 1984, p. 5.

39. Newsletter from United Electrical, Radio, and Machine Workers of America (UE), Pittsburgh, Penn., May 1993; see also *New York Times*, September 28, 1991.

gain, many union supporters may have quit or been fired, while new employees are being screened for union sympathy. After bargaining begins, the company still can resist reaching an acceptable contract agreement.[40]

Through the 1980s and early 1990s, lockouts increased dramatically. A lockout occurs when management refuses to negotiate a contract with the union, deliberately forcing workers out on strike; then the company fires the strikers and brings in permanent replacements to break the union. This is why strike activity has fallen markedly. The threat of permanent worker-replacement in effect has eliminated the right to strike and seriously hampered the right to unionize.[41]

If unions are in decline, it is not because workers do not like them. By a margin of 60 to 23 percent, Americans believe unions have been good for working people. Almost four out of five citizens favor laws that would protect the right of workers to organize without being fired by their bosses.[42] The causes of decline are the repressive, one-sided conditions under which organized labor has been forced to operate.

To juxtapose "Big Labor" with Big Business, as do some political science textbooks, is to forget several important facts. First, businesspeople have a near monopoly on the top decision-making posts in government. Second, government has historically been friendly to business and hostile to labor. Government security agencies such as the FBI have a history of spying on unions, sometimes in cooperation with management.[43] Third, while labor can sometimes play an effective role in support of social legislation, it cannot match business in material resources and political muscle. Nor can it match business ownership of the major media and the hundreds of millions of dollars business spends propagandizing issues through the press. Total corporate profits are about 500 times greater than the total income of labor unions.[44]

In recent electoral campaigns, business outspent labor by about four to one. If we add the huge sums given to lawmakers and lobbyists between elections or spent on referenda campaigns and the money from individual fat cats and wealthy candidates, the ratio is more lopsided than that.[45] Far from having too much power, unions have been fighting for their lives

40. Richard Bensinger, "Dirty Campaigning," *Solidarity* (publication of the United Auto Workers), August 1993, p. 28; "Stealing Workers' Right to vote," *1199 News*, November 1992, p. 4.

41. *Economic Notes,* January/February 1988, p. 4, and January/February 1991, pp. 1–2.

42. *Economic Notes,* January/February 1992, p. 3.

43. Chuck Fogel, "Spying on the Union," *Solidarity,* March 1988, pp. 11–16; Tim Wheeler and Ron Johnson, "Files Reveal Four Years of FBI Spying on Unions, Peace Groups," *People's Daily World,* January 28, 1988.

44. *Guardian,* February 18, 1981.

45. *Washington Post,* February 21, 1982. In the 1992 campaign the total contributions by unions to both parties, $1.24 million, was dwarfed by the $17.1 million given by business

against hostile laws, court rulings, NLRB decisions, and government witch-hunting that purged the labor movement of communists—who were among its most effective leaders and most dedicated organizers.[46]

Some people complain that unions are corrupt and undemocratic. To be sure, some union leaders become union dealers, powerful and autocratic in relation to their own membership, voting themselves sumptuous salaries, colluding with gangland thugs to intimidate the rank and file into submission, cooperating in management speedups, and doing little for the membership. In return, they win management's ready acceptance as a union. Yet this kind of corruption tends to be concentrated in less than 1 percent of all locals.[47] In contrast, as noted in chapter 8, 60 percent of the 582 largest U.S. companies have been guilty of fraud, bribes, illegal kickbacks, tax evasion, or other criminal acts. Business also plays fast with labor's money. During the 1980s almost two thousand companies removed $21 billion from employees' pension funds, and stole additional billions by substituting inferior pension plans for the ones that workers had originally paid into. By 1993, many employees retirement annuities were at risk.[48]

Unions have been attacked for causing both inflation and recession. However, as noted in chapter 2, wage demands do not drive up prices but usually lag behind price-profit growth. Labor's share of the national income has declined in the last dozen years, yet inflation continues. As for recession, it is argued that unions drive up labor costs, forcing companies to mechanize, cut back on jobs, and relocate to cheaper labor markets. But

---

corporations, three-fourths of which went to the Republican party: *New York Times*, April 19, 1992.

46. Richard Boyer and Herbert Morais, *Labor's Untold Story* (New York: United Electrical, Radio, and Machine Workers, 1972), pp. 340–380. Instead of being interested in ridding unions of gangster influence, corporations and government were more interested in going after communists in the labor movement, including many who performed heroically against mobsters: Dan Moldea, *Dark Victory: Ronald Reagan, MCA, and the Mob* (New York: Penguin Books, 1987), pp. 66–70.

47. Even one of the more corrupt unions, the International Brotherhood of Teamsters (IBT), has had honest leadership in about 600 of its 700 locals (the other hundred have been linked to organized mobsters). A rank-and-file movement within the IBT elected reformist Ron Carey as Teamsters president. Carey got rid of double-dipping union officials and their jets and limousines, and hired hard-working labor activists who want to revitalize the union and mobilize around progressive issues: Kenneth Crowe, *Collision: How the Rank and File Took Back the Teamsters* (New York: Scribner's, 1993). Instead of welcoming such moves, the Republican administration in Washington put the IBT in trusteeship and appointed two corporate lawyers (including former FBI and CIA director William Webster) to exercise full authority over the union, doing more to hamstring than help the IBT revitalize itself: Frank Dobbs, "Can Carey Reform The Teamsters?" *Nation*, February 15, 1993. As of February 1994, President Clinton had failed to lift the trusteeship.

48. John Parsons, "Dipping Into Pensions," *Economic Notes*, November/December 1986, pp. 8–9; Donald Barlett and James Steele, *America: What Went Wrong?* (Kansas City: Andrews and McMeel, 1992), pp. 171–183; *New York Times*, April 22, 1993.

most downgrading, restructuring, and relocating during the 1980s and early 1990s came when labor costs were in decline. Labor has been the victim, not the cause, of recessions.

To be sure, under capitalism the demands of labor are not automatically accommodated and do create problems for the capital accumulation process. But given management's drive to depress the condition of labor and given the boom-and-bust cycles endemic to capitalism, it is a bit much to give the capitalists credit for the boom while blaming the workers for the bust.

If unions are bad for the economy, we might expect that as they decline, the economy would flourish. But the very opposite has happened. Organized labor has lost membership from 1970 to 1993, but there has been no great economic resurgence; instead there were several severe recessions. In states where unions have been traditionally weak (e.g., Alabama, South Carolina, and Mississippi), the standard of living has been lower than in states where unions have a stronger presence. So with Third World countries that have weak or nonexistent unions as compared to the better unionized and more prosperous nations of Western Europe and Scandinavia.[49] Unions correlate with prosperity rather than with poverty.

It is argued that unions are of no help and some harm to workers. The opposite is true. Union members make more money than nonunion workers. Even the latter benefit from the struggles of organized labor when their bosses make concessions in order to keep unions out.[50] Criticisms and challenges from unions tend to produce better management performance.[51] The higher the unionization rate, the more equal is the distribution of income. Conversely, as unions have declined, income distribution has become more skewed in favor of the rich.[52] Occupational conditions and safety inspections generally are better at unionized workplaces than nonunion ones.[53]

Far from being the autocratic, all-powerful bullies they are made out to be by media and government, labor unions are a vital part of whatever democracy we have. They are one of the few institutions in which ordinary working people can give an organized response to the issues affecting their lives. The rank and file participate in union elections at higher rates than in

---

49. Wages and work conditions in the United States compare unfavorably with those of the more strongly unionized nations of Canada, Scandinavia, and Western Europe: *1199 News*, November 1992, p. 5; *Economic Notes*, September/October 1991, p. 12.

50. *Economic Notes*, May/June 1990, pp. 4–5.

51. Richard Freeman and James Medoff, *What Do Unions Do?* (New York: Basic Books, 1984).

52. Study by Rudy Fichtenbaum, "How Unions Affect the Distribution of Income," summarized in *Economic Notes*, July/August 1993, p. 7.

53. "OSHA Enforcement," *Economic Notes*, January/February 1991, p. 3.

national elections. In most unions the entire membership gets to vote on a contract.[54] Unions have played an important role in the passage of major civil-rights bills and have supported single-payer health insurance, low-income housing, mass transportation, consumer protection, public education, and progressive tax reform. They have opposed the North American Free Trade Agreement (NAFTA) and other circumventions of popular sovereignty. Unions have backed environmental controls and peace movements in coalitions with other organizations. Some of the more progressive unions broke with the militaristic cold-war mentality of the AFL-CIO leadership and supported nonintervention in Central America.

For organized labor to reverse its ill fortunes, it needs repeal of the anti-labor laws that undermine its right to strike and hamstring its ability to organize and win decent labor contracts from management.[55] The NLRB must once again become an agency that defends—rather than undermines—the right to collective bargaining. Labor must struggle for the repeal of NAFTA and against the General Agreement on Tariffs and Trade (GATT). It must show itself willing to fight hard against corporate cutbacks. Union leaders must avoid a collaborationist policy with management. Labor must use the billions of dollars in pension funds to invest in housing rehabilitation, community development, and other social programs beneficial to its rank and file.[56] And AFL-CIO leaders must stop promoting a reprehensible U.S. foreign policy that supports oppressive regimes, undermines independent labor unions in the Third World, and preserves cheap labor markets abroad—to which U.S. jobs are then exported.[57]

Human labor is the basis of our well-being and survival. Everywhere in the world, including the United States, it deserves far better treatment than it is getting.

---

54. Freeman and Medoff, *What Do Unions Want?*

55. The Clinton administration is pledged to legislation that would prohibit management from permanently replacing strikers with scabs. At the time of this writing (April 1994), no action has been taken by the Clinton administration.

56. See reports on pension investment strategies in *Economic Notes*, November/December 1992, pp. 2–3, and May 1993, p. 8.

57. Jonathan Tasini, "American Labor Needs a Revolution," *Oakland Tribune*, September 6, 1993; Laurie Jo Hughes, "AIFLD: American Intervention Against Free Labor Development," *Nicaragua Monitor* (publication of Nicaragua Network Education Fund, Washington, D.C.), December 1991/January 1992, pp. 1–3.

13

Congress: The Pocketing of Power

The framers of the Constitution separated governmental functions into executive, legislative, and judicial branches and installed a system of checks and balances to safeguard against both the usurpation of power by a tyrannical few and attacks on wealth by the democratic many. The Congress they created is a bicameral body, divided into the House of Representatives, whose seats are distributed among the states according to population, and the Senate, with two seats per state regardless of population. Thus California, with sixty-six times as many people as Wyoming, has the same number of senators.[1]

The people elected to Congress are not demographically representative of the nation. Women are 52 percent of our population but less than 7 percent of the Congress. African Americans are some 14 percent of the population but have less than 5 percent of the legislative seats. Occupational backgrounds are heavily skewed in an upper-class direction. Although they are only a small fraction of the population, lawyers (many of them corporate attorneys) compose about 50 percent in both houses. Bankers, investors, entrepreneurs, and business executives compose the next largest group. There are almost no blue-collar persons or other ordinary working people in Congress.[2]

---

1. Nine states—California, New York, Florida, Texas, Pennsylvania, Illinois, Ohio, Minnesota, and New Jersey—contain almost 52 percent of the population but only 18 percent of the Senate's seats.

2. U.S. Bureau of the Census, *Statistical Abstract of the United States: 1992* (112th edition) Washington, D.C., 1992, p. 264; *Congressional Quarterly Weekly Report,* 41, January 1985, pp. 34–41.

A CONGRESS FOR THE MONEY

Rather than slates of candidates backed by a cohesive party organization united around a common program, elections are individualized district-by-district contests, fueled more by personalized candidate appeals and image manipulation than by substantive issues. As already noted, the major campaign weapon is money. "Congress is the best money can buy," said the humorist Will Rogers over a half-century ago. The quip is truer than ever. In recent decades, congressional election expenses have climbed more than 300 percent faster than the cost of living.[3] Presidential and congressional elections (including primaries) totaled $1.6 billion in 1988, and $2.1 billion in 1992.[4]

In 1992, business interests outspent labor by more than five to one.[5] Coming from corporations, trade associations, and rich individuals, most campaign money finds its way into the coffers of the more conservative of the two capitalist parties. GOP campaign committees raise several times more than their Democratic counterparts.[6] However, money respects class lines more consistently than party lines, only class lines. The more conservative members of the Democratic party also do quite well. Both capitalist parties (but none of the anticapitalist ones) receive millions of dollars from special-interest political action committees (PACs).[7] To hedge their bets, big donors often give money to candidates who are running against each other, thereby trying to ensure the cooperation of whomever wins.[8]

---

3. *Washington Post* editorial, February 26, 1988; Philip Stern, *The Best Congress Money Can Buy* (New York: Pantheon, 1988).

4. Herbert Alexander and Monica Bauer, *Financing the 1988 Election* (Boulder, Colo.: Westview, 1991); also telephone interview with Federal Elections Commission staff member, December 29, 1993. In 1990, successful candidates for the Senate raised, on average, nearly $4 million each: newsletter, Common Cause, Washington, D.C., April 1991. In the 1990 gubernatorial race in California, the two major-party candidates spent $35 million between them; the Texas gubernatorial race that year cost $33 million: *Seattle Times,* November 4, 1990.

5. *Wall Street Journal*/NBC poll reported in *People's Weekly World,* October 31, 1992.

6. *Washington Post,* June 30, 1989. Big campaign donors who sat on the boards of directors of the top defense corporations favored Republicans over Democrats by almost six to one: Tom Koenig, "Business Support for Disclosure of Corporate Campaign Contributions," in Michael Schwartz (ed.), *The Structure of Power in America* (New York: Holmes & Meier, 1987), p. 88.

7. G. William Domhoff, *Fat Cats and Democrats* (Englewood Cliffs, N.J.: Prentice Hall, 1972), and David Corn's report in *Nation,* September 30, 1991, p. 364; Howard Reiter, *Parties and Elections in Corporate America* (New York: St. Martin's Press, 1987), pp. 265–266. Democratic incumbents with strategic committee seats are well funded by business interests: *Washington Post,* June 19, 1990.

8. To cite one of many examples of "switch hitting" or "double giving", the American Bankers Association contributed $10,000 to assist a Republican senator's reelection effort. When he lost, the bankers unabashedly gave his victorious Democratic opponent $10,000, thereby hoping to ensure the newcomer's cooperation: *Washington Post,* March 26, 1987.

Generous funds are often given to lawmakers who run unopposed—not to buy victory but to ensure influence over the preordained victor.

Members of Congress go where the money is, scrambling for congressional committee assignments that deal with issues of greatest interest to big donors. In 1989–90, the top nine Senate recipients of donations from weapons makers and the top ten House recipients—receiving together over $2.2 million—were all members of committees that dealt with defense contracts. PACs with direct interest in banking gave members of House and Senate banking committees $5.8 million over a two-year period. But Henry Gonzalez (D-TX), chair of the House committee, who believes banks should be regulated in the public interest, received but a pittance. The sugar lobby gave $3.3 million over a seven-year period, with prosugar legislators receiving seven times more than others.[9]

There is a century-old saying, "The dollar votes more times than the man." The power of money works ceaselessly to reduce the influence of citizens who have nothing to offer but their votes. Most senators and many House members get the greater part of their money from outside their districts or home states. Senator Robert Dole (R-KS) worked hard for a billion-dollar tobacco subsidy. He also received generous contributions from the tobacco industry. But tobacco is virtually an unknown crop in Kansas, the state that elected him, so whom was he representing?[10]

Many legislators profess to be uninfluenced by the money they accept. Thus Senator Durenberger (R-MN) maintained that the $62,775 he received from the chemical industry "hasn't had any effect on me. These people contributed in the hope that I'd be a senator, and not on the condition that I'd vote for their legislation."[11] But was the chemical industry so keen on having Durenberger be a senator because they were utterly taken by his personal qualities? More likely it was because he voted the way they liked on most issues. Politicians can claim that money does not influence their votes, but their votes influence the money flow. Big donors might be strung along now and then, contributing in the hope of buying a legislator's eventual support, but they do not long reward those who habitually oppose them.

---

9. *New York Times*, August 6, 1991; *PACs and Lobbies*, newsletter, Edward Zuckerman (ed.), Washington, D.C., June 1990; *Too Sweet to Resist: The Congressional Appetite for Sugar PAC$*, report by the Public Voice for Food and Health Policy, Washington, D.C., 1990; *Washington Post*, June 19, 1990.

10. *New York Times*, April 16, 1990; Stern, *The Best Congress Money Can Buy*, pp. 84–85. Members of Congress are less inclined to vote against their largest contributors than against what seems to be the interests of their district. Thus, senators who received the largest sums from defense-contract PACs were almost twice as likely to support higher military spending than those who received little, regardless of how much defense industry existed in their respective states: study by Military Spending Research Services, reported in *Washington Post*, January 23, 1987.

11. Quoted in *Washington Post*, November 17, 1980.

Not many oppose them. In six years, members of Congress took $36.5 million from the banking industry. In return, bankers were granted dereg- ulation and bailout legislation that will cost the U.S. public $500 billion. Utilities contributed over half a million dollars plus thousands more in speaking fees to members of the House Ways and Means Committee. In return, the committee defeated a proposal that would have speeded up refunds to consumers of excess taxes collected by utilities (excess collec- tions of future taxes—amounting to $19 billion—that were no longer due because of tax reductions given to utilities). Other well-placed contribu- tions by wealthy interests have brought similar rewards.[12]

PAC representatives and other lobbyists often are primarily concerned about having a member of Congress help them get some revision, protec- tion, or exemption that usually applies only to themselves into legislation. With those specific but unpublicized favors safely inserted, the special- interest contributor may no longer care how the legislator then votes on the final bill. Though each individual insertion is relatively minor, the cumu- lative impact is great, contributing to the inability to create fundamentally reformist legislation.[13]

Legislators themselves admit they feel obliged to accommodate big con- tributors.[14] One House candidate, outspent and defeated by his conser- vative opponent, noted: "Campaign money becomes an overriding factor. Constant trips to raise money eat you up and get in the way of talking about issues and meeting voters. . . . [Many candidates] are tempted to compro- mise their positions in return for PAC money."[15] At a Senate Democratic Caucus, Senator Harold Hughes said his conscience would not allow him to continue in politics because of the way he had been forced to raise money. Senator Hubert Humphrey concurred:

> In all his years in politics [Humphrey] said, nothing was as demeaning and degrading as the way he had to raise money. He was in a highly emotional state as he told of how ashamed he was of the things he had to do to extract campaign money from contributors. He spoke of how politicians are treated by those who

---

12. Stern, *The Best Congress Money Can Buy,* passim; *Washington Post,* July 31, 1987, and September 6 and October 12, 1989; *New York Times,* September 15, 1993. There are "$10,000 clubs" providing special opportunities for big contributors to meet regularly and informally with senators who occupy influential posts: *Washington Post,* February 3 and 6, 1987. Members of Congress also solicit lucrative speaking engagements from special interest groups: *Washington Post,* July 30, 1990.

13. Dan Clawson, Alan Neustadt, and Denise Scott, *Money Talks: Corporate PACs and Political Influence* (New York: Basic Books, 1992).

14. For specific testimony, see Mark Green, "When Money Talks, Is It Democracy?" *Nation,* September 15, 1984, pp. 200–204.

15. Thomas Cronin quoted in Dom Bonafede, "Textbook Candidate," *PS,* Winter 1983, p. 55.

contribute, of how candidates literally had to sell their souls. Both Hughes and Humphrey clearly touched a nerve in those present at the caucus.[16]

It has been argued that money is not a major influence on elections, since better-financed candidates sometimes lose. True, the bigger spenders may not always win but they usually do, as has been the case over the last decade in over 80 percent of House and Senate races.[17] In any case, who wins is not the only way to measure the influence of campaign funding. Money also determines who runs. Candidates sometimes are backed by party leaders explicitly because they have personal wealth and are therefore more likely to wage an effective campaign.[18] Conservative losses would probably be much greater if they did not enjoy such a financial superiority in key races.

In the 1982 New York gubernatorial contest, Lewis Lehrman, a political unknown and ultraconservative, came from way behind in the opinion polls to within three points of defeating the popular Democrat Mario Cuomo. Would he have done as well without the $14 million of his personal fortune which he expended on a massive media campaign against Cuomo? Would he have even been nominated to head the GOP ticket? Would Cuomo have won without the $6 million *he* spent in the campaign? Even if the candidate who wins spends less, he or she usually spends quite a lot. The winning candidate may not need to have the most funds but must have enough. Without money there is no campaign to speak of—as poorly funded minor-party candidates have long known.

A SPECIAL-INTEREST COMMITTEE SYSTEM

Once elected, how do the legislators go about their work? For years, power in Congress rested with the twenty or so standing (i.e., permanent) committees in each house that determined the destiny of bills: rewriting some, approving a few, and burying most. The committees were dominated by chairpersons who rose to their positions by seniority—that is, by being repeatedly reelected, a feat best accomplished in a safe district or predominantly one-party state. This explains why Southern Democrats monopo-

---

16. James Abourezk, "Clear Out PACs, Clean Up Congressional Campaigns," release by Institute for Policy Studies, Washington, D.C., March 18, 1986. Then-Senator Abourezk was himself attending the caucus.

17. Other variables such as incumbency, the candidate's image and personality, the issues, and a strong campaign organization have an impact of their own. But some of these in turn are much helped by money.

18. Frank Lynn, "With Eye to November, Dyson Stresses Wealth," *New York Times*, August 26, 1986.

lized the chairmanships for years. Seniority increased a legislator's influence within Congress and thereby attracted an increasing amount of moneyed support, which helped ensure reelection and seniority. With two-party competition growing in the South, committee chairpersons have started coming from non-Southern states and less conservative urban and suburban districts.

Although seniority remains the rule in both houses, the House Democratic Caucus instituted a number of changes to weaken the hold of committee chairpersons, removing several from their positions and expanding the powers of subcommittees.[19] No longer can chairpersons arbitrarily select subcommittee chairpersons, nor stack a subcommittee with members of their own choice, or cut its budget. Totaling 241 in the House and Senate combined, the subcommittees have staffs of their own and fixed legislative jurisdictions. Advancement within the subcommittees, as within the full committees, is still mostly by seniority. Departures from seniority occur more frequently than in earlier decades and probably a little more frequently in the House than in the Senate. On occasion, the House Democratic Caucus will pass over the most senior person when selecting a committee chairperson or remove one who has not worked well. Chairmanships are sometimes contested in caucus elections by several candidates.[20]

House Democrats have restored some powers to the Speaker of the House, giving the speaker more input in the selection of committee members and in the formulation of policy. But as legislators rely less on party leaders for campaign funds and a place on the ballot, the leadership exercises less leverage over them. The atomized campaign system makes for a more atomized legislature. House rules limit the powers of committee chairpersons but not subcommittee chairpersons, some of whom do not always act in a democratic way.

The fragmented committee system in Congress, then, has been replaced by a still more fragmented "subcommittee system," lacking a central leadership to garner support for popular constituencies deprived of lobbyists and PACs. In agriculture, for instance, cotton, corn, wheat, peanut, tobacco, and rice producers compete for federal support programs; each interest is represented on a particular subcommittee of the Senate and House Agricultural Committees by senators and representatives ready to do battle on their behalf. The fragmentation of power within the subcommittees simplifies the lobbyist's task of controlling legislation. It offers the

---

19. Representative Les Au Coin (D-OR) describes subcommittees as "sovereign states": *Washington Post,* July 17, 1989.

20. *Washington Post,* December 6, 1990. Both parties in both houses have a caucus (or "conference") consisting of the entire membership of the party in that particular house. It elects the majority (or minority) leader and party whips. The majority-party caucus also elects the committee and subcommittee chairs.

special-interest group its own special-interest subcommittee. To decentralize power in this way is not to democratize it. The separate structures of power tend to monopolize decisions in specific areas for the benefit of specific groups. Into the interstices of these substructures fall the interests of large segments of the unorganized public.

Whether Congress is organized under a committee system, a subcommittee system, or a strong centralized leadership—and it has enjoyed all three in its history—it seems unchanging in its dedication to business interests. Some examples:

> A Senate reclamation law revision exempts the big irrigators in the West from acreage limitations, continuing hefty tax subsidies. A House committee relieves asbestos producers of sharing the cost of removing their cancer-causing insulation from schoolhouses. A 2-year-old strip mine control law is dealt a stunning blow in the Senate under pressure from coal companies.
>
> Hospital cost-containment legislation is bottled up by a powerful hospital-doctor lobby that contributed more than $1.6 million to campaigners. . . . Sugar producers are voted a 15.8 cents-a-pound price increase and milk producers' price supports are extended by a House committee. Sand and gravel and limestone pit operators win an exemption from safety training requirements. The House waters down a windfall profits tax proposed on the affluent oil industry, whose PACs spent better than $1 million in the last two congressional elections.[21]

One could go on. In 1989, meeting late into the night, the Senate Finance Committee voted a series of obscure provisions into a tax bill that served the few at the expense of the many, including nearly $1 billion in estate planning benefits to family business owners; $500 million in alcohol fuel benefits, much of it going to one giant processor; $58 million to private interests to build sports stadiums and convention centers; a $140 million tax shelter for timber growers; a tax exemption for gifts of appreciated property; $112 million in estate tax benefits to wealthy grandparents who want to pass assets on to grandchildren; and an expansion of tax deductions on individual retirement accounts, mostly for upper- and upper-middle income people, altogether costing the Treasury $12.6 billion over five years.[22]

Congress produces an array of protections, grants, subsidies, leases, franchises, in-kind supports, direct services, noncompetitive contracts, loan guarantees, loss compensations, and other forms of public largesse for narrow private interests. Some appropriations, known as "pork barrel" (or just "pork"), provide funds for projects that are not the most essential or economical but are highly visible representations of the legislator's ability to

---

21. *Washington Post,* September 23, 1979.
22. *Washington Post,* October 5, 1989, and September 27, 1989 for additional examples.

bring home the federal bacon.[23] Recent budgets suggest that pork is no longer a significant item, if ever it was. When the Reagan administration announced it would reveal the ugly excesses of congressional pork-barrel spending, it came up with projects totaling $3 billion or one-third of 1 percent of a $1 trillion budget.[24]

Congress also knows how to save money. In recent years, it has refused to provide $9 million for a disease-control center dealing with tuberculosis. It cut five million doses out of the federal immunization program for children, for a grand saving of $10 million, and reduced venereal-disease programs by 25 percent despite increases in venereal afflictions. To teach people rugged self-reliance, Congress has cut food programs for infants and senior citizens, assistance programs for the disabled, home-care and therapy programs for the infirm and handicapped, and medical care, job, and housing programs for the poor and elderly.[25] The Clinton administration has not restored any significant amounts to these programs.

What has failed to appear on Congress's agenda is any notion of major structural changes in class and power, of moving the economy toward nonprofit forms of production for social use rather than production for corporate gain. As an integral product of the existing politico-economic system, Congress is not likely to initiate a transformation of that system.

When public opinion is aroused, Congress is likely to respond by producing legislation that appears to deal with the problem while lacking real muscle. Thus we are treated to a lobbyist-registration act that does little to control lobbyists and an occupational-safety act that has grossly insufficient enforcement provisions. Congress sometimes is capable of ignoring strong public sentiments. After years of large peace demonstrations and with opinion polls showing a majority against the Vietnam intervention, the legislators were still voting huge appropriations for the war by lopsided majorities. In the face of a nationwide consumer meat boycott and a deluge of letters and calls protesting inflation, Congress chose to listen to "cattlemen, banking and business interests and food merchants" and voted down all proposals for price freezes.[26] In 1982 a massive grass-roots movement for a bilateral, verifiable freeze on nuclear weapons swept the country like few things in our history, yet Congress continued to vote for major escalations

---

23. A few examples: $6.4 million for the construction of a gondola system to attract tourists to Kellogg, Idaho; $500,000 to renovate the birthplace home of bandleader Lawrence Welk and build a nearby motel for tourists; and $7 million for grants to research new methods for building wooden bridges: *Washington Post,* June 4, 1989; September 11, 1989; December 1, 1990; and *City Paper,* March 1, 1991.

24. *Washington Post,* March 21, 1988. Reagan did not look at Pentagon spending, however, which contains much more pork than the nonmilitary budget: Major Garrett, "House Packs Pork in Pentagon Bill," *Washington Times,* May 31, 1991.

25. See discussion and citations in chapter 7.

26. *Washington Post,* January 17, 1982.

in nuclear weapons systems. In 1986 opinion polls showed that by large majorities the public opposed aid to the Nicaraguan mercenaries who were waging war against Nicaragua from U.S.-furnished bases in Honduras, yet Congress voted $100 million in aid to the mercenaries.

At other times lawmakers will heed an aroused public—especially as election time approaches. Before the 1982 and 1986 congressional elections, even under the threat of President Reagan's vetoes, the Congress pushed through a number of important human services and environmental programs. But normally the populace exercises an influence over our lawmakers that is more episodic than durable.

Congress is inclined to remove itself from scrutiny whenever the people get too interested in its affairs. Congressional committees hold many of their sessions behind closed doors. While public-interest advocates are often kept in the dark, business groups are kept informed. "The thing that really makes me mad is the dual standard," complained a Senate committee staff member. "It's perfectly acceptable to turn over information about what's going on in committee to the auto industry or the utilities but not to the public."[27]

Secrecy can envelop the entire lawmaking process. A bill cutting corporate taxes by $7.3 billion was (1) drawn up by the House Ways and Means Committee in three days of secret sessions, (2) passed by the House under a closed rule after only one hour of debate with (3) about thirty members present for the (4) non-roll-call vote. Sometimes the lawmakers themselves do not know what is going on. In 1984, during conference committee negotiations on a bill to reduce the deficit, Representative Dan Rostenkowski (D-IL), Senator Robert Dole (R-KS), and Donald Regan, then-Secretary of the Treasury and former Wall Street executive for Merrill Lynch, slipped a provision into the final package allowing some commodity traders (including Merrill Lynch) to roll their tax liability forward year after year. Most of the Congress knew nothing about this $1.3 billion tax dodge.[28]

Some of the most significant legislation is drafted clandestinely. Without benefit of public hearings and public debate, a coterie of high-placed government officials and corporate executives secretly put together the North American Free Trade Agreement, a two-thousand page bill that imposed momentous and tailor-made changes on the relationship between popular sovereignty and capitalism, to the great advantage of the latter.[29] In November 1993, the bill was given a promotional media blitz by the Clinton

---

27. Mark Green et al., *Who Runs Congress?*, 2nd ed. (New York: Bantam Books, 1972), p. 56. On closed-door dealings in the House Appropriations Committee, see *Washington Post,* July 17, 1989.

28. Both Rostenkowski and Dole accepted thousands of dollars in campaign contributions from these same Wall Street firms: *Washington Post,* June 3, 1985.

29. Jeremy Weintraub, "Citizens Shut Out," *Progressive,* January 1993, p. 21.

administration and presented to the House of Representatives with a "fast-track" proviso that it be voted on without amendment, with only two days set aside for debate.

Capitol Hill exerts an influence on executive agencies in order to get government contracts, government posts, and favorable administrative rulings for business clients. In this capacity, the legislator again acts as little more than an extension of the lobbyist. One ex-lobbyist concludes that the lobbyist's main job is to circumvent existing laws and get preferential treatment "for clients who have no legal rights to them." To achieve this he pays cash to "one or more members of Congress—the more influential they are, the fewer he needs."[30]

While moneyed interests may not always get their way, they usually do. If money were not effective, why would those who have it spend so much on politics? Certainly corporate heads do not feel contributions are wasted. The chair of the American Can Corporation commented on his company's PAC contributions: "I've got to admit the money does have an impact. There is no doubt about it."[31]

HELPING THEMSELVES: THE VARIETIES OF CORRUPTION

Members of Congress will sometimes act as pressure politicians without prodding from any pressure group, either because they are so well funded by the group or have lucrative holdings of their own in the same industry. Legislators with large farm holdings sit on committees that shape agricultural programs that directly benefit them. Fully a third of the lawmakers hold outside jobs as lawyers or officers of corporations, banks, and other financial institutions that closely link them with the very industries they were elected to oversee.[32] More than a third of the senators make money every time the military budget increases; they have investments in firms that rank among the top defense contractors. Almost half the Senate and over a hundred House members have interests in banking, including many who sit on committees that deal with banking legislation. What is called "conflict of interest" in the judiciary and executive branches is defined as "expertise" in the Congress by lawmakers who use their public mandate to legislate on behalf of their private fortunes.

---

30. Robert Winter-Berger, *The Washington Pay-Off* (New York: Dell, 1972), p. 14. Winter-Berger offers some astonishing eyewitness testimony in his book.

31. William May quoted in Mark Green and Jack Newfield, "Who Owns Congress?" *Washington Post Magazine,* June 8, 1980, p. 12.

32. *Washington Post,* September 5, 1979 and February 7, 1985.

Plutocracy—rule for the rich by the rich—prevails in Congress. With unusual candor, Senator Daniel Patrick Moynihan (D-NY) remarked: "At least half of the members of the Senate today are millionaires. . . . We've become a plutocracy. . . . The Senate was meant to represent the interests of the states; instead, it represents the interests of a class."[33] The lower chamber too is going upper class, in what one critic called an "evolution from a House of Representatives to a House of Lords."[34] Because of a Supreme Court ruling that allows wealthy candidates to expend as much as they want of their own money on their own campaigns, rich individuals have an additional advantage in gaining party nominations. Furthermore, because most PAC contributions go to incumbents, it is more desirable than ever for challengers to have a private source of wealth. Thus the new House members of the 99th Congress had 400 percent more in personal assets than had the new members of the previous Congress.[35]

The people who represent us in Congress are certainly not financially representative of us. Almost all have personal incomes that put them in the top 1 percent bracket. As Philip Green notes, our rulers experience a vastly different life from those over whom they rule. Transportation policy is made by people who fly in heavily subsidized private planes and who never have to search for a parking space or endure the suffocation of a rush-hour bus. Agricultural policy is shaped by legislators who never tried keeping a family farm going. Safety legislation is devised by lawmakers who never worked in a factory or mine. Medical policies are made by persons who never have to wait in a crowded clinic.[36] The same legislators who impose austerity programs on working people vote themselves pay raises and a tax-free income.[37]

Some members of Congress pilfer from the public treasure. They travel for fun at government expense under the guise of conducting committee investigations; they place relatives on the payroll and pocket their salaries

---

33. Quoted in *New York Times,* November 25, 1984.

34. Mark Green quoted in Steven Roberts, "The Rich Get Richer and Elected," *New York Times,* September 24, 1985.

35. Roberts, "The Rich Get Richer . . ." The legislators financial disclosure do not cover their net worth and are often "incomplete, misleading or useless": *Congressional Quarterly,* September 2, 1978. Thorough disclosures would likely reveal more millionaires: *Washington Post,* May 21, 1982. Millionaire representatives are found at the state level as well. In a poor state like West Virginia, an estimated half of the state legislators are millionaires, many of them coal-mine owners; almost none are environmentalists: Jean Callahan, "Cancer Valley," *Mother Jones,* August 1978, p. 40.

36. Philip Green, *Retrieving Democracy* (Totowa, N.J.: Rowman and Allanheld, 1985), pp. 177–178.

37. In 1981, members of Congress voted enough new tax breaks for themselves so as to avoid paying any income taxes: *Washington Post,* January 14, 1982.

or take salary kickbacks from staff members; they charge both the government and a private client for the same expense; they use unspent travel allocations and unspent campaign contributions for personal indulgences; they keep persons on the staff payroll whose major function is to perform sexual favors.[38]

Rich corporate interests do their share to make life more pleasant for key legislators, providing them with generous speaking honoraria, expense-paid trips to luxury resorts (spouse included), and repeated use of the company's private jets.[39] Of course, lawmakers insist such things do not influence their votes, but there is no way to measure what effect gifts might have: a speech made (or not made), a bill not introduced, a committee hearing not called. Such actions and inactions have an important effect on legislative output.[40]

Venality takes more serious forms. Since World War II, scores of lawmakers or their aides have been indicted or convicted of bribery, influence peddling, extortion, and other crimes. And those were only the ones unlucky enough to get caught. Numerous other members have retired from office to avoid criminal charges. The House and Senate ethics committees are charged with overseeing and enforcing ethics codes, but they lack sufficient inclination and staff to do so.[41] In regard to thousands of its own employees on Capitol Hill, Congress ignores the rules governing civil rights, minority employment, and occupational safety and remains one of the worse employers in the nation.[42]

If, as they say, power corrupts, it usually gets a helping hand from money. Members of Congress are not the only culprits. For years there have been reports of corruption involving federal, state, and local officials throughout the nation. In just one six-year period, the number of public officials convicted included three cabinet officers, three governors, thirty-four state legislators, twenty judges, five state attorneys-general, twenty-

---

38. *New York Times,* January 22, 1989; *Washington Post,* February 10, 1989; Shiela Kaplan, "Join Congress, See the World," *Mother Jones,* September/October 1986, pp. 18–24. Worried about the public's image of Congress as a privileged preserve, congressional leaders pruned some of the perks that members enjoy. *Washington Post,* April 4, 1992.

39. For numerous examples see *Washington Post,* May 23 and October 12, 1989; March 8 and June 21, 1991; and *New York Times,* January 22, 1989.

40. Richard Cohen, "Beware Congressmen Accepting Gifts," *Washington Post,* July 16, 1987.

41. The chair of the Senate Ethics Committee in the 98th Congress, Malcolm Wallop (R-WY), believed that senators should not have to disclose their financial holdings and could decide their own conflict of interest. He even criticized the whole idea of a code of ethics. No wonder his colleagues picked him for the job: *Washington Post,* December 31, 1982.

42. *Washington Post,* April 5, 1988. The reference is to staff employees and to the people in the congressional mail rooms and restaurants, and janitorial and maintenance crews.

eight mayors, eleven district attorneys, 170 police officers, and a U.S. vice-president, Spiro Agnew, who pleaded no contest. A U.S. president, Richard Nixon, escaped impeachment and jail by resigning from office.[43]

Officials in various executive agencies have received illegal favors and gratuities from companies or have owned stock in firms under their jurisdiction, in violation of federal rules. A GAO study found over 77,000 cases of fraud in federal agencies during a two-and-a-half-year period; nearly half were in the Pentagon. Only a small portion of the individuals involved were prosecuted.[44] In 1975, fifty-three federal executive officials were indicted for crimes; by 1985, the number had jumped to 563.[45] The Nixon administration was implicated in scandals involving the sale of wheat, an out-of-court settlement with ITT, price supports for dairy producers, corruption in the Federal Housing Administration, stock-market manipulations, and political espionage (the Watergate affair).

The career of Nelson Rockefeller provides an impressive example of money doing its thing. When he was being considered for appointment to the U.S. vice-presidency to replace Spiro Agnew (who had just resigned in exchange for the dropping of charges of bribery, extortion, and income-tax evasion), Rockefeller admitted to having given nearly $1.8 million in gifts and loans to eighteen New York and federal public officials, including $50,000 to Henry Kissinger, an erstwhile Rockefeller employee, three days before Kissinger became national security advisor to President Nixon. At a Senate hearing, Rockefeller insisted these payments were simply manifestations of his esteem for the recipients. "Sharing has always been part of my upbringing," he told the senators, none of whom doubled over with laughter. None of them reminded him that New York law prohibits public employees from accepting any gift greater than $25. Nor did they wonder aloud whether a "gift" to public officials who make decisions affecting one's private fortune might not better be called a "bribe." Instead they confirmed Nelson Rockefeller as vice-president of the United States.[46]

Every administration has had its scandals but the number of high-level members of the Reagan administration accused of unethical or illegal conduct was without precedent—110 by early 1986, with the number climbing well beyond that as the Iran-contra affair unfolded later that year. These

---

43. *Washington Post,* January 1 and December 10, 1981 and February 21, 1984; *New York Times,* October 1985 and March 15 to March 27, 1986. For more recent examples, see *Los Angeles Times,* February 8, 1989 and October 15, 1990; *Washington Post,* January 13, June 30, July 30, and September 22, 1990; *New York Times,* February 10, 1991 and January 21, 1993.

44. *Washington Post,* October 10, 1981.

45. U.S. Justice Department, *Report to Congress on the Activities and Operations of the Public Integrity Sector for 1986* (Washington, D.C.: Government Printing Office, 1987).

46. *Newsweek,* October 21, 1974; *New York Times,* October 7, 1974.

"To close on an upbeat note, I'm happy to report we received twenty-two per cent more in kickbacks than we paid out in bribes."

included at least three cabinet members, a CIA director, several White House staff members, several advisors and aides from the National Security Council, and numerous administrative agency heads. The charges included fraud; illegal or improper stock dealings; tax-code violations; failure to make proper financial disclosures; perjury; obstructing congressional investigations; accepting illegal or improper loans, gifts, and favors; and using public resources to aid personal interests. Only a few went to jail, many resigned, and many stayed on, including Attorney General Edwin Meese.[47]

Some observers see corruption as a more or less acceptable fact of life. Passing a little money under the table is just another way of oiling the wheels of government and getting things done.[48] But corruption has gone beyond

47. See the detailed compilation in the *Washington Post*, April 27, 1986. A Justice Department report sharply criticized Attorney General Meese for serious violations of standards. Questioned during various investigations, Meese seemed to suffer amnesia, being unable to remember a whole host of shady financial dealings in which he was directly involved. Before a Senate committee his memory lapsed seventy-nine times: *Washington Post*, February 5, 1988 and January 17, 1989. On corruption in the Reagan administration after 1986, see *Washington Post*, September 24, 1988; *New York Times*, July 27, 1988 and May 1, 1990.

48. An example of this quaint approach to corruption is Peter deLeon, *Thinking About Political Corruption* (New York: M.E. Sharpe, 1993).

the petty bribe to reach momentous proportions. Rather than being a violation of the rules of the game, corruption is the name of the game. It is not so much a matter of finding a few bad apples as noting that the barrel itself is rotten. Corruption in government promotes policies that lead to permanent public indebtedness, inefficiency, and waste; it drains the public treasure to feed the private purse; it vitiates laws and regulations that might otherwise safeguard occupational, health, environmental, and consumer interests; it undermines equal protection of the law, producing favoritism for the few who can pay and injury and neglect for the many who cannot.

Besides denouncing corruption we should understand the politico-economic system that makes it ubiquitous. The need for corporate interests to use large sums of money to win decisions that bring in vastly larger sums is strong, especially since those who would be the guardians of the law themselves have their palms out or are in other ways beholden to the corrupting powers. If the powers and resources of the social order itself are used for the maximization of private greed and gain, and if the operational ethic is "looking out for number one," then corruption will be chronic rather than occasional, a systemic product rather than merely an outgrowth of the politician's flawed character.

THE LEGISLATIVE LABYRINTH

As intended by the framers of the Constitution, the very structure of Congress has a conservative effect on what the legislators do. The staggered terms of the Senate—with only one-third elected every two years—are designed to blunt any mass sentiment for a sweeping turnover. The division of the Congress into two separate houses makes legislative action all the more difficult, often giving an advantage to those who desire to prevent reforms. A typical bill before Congress might go the following route: after being introduced into, say, the House of Representatives, it is committed to a committee, where it can be pigeonholed or gutted by the chairperson, or parceled out to various subcommittees for extensive hearings, where it might then meet its demise. Or it might be reported out of subcommittee to full committee either intact or greatly diluted or completely rewritten. In the event it is reported out of the full committee, the bill is sent to the Rules Committee, which might pigeonhole it, thus killing it. Or the Rules Committee could negotiate with the standing committee for a rewriting of certain provisions. Or the House might vote—by at least two-thirds—to bypass or take the bill away from the Rules Committee and bring it directly to the House floor for debate and a vote. Usually the Rules Committee provides a rule for the bill, regulating the amount of time for debate and what provisions may or may not be open for amendment. Then the bill goes to the House, which can reject or amend the rule. The House resolves itself into the Committee of the Whole House (allowing suspension of House rules, including quorum requirements) to debate, amend, pass, or reject the bill, or recommit it to the originating committee for further study. If passed by the Committee of the Whole, the House reconstitutes itself and then decides the bill's fate.

If the bill is passed by the House it is sent to the Senate, which either places it directly on its calendar for debate and vote or refers it to a standing committee to repeat the same process of subcommittee and committee hearings and amendments. It can die in committee or be sent to the Senate floor. The Senate might defeat the bill or pass the House version either unchanged or, more likely, amended. If the House refuses to accept the Senate amendments, a conference committee is put together consisting of several senior members from each house. Should the conference committee be able to reach a compromise, the bill is returned to both houses for a final vote.[49] If passed by both houses, the bill goes to the president who either signs it into law or vetoes it. (A bill that does not make it through both houses before the next congressional election must be reintroduced and the entire process begun anew.) The president's veto can be overridden only by two-thirds of the members of each house who are present and voting. If the president fails to sign the legislation within ten days after passage, it automatically becomes law unless Congress adjourns in that time, in which case it has been "pocket vetoed" and so dies.

The bill that survives this legislative labyrinth to become law may be only an *authorization* act—that is, it simply brings some program into existence. Congress then must repeat the entire legislative process for an *appropriations* bill to finance the authorized policy—something the lawmakers occasionally fail to do. Congress's task is made no easier by the duplication of bills and overlapping committee jurisdictions.

Various dilatory tactics, from time-consuming quorum calls to Senate filibusters, help to thwart legislative action. Senate rules allow a small but determined number of senators to filibuster a bill to death or dilute it by exercising the threat of filibuster. This right of unlimited debate is a peculiarity the Senate has retained from its earliest days to preserve its historic role of blunting the majoritarian will of a democratic government. Today a filibuster can be broken with a cloture petition that requires sixty votes, which is not easily achieved. In the 1980s and early 1990s, the Republican

---

49. More than one conference committee has rewritten a bill on its own. In 1985, a House-Senate conference committee approved a $302.5 billion military budget that restored money for all of the twenty-two weapon systems that either the House or Senate had voted to kill: *New York Times,* July 26, 1985.

minority used the filibuster far more frequently than did Democrats. During 1993 alone, the first year of the Clinton administration, the Senate Republicans forced cloture votes on some sixty bills.[50]

About 80 percent of the bills never make their way out of the legislative labyrinth to become law. Many of these are better left buried. But the lawmakers' wisdom is not the only determinant of what gets through; class power is also at work. Corporate and financial interests usually get what they want and stymie what they oppose. Legislation that is intended to assist the needy moves along the slow track: a $100 million bill to fund summer jobs for unemployed youth is debated in Congress for eight months, with dozens of attempts at crippling amendments; a pilot project supplying school breakfasts for a small number of malnourished children is debated at agonizing length. But when Continental Illinois Bank is about to go bankrupt, billions of dollars are handed out practically overnight without any deliberation by the appropriate congressional committees. Hundreds of billions are readily handed over in the savings and loan bailout. Billions for new weapons systems are passed in a matter of days. The North American Free Trade Agreement is rammed through without amendment in two days. And domestic programs that had taken many years of struggle to achieve are cut by many billions of dollars in a few weeks. The major financial interests may not always get all they want, but they seem to have the fast track in Congress.

One Democratic senator reminded his party colleagues that they were too responsive to moneyed interests and were neglecting to keep up appearances as "the party of the people." In a speech on the Senate floor urging that the scientific patents of the $25 billion space program not be given away to private corporations but applied for public benefit, Russell Long (D-LA) candidly remarked: "Many of these [corporate] people have much influence. I, like others have importuned some of them for campaign contributions for my party and myself. Nevertheless, we owe it to the people, now and then, to save one or two votes for them. This is one such instance. . . . We Democrats can trade on the dubious assumption that we are protector of the public interest only so long if we permit things like these patent giveaways."[51] Here Senator Long provided a perfect example

---

50. The Republicans filibustered against bills that supported arms control, public financing of congressional campaigns, limits on private campaign spending, legal abortions at military hospitals, human rights conditions on military aid to El Salvador, a modest tax-rate increase for the rich, accessible voter registration for the poor and unemployed, outlawing the use of scabs as permanent replacements of strikers, and a $16.3 billion jobs program: *New York Times*, August 9, 1987 and April 8, 1993; *Washington Post*, June 17, 1987; August 13, 1991. For instances of Democratic use of the filibuster, see *Washington Post*, November 16, 1989; *New York Times*, November 2, 1991.

51. *Washington Monthly*, April 1972, p. 18.

of how the need to maintain democratic appearances can sometimes lead to taking an actual democratic stance.

Special-interest legislators often achieve working majorities in Congress by "logrolling," a process of mutual support that is not the same as compromise. Rather than checking one another as in compromise situations, and thus blunting the selfish demands of each, interest groups end up backing one another's claims at the expense of those who are without power in the pressure system. For example, legislators hoping to maintain a price support program for sugar interests will swap votes with legislators seeking to protect steel subsidies.[52]

For some members of Congress getting reelected is their major concern; for others it is their only concern. In any case, the great majority of them are quite successful at it. In the nineteenth century, half or more of every new House was made up of freshmen representatives. In recent years the turnover has dropped to between 10 and 20 percent, and this includes members who retire or die. In the last two decades, incumbents who sought reelection have won over 90 percent of the time.[53] There are several reasons for this:

Campaign funding. By definition, incumbents are persons who have already demonstrated an ability to muster enough money and organization to win. Once in office, they have opportunities to gather additional financial support. Senate incumbents raise twice as much money as challengers, and House incumbents raise over three times more.[54]

Constituent service. Members of Congress build support by doing casework for constituents (such as, locating a Social Security check or getting someone into a veterans hospital). Members devote large portions of their staffs to working in the district home office.[55] They do little favors for little people and big favors for big people, gathering votes from the former and campaign money from the latter.

Exposure and name recognition. Incumbents use their franking privileges (free mailing) to correspond with constituents and send out news-

---

52. *New York Times*, October 2, 1985.

53. Charles Jones, *The United States Congress* (Homewood, Ill.: Dorsey Press, 1982), p. 79. Sometimes the reelection rate is as high as 98 percent: *Washington Post*, August 28 and November 13, 1988. In 1992, 92 percent of those who sought reelection to the 103rd Congress were successful, according to my calculations based on figures taken from *Congressional Quarterly* (Special Report), Washington, D.C., December 11, 1993, p. 16.; and *New York Times*, November 5, 1992.

54. U.S. Bureau of the Census, *Statistical Abstract of the United States: 1992* (112th ed.), Washington, D.C., 1992, p. 275. Some sources estimate a higher spending disparity: Report by Common Cause staff, *Half of Senate Incumbents Seeking Election in 1990 Are Financially Unopposed*, Washington, D.C.: Common Cause, October 1990; *New York Times*, August 27, 1992.

55. *New York Times*, October 28, 1990.

letters and promotional sheets that herald the officeholder's virtues and accomplishments.[56] Members issue press releases, get their names in hometown media, and generally enjoy a long headstart over potential challengers in self-advertising and name recognition.

One-party dominance. Some states and districts are demographically inclined toward one party or another, and many districts are gerrymandered to concentrate party strength in lopsided ways. In the 1990 election, four senators, two from each party, and eighty-one House members (thirty-five Republicans and forty-six Democrats) ran against no major party opponent at all. Convinced that they cannot muster the money or votes to win, potential challengers walk away from races.

Earlier retirements. With the workload and fund-raising tasks becoming ever more onerous, officeholders are retiring from Congress in growing numbers; a record high of 20 percent voluntarily departed in 1992.[57] Those who face tough reelection challenges usually are more inclined to quit than those who occupy comfortably safe seats. As more of them retire, fewer are defeated at the polls.[58]

Term Limits

Conservatives had nothing against limitless incumbency when conservative Southern Democrats or Republicans occupied the influential committee leadership positions, but now that senior positions are going to moderately liberal and even progressive Democrats, including members of the Congressional Black Caucus, conservatives have become the moving force behind term limitations.[59] Recently, the issue of term limits has received wide exposure in the business-owned news media and financial backing from conservative organizations. In 1992, well-funded initiatives to limit congressional terms to six or twelve years (depending on the state) won voter endorsements in fourteen states.[60]

---

56. In one session, Senator Alfonse D'Amato (R-NY) spent $2.65 million of taxpayer money in franked mailings that totaled 16.7 million pieces to his constituents: *Washington Post,* January 3 and July 18, 1990.

57. Calculations based on sources cited in footnote 53.

58. There are various reasons lawmakers retire. The inability to effect important changes frustrates some, while highly lucrative jobs in private industry entice others. The consolation of a generous pension is an additional inducement.

59. For instance, George Will, *Restoration* (New York: Free Press, 1992).

60. *San Francisco Chronicle,* November 4, 1992; *Seattle Post-Intelligencer,* August 31, 1992. The initiatives apply to the respective congressional delegations from the fourteen states and limit terms to six to twelve years, depending on the state.

While promising to revitalize the legislative process and improve congressional performance, term limits will more likely do the opposite, creating a rotating amateur Congress that faces a professional, long-entrenched national security state and professional bureaucracy. Congress would be composed largely of freshman and sophomores who would still need large sums of money to get re-elected and be even more dependent on and vulnerable to professional lobbyists and big contributors. Members would also be increasingly dependent on congressional staffers, who are elected by no one, including committee and subcommittee staffers who sometimes serve for decades. And when one recalls that it takes many years of struggle to pass major public-interest legislation, we might wonder who in Congress will be able to stick around long enough to see things through—especially since term limits would wipe out whatever progressive leadership that now exists—which is the real objective of the major sponsors of term limits.[61]

A TOUCH OF DEMOCRACY

Behind Congress there stands the entire corporate social order, with its hold over the material resources of society; its control of information and mass propaganda; its dominant influence over most cultural institutions; its well-placed policymakers, organized pressure groups, high-paid lobbyists, influence peddling lawyers, and big corporate contributors. Given all this, it is surprising that any democratic victories are won in Congress. Yet, progressive elements do manage to get things through from time to time. The lawmakers are not entirely untouched by popular pressures. Votes still count and therefore so do voters. Many worthwhile laws bring needed jobs and services to the ordinary folks back home, be it a post office, a cancer clinic, a program for the handicapped, or an adult training project.

The legislators also perform democratic watchdog functions over administrative agencies, checking to see why a Labor Department field office is not functioning, why a Social Security office is being closed, why vacancies in an agency investigating racketeering have not been filled, why a report on wage rates at rural hospitals has not been released, why compensation has not been made to veterans injured in mustard gas experiments, and other such matters. This watchdog function is an important democratic

---

61. Some conservatives, most notably President Nixon and President Reagan, have wanted to abolish the 22nd Amendment, which places a two-term limit on presidential incumbents. They had no problem with limitless incumbency for Republican presidents. No conservatives have urged term limits on Supreme Court justices or federal judges; the judiciary is heavily populated with relatively young conservative ideologues. They target only Congress and those state legislatures in which the Democrats have a long-standing majority.

pressure on behalf of ordinary people, prodding a recalcitrant and often secretive bureaucracy.[62]

Despite the conservatism of the Reagan–Bush years, Congress approved the expansion of Medicare, strengthened major civil rights statutes, federal ethics standards, and environmental programs. It strengthened programs for AIDS victims, drug addicts, and the homeless, and extended unemployment insurance and new protections for workers facing mass layoffs. Congress passed a plant-closing notification bill and imposed sanctions on South Africa because of its racist apartheid policy. Congress, then, is not just a special-interest arena. It is also a place where larger critical issues are sometimes raised. There are dedicated legislators who often respond to the needs of the many rather than the greed of the few, impelled both by their own political commitment and by popular pressure. What victories they win are almost always hard-fought and hard-won, for the high ground is usually occupied by the conservative coalition, composed mostly of Republicans and Southern conservative Democrats who, shored up by the awesome power of big business, frequently manage to block or seriously maul any liberal agenda for change.[63] And when the White House also is on their side, conservatives score decisive victories against the hardwon gains of labor and the Left.

In sum, Congress is still a place where democratic inputs can be registered, where progressive forces occasionally can mount attacks against a conservative status quo or maintain some (partially successful) defense against right-wing rollback. However, the overall evidence suggests that the moneyed powers are the predominant influence, and that officeholders do more to sustain than to change the existing system of class power and privilege.

A more democratic Congress would be one that is more responsive to voters and less dependent upon rich individuals and corporate and trade PACs for financial support. How can that be achieved? The only money that comes with no strings attached comes from each citizen equally—from all the taxpayers, through their government—money that does not obligate the officeholder to any special interest or privileged group.[64] What is needed is a system of public campaign financing that neutralizes the influence of private moneyed interests. We need full public funding of House

---

62. The most useful watchdog of government, the General Accounting Office (GAO), created by Congress to investigate everything from military waste to environmental abuse, operates at the request of specific legislators and reports directly to Congress.

63. "Recent evidence supports the view that major business lobbies appear to be able to exercise a de facto veto over measures they oppose. If business lobbies don't object, reform measures can become law; if they do, they can't": Mark Green and Michael Calabrese, *Who Runs Congress?* 3rd ed. (New York: Bantam, 1979), p. 28.

64. Stern, *The Best Congress Money Can Buy*, p. 180.

and Senate elections and primaries. Candidates who accept public funding would have to agree to limit their spending to the amount of the public grant. Those who decline taxpayer money would be free of that spending limit—but their opponents would then qualify for matching funds equal to any amount spent by the privately funded candidate. Limitless private funding would be allowed—but it would be neutralized and equalized by public funding.

In addition, prohibitions should be placed on lobbyists' perks, the honoraria, free travel, and other gifts and services that are little more than legalized bribery.

Finally, broadcast media should be required to set aside free and equal time for all candidates during campaigns. The air waves are the property of the American people, part of the public domain. While broadcasters are granted licenses to use the air waves, they do not own them. It is no infringement on their free speech to oblige them, as a public service, to make some portion of broadcast time available to office seekers who want to exercise *their* free speech.

With public financing of campaigns, limits on private perks, and free access to media, candidates and officeholders would be liberated from the incessant task of raising money and from slavish obligations to the moneyed interests. And major public office would be accessible to others besides the rich or those supported by the rich, something fairly fought for rather than bought.[65]

---

65. Marty Jezer and Randy Kehler, "Let's Have *Real* Campaign Reform," *Nation*, November 2, 1992, pp. 496–499; Stern, *The Best Congress Money Can Buy*, pp. 180–181. Public funding features already exist in the financing of presidential elections. In November 1993 the House passed the Congressional Campaign Spending Limit and Election Reform Act, to provide partial public funding of candidates who agree to comply with federal spending caps. Bills that provide public funding and voluntary spending limits have been filibustered in the Senate by well-financed Republican senators: *New York Times*, March 8, 1993.

14

The President: Guardian of the System

In this chapter our task is to take a nonworshipful look at what presidents do and why they do it. The president, we are told, plays many roles: chief executive, "chief legislator," commander-in-chief, head of state, and party leader. Seldom mentioned is the role of guardian and representative of capitalism. The president is the embodiment of the executive-centered state system that defends American corporate interests at home and abroad.

SALESMAN OF THE SYSTEM

As authoritative figures whose opinions are widely publicized, presidents do their share to indoctrinate the American people into the ruling-class ideology. Every modern president has had occasion to praise the "free enterprise system" and denounce collectivist alternatives. One description of President Ford could easily apply to any number of other presidents: "[He] follows the judgment of the major international oil companies on oil problems in the same way that he amiably heeds the advice of other big businesses on the problems that interest them. . . . He is . . . a solid believer in the business ideology of rugged individualism, free markets and price competition—virtues that exist more clearly in his mind than they do in the practices of the international oil industry."[1]

---

1. William Shannon, *New York Times*, July 22, 1975. When I refer to the president as *he*, I only am recognizing that every president thus far has been a man. I do not mean to imply that the male gender has a natural or interminable hold on the office.

The president is the top salesman of the system, conjuring up reassuring images about the state of the union. He would have us believe that our social problems and economic difficulties can be solved with enough "vigor" and "resolve," as John Kennedy used to say; or with "hard work" and "toughing it out," as Richard Nixon put it; or with a return to "self-reliance" and a "spiritual revival," as Ronald Reagan urged. "America is number one," proclaimed President Nixon, while millions of his unemployed compatriots were feeling less than that. "America is standing tall. America is the greatest," exulted President Reagan to a nation with thirty-five million citizens living below the poverty level, a record trade deficit, and a runaway national debt. Prosperity, our presidents tell us, is here or not far off—but so are the nation's many wild-eyed enemies, be they communists, revolutionaries, terrorists, "fanatical" Islamics, or whatever. There is no shortage of adversaries abroad supposedly waiting to pounce upon the United States, thwarted only by huge U.S. military budgets, covert actions, and a strong internal security system. Presidents usually downplay crises relating to the economy and emphasize the ones needed to justify arms spending and interventionism abroad.

Whether Democrat or Republican, liberal or conservative, the president tends to treat capitalist interests as synonymous with the nation's well-being. Presidents greet the accumulation of wealth as a manifestation of a healthy national economy, regardless of how that wealth is applied or distributed. America will achieve new heights spurred on "by freedom and the profit motive," President Reagan announced. "This is a free-enterprise country," said President Clinton. "I want to create more millionaires in my presidency than Bush and Quayle did."[2] Presidents will describe the overseas investments of giant corporations as "U.S. interests" abroad, to be defended at all costs—or certainly at great cost to the populace. A president's primary commitment abroad is not to democracy as such but to free market capitalism.[3]

At the Constitutional Convention, the wealthy planter Charles Pinckney proposed that no one qualify for the presidency who was not worth at least $100,000—a munificient sum in 1787. While the proposal was never written into the Constitution, it seemingly has been followed in practice. Since World War II, and frequently before then, almost all presidential candidates on the Republican and Democratic tickets have been millionaires

2. Reagan quoted in *Seattle Times,* January 15, 1989; Clinton speaking on "MacNeil-Lehrer News Hour," PBS, October 27, 1992.

3. In an address before the United Nations, September 27, 1993, President Clinton said: "Our overriding purpose is to expand and strengthen the world's community of market-based democracies." In fact, U.S. presidents have supported any number of market-based autocracies as in Turkey, Indonesia, Zaire, Morocco, Kuwait, Saudi Arabia, Thailand, Guatemala, and the like.

either at the time they first campaigned for the office or by the time they departed from it. In addition, presidents have drawn their top advisers and administrators primarily from industry and banking and have relied heavily on the judgments of corporate leaders.[4]

It is probably not easy for a president to remain keenly aware of the travails and deprivations endured by ordinary working people. He lives like an opulent potentate in the White House, a rent-free, 132-room mansion set on an eighteen-acre estate, with a domestic staff of about one hundred, including six butlers and five full-time florists, a well-stocked wine cellar, tennis courts, a private movie room, a gymnasium, a bowling alley, and a heated outdoor swimming pool. In addition, the president has the free services of a private physician, a dozen chauffeured limousines, numerous helicopters and jets, including Air Force One. He also has access to the imperial luxuries of Camp David and other country retreats, free vacations, a huge expense allowance—and for the few things he must pay for—a $200,000 annual salary.[5]

Journalists and political scientists have described the presidency as a "man-killing job." Yet presidents take more vacations and live far better and longer than the average American male. After leaving office they continue to feed from the public trough. Four ex-presidents (Ford, Carter, Reagan, and Bush) are millionaires, yet each receives from $500,000 to $700,000 in annual pensions, office space, staff, and travel expenses, along with full-time Secret Service protection costing $5 million a year for each.[6]

Presidents and presidential candidates regularly evade federal limits on presidential campaign spending through a loophole that allows big contributors to give what is called "soft money" directly to state political parties.[7] Contributors may disclaim any intention of trying to buy influence, but if it should happen that after the election they find themselves or their firms burdened by a problem that only the White House can handle, they see no reason why they shouldn't be allowed to exercise their rights like other citizens and ask their elected representative, who in this case happens to be their friend, the president of the United States, for a little help.

For their part, presidents seem as capable of trading favors for money as any influence-peddling, special-interest politician—only on a grander scale.

---

4. For more on the social background of leaders, see chapter 12.

5. President Bush's numerous vacations to his country estate in Maine cost taxpayers from $50,000 to $100,000 a day, at a time he was calling on these same taxpayers to tighten their belts: Eugene Carroll Jr., correspondence, *Washington Post*, September 15, 1990.

6. *San Francisco Chronicle*, November 9, 1992. A group of self-described "independently wealthy" individuals contributed $156,000 each and bought a $2.5 million home in fashionable Bel Air, California, which they gave to Reagan when he left office: Mark Shields' column in *Washington Post*, January 28, 1989.

7. *Los Angeles Times*, December 10, 1988.

The Nixon administration helped settle a multibillion-dollar suit against ITT and received a $400,000 donation from that corporation. Reagan pushed through the deregulation of oil and gasoline prices and received huge contributions from the oil companies.[8] President Bush's Team 100, consisting of 249 wealthy financiers and corporate CEOs, put up at least $100,000 each to help elect Bush in 1988. In return, they enjoyed White House pork-barrel handouts, special dispensations on regulatory and legal matters, and appointments to choice ambassadorships.[9]

It is said that the greatness of the office lends greatness to its occupant, so that even persons of mediocre endowment grow in response to the presidency's responsibilities and powers. Closer examination reveals that presidents have been just as readily corrupted as ennobled by high office,

---

8. *New York Times,* January 11 and June 15, 1973; Anthony Sampson, *The Sovereign State of I.T.T.* (New York: Stein & Day, 1973); Juan Williams, "Reagan is the Real King of the Special Interest Groups," *Washington Post,* April 1, 1984.

9. See the study "Team 100 All-Stars," *Common Cause Magazine,* April/May/June 1992. Bush received a total of $900,000 from persons he later appointed to ambassadorships; many had no political or diplomatic experience: *Harper's* August 1992, p. 11; Warren Lenhart, *Ambassadorial Appointments: The Congressional Debate Over Qualifications and Implications for U.S. Policy,* Congressional Research Service, Report 91–385F, Washington, D.C., May 1, 1991. President Clinton demanded that Saudi Arabia award a $4 billion contract to AT&T. Intensive sales pressure from the Clinton administration induced the Saudis to order $6 billion in passenger jets from U.S. firms, bypassing European competitors: *New York Times,* April 27, 1994.

inclined toward self-righteous assertion, compelled to demonstrate their military "toughness" against weaker nations, and not above operating in unlawful ways. Thus, at least six presidents employed illegal FBI wiretaps to gather incriminating information on rival political figures.[10] The White House tapes, which recorded the private Oval Office conversations of President Nixon, showed him to be a petty, vindictive, bigoted man who manifested a shallowness of spirit and mind that the majestic office could cloak but not transform.[11] President Reagan repeatedly fabricated stories and anecdotes about nonexistent events. The Iran-contra affair revealed him to be a deceptive manipulator who pretended to support one policy while pursuing another, and who felt himself to be unaccountable to Congress and to the law.[12]

THE TWO FACES OF THE PRESIDENT

Presidents conjure up fine-sounding labels and images to enhance their popular appeal. Roosevelt had his "New Deal," Truman his "Fair Deal," Kennedy his "New Frontier," Johnson his "Great Society," Reagan his "American Renaissance," and Bush his "thousand points of light."

Consider John Kennedy, a liberal president widely celebrated for his devotion to the underdog. In foreign affairs, Kennedy spoke of international peace and self-determination, yet he invaded anticapitalist Cuba. He drastically increased military expenditures, instituted new counterinsurgency programs throughout the Third World, and sent military advisors to Vietnam. In domestic matters Kennedy presented himself as a champion of civil rights, yet he refrained from taking legal action to support antidiscrimination cases and did little to prevent repeated attacks against civil-rights organizers in the South. He talked as if he were a friend of working people, yet he imposed wage restraints on unions at a time workers' buying power was stagnant or declining, and he opposed introduction of the thirty-

---

10. *Washington Post,* December 12, 1983; Anthony Summers, *Official and Confidential: The Secret Life of J. Edgar Hoover* (New York: G. P. Putnam's Sons, 1993), passim.

11. James Perry, "A Remembrance of Things Past–The Nixon Tapes," *Wall Street Journal,* June 5, 1991. Official audits revealed that President Nixon spent over $2.4 million of taxpayers' money on improvements of his private estate and underpaid his taxes by $444,022. On occasion, he requested the IRS to stop auditing the incomes of close friends and go after enemies: *New York Times,* June 21, 22, and 25, 1973, and April 4, 1974.

12. On Reagan's fabrications, see Mark Green and Gail MacColl, *Ronald Reagan's Reign of Error* (New York: Pantheon, 1983). On his misrepresentations regarding Iran-contra, see *Washington Post* and *New York Times* from November 26, 1986 onward. For other shady dealings involving savings and loans that serviced Mafia and CIA people: Pete Brewton, *The Mafia, CIA & George Bush* (New York: Shapolsky, 1992), pp. 213–215.

five-hour work week. Kennedy also instituted tax programs and deficit-spending policies that carried business profits to all-time highs without reducing unemployment.[13]

One of the president's many roles is "chief liar," performed by offering the public a deceptive admixture of populist rhetoric and conservative policy. Richard Nixon and Gerald Ford both voiced their support for environmentalism and then opened new forest lands for commercial exploitation and strip mining. Both gave lip service to the problems of the Vietnam veteran, the plight of the elderly, and the needs of the poor, yet cut benefits to these groups.[14] President Jimmy Carter promised to cut the military budget and instead increased it. He promised to reduce arms sales, but under his administration arms sales rose to new levels. He talked of helping the needy, but proposed cutbacks in summer youth jobs, child nutrition programs, and other benefits. After campaigning as a friend of labor, Carter went on to oppose most of the AFL-CIO legislative program. Like his predecessors, he also advocated multibillion-dollar credits and subsidies for big business.[15]

The gap between rhetoric and policy became a virtual chasm during the Reagan years. President Reagan called for a "war on drugs," but substantially cut funding for drug treatment and drug enforcement. He lauded our veterans for their great sacrifices, but offered a budget that cut veterans' health-care. Before an African American audience in Washington, D.C., Reagan described himself as a champion of racial equality; in fact he had advocated tax breaks for segregated private schools, drastically reduced enforcement of civil-rights laws, and cut inner-city assistance programs.

Reagan called for honest government, but vetoed an ethics bill passed by Congress. He announced that his tax cuts had benefited the poor and not the rich—though the figures said otherwise. He claimed to be a vigorous defender of the environment, while in fact he protected polluters, pil-

---

13. Ian McMahan, "The Kennedy Myth," *New Politics,* Winter 1968, pp. 40–48; Richard Walton, *Cold War and Counter-Revolution: The Foreign Policy of John F. Kennedy* (Baltimore: Penguin, 1972); Bruce Miroff, *Pragmatic Illusions* (New York: McKay, 1976). Nevertheless, Kennedy was hated by right-wingers because of his call for a reevaluation of our attitudes toward the Soviet Union, his differences with the Federal Reserve System and the steel industry, his friendliness with civil rights leaders, his atmospheric test-ban treaty with the Soviets, his attempts at bringing the CIA under White House control, and his unwillingness to attempt another invasion of Cuba and initiate a massive land war in Vietnam.

14. For instance, *New York Times,* September 11 and October 8, 1975; also David Wise, *The Politics of Lying* (New York: Vintage, 1973), which treats patterns of manipulation and deception in the Eisenhower, Kennedy, Johnson, and Nixon administrations.

15. Christopher Lydon, "Jimmy Carter Revealed: He's a Rockefeller Republican," *Atlantic Monthly,* July 1977, pp. 50–59; Frank Browning, "Jimmy Carter's Astounding Lies," *Inquiry,* May 5, 1980, pp. 13–17.

laged public lands, undermined environmental regulations, and left the earth a sadder, dirtier, more radioactive place.[16] He repeatedly called for the rule of law in domestic and international affairs, yet relied on the rule of the CIA when dealing with Third World countries, committing acts of war against Nicaragua, then refusing to accept the lawful jurisdiction of the World Court when Nicaragua brought the case before the court.[17]

Then came President George Bush, who proclaimed himself the "education president," yet slashed education funds for disadvantaged children and others. As the self-professed "environment president," he withdrew vast areas of wetlands from federal protection and opposed international measures against global warming and ozone depletion. He spoke of preserving family values, but vetoed a bill that would allow workers to take unpaid leave so they might care for an ill family member or newborn child. Bush proclaimed his commitment to science, then reduced the number of presidential science grants.[18] He invaded Panama ostensibly to arrest President Noriega for dealing in drugs, but had maintained close relations with various CIA-linked drug traffickers for years.[19]

"The courage to change" was the campaign theme that got Bill Clinton elected president in 1992. He promised labor-law reform, but after more than a year in office had done nothing to liberate workers from restrictive organizing rules and one-sided enforcement procedures. He talked of helping the economically deprived, yet failed to restore the human-service cuts imposed by Reagan and Bush, including the 30 percent reduction in summer jobs for low-income youth. Clinton actually decreased public service spending from what it was under Bush, including a $3 billion reduction for low-income housing. He proposed limiting welfare assistance to two years, while neglecting to fund any serious job and day-care programs for single mothers who would be thrown off welfare. When his modest $16 billion job package was stalled in the Senate, he let it die without a fight. He did little of note to strengthen occupational safety enforcement. He reassured the public that some of the unfair tax burden would be shifted back onto the rich, but proposed only a modest raise in the upper-bracket tax rate, with enough loopholes to allow the rich to recoup their losses. He vowed to protect the environment, then backed a plan to open ancient

---

16. James Nathan Miller, "Ronald Reagan and the Techniques of Deception," *Atlantic Monthly*, February 1984, pp. 62–68; *Washington Post*, August 29, 1982, June 17 and 19 and July 13, 1984, September 27, 1986; *New York Times*, July 30 and 31, 1982; December 27, 1985; *Seattle Times*, January 15, 1989.

17. *Washington Post*, April 9 and 12, 1984. The World Court found the United States in violation of international law in its aggression against Nicaragua.

18. *New York Times*, February 20 and June 30, 1990; *Washington Post*, October 29, 1991.

19. Peter Dale Scott and Jonathan Marshall, *Cocaine Politics* (Berkeley: University of California Press, 1991).

forest reserves to timber operations, and softened penalties for oil-spill polluters.[20]

In foreign affairs, Clinton talked of charting a new course but tread the same path as his predecessors. He bombed Iraq on a slender pretext. He continued Bush's armed intervention in Somalia, eventually withdrawing troops only because of the public outcry regarding the losses sustained. Like numerous administrations before him, Clinton maintained a crippling embargo against Cuba. As of April 1994 he had done next to nothing to restore democracy in Haiti. He proposed a missile defense budget equal to the one accepted by Bush, despite the end of the cold war. Clinton signaled his intention to increase funding for intelligence operations and maintain the CIA at its ongoing level. After a year in office, he had yet to fill hundreds of administrative posts, showing himself quite happy with the Reagan and Bush holdovers. Most of his own appointees were of corporate background. Some of the few liberal nominees he offered up, such as Lani Guinier, were quickly withdrawn when they met with conservative opposition.[21] The president who talked about "the courage to change" did not seem interested in changing much of anything.

The President's Systemic Bind

If presidents tend to speak one way and act another, it is due less to some inborn flaw shared by the varied personalities who occupy the office than to the nature of the office itself. Like any officeholder, the president plays a dual role in that he must satisfy the major interests of corporate America and at the same time make a show of serving the people. He differs from other politicians in that the demands and expectations of his office are greater and therefore the contradictions deeper. More than any other officeholder, he deals with the overall crises of capitalism, for he is the chief executive and the only nationally elected leader (along with the vice-president), hence the focus of mass attention and expectation. Like other politicians, perhaps more so, the president is caught between the demands of democracy and the powers of plutocracy.

Although some presidents may try, they discover they cannot belong to both the corporations and the people. Occasionally a president may be instrumental in getting Congress to allocate monies and services for the

20. *Nation,* May 17, 1993; Jeffrey St. Clair, "Ancient Forests Meet the Press," *Lies of Our Times,* November 1993, pp. 3–6; Victor Perlo, "Economic Betrayal in Washington," *People's Weekly World,* August 28, 1993; *San Francisco Chronicle,* January 8, 1994.

21. James Petras, "President Clinton Wall Street Populist," Z *Magazine,* April 1993, pp. 18–22; *New York Times,* January 10, 1994.

U.S. public, but whatever his intentions, he cannot solve the deep structural problems of the political economy, for he cannot both serve capitalism as capitalism needs to be served and at the same time drastically transform it.

While members of Congress are the captives of the special interests, the president, elected by the entire country, tends to be less vulnerable to pressure groups and more responsive to the needs of the unorganized public—at least this is what political scientists taught after years of observing Democratic presidents like Roosevelt, Truman, and Kennedy tussling with conservatives in Congress. But as noted, the chief executive exchanges special favors with special interests. In addition, he must do for the capitalist system what individual capitalists cannot do. He must reconcile conflicts between various business interests, usually deciding in favor of heavy industry and big finance as against light industry and small business.

The president sometimes must oppose the interests of individual companies or industries, keeping them in line with the overall needs of the corporate economy. Hence he might do battle with an industry like steel, as did Kennedy, to hold prices down in order to ease the inflationary effects on other producer interests. When engaged in such conflicts the president takes on an appearance of opposing the special interests on behalf of the common interest. In fact, he might be better described as *protecting the common interests of the special interests.* This role is not usually appreciated by the business community, who will attack a president for any "anti-business" challenge, thereby enhancing the impression that he is the defender of the public interest.

It is usually the president's task to convince the business class that new concessions like minimum-wage laws and social programs are needed to defend the old order. As the prime elected officeholder accountable to a national constituency, and as the focus of popular expectation and constant attention from the media, the president feels more pressure than others to solve the nation's problems. It is his task, if anyone's, to ameliorate popular discontent and discourage disturbances and protests. Presidents, especially liberal ones, have played key roles in the process of reform. For this they may incur the wrath of conservatives who see such things as the beginning of the end.

The success any group enjoys in winning White House intercession has less to do with the justice of its cause than with the place it occupies in the class structure. If a large group of migrant workers and a small group of aerospace executives both sought the president's assistance, it would not be difficult to predict which of them would more likely win it. Witness these events of April 1971:

1. Some 80,000 to 90,000 migrant farm workers in Florida, out of work because of crop failures and exempted from unemployment compensation,

were without means of feeding themselves and their families. The workers demonstrated peacefully in large numbers outside President Nixon's vacation residence in Florida, hoping to get the White House to intercede. They were met only by the police, who dispersed them with swinging clubs. Eventually the farm counties were declared disaster areas. But the government emergency relief money ended up in the hands of the big commercial growers, who had sustained the crop losses. Since the migrant workers had no state residence, they did not qualify for relief.[22]

2. During the very week the farm workers were being clubbed by police, leaders of the aerospace industry placed a few telephone calls to Washington and were invited to meet quietly with the president to discuss their companies' problems. Later that same day the White House announced a $42 million authorization to the aerospace industry to relocate, retrain, and in other ways assist its top administrators, scientists, and technicians. The spending plan, an industry creation, was accepted by the government without prior study.[23]

Is the president responding to a "national interest" or a "special interest" when helping the giant firms? Much depends upon how the labels are applied. Those who believe the national interest necessitates taking every possible measure to maintain the profits and strength of the industrial and military establishment, of which the aerospace industry is a part, might say the president is responding to a national interest. Certainly almost every president in modern times might have acted similarly. In addition, it might be said that farm workers represent a marginal group, therefore a limited special interest. The president's first responsibility is to tend to our industrial economy. In fact, the argument goes, when workers act to disrupt and weaken the sinews of industry, as have striking coal miners, railroad operators, and steel workers, the president may see fit to deal summarily with them.[24]

Other people would argue that the national interest is not served when giant industries receive favored treatment at the expense of workers, tax-

---

22. Tom Foltz, "Florida Farmworkers Face Disaster," *Guardian*, April 3, 1971, p. 4.

23. *New York Times*, April 2, 1971.

24. When Ronald Reagan complained about the "special interests" attempting to thwart his desire to serve the national interest with his budget-cutting efforts, he was using a motif long propagated by political scientists who defined "special" and "national" interests by some abstract measure (particular versus broad) and not by the class interest involved (owners versus employees and consumers). Thus, Reagan was able to portray the social needs of working people as limited, parochial "special" interests, while the big companies had "national," indeed international, interests. (It is the same argument made by present-day apologists for the framers of the Constitution: see chapter 4.) When asked whether a U.S. military foray into Bolivia, ostensibly to catch drug traffickers, was in the national interest, President Reagan said, "Anything we do is in the national interest": *Washington Post*, December 29, 1986,

payers, and consumers. That the corporations have holdings that are national and often multinational in scope does not mean they represent the interests of the nation's populace. The "national interest" or "public interest" should encompass the ordinary public rather than a handful of big commercial farm owners, corporate elites, and their well-paid technicians and managers. Contrary to an established myth, the public monies distributed to these favored few do not "trickle down" to the mass of working people at the bottom—as the hungry farm workers can testify.[25]

Whichever position one takes, it becomes clear that there is no neutral way of defining the national interest. Whatever policy the president pursues, he is helping some class interests rather than others. It is a matter of historical record that presidents usually have chosen a definition of the national interest that serves the giant conglomerates. As the most powerful officeholder in the land, the president is more readily available to the most powerful interests and rather inaccessible to us lesser mortals.

A LOADED ELECTORAL COLLEGE

Much of the president's legitimacy as national leader rests on the premise that he alone is elected by the entire nation. In fact, under Article 2, Section 1 of the Constitution, presidents are not directly elected by the people but by a majority of "electors," appointed in such manner as the various state legislatures might direct. The number of electors each state has is equal to the number of its representatives and senators. When voting for the president we are actually voting for one or another slate of party-designated electors who are morally—but not legally—pledged to vote as we expect.[26] The "Electoral College," as it has come to be known, remains an undemocratic anachronism, designed by the framers of the Constitution to act as a filter of "popular passions." In keeping with their class prejudices and interests, they assumed that the electors would generally be propertied and educated gentlemen who supposedly would not succumb to self-interested choices as might ordinary voters.

---

25. Studies show that nations with a great gap between rich and poor also have low economic growth. Conversely, nations with greater income equality enjoy healthier economic growth: *New York Times*, January 8, 1994.

26. If no candidate gets a majority of the Electoral College, the president is chosen by the House of Representatives, with each state delegation casting only one vote. The 23rd Amendment gave the District of Columbia a number of electors equivalent to the least populous state (three), which in addition to the number of senators (100) and representatives (435) brings the Electoral College to 538. The Constitution prohibits any member of Congress or any other government official from serving as an elector.

By awarding the state's entire electoral vote on a winner-take-all basis to the candidate who wins a plurality of the popular vote, the Electoral College creates artificial or exaggerated majorities. Thus, in 1984 Reagan won 58.8 percent of the popular vote but 97.5 percent of the Electoral College. The distribution of popular votes sometimes becomes more important than the actual number of votes. In 1976 Gerald Ford would have won election with a shift of a mere 5,558 votes in Ohio and 3,686 in Hawaii, giving him a majority of electoral votes (270), leaving Carter with a popular majority of 50.4 percent and over 1.5 million more votes. On three occasions in the nineteenth century, the Electoral College elected presidents who ran second in popular votes.

This method of election distorts the significance of votes, as does any winner-take-all system. In any state that is heavily Democratic or Republican, voters of the outnumbered party can stay home, correctly understanding that their votes will not count. Furthermore, electors are not legally bound to abide by the popular vote. Since 1796 at least fifteen electors have failed to support their party's candidate. Thus, in 1960 a Nixon elector from Oklahoma voted for Senator Harry Byrd, as did six of the eleven Alabama electors pledged to John Kennedy. Supreme Court Justice Robert Jackson referred to electors as "free agents."[27]

The Electoral College also distorts the popular vote by giving each state, regardless of its population, two extra votes (equivalent to its seats in the U.S. Senate). Since the Republicans control a number of relatively less-populated Western and Southern states, this gives them proportionately more electoral votes per popular votes. It is also nigh impossible for a third-party candidate, with a thinly spread as opposed to a concentrated regional base, to make a showing in the Electoral College, therefore further discouraging voters from considering third-party candidates.[28]

With direct election of the president there would be no distortion of the popular vote. Every vote would count. And there would be no possibility of having to throw an election into the House of Representatives, where further distortions can occur. An attempt to introduce a constitutional amendment through Congress for the direct election of the president failed in 1977–78, because of the opposition of members from smaller states advan-

---

27. Twenty-six states, representing 268 electoral votes, have passed laws requiring electors to follow the popular vote. The Supreme Court has declared these laws constitutional but has not said whether they are legally enforceable.

28. It is argued that by treating the large states as giant blocks of electoral votes, the Electoral College enhances their importance, and since large states like New York and California tend to be liberal, this works to the advantage of liberals. But there is no set correlation between state size and ideology. California and New York have produced their share of conservatives.

taged by the two extra elector votes. In 1980, a Gallup poll found that 67 percent of U.S. citizens favored direct presidential elections and only 19 percent were opposed.[29]

THE "NEW FEDERALISM" PLOY

President Reagan sought "to curb the size and influence of the federal establishment" by giving many social programs back to the states (when not able to abolish them outright). This "New Federalism," as it was called, supposedly would revitalize state governments. In actuality, states and cities were given greater responsibility for dealing with major social problems while federal revenue sharing was cut drastically. In the 1980s, federal aid to state and local governments fell by $34 billion in real terms, leading to harsh cuts in housing, health, and services to low-income elderly and youths. Spending for programs like community development and mass transit dropped by over 70 percent.[30] The remaining federal monies were allocated in block grants to the state governments instead of directly to the needy urban areas, as previously. The effect was to create new bureaucracies at the state level that shortchanged the cities and doled out funds to relatively prosperous small towns and suburban communities.[31]

The "New Federalism" sought to shift public power—at least in the area of human services—back to smaller units of government, thus reviving a dream, so dear to conservatives, of a marriage between Big Business and Little Government, one that allows business to play off states and communities against each other in order to extract more tax breaks and subsidies from them. It is easier for Dupont Corporation to control the tiny state of Delaware than deal with the federal government as a whole. More powerful and richer than Alaska, Exxon would like to see that sparsely populated state given complete control over all federal oil and natural resources within its boundaries—in effect giving Exxon easier access to those resources.

On occasions when various states impose progressive regulations upon business, conservatives discard their states-rights posture and act like early

---

29. See comments by Theodore Arrington and opposing arguments by Saul Brenner in "Should the Electoral College be Replaced by the Direct Election of the President? A Debate," *PS*, Spring 1984, pp. 238–239; also Harvey Zeiderstein, *Direct Election of the President* (Lexington, Mass.: Heath, 1973). Short of abolishing the Electoral College, a state could allocate its electoral votes to candidates in proportion to their popular vote in that state. A bill to do so has been proposed in Washington state. Maine and Nebraska give two electoral votes to the statewide winner and the others for the candidate who carries each congressional district.

30. Carol O'Cleireacain, "The 'New Federalism,'" *Economic Notes*, March/April 1991, p. 6.

31. Howard Kurtz, "Hostility to 'New Federalism' Is Bipartisan Among Mayors," *Washington Post*, December 10, 1984; also *Washington Post*, January 7, 1987.

Hamiltonian federalists, using the central government to override state powers. For instance, the Reagan administration argued that the states were prohibited from establishing nuclear-plant emission standards more stringent than those imposed by federal authorities, and that state laws protecting companies from corporate takeovers were invalid because the matter was exclusively within the province of the federal government.[32]

Since 1787, conservatives have been for stronger or weaker state powers depending on which arrangement served owning-class interests on a particular issue. The conservative understands that abstract notions such as states' rights are not an end unto themselves but a means of serving the moneyed class, and when they fail to do so, they are quietly put aside for more effective measures. This is not a matter of compromising conservative principles but of uncompromisingly pursuing ruling-class interests by whatever means available.

THE PRESIDENT VERSUS CONGRESS: WHO HAS THE POWER?

A glance at the Constitution seems to indicate that Congress is the more powerful branch of government. Article 1 gives Congress the power to declare war, make the laws of the land, raise taxes, and spend money. Article 2 seems more limited in its scope; it gives the president the power to appoint ambassadors, federal judges, and senior executive officers (subject to Senate confirmation) and to make treaties (subject to ratification by two-thirds of the senators present). The president can veto laws (but the veto can be overridden by a two-thirds vote in Congress), can call Congress into special session, and do a few other incidental things. The president has two more significant functions: to see that the laws are faithfully executed and to serve as commander-in-chief of the armed forces. By all appearances, it is Congress that determines policy and lays down the law and it is the president who does Congress's bidding.

The reality is something else. In the last century or so, with the growth of industrial capitalism at home and abroad, the role of government has grown enormously at the municipal, state, and federal levels and in the executive, legislative, and judicial branches. But the tasks of serving capitalism's vast needs and interests in war and peace have fallen disproportionately on the level of government that is national and international in scope—the federal—and on the branch most suited to carrying out the necessary technical, organizational, and military measures—the executive.

---

32. Alan Morrison, "New Federalism Holes," *New York Times,* September 20, 1982.

The executive branch today is a vast conglomeration of fourteen departments, and hundreds of agencies, commissions, and bureaus. Many of these units are designed to accommodate special interests in transportation, commerce, mining, shipping, banking, veterans affairs, education, and agriculture, to name only some. In addition, the Executive Office of the President, a bureaucracy unto itself, contains a number of administrative units to help the president formulate and coordinate overall policy. There is the Office of Management and Budget, which puts together both the president's budget and his legislative program and sometimes enforces White House policy in the bureaucracy. Also within the Executive Office is the National Security Council (NSC), created after World War II for the purpose of overall planning and coordination of military, international, and domestic policies related to national security. The NSC is the White House's instrument (along with the Defense Department and to a lesser extent the State Department) for managing counterinsurgency in the Third World, the cold war, and U.S. global corporate hegemony. The CIA reports directly to the NSC.

The growth of presidential powers has been so great as to have occasioned a relative decline in the powers of Congress (even though legislative activity itself has increased greatly over the years). This is especially true in international affairs. The end result is a presidency that tends to eclipse Congress—and sometimes the law itself. The president commands a number of resources that give him a decided edge over Congress:

Personal lobbying. The president directly seeks the support of members of Congress. He flatters them with invitations to dine at the White House, appeals to their personal and party loyalty, and promises White House support during the next election campaign. Lawmakers sometimes come to feel they would not look good going against the president. The prestige of the presidency itself lends persuasion to this pressure.

Superior media exposure. Commanding the kind of media attention that most politicians can only dream of, the president is able to define the issue agenda more readily than legislative leaders. Transmitted by a dutiful press, the president's appeals shape the climate of opinion in which Congress must react. One study found that on only five of thirty-six occasions that President Reagan appeared in a formal address on evening television was the congressional opposition given an opportunity to respond directly to him on the same network. Live network coverage of the president's messages seems "to have had an unmistakable impact on measures being considered by Congress."[33]

---

33. Report on Media Access by the Library of Congress, Washington, DC, October 3, 1984. Under the Clinton administration, the press gives much more exposure to GOP Senate minority leader Robert Dole than it ever gave to Democratic leaders during the Reagan–Bush years.

Pork barrel and other special favors. The president can reward supportive lawmakers and punish uncooperative ones. The lawmaker who votes the way the president wants on crucial bills is more likely to get that veterans' hospital built in his or her district, or support for an emergency farm bill, or a federal contract for a shipyard back home. To sway votes on behalf of the North American Free Trade Act (NAFTA), President Clinton doled out hundreds of millions of dollars in pork projects, special protections, subsidies, and cuts in cigarette taxes and grazing fees.[34]

Unitary office. There being only one president but many legislators, the chief executive has the advantage of unitary initiative and action. Almost by definition, a legislature is a cacophony of voices and interests, not structured as a command post, and usually not productive of cohesive national policy. Today, the executive plays a greater role in shaping the legislative agenda than do the legislators. One hears of "the president's program" rather than "Congress's program." Approximately 80 percent of major laws originate in the executive branch.

Control of information. In just about every policy area—from weapons systems to management of timber lands—the executive controls the crucial information. Congress frequently goes along because it depends so heavily on what the executive departments have to say. At times, presidents place themselves and their associates above congressional investigation by claiming that the separation of powers gives them an inherent right of "executive privilege." Executive privilege has been used to withhold information on everything from undeclared wars to illegal campaign funds and burglaries, yet it has no existence in the Constitution or any law. A president who can decide at his own discretion what he will or will not tell Congress and the public ends up exercising unaccountable power. We are left with no defense against deception and executive self-interest. Executive privilege deprives Congress of the information it needs to discharge its constitutional responsibilities, including its right to examine the manner in which its laws have been executed.[35]

National security and unaccountability. The president's claim to executive privilege is nowhere more pronounced than in the area of "national

---

34. *Wall Street Journal,* November 10, 1993; *Washington Times,* November 11, 1993; *Houston Post,* November 12, 1993; and printout reports from Public Citizen, Washington, D.C., n.d. Clinton used the carrot as well as the stick. He slashed space-station jobs from Alabama after that state's Democratic senator publicly criticized him for failing to cut spending sufficiently: *San Francisco Examiner,* March 27, 1993.

35. See Raoul Berger, *Executive Privilege, A Constitutional Myth* (Cambridge, Mass.: Harvard University Press, 1974). The Supreme Court collaborated in the fabrication of the concept of "executive privilege," deciding that a "presumptive privilege" for withholding information (in noncriminal cases) belonged to the president: *United States v. Nixon* (1974). Indeed, "presumptive," with no basis in law.

security." The president and his various intelligence agencies remove whole policy areas from public scrutiny and congressional oversight. A report by two House subcommittees dealing with foreign affairs complained of the "unwillingness of the executive branch to acknowledge major decisions and to subject them to public scrutiny and discussion."[36] Congress unknowingly funded CIA covert operations in Laos and Thailand that were in violation of congressional prohibitions. The legislature ordered a halt to expansion of a naval base in the Indian Ocean, only to discover that construction was continuing. Many members of the Senate had not heard of the automated battlefield program for which they voted secret appropriations.[37]

International crises and wars. "War is the true nurse of executive aggrandizement," wrote James Madison in 1787. About two hundred years later, U.S. presidents invaded the sovereign states of Grenada and Panama, and supported proxy wars against Cuba, Angola, Mozambique, Afghanistan, Cambodia, and Nicaragua, forcibly overthrowing governments without a declaration of war and engaging in unlawful arms sales and illegal acts of war, including the arming and training of mercenary forces, without a declaration from Congress.[38] The CIA overspent its legal limits in the covert war against Nicaragua. U.S. planes and bases were used for support in the Nicaraguan war, against the expressed will of Congress. And CIA flight crews were not only ferrying arms to the contra mercenaries (without congressional knowledge) but were smuggling cocaine and other drugs on their return trips to the United States.[39] Recent presidents have asserted what

---

36. *New York Times,* January 22, 1973. By entering into "executive agreements" with foreign nations, the president can even circumvent the Senate's power to ratify treaties. The Reagan administration argued that testimony given by its officials during treaty ratification hearings need not reflect a treaty's true meaning. Some senators protested, noting that such a procedure undermined the Senate's constitutional duty to ratify a treaty because the Senate would have no certainty about what it was actually approving: *Washington Post,* February 7, 1988.

37. Paul Dickson and John Rothchild, "The Electronic Battlefield," *Monthly Review,* May 1971, pp. 6–14. President Nixon claimed he had "inherent executive power" under the Constitution to commit even criminal acts when impelled by what he considered to be national security considerations. In a TV interview on the David Frost show, May 19, 1977, he said, "When the president does it, that means it is not illegal." Scratch a president and you find a divine-rights monarch.

38. The president's "black budget," a secret account used to fund secret wars against established governments, had grown to $39 billion a year by 1989: Tim Weiner, *Blank Check, The Pentagon's Black Budget* (New York: Warner Books, 1990). While Congress debated whether to declare war on Iraq, President Bush announced, "I don't care if I get one vote in Congress. We're going in": quoted in *New York Times,* August 18, 1992. It was not the intent of the framers of the Constitution to confer upon the president any power to start a war. That power was intended for Congress alone.

39. Jonathan Bennett, "Embargo May Violate U.S. and International Law," *Guardian,* May 15, 1985; Tim Weiner, "Anti-Drug Unit of CIA Sent Ton of Cocaine to U.S. in 1990," *New York Times,* November 20, 1993; Scott and Marshall, *Cocaine Politics,* passim.

amounts to a monopoly of power to make foreign policy.[40] In sum, the White House has repeatedly undermined Congress's power to declare war, make laws, appropriate funds, and exercise legislative oversight.

Rule by executive order. The president frequently issues decrees on his own, without authorization from Congress. Thus, Reagan abrogated the outstanding treaty of commerce and friendship with Nicaragua to wage a war of attrition against that country. On another occasion he issued an executive order that authorized intelligence agencies to conduct domestic surveillance and covert operations against U.S. citizens within the United States, in violation of the limitations set forth in the National Security Act of 1947. Both Reagan and Bush used executive orders to take wetlands out of protection and grant favorable deregulations to industry. It has become the practice to treat such executive orders as if they had the force of law, when actually they do not. By using executive orders to create important departures from the law, the president is unilaterally concocting his own laws for his own purposes, something not allowed by the Constitution.

Levers of power. The Supreme Court has long been aware that its decisions have the force of law only if other agencies of government choose to carry them out. In recent years Congress has been coming to the same realization, developing a new appreciation of the executive's power to command directly the personnel, materials, and programs needed for carrying out decisions. The peculiar danger of executive power is that it executes. Presidents have repeatedly engaged in acts of warfare without congressional approval because they command the military forces to do so. The executive alone has the power of implementation, acting (or refusing to act) with the force of state, to exercise extraordinary and sometimes unlawful initiatives of its own. Some instances drawn from the Reagan and Bush years illustrate how the executive can circumvent the law at home and abroad:

1. Although price-fixing by retail business has been outlawed since 1911, the Justice Department's antitrust division through the 1980s simply refused to enforce the law.

2. The Reagan administration terminated Social Security benefits for hundreds of thousands of disabled Americans. When federal courts found the rulings to be illegal, the administration announced it would simply ignore the unfavorable court decisions.

3. When a federal judge ordered the Bush administration to make surplus federal property available to the homeless under a 1987 law, the White House ignored the order.

---

40. For instance, assertions by the Reagan administration that Congress could not limit the president's "constitutional and historical power" to conduct foreign affairs, including raising money for counterrevolutionary armies: *New York Times,* May 15, 1987.

4. Both the Reagan and Bush administrations refused to spend billions appropriated by Congress for housing and low-income programs, and impounded billions intended for improvements in mass transit and air safety.

5. Congress prohibited military sales to Guatemala, yet the White House agreed to sell $14 million worth of military equipment to that government, asserting that since the sale would be a cash transaction, it would not violate the congressional ban.

6. The General Accounting Office (GAO) released a report showing that the Reagan administration violated U.S. law in its preparations for increased intervention in Central America and military construction in Honduras.

7. The GAO revealed in June 1993 that the Pentagon had deliberately misled Congress during the 1980s about the cost, performance, and need for nuclear weapons systems.

8. The White House halted or interfered with U.S. law enforcement efforts to keep narcotics out of the United States, for fear of jeopardizing the war effort against Nicaragua.

9. President Bush refused to undertake a needs assessment, as mandated by Congress, as a step toward developing a humanitarian aid program for Cambodia and instead used the money to fund an antigovernment guerrilla war.[41]

Congress itself has sometimes collaborated in the usurpation of its power, granting each president, and a widening list of executive agencies, confidential funds for which no detailed invoices are required. The legislators sometimes have preferred to pass on to the president the task of handling crises.[42] Under the guise of limiting presidential power, Congress sometimes expands it. The War Powers Act of 1973 requires the president seek congressional approval within sixty days for any military action he has launched is a case in point. The Constitution does not grant the president power to engage in warfare without prior congressional approval. Even these expanded and unconstitutional limits have been violated. Thus the War

---

41. For these various examples, see *New York Times*, March 25, 1986; *Los Angeles Times*, November 4, 1984; letter to Secretary of State George Shultz from Representative Robert Mrazek and seven other members of Congress, protesting arms sales to Guatemala, October 5, 1988; General Accounting Office report B–213137, "Propriety of Funding Methods Used by the Department of Defense in Combined Exercises in Honduras," Washington, D.C., June 22, 1984; GAO report summarized in *People's Weekly World*, August 21, 1993; "U.S. Slammed on Aid to Khmer Rouge," *Guardian*, August 1, 1990 and May 8, 1991; Senate Committee on Foreign Relations, *Drugs Law Enforcement and Foreign Policy* Washington, D.C.: Government Printing Office, 1989).

42. Ann Nocenti and Brian Tenenbaum, "The Great Compromise," *Lies of Our Times*, June 1991, p. 9.

Powers Act allows the president to engage U.S. troops only in case of an attack on the United States or its territories, possessions, or armed forces. In invading Grenada and Panama, and sending "military advisors" to El Salvador and Honduras, who sometimes engaged in combat actions, two presidents violated the act. In each of these instances Congress was not consulted.

The Constitution does not grant the president the right to wage covert actions against other nations, yet President Bush made such a claim, stating he would notify Congress of covert operations about to be launched—unless he decided not to, "based on my assertion of the authorities granted this office by the Constitution."[43]

Many of the restrictions imposed on the executive by Congress are more form than substance. Thus, despite the National Emergencies Act of 1976, which terminated all emergency powers previously granted to presidents, there exist some 470 statutes that enable the chief executive to claim potentially dictatorial powers, even if only for a specified time, to seize private properties, declare martial law, suspend habeas corpus, confiscate all means of transportation, and restrict travel.

It would be wrong to conclude from all this that the legislative branch has been reduced to a mere rubber stamp. From time to time Congress has fought back. Both houses now have budget committees with staffs that can more effectively review the president's budget. Along with the investigations conducted by its standing committees and subcommittees, Congress has the General Accounting Office which, as already noted, is independent of the executive branch and reports directly to the legislature. The GAO plays an important role in uncovering executive waste, wrongdoing, mismanagement, and nonenforcement of the law. The Democratic-controlled House of Representatives resisted a number of President Reagan's proposals, voting against chemical weapons, against antisatellite weapons testing, for a year-long ban on nuclear testing, and for less military spending than the White House wanted. Congress restored a number of worthwhile items that Reagan and Bush sought to cut, including library programs, public health services, rental housing grants, student incentive grants, soil conservation programs, and emergency food and shelter funds. Yet in most of these kinds of battles the high ground belongs to the president—especially if he is a conservative.

Years ago, liberals, who saw how a conservative leadership in Congress managed to thwart the desires of liberal presidents like Truman and Kennedy, concluded that the national legislature had too much power and the executive not enough. But having witnessed conservative presidents like Nixon and Reagan effect their will over Congress, some of these same liberals concluded that the president was too powerful and Congress too

---

43. David MacMichael, "Overt Inaction," *Nation*, September 17, 1990, p. 261.

weak. Actually, there was something more to these complaints than partisan inconsistency. In the first instance, liberals are talking about the president's insufficient ability to effect measures that might benefit the working populace. And in the second, they are talking about the president's ability to make overseas military commitments and to thwart social-welfare legislation at home.

What underlies both complaints is the realization that the president tends to be more powerful than Congress when he assumes a conservative stance and less powerful when he wants to push in a progressive direction. This reflects the entire distribution of politico-economic class power, including media influence, lobbying, campaign contributions, weakened labor unions, low voter-participation among working people, and various other factors mentioned in this book. It is also a reflection of the way the Constitution itself structures things. As the framers intended, the system of separation of powers and checks and balances is designed to give the high ground to those who resist social change, be they presidents or legislators. Neither the executive nor the legislature can single-handedly initiate reform, which means that conservatives need to control only one or the other branch to thwart domestic actions (or in the case of Congress, key committees in one or the other house) while liberals must control both houses and both branches.

Small wonder conservative and liberal presidents have different kinds of experiences with Congress. Should Congress insist upon passing bills that incur his displeasure, the conservative president need control only one-third plus one of either the House or the Senate to sustain his vetoes. If bills are passed over his veto, he can still undermine legislative intent by delaying enforcement under various pretexts relating to timing, efficiency, and other operational contingencies. The conservative president can defer spending or even rescind it completely on specific projects, as long as Congress passes a resolution approving the cut within forty-five days, which Congress often does.[44]

The techniques of veto, decoy, and delay used by a conservative president to dismantle or hamstring domestic programs are of little help to a less conservative president who might claim an interest in social change, for the immense social problems he faces cannot be solved by executive sleight-of-hand. What efforts presidents do make in the field of social reform are frequently thwarted or diluted by entrenched conservative powers within and without Congress. It is in these confrontations that the Congress gives every appearance of being able to frustrate presidential initiatives.

---

44. Norman Ornstein, "A Line-Item Veto: Who Needs It?" *Washington Post*, August 11, 1985. Because George Bush, a conservative president, had no domestic agenda, other than to want to abolish capital gains taxes, he occupied the high ground, Democrats in Congress complained. "He can pick and choose what he will allow to pass," noted one. "It's only when he wants to get things done, then we have some leverage": *Washington Post*, June 24, 1991.

The Reagan years lent confirmation to the above analysis, albeit with a new twist, for here was a conservative president who was not obstructionist but activist, one who sought a major transition in taxing and spending policies. The obstructionist defenses that Congress uses so well against progressive measures were less successful against Reagan, as a coalition of Republicans and "boll weevil" conservative Democrats, backed by corporate and moneyed interests outside Congress, gave the president most of what he wanted, curtailing or diminishing in one session progressive programs developed over the last fifty years. The same coalition gave President Clinton and corporate America their NAFTA victory in record time. So was demonstrated a new variation on an old theme: the system moves most swiftly when directed with concerted effort toward conservative ends.

With an activist conservative president like Ronald Reagan dedicated to rolling back social services and advancing the prerogatives of the corporate class and the military, liberals developed a new appreciation for congressional resistance to presidential initiatives. During the New Deal and Fair Deal days of liberal dominance of the White House, liberals advocated a strong presidency and warned against turning the president into an ineffectual lame duck by restricting the number of terms he might serve. Having endured twenty years of Roosevelt and Truman, conservatives were convinced that their main task was to trim the power of the federal government and of the presidency in particular. So they fought successfully for the Twenty-second Amendment (1951) which limited White House occupancy to two terms.

Likewise, in the 1950s liberals were urging that the president be given a freer hand in foreign policy, while conservatives were pushing for the Bricker amendment, a measure that would have given the states a kind of veto over the executive treaty power reminiscent of the Articles of Confederation. Liberals talked about giving the president an item veto (allowing him to veto specific items in a bill while accepting other portions of it) so that he might better resist special-interest legislation. Conservatives treated the item veto as just another example of executive usurpation.

By the 1980s we heard a different tune. Conservatives now better appreciated the uses of a strong presidency in advancing the causes of military spending and of multinational corporate capitalism at home and abroad. Furthermore, given their ability in recent times to win the presidency (four out of the last five times) and their superior ability to raise the enormous sums needed for that endeavor, conservatives, including those on the Supreme Court, now favored an expanded executive power.[45] A conservative president, Ronald Reagan, broadened the realm of unaccountable execu-

---

45. For a sample of prominent conservative policymakers who now complain that the president is overpowered by Congress, see L. Gordon Crovitz and Jeremy Rabkin (eds.) *The*

tive initiative and secrecy. He also requested an item veto. And in 1988 he and other conservatives called for repeal of the Twenty-second Amendment, so the president might again enjoy an indefinite number of terms.

In contrast, liberals now railed against the "imperial president."[46] They talked about holding firm with the War Powers Act and making the executive more accountable to Congress. Under their breaths they were thankful for the Twenty-second Amendment, and few of them still called for an item veto. They had discovered that a presidency that so grew in power under their domain could become a powerful conservative instrument.

Change from the Top?

Presidents, along with mayors and governors, have complained that the problems they confront are of a magnitude far greater than the resources they command. We can suspect them of telling the truth. The liberal executive leader who begins the term with the promise of getting things moving is less likely to change the political-corporate class system than be reined in by it. Once in office, he finds himself staggered by the vast array of entrenched powers working within and without government, and he finds it difficult to move in reformist directions without incurring the hostility of those who control the economy and its institutional auxiliaries. So he begins to talk about being "realistic" and working with what is at hand, now tacking against the wind, now taking one step back in the often unrealized hope of taking two steps forward, until the public begins to complain that his administration bears a dismaying resemblance to the less dynamic, less energetic ones that came before.[47]

In the hope of maintaining his efficacy, the chief executive begins to settle for the appearance of efficacy, until appearances are all he is left struggling with. It is this tugging and hauling and whirling about in a tight circle of options and ploys that is celebrated by some as "the give-and-take of democratic interest-group politics." To less enchanted observers, the failure of reform-minded leaders to deliver on their promises demonstrates the difficulty of working for major changes within a politico-economic system structured to resist change.

Fettered Presidency: Legal Constraints on the Executive Branch (Washington, D.C.: American Enterprise Institute, 1989).

46. And, of course, some conservatives now rail against an "imperial Congress": Norman Podhoretz, "The Imperial Congress," *Washington Post*, December 23, 1986.

47. In the case of Clinton, it has been less a tactical retreat and more a quick plunge into the ranks of corporate conservatism, as he shows himself to be almost as Republican as the Republicans in both domestic and foreign affairs: see Norman Solomon, *False Hope: The Politics of Illusion in the Clinton Era* (Monroe, Maine: Common Courage Press, 1994).

The executive has grown in power and responsibility along with the increasing concentration of monopoly capital. As already noted, a centralized nationwide capitalist economy needs a centralized nationwide state power to tend to its needs. By the same token, as U.S. corporate interests grew to international scope and were confronted with challenges from various anti-imperialist forces, so the president's involvement in international affairs grew—and so grew the military establishment intended to defend "U.S. interests" abroad. The president can intervene in other countries in a variety of ways, destroying the social support systems of whole nations, as demonstrated by the destruction of Iraq. Such powers do not advance the democratic interests of the American people, nor are they so designed. The immense military power the president commands, supposedly to make us all much safer, actually gives the chief executive an increasingly destructive and undemocratic power. As the executive power grows in foreign affairs, so the president's power over the American people becomes less accountable and more dangerous.

Although the president and the government are often held responsible for the economy, they do not have that much control over it. The purpose of executive economic involvement is to sustain and advance the process of "free-market" capital accumulation. There is, then, not likely to be much progressive change from the top, no matter who is in the White House, unless there is also widespread social unrest and a mass mobilization for fundamental reforms.

15

The Political Economy of Bureaucracy

Conservatives would have us believe that bureaucracy is a malady peculiar to the liberal welfare state or to socialism. In fact, bureaucracy can be found in just about every area of modern capitalist society; in hundreds of giant business corporations; in universities, religious establishments, and other private organizations; in the military, FBI, and CIA; as well as in government. Bureaucracy is a technically superior method of organization, in the way that machine production is superior to nonmachine production. A model bureaucracy has the following characteristics: (1) the systematic mobilization of human energy and material resources for the fulfillment of explicitly defined policy goals or plans; (2) the use of trained career personnel who occupy nonhereditary offices of specified jurisdictions; (3) the specialization of skills and division of labor, coordinated by a hierarchy of command that is accountable to some authority or constituency.[1] Bureaucracy can be used to administer a national health program or run a death camp. Much depends on the politico-economic context in which it operates.

The growth of bureaucracy and government in general is less the result of the self-interested behavior of politicians and bureaucrats and more a response to public and corporate demands for an array of services.[2]

---

1. See Max Weber's classic statement, "Bureaucracy," in Hans Gerth and C. Wright Mills (eds.), *From Max Weber: Essays in Sociology* (New York: Oxford University Press, 1958), pp. 196–244.

2. William Berry and David Lowery, *Understanding United States Government Growth: An Empirical Analysis of the Postwar Era* (New York: Praeger, 1987).

THE MYTH AND REALITY OF INEFFICIENCY

Bureaucracies have certain bothersome characteristics that seem to inhere in the nature of the beast. For instance, the need for consistent and accountable operating procedures can create a tendency toward inertia, red tape, and a limited capacity to respond to new initiatives. The need to divide responsibilities over widely dispersed areas can cause problems of coordination and accountability. Highly centralized supervision, in turn, can create problems of congestion, inflexible responsiveness, and an unwillingness of subordinates to assume responsibilities. And for the average citizen there is the problem of the incomprehensible forms and labyrinthine runarounds orchestrated by the petty autocrats and uncaring paper pushers who sometimes inhabit both public and private bureaucracies.

Despite these problems, bureaucracies perform crucial and complex tasks—for better or worse—that could not be accomplished without the systematic administrative capacity that is the hallmark of modern organization. "The feat of landing men on the moon," observes Duane Lockard, "was not only a scientific achievement but a bureaucratic one as well."[3] The same might be said of the Vietnam War, the Social Security system, and the farm, highway, housing, and defense programs.

According to the prevailing ideology of corporate America, public bureaucracy is expensive, inefficient, and a drain on the more productive private economy. The conservative remedy is the hand over public programs to private contractors ("privatization") or abolish them altogether. This conservative attack on government diverts attention from the realities of class privilege and class power. When things go wrong with the economy, the conservative critics blame not the corporate interests that own and control the economy but the government that dares to tamper with the free market.

Conservatives insist that government should be "run more like a business." One might wonder how that could be possible, since government does not market goods and services for the purpose of capital accumulation. Government deals with complex social problems, conflicting goals, and competing constituencies. Exactly what businesses should government imitate? the fifty thousand firms that go bankrupt every year? or the large successful corporations—themselves giant bureaucracies and recipients of generous public subsidies—that regularly skirt the law and cater only to those who have sufficient cash or credit? Do we want government run like the giant firms that are controlled by nonelective directors, who answer to no one but themselves and a few banks and big investors?

---

3. Duane Lockard, *The Perverted Priorities of American Politics* (New York: Macmillan, 1971), p. 282.

If we run government like a business (whatever that means), then who will take care of the costly, nonprofit public services that business relies on for its existence? For instance, while much has been made of the regulatory costs imposed on the automobile industry, little attention is given to the hundreds of billions of dollars that government must come up with for roads and highways and the dislocation costs to surrounding communities, for which government must take the heat. In such instances, is government a burden on the auto industry, or is it the other way around?[4]

There are inefficiencies and waste in private business as well as public administration, but the former are rarely publicized. Seldom mentioned is the fact that administrative expenses are generally lower in the public than the private realm. For instance, administrative costs for the government's Medicare program are less than three cents per dollar, while administrative costs of private health insurance are twenty-six cents per dollar.[5] Government administrators generally work longer hours for less pay than managers in private bureaucracies.[6]

Conservatives want to eliminate social spending programs not because they don't work but because they often do. When public programs attend to social needs with not-for-profit services, they are demonstrating the parasitic irrelevance of an owning class. Thus, Conrail demonstrated that a government-owned rail system could give better service at less cost than the investor-owned lines it replaced. But this very success is intolerable to conservatives who correctly see nonprofit public ownership as a threat to the private-profit system. So, Conrail was "privatized" (sold back to private investors) at a bargain price.[7]

Government programs also impose limits on profit maximization. Environmental protections and occupational safety do save lives and benefit the public but they can cut into profits by adding to production costs. They place limits on industry's ability to use human labor and the environment solely as it sees fit. Public housing did dramatically reduce overcrowding between 1940 and 1980,[8] but it also created a supply of residences that competed with the private housing industry. Rent control did keep millions of units af-

4. H. Brinton Milward and Hal Rainey, "Don't Blame the Bureaucracy," *Journal of Public Policy*, 3, 1983, pp. 151–152.

5. Pacifica Network News, September 14, 1993. On the comparison of public and private management costs and the relative efficiency of public administration, see John Schwarz, *America's Hidden Success*, rev. ed. (New York: W. W. Norton, 1988); also Charles Goodsell, *The Case of Bureaucracy*, 2nd ed. (Chatham, N.J.: Chatham House, 1985).

6. Between 1969 and 1985 there was a 40 percent decline in purchasing power of top federal salaries and a 68 percent rise in the real income of corporate executives: Carl Brauer, "Lost In Transition," *Atlantic Monthly*, November 1988, p. 75.

7. *Washington Post*, March 27, 1987.

8. Schwarz, *America's Hidden Success*, pp. 59–69.

fordable but it cut into landlord profits.[9] Without federal assistance programs the number of people who live in illness and destitution would easily double.[10] But business believes the money would be better spent in the private-profit sector. Such federal programs redistribute income in a downward direction to those who have less rather than to those who want it all.

Federal funds to ameliorate inequality in education produced strong scholastic gains among low-income students in inner-city schools and others in the lowest performance quartile.[11] Social Security has been a more reliable retirement program than private pension plans and has substantially reduced the elderly poverty rate over the last half century.[12] The efficacy of public programs can be appreciated when the programs are abolished or diminished. The cuts in public housing and rent control have been accompanied by a rise in homelessness. The closing of venereal disease clinics has fueled an increase in VD cases. The heartless cuts in welfare payments introduce more hunger among children. The reduction of education funding increases the number of substandard, overcrowded schools. The deregulation of the airline industry has reduced aviation safety.[13] An elimination or watering down of worker-safety rules, safety information on medical devices and consumer products, clean-air standards, and pesticide controls "is costing the nation dearly in human life and a damaged environment."[14]

Public administration carries out tasks that private business could not handle. Consider the much maligned post office: what private corporation

9. Rent control generally accomplishes its objective of holding down housing costs for renters while allowing landlords to make reasonable profits: Margery Turner, *Rent Control and the Availability of Affordable Housing in the District of Columbia* (Washington, D.C.: Urban Institute, 1988).

10. One dollar invested in prenatal care and infant feeding programs saves $3 in immediate hospital costs. One dollar spent on childhood immunization saves $10 in later medical expenses: *Youth and Families,* report by House Select Committee on Children, Washington, D.C.: Government Printing Office, 1988; also study by Mathematica Policy Research, reported in *New York Times,* November 1, 1990.

11. *Washington Post,* June 21, 1983. On effective poverty programs, see *San Francisco Chronicle,* August 31, 1992, and Lisbeth Schorr, *Within Our Reach: Breaking the Cycle of Disadvantage* (Garden City, N.Y.: Doubleday Anchor, 1988).

12. Merton Bernstein and Joan Brodschaug, *Social Security: The System That Works* (New York: Basic Books, 1988); Paul Kleyman, "Scapegoating the Elderly," *Propaganda Review,* Winter 1990, pp. 10–13. Job Corps programs still bring positive results: *Washington Post,* September 2, 1991. In one decade, government requirements for smoke detectors, seat belts, speed limits, emergency public health facilities, and safety features on consumer products have helped produce a 21 percent drop in accidental fatalities, according to the National Safety Council: *New York Times,* October 7, 1990.

13. Paul Stephen Dempsey, "'91 A Year of Aviation Disasters, Thanks to DeRegulation," *Seattle Times,* January 7, 1992.

14. Christine Triano and Nancy Watzman, *Voodoo Accounting,* a report by Public Citizen and OMB Watch, Washington, D.C., 1992.

would deliver a letter 3,000 miles, door to door, for the price of a postage stamp, or forward your mail to a new address at no cost? In recent times, however, Republican administrations attempted to put the U. S. Postal Service on a more "profit-motivated" basis. They contracted out postal jobs to low-wage nonunion workers, reduced delivery standards, gave away millions of dollars in top-management bonuses, and disregarded health and safety regulations for postal workers—all of which brought a marked deterioration in service.[15]

This is not to make light of government waste. The General Accounting Office found that the federal government—under a supposedly economy-minded conservative administration—lost billions of dollars in the 1980s because of poor management in major agencies, the most costly being the Pentagon and the National Aeronautics and Space Administration (NASA).[16] But business seldom complains about wasteful military and space spending—there is too much profit to be had in that kind of largesse. Nearly one-fourth of today's federal budget goes to private contractors.[17] Here too, one hears little complaining from industry about government expenditures.

Business attacks against bureaucracy help direct public discontent away from corporate America and toward government. Such attacks ignore the many costly public expenditures that end up as subsidies to private business. Thus, in cities throughout the nation, working-class neighborhoods have been razed to make way for shopping malls, industrial parks, sports arenas, and convention centers, built with public funds. While business benefits from such ventures, the public monies invested are seldom recovered and the projects often become multimillion dollar debts and continual drains on municipal budgets. These public subsidies of private gain are a large part of the U.S. urban fiscal crisis.[18] Instead of contrasting the profitability of private business with the debt-ridden costliness of government, we would do better to see the causal connection between the two. "The

---

15. Michael Parenti, "Don't Dump on the Post Office," *The New Haven Advocate,* February 5, 1986; and the American Postal Workers Union press release, Washington, D.C., November 1991.

16. One audit found spending abuses by NASA officials and contractors in virtually every aspect of NASA's operations. The waste, estimated at over $3.5 billion, was "only the tip of the iceberg" according to federal auditors: *New York Times,* April 23, 1986. Delinquent debts and taxes have continued to grow and were reported at over $89 billion by 1989: U.S. General Accounting Office, Report to Congress: *Financial Integrity Act,* Washington, D.C.: November 1989.

17. John Hanrahan, *Government by Contract* (New York: W. W. Norton, 1983). In 1992 the White House acknowledged that private contractors doing government work are often left unsupervised and waste billions of dollars: *New York Times,* December 2, 1992.

18. Susan Fainstein and Norman Fainstein, "The Political Economy of American Bureaucracy," in Carol Weiss and Allen Barton (eds.) *Making Bureaucracies Work* (Beverly Hills, Calif.: Sage, 1980), p. 285; Jerome Ellig, "Public Stadiums Aren't Worth the Price," *Washington Post,* September 20, 1987.

very governments which have continually . . . subsidize[d] business are then charged with inefficient performance by the business class."[19]

Sometimes government agencies perform inefficiently because their missions are impossible. During the 1960s, a few agencies, like the Office of Economic Opportunity, were assigned the task of "eradicating" poverty, an undertaking that could be accomplished only with a major transformation of the economic system. As noted earlier, government in capitalist America is not allowed to make a profit—which could then be put back into the public treasury. Unused offices in a U.S. government building may not be rented, even if this benefited the public treasury, for it would put government in competition with private rentals. Government is allowed to operate only in the unprofitable "markets" that business does not want. Thus, public hospitals show none of the profits of private ones because they handle the people who cannot afford the health insurance and other astronomical cost of private health care. Likewise, low-income public housing provides shelter for those financially excluded from the private housing market. And public welfare administers to those who cannot sell their labor on the private job market.

Government bureaucracies have little control over the production process, over what is produced, how, where, and by whom.

> Thus . . . the Department of Energy is supposed to ensure an adequate supply of gasoline, but it cannot even command accurate data from the oil companies, much less itself extract petroleum from the ground and process it. The Department of Housing and Urban Development can subsidize low-income housing, but it can neither build units itself nor divert private investment from middle-class suburban development. In each case the public bureaucracy is inefficient and ineffective. But its problems are foreordained by the conditions under which public agencies operate.[20]

SECRECY, DECEPTION, AND UNACCOUNTABILITY

Business, we are told, answers to the public through the competition of the free market, while government strives for secrecy and unaccountability. In fact, as just noted, government is more the object of public scrutiny than is business. People expect government to solve problems because they have no expectation that business will. They blame government precisely because they feel, correctly, that it is more controllable than business.[21]

---

19. Fainstein and Fainstein, "The Political Economy of American Bureaucracy," p. 285.
20. Ibid. p. 286.
21. Ibid., p. 283.

This is not to deny that both public and private bureaucracies have a strong tendency toward secrecy. In the federal bureaucracy, as in most other organizations, be it the church, the police, the university, the military, or the corporation, there is more concern about the damaging effects that might be caused by disclosures of wrongdoing than about the wrongdoing itself. Most of the secrecy in public bureaucracy is on behalf of private business, the military, and the dirty operations of the CIA and other such agencies.[22] The government has suppressed information concerning bank bailouts and health and safety problems that might prove troublesome to powerful business interests, including data on toxic waste disposal and on the harmful features of certain medical drugs, pesticides, and nuclear plants.[23]

The government withheld information regarding the medical problems of 30,000 American soldiers and thousands of Utah residents exposed to nuclear tests in the 1950s, and the ill effects of defoliants upon military personnel in the Vietnam War.[24] It secretly conducted germ warfare tests in U.S. urban areas and radiation tests on at least 800 unsuspecting subjects.[25]

The more secrecy, the more opportunity for officials to do what they want without having to answer for it. The executive branch withholds about sixteen million documents a year. Despite a 1977 law requiring most government agencies to open their meetings to the public, a decade later about half of all such meetings were still being conducted in secret.[26] President Reagan issued a presidential directive that forced some two million government workers to take a pledge of secrecy. He required almost 300,000 federal employees to agree to lifetime government censorship of their writings and speeches.[27] Administrations have sought to undercut the Freedom of Information Act by expanding the restrictive classifications of documents,

22. For numerous examples, see *Government Secrecy: Decisions Without Democracy* (report by People for the American Way, Washington, D.C., 1988); *New York Times,* August 18, 1988; *Christian Science Monitor,* October 16, 1990; *Los Angeles Times,* February 16, 1990; and the discussion in chapter 9.

23. *New York Times,* September 27 and December 1, 1992 and November 2 and 9, 1993; *Washington Post,* July 10, 1989 and September 22, 1991; Jim Sibbison, "The EPA Speaks," *Lies of Our Times,* June 1990, p. 4.

24. Howard Rosenberg, *Atomic Soldiers* (Boston: Beacon Press, 1980); Harvey Wasserman and Norman Soloman, *Killing Our Own* (New York: Delacorte, 1980); *New York Times,* August 10, 1990; Carole Gallagher, *American Ground Zero* (Cambridge, Mass.: MIT Press, 1993).

25. Leonard Cole, *Clouds of Secrecy: The Army's Germ Warfare Tests Over Populated Areas* (Totowa, N.J.: Rowman and Littlefield, 1988); *New York Times,* January 1 and 5, 1994.

26. *Wall Street Journal,* September 25, 1986.

27. In 1985 alone, a total of 14,144 books, articles, and speeches were subjected to prior government censorship. Reagan instituted polygraph tests for public employees to track down press leaks. But he never responded to suggestions that he himself take a lie detector test to see if he was telling the truth about his role in the Iran-contra affair. In April 1993, President Clinton set up a taskforce to consider ways to avoid overclassification and speed up government declassification of documents.

blocking out more and more information on the documents that are released, imposing long delays on releasing materials, and charging exorbitant copying fees.[28]

With secrecy come unaccountability and corruption. The Agricultural Department has given billions of dollars worth of contracts to agribusiness firms that have been caught rigging bids, fixing prices, and defrauding government programs.[29] Hordes of speculators and fast-buck investors, risking almost no money of their own, used mortgage loans from the Department of Housing and Urban Development, plus millions in tax credits, to acquire and rent properties at federally subsidized rates, with hundreds of millions in profits for themselves. Housing grants and mortgage insurance, intended for affordable housing for low-income elderly, have gone to luxury and resort projects instead.[30]

Members of Congress are not the only ones who accept special services from special interests. Top officials in the executive branch have enjoyed the free use of vacation homes, company planes, and luxury hotels; easy-term loans; artificially large honoraria for appearances sponsored by interest groups; and the opportunity to sell their assets at inflated prices or buy properties at artificially low prices.[31] Fifty-three federal officials were indicted for corruption in 1975. Ten years later it was 563.[32]

Presidents often stand by subordinates who are accused of wrongdoing, supposedly out of "loyalty" to them. Usually they are bound to their underlings by something stronger than loyalty, namely self-interest. A subordinate abruptly cut loose might turn into a damaging source of disclosure. During the Watergate affair, the one aide President Nixon tried to throw to the wolves, John Dean, ended up singing the entire conspiracy libretto to Congress and the world. Generally, it is best for presidents who are implicated in an illegal affair, as was Nixon in Watergate and Reagan and Bush

---

28. Richard Curry (ed.) *Freedom at Risk: Secrecy, Censorship and Repression in the 1980s* (Philadelphia: Temple University Press, 1989); Walter Karp, *Liberty Under Siege* (New York: Henry Holt, 1988); Steve Weinberg, "Trashing the FOIA," *Columbia Journalism Review,* January/February 1985, pp. 21–28. Thirty years after the assassination of President John Kennedy, the government still refuses to release hundreds of thousands of pertinent documents, all the while maintaining that there is nothing to hide and the case is closed. Of the documents that have been released, many are heavily censored. Many pertinent documents are missing. See newsletters dedicated to opening the archives and conducting a new investigation into the murder: *Probe* (Hollywood, Calif.) and *Prologue* (Washington, D.C.).

29. *New York Times,* October 12, 1993.

30. Officials involved received hundreds of thousands in "consulting fees." An investigation found at least 28 of HUD's 489 programs suffered significant instances of fraud, mismanagement, and favoritism: *New York Times,* August 13, 1989.

31. *New York Times,* June 23, 1991; Dan Moldea, *Dark Victory* (New York: Penguin, 1987), pp. 236–237. Rich backers bought land owned by President Reagan at many times its market value: ibid., pp. 240–241.

32. *In These Times,* January 27–February 2, 1988.

in Iran-contra, to do everything to firm up the skittish line of persons who stand between them and the law.

Public servants who become "whistleblowers" by going public about some wrongdoing risk their careers. A federal employee who tried to warn the government that it was wasting millions on a foreign aid program had his job abolished. Another who exposed instances of patient abuse at a Veterans Administration hospital was labeled a troublemaker and fired. An Air Force engineer was fired for telling the truth about the costs of building the C–5A cargo plane. A Pentagon auditor, who discovered that contractors were padding expenses, was told to resign his job by his superiors. When a Census Bureau demographer reported that President Bush's war against Iraq had resulted in 158,000 Iraqi deaths, including 71,807 women and children, she was informed she would be fired. A U.S. Attorney was dismissed for disclosing that the CIA was trying to block prosecution against a crime figure. When several scientists announced that current radiation safety standards were at least ten times too low, the Department of Energy fired them, confiscated their data, and launched character assassinations.[33]

These are not isolated instances. The special board created to handle whistleblower complaints had a backlog of 1,000 cases only four months after its creation. Whistleblowers in the U.S. Army are routinely subjected to reprisals and threats and some are even railroaded into mental hospitals. Whistleblowers in private industry face harassment and job loss. Once unemployed, they find few job opportunities in either government or industry. Instead of being rewarded for their honesty, they are punished.[34]

To prevent federal employees from "committing truth," the White House has sought greater power to control and punish disclosures—even of unclassified materials. It has argued in several cases that government information is government property; therefore, employees who take and release such information are guilty of theft. Former Attorney General Bell denounced Justice Department personnel who leaked information to the press regarding FBI wrongdoings as having violated their oath to uphold the law.[35] Thus, leaking information about crimes is itself treated as a

---

33. Ralph Nader, Peter Petkes, and Kate Blackwell (eds.), *Whistleblowing* (New York: Bantam, 1972); A. Ernest Fitzgerald, *The Pentagonists: An Insider's View of Waste, Mismanagement, and Fraud in Defense Spending* (New York: Houghton Mifflin, 1989); Dina Rasor, *The Pentagon Underground* (New York: Times Books, 1985); *Washington Post,* June 17, 1988; July 16, 1990; March 6, 1992; *America's CENSORED Newsletter,* October 1992. p. 1.

34. *Washington Post,* March 31, 1987; CBS-TV report, January 8, 1994. About 95 percent of whistleblowing cases involving occupational safety in private industry are decided in favor of the company. The government repeatedly revealed names of whistleblowers to employers, and the whistleblowers soon found themselves unemployed: Joseph Kinney, *Safer Work* (Chicago: National Safe Workplace Institute, 1988).

35. *New York Times,* May 18, 1977, and July 12 and August 8, 1978.

crime. Note that such secrecy and coverup does not inhere in the bureaucratic process as such, but is imposed by White House officials. Politics, not bureaucracy, is in command.

BUREAUCRATIC ACTION AND INACTION

Many of the rulings of bureaucratic agencies, published daily in the Federal Register, are as significant as major pieces of legislation, and in the absence of precise guidelines from Congress, they often take the place of legislation. Thus, without a word of public debate, the Price Commission approved more than $2 billion in rate increases for utilities, thereby imposing upon the public an expenditure far greater than what is contained in most bills passed by Congress. Under a White House directive, the Social Security Administration used "stricter eligibility" rules to deprive 265,000 disabled persons of public assistance. By administrative fiat, the Reagan administration shifted most Federal Emergency Management Agency funds— intended by Congress for natural disaster relief—to secret military programs. Likewise, the Bush administration shifted over $450 billion in Social Security funds to help cover the deficit and reclassified the multibillion-dollar savings-and-loan bailouts as "off-budget."[36]

The political process does not end with the passage of a bill but continues at the administrative level, albeit in more covert fashion, influencing how a law is administered. In the 1980s and early 1990s, the Environmental Protection Agency failed to enforce a program devised by Congress to ensure safe disposal of hazardous wastes. Enforcement of environmental laws was so spotty that half the nation's wetlands have been lost. (Wetlands are valued as wildlife habitats and for their role in flood control.) The Office of Surface Mining (OSM) allowed widespread mining without environmental controls, resulting in thousands of miles of landslides and polluted streams. More than half the mine owners who were directed to halt illegal operations ignored the order. Some $200 million in fines imposed on the owners went uncollected. The Occupational Safety and Health Administration dropped its policy of surprise visits to work sites and began relying on the safety records kept by the companies themselves. The Consumer Product Safety Commission cut its staff in half and adopted a voluntary compliance program that allows companies to come up with their own safety remedies.[37]

---

36. *New York Times*, February 9 and April 7 and 21, 1983; January 31, 1990; Associated Press report, February 22, 1993.

37. For these and other instances of nonenforcement, see *Washington Post*, January 26 and May 8, 1983; January 17, 1987; October 2, 1988; January 3, 1990. The Clinton administration has done little to bolster regulatory efforts on behalf of workers and consumers.

The list goes on. The White House withheld millions of dollars in congressionally approved aid to abused children and chronically ill elderly.[38] The Internal Revenue Service was so lax regulating the railroad workers retirement system that railroad owners underpaid the pension fund by about $73 million in three years.[39] There has been lax enforcement or nonenforcement of consumer protection laws, civil rights, collective bargaining rights, and protection of public lands and parks.[40] Without public debate or the reversal of any law, President Reagan ordered most regulations to be judged by the costs imposed on business, irrespective of whether they protected us against illness or injury.[41] In sum, most nonenforcement is not the result of bureaucratic inertia but political intent, arising from the hostility of policymakers toward those government regulations that interfere with the maximization of profits.

Often, agencies are not sufficiently staffed to handle the enormous tasks that confront them. The federal government has twenty-five inspectors to monitor the transportation of hazardous wastes over the entire country. The EPA staff can monitor but a fraction of the 1,000 new potentially toxic chemicals that industry pours into the environment each year. Representatives of a farm-workers union complained that enforcement of existing laws, not enactment of new ones, was needed to alleviate the housing and safety problems faced by farm workers.[42]

While some laws go unenforced, others are so transformed during implementation as to subvert their intent. We have already noted how this was done to the Freedom of Information Act. A few more examples might suffice: (1) a House subcommittee charged that the Merit System Protection Board created by Congress to protect whistleblowers had been administered so as to afford even less protection than before, requiring whistleblowers to carry the burden of proof in ways not authorized by statute; (2) the Clean Air Act passed by Congress was gravely weakened by administrative fiat when the EPA decided to relax national smog standards by more than 50 percent; and (3) without changing a word of the federal strip-

---

38. *New York Times*, April 21, 1987.

39. *Washington Post*, August 17, 1990.

40. U.S. House of Representatives, Government Operations Committee, *Mismanagement of the Office of Human Development Services* (Washington, D.C.: Government Printing Office, 1987); *Nation*, June 21, 1993; *Washington Post*, September 26, 1991; *New York Times*, November 22, 1988. The toughest enforcement seems to be delivered upon relatively powerless individuals. Thus a 57-year-old mechanic in Pennsylvania, who deposited clean topsoil on a ragged, weed-covered lot bordering a state highway and a junkyard, was sentenced to three years in prison and $202,000 in fines because the government maintained that the property was wetlands. It was the harshest sentence ever imposed in an environmental case: *Washington Post*, January 3, 1990.

41. Alison Mitchell, "The Silent Shift of Power," *Newsday*, May 4, 1986, p. 7.

42. *Guardian*, September 17, 1980.

mining law, the government systematically weakened it by relaxing regulations and getting rid of conscientious enforcers.

Consider the fate of three consientious public servants. John O'Leary was a director of the Bureau of Mines, who began enforcing safety mine regulations as required by law. The mine companies made known to the White House their strong desire to be rid of the troublesome O'Leary and he was removed from office. His successor, a former CIA employee, re-established cozy relations with the mine owners, making personal appearances at corporate gatherings and riding in company planes.[43]

Then there was Bruce Boyens, an OSM enforcer who pressured coal companies to restore the natural landscape of hills and mountains they had laid bare, and who faced down the threats of coal operators and called in federal marshalls to subdue them. He was transferred to Washington. "OSM called it a salute to his expertise. Boyen, who had no choice, took it as a 'get out' [order]."[44]

Also Gerald Scannell, who as OSHA administrator pursued a more vigorous policy of occupational safety than his predecessors, authorizing larger penalties and fines for violations. For doing so, he was forced out.[45]

In each of these instances, it was not "bureaucratic usurpation" as such that thwarted legislative intent, but the political will of the policymakers on top. In his 1994 State of the Union message, President Clinton boasted of his plan to reduce the federal bureaucracy by almost a quarter of a million employees. One might wonder which bureaucrats he had in mind: the high-paid Pentagon flacks who push for multibillion dollar weapons systems that feed the corporate pot of gold? or administrative workers in the already downsized and demoralized Social Security Administration, who serve the needy elderly and handicapped? The president did not say if he was cutting fat or bone. But it might be noted that while supposedly downsizing the government, he proposed an increase in the military budget from $265 billion to $277 billion.

People who insist that things do not get done because that is the nature of the bureaucratic beast seem to forget that only certain kinds of things do not get done, while other things are accomplished all too well. The law making some thirteen million children eligible for medical examination and treatment, supported by public health advocates and progressives, had the same legal status as the law to develop a multibillion-dollar "Star Wars" outer space weapon system, backed by the White House, giant industrial contractors, research institutes, Pentagon brass, and members of Congress, whose patriotism was matched only by their desire to keep their campaign

---

43. *Christian Science Monitor,* April 8, 1970; *Washington Post,* June 17, 1973.
44. *Washington Post,* June 6, 1982.
45. *People's Weekly World,* January 25, 1992.

coffers filled by appreciative corporate donors. If anything, the Star Wars program was of vastly greater technical and administrative complexity. Yet it moved full steam ahead, while the children's health program moved hardly at all. Several years after the program's inception, almost 85 percent of the youngsters had been left unexamined, causing "unnecessary crippling, retardation, or even death of thousands of children," according to a House subcommittee report.[46]

Again, the important difference between the two programs was not bureaucratic but political. The effectiveness of a law or a bureaucratic program depends on the power of the groups supporting them. Laws that serve powerful clientele are likely to enjoy a vigorous life, while laws that have only the powerless to support them are often stillborn. Those parts of the bureaucracy that service the capitalist class are relatively free from attack and from complaints about bureaucratic meddling. Such administrative units are accountable, not to the citizenry but to the corporate interests they serve.

Red tape, often seen as an inevitable by-product of bureaucracy, may actually be used as a deliberate means of immobilizing programs that incur the disfavor of powerful politico-economic interests. Hostile toward school-lunch programs, the Reagan administration imposed extensive income-verification systems on school districts. The complicated paperwork cost the districts tens of thousands of dollars and threatened to end lunch services in some districts—while turning up very few instances of children getting lunches who were not eligible for them.[47]

The capitalist political economy is the graveyard of reform-minded administrative bodies. An agency like the Office of Economic Opportunity, which tries to represent low-income interests and invites the participation of have-nots in urban programs, runs into powerful opposition and eventually is abolished. An agency set up to regulate industry on behalf of consumers, workers, or the environment may possess a zeal for reform in its youth, but before long the news media either turn their attention to other things or present an unsympathetic picture of the agency's doings. The president, even if originally sympathetic, is now occupied with more pressing matters, as are the agency's few friends in Congress. But the industry that is supposed to be brought under control remains keenly interested and ready to oppose government intrusions. First, it may challenge the agency's jurisdiction or even the legality of its existence in court, thus preventing any regulatory actions until a legal determination is made. If the agency survives this attack, the industry then hits it with a barrage of arguments and

---

46. UPI dispatch, October 8, 1976.
47. The news report on this in the *Washington Post,* December 29, 1983, was headlined: "Bureaucracy Is Upsetting Schoolchildren's Lunch" even though the facts of the story indicated another culprit.

technical information, sufficiently impressive to win the attention of the agency's investigators. The investigators begin to develop a new appreciation of the problems industry faces in maintaining profitable operations.[48]

If the agency persists in making unfavorable rulings, businesspeople appeal to their elected representatives, to a higher administrative official, or, if they have the pull, to the president himself. In its youthful days after World War I, the Federal Trade Commission (FTC) moved vigorously against big business, but representatives of industry prevailed upon the president to replace "some of the commissioners by others more sympathetic with business practices: this resulted in the dismissal of many complaints which had been made against corporations."[49] Some sixty years later, the pattern was to repeat itself. Staffed by consumer advocates, the FTC began vigorous action against questionable practices by insurance companies, funeral-home operators, doctors, and others, only to find itself under fire from Congress and the business community. It was not long before the FTC had its jurisdictional powers abridged and its budget cut.[50]

Frequently, members of Congress demand to know why an agency is bothering their constituents or their campaign contributors. Administrators who do not want unfavorable publicity or a cut in their appropriations are likely to apply the law in ways that satisfy influential legislators.[51] Some administrative bodies, like the Army Corps of Engineers, so successfully cultivate support among powerful members of Congress and their big-business clientele that they become relatively free of supervisory control from department heads or the White House.[52]

---

48. For instance, a report by the National Academy of Sciences found that the EPA "is inevitably dependent" on the industries it regulates for much of its information and that such information is easily withheld or distorted to serve industry's ends: *New York Times,* March 22, 1977.

49. Edwin Sutherland, *White Collar Crime* (New York: Holt, Rinehart and Winston, 1949), p. 232.

50. For the full story, see Michael Pertshuk, *Revolt Against Regulation* (Berkeley: University of California Press, 1982). In similar fashion, EPA had its budget cut, drastically reducing its already limited capacity to regulate. The Consumer Product Safety Commission had its staff cut from 975 to 519 in the early 1980s. The commission was then stacked with conservatives who had no background and no interest in product safety: *Washington Post,* February 2, 1989.

51. E. Pendelton Herring, "The Balance of Social Forces in the Food and Drug Law," *Social Forces,* 13, March 1935, p. 364. With a limited budget of only $2 million in 1949, the Food and Drug Administration proceeded against thousands of violators. Today, with a budget a hundred times larger, FDA rarely takes action against major food or drug companies. It has learned discretion. The result is that the pharmaceutical industry is an unregulated monopoly. Each company has a monopoly on most of the drugs it markets and can charge whatever price it likes. So Americans spend $67 billion yearly on prescription drugs: *New York Times,* January 16, 1993.

52. It was discovered that the Army Corps of Engineers was illegally overseeing more than three hundred oil and gas leases. It had failed to collect most of the royalties on these leases

Given a desire to survive and advance, bureaucrats tend to equivocate in the face of controversial decisions, moving away from dangerous areas and toward positions favored by the strongest pressure groups. With time, the reform-minded agency loses its crusading spirit and settles down to serving the needs of the industry it is supposed to regulate. The more public-spirited staff members either grow weary of the struggle and make their peace with the corporations or depart, to be replaced by personnel who are acceptable to, if not indeed the nominees of, the industry.[53]

Many career administrators eventually leave government service to accept higher-paying jobs in companies whose interests they favored while in office. This promise of a lucrative post with a private firm can exercise a considerable influence on the judgments of an ambitious administrator. During the 1970s, a total of 343 Pentagon officers and civilians and seventeen high officials of the military-oriented space agency left their government jobs to become Northrop executives—while seventeen top Northrop people went to restock these military agencies.[54]

Among the few things working in favor of public interest regulations are public-interest groups. Most enforcement cases against powerful corporate polluters, for instance, are initiated by environmental and local citizens groups. The Environmental Protection Agency rarely initiates action and usually opposes tough environmental laws, expending more effort attempting to remove companies from regulation than getting them to abide by the law. Environmental groups sue to make EPA do what the law already requires it to do. EPA uses taxpayers' money in such cases to protect its right not to do what the taxpayers want it to do. It often takes years of struggle before EPA will act.[55]

SERVING THE "REGULATED"

There are regulatory agencies that are under the command of various executive departments, such as the Occupational Safety and Health Administration (Labor Department) and the Drug Enforcement Administration (Justice Department). And there are independent regulatory commissions, such as the Federal Communications Commission, Federal Trade Commission, and Interstate Commerce Commission, that operate just outside the

---

and could not account for the sums that had been collected: *Washington Post,* March 27, 1987.

53. Grant McConnell, *Private Power and American Democracy,* p. 288.

54. Victor Perlo, "What is the Military-Industrial Complex," *Political Affairs,* June 1983, p. 30.

55. William Sanjour, "Why EPA Is Like It Is," *Everyone's Backyard,* February 1991, pp. 18–19.

executive branch, making quasi-judicial rulings that can only be appealed to the courts. They report directly to Congress but their personnel are appointed by the president, with Senate confirmation. For reasons just discussed, both these kinds of agencies frequently become protectors of the industries they are supposed to regulate, granting monopoly privileges to big companies that cost the public billions a year. So, the Interstate Commerce Commission continues its long devotion to the railroad companies; the Federal Communications Commission serves the telephone companies and the media networks; the Federal Elections Commission safeguards the two-party monopoly; the Food and Drug Administration devotes more energy to protecting the profits of the food and drug companies than the health of people; the Securities and Exchange Commission regulates the stock market mostly for the benefit of large investors; the Federal Energy Regulatory Commission maintains a permissive policy toward energy producers.

So with other units of government: the Department of Transportation defers to the oil-highway-automotive combine; the Agriculture Department promotes giant agribusiness; the Army Corps of Engineers and the Bureau of Reclamations continue to mutilate the natural environment on behalf of utilities, agribusiness, and land developers; the Department of Interior serves the oil, gas, mining, and timber companies; and above all, the Pentagon supports the defense industry with hundreds of billions of dollars yearly.

Congressional oversight of the hundreds of government agencies is scant and sporadic, a Senate report concluded, largely because members of Congress fear reprisals from powerful economic interests that are regulated. This "iron triangle" of bureaucratic unit, congressional committee, and corporate interest gets its way on most things.[56]

The political appointees who preside over the various administrative units of government are usually so tightly bound to private interests that it is often difficult to tell the regulators from the regulated. As noted earlier, many of them are persons who previously were employed by the "regulated" industry. Eleven of the top sixteen officials appointed in the 1980s to head the Department of the Interior were linked to the five major industries regulated by the department. Administrators who have supervised such things as water-development, land-use, nuclear-energy, consumer-protection, occupational safety, and food and drug regulations have had a

---

56. Senate Government Operations committee report: *New York Times*, February 10, 1977. Agencies that do not serve powerful interests, but only powerless people, are much more vulnerable to White House control; see Ronald Randall, "Presidential Power versus Bureaucratic Intransigence: The Influence of the Nixon Administration on Welfare Policy," *American Political Science Review*, 73, 1979, pp. 795–810.

history of previously serving as lobbyists, lawyers, and managers for the business firms they were to regulate.[57]

Federal meat-inspection laws have been administered by officials with a history of opposition to meat inspection. Public housing programs have been supervised by businesspeople openly hostile to public housing. Civil rights enforcement has been delegated to individuals who are opponents to civil rights. Conservation and environmental programs have been given over to people who have been openly antagonistic to such programs. Nuclear-weapons plant cleanup has been entrusted to persons with records of notorious permissiveness toward the nuclear industry. Energy programs have been administered by former oil executives who want nothing to do with the development of alternative energy sources. The Arms Control and Disarmament Agency has been dominated by high-placed persons from the military-industrial complex.[58]

Once again, the problem is not in the nature of bureaucracy as such but in the politico-economic use to which bureaucracy is put. It is not that anonymous and unaccountable bureaucrats have usurped power for themselves. A closer look shows that career bureaucrats pretty much do as they are told by their administrative bosses. The professional ethic of most bureaucrats is: remain neutral and wait for the policy line to be set from above. "Bureaucratic failures" are usually better described as successful uses of political power to undermine regulations and laws that prove troublesome to corporate interests. Conservative administrations appoint administrators who do not think government works, at least not in public-service areas. This puts them into conflict with careerists who believe that government can work if made to do so. Careerists who buck the conservative tide may be passed over for promotion, or given negative job evaluations, undesirable transfers, unpleasant tasks, or nothing to do, causing many to leave government service.[59]

It is not enough to bemoan the fact that government agencies end up as captives of interests they are supposed to regulate; rather we should understand how this situation results from the politico-economic realities in which administrators operate. In a capitalist society the special interests are the

57. *New York Times*, December 6, 1991; February 5 and December 8, 1993; *Washington Post*, January 19, 1986; May 26 and November 15, 1989; *Guardian*, March 27, 1985.

58. *Washington Post*, October 17 and November 19, 1989: *In These Times*, August 7–20, 1991, pp. 4–5; Barry Mehler, "Rightist on the Rights Panel," *Nation*, May 7, 1988, pp. 640–641, and October 9, 1989, p. 372; Sidney Lens, "The Doomsday Strategy," *Progressive*, February 1976, p. 28. The chair of the Legal Services Corporation (LSC), a Reagan-appointee, told a House committee that he believed the LSC should not exist because it was an unconstitutional entity: *Washington Post*, August 8, 1989.

59. The U.S. Chamber of Commerce reportedly had a "hit list" of career bureaucrats whom it wanted removed from the EPA and from the Departments of Justice, Labor, and Energy: *Washington Post*, September 6 and 7, 1984.

systemic interest, controlling the economic life of the society. Hence, regulation of the capitalist economy on anything but its own terms eventually does not work, not merely because industrialists employ shrewd lobbyists who can manipulate timid and compliant bureaucrats, but because industry is the economic system and sooner or later government must meet that system on its own terms or change to another. Within the imperatives of the capitalist system, regulation too often becomes a way to rig prices at artificially high levels, control markets for the benefit of large producers, secure high profits, and allow private corporations more direct and unchallengeable access to public authority.

PUBLIC AUTHORITY IN PRIVATE HANDS

The ultimate subservience of public power to private interest comes when government gives, along with its funds and services, its very authority to business in such areas as agriculture, medicine, industry, and trade. Control of federal lands and water has been handed over to local "home-rule" boards dominated by the large ranchers, who thereby successfully transform their economic power into a publicly sanctioned authority.[60] Likewise, "agriculture has become neither public nor private enterprise. It is a system of self-government in which each leading farm interest controls a segment of agriculture through a delegation of national sovereignty," a condition that has prevailed through successive administrations in the White House.[61] The private codes that trade associations develop to govern the specifications of goods produced by their respective industries are frequently written directly into statutes, thus taking on the force of law.[62]

One congressional committee, investigating relations between government and industry, complained of a "virtual abdication of administrative responsibility" on the part of officials in the Department of Commerce, their actions in many instances being "but the automatic approval of decisions already made outside the Government in business and industry."[63] In every significant line of industry, advisory committees staffed by representatives of leading firms work closely with government agencies, making most of the important recommendations. In trying to assess their roles, it is difficult to determine where lies the distinction between advice and

---

60. McConnell, *Private Power and American Democracy*, p. 210.
61. Theodore Lowi, *The End of Liberalism* (New York: W. W. Norton, 1969), pp. 103–104.
62. Jack Walker, "The Origins and Maintenance of Interest Groups in America," *American Political Science Review*, 77, 1983, p. 397.
63. From a congressional report cited in McConnell, *Private Power and American Democracy*, p. 275. On the special public privileges of business, see also Charles Lindblom, *Politics and Markets* (New York: Basic Books, 1977).

policy making. There are several thousand committees and boards that meet regularly with administrative leaders, costing the government many millions a year to finance. The most influential of these deal with banking, chemicals, communications, commercial farming, oil, and utilities. Their reports become the basis for administrative actions and new legislation. With the coercive power of the state backing their decisions, they secure advantages over smaller competitors, workers, and consumers of a kind less easily gained in open competition. The meetings of these business advisory committees are not open to the press or public.

In many state and municipal governments, as in the federal government, business associations—dominated by the biggest firms—are accorded the power to nominate their own personnel to public licensing boards and other administrative bodies. The transfer of public authority to private hands frequently is treated as "voluntaristic" and "decentralized" forms of policymaking. In fact, these measures transfer sovereign authority to favored private producers without their being held democratically accountable. There exists, then, unbeknownst to most Americans, a large number of private decision makers who exercise public authority without having to answer to the public and who determine official policy while remaining primarily obligated to their private businesses. They are what might be called the "public-privateers." Included in this category are the various quasi-public corporations, institutions, foundations, boards, councils, "authorities," and associations, one of the most powerful being the Federal Reserve Board, which controls the nation's interest rates and money supply.

In 1913, at the behest of the major banks, Congress and President Woodrow Wilson created the Federal Reserve System. Its key architect was Nelson Aldrich, father-in-law of John D. Rockefeller Jr. All federally charted banks and many state banks are members of the "Fed," as it is called. The Fed's seven-person board of governors is appointed to staggered fourteen-year terms by the president, who can make only two appointments during his four-year term. Once appointed, the board members in effect answer to no one but the banking industry. The five regional members of its most powerful policy committee are selected not by the president but by bankers from the various regions. The Fed expands the money supply by buying government securities, and contracts it by selling these securities. In effect, the government pays hundreds of billions a year—in interest on the securities—for the Federal Reserve Notes we use as currency.

The Fed operates in total secrecy, refusing to allow Congress or the White House audit its books and refusing to release information to public-interest groups. Congress holds an agency accountable primarily by controlling its appropriations. But the Fed evades this control by drawing its operating funds from the billions it collects (from taxpayers) in interest on government securities. Generally the Fed pursues a conservative, deflationary policy, making it difficult for the president and Congress to prime a sluggish economy. The Fed's autonomy supposedly demonstrates its "independence" from politics. But everything it does has a policy effect, usually favorable to banking and other conservative interests. In sum, the big bankers have public authority to act as nonelected oligarchs, who can manipulate the economy in defiance of the preferred agenda of elected officials.[64]

Numerous "public authorities" at the federal, state, and local levels (such as the Port Authority of New York) carry out a range of activities. They all have several things in common: they are authorized by state legislatures or Congress to function outside the regular structure of government, and because of their autonomous corporate attributes, they are seldom subjected to public scrutiny and accountability. The public authorities of some states have run up debts that total more than twice the state's debt. To meet their obligations, they float new bond issues—none of which are passed upon by voters—and thus make demands on future tax revenues. They are creatures that have the best of both worlds, feeding off the public treasury while remaining accountable only to themselves.

The use of public authority to protect private interests extends overseas. When the Peruvian generals nationalized the holdings of private American oil companies, the president sent a special envoy to protest the move and negotiate for reacquisition. When the Bangladesh government sought to ban the importation of hundreds of useless or harmful drugs from the United States, the State Department sent an official committee (composed of representatives of drug companies) to that country to argue against the ban. Agents of ITT met with the CIA, and the White House to consider ways of preventing a democratically elected socialist from taking office in Chile. The private interests do not merely benefit from public policy; they often make policy by selecting key officials, directing World Bank loans and foreign aid investments, and offering recommendations that are treated as policy guidelines—in sum, using the United States government to pursue their interests abroad.[65]

The corporate interests exert an influence that cuts across particular administrative departments. Within a government fragmented into hundreds of administrative units, they form cohesive and sometimes overlapping blocs around major producer interests like oil, steel, banking, pharmaceu-

---

64. Morton Mintz and Jerry Cohen, *Power, Inc.* (New York: Bantam, 1977), pp. 104–106, 109–117; Bernard Nossiter, "The Myth of an Independent Fed," *Nation,* December 31, 1990, pp. 837–838. In 1963, President John Kennedy issued silver-backed Treasury notes as currency—to begin replacing Federal Reserve Notes. The printing of that currency was stopped shortly after Kennedy was assassinated.

65. On how the World Bank promotes private investment in the Third World, see Cheryl Payer, *The World Bank* (New York: Monthly Review, 1983).

ticals, transportation, and armaments. These blocs are composed of high-level bureaucrats, regulatory commissioners, senior members of Congress, lobbyists, newspaper publishers, members of trade associations, and executives of business firms, operating with all the autonomy and unaccountability of principalities.

MONOPOLY REGULATION VERSUS PUBLIC-SERVICE REGULATION

If government is capitalism's provider and protector at home and abroad, and if government and business are so intermingled as to be often indistinguishable, then why are businesspeople so critical of "government meddling in the economy"? There are a number of explanations. First, as previously noted, businesspeople are not opposed to government regulation as long as it is favorable to them. The railroad owners are quite happy with regulation by the ICC; the media networks do quite well with the FCC; the nuclear industry finds shelter in the NRC; and the oil industry is perfectly at home with the National Petroleum Council.

It is necessary to distinguish between monopoly regulation and public-service regulation. *Monopoly regulation* limits entry into a market, subsidizes select industries, sets production standards that only big companies can meet, weakens smaller competitors, and encourages monopoly pricing. This kind of government regulation has long been the rule in the agribusiness, telecommunications, energy, oil, pharmaceuticals, and some other industries. Virtually this entire regulatory edifice was constructed in response to the needs and demands of the business community. Today, business demands for monopolistic regulation continue unabated even with all the talk about "deregulation."[66]

In contrast, *public-service regulation* is democratically based. It attempts to restrict business conduct and protect public interests. Public-service regulations, such as environmental protections, antitrust laws, and worker-safety and consumer safeguards, are anathema to business. Deregulation in the public-service realm does not make business more productive or even more competitive; if anything it removes a set of competing interests—those of the public—and simply leaves business freer to pursue profits without incurring any obligation for the social costs of that pursuit. Deregulation has given the mining companies a free hand to strip-mine and

---

66. Berry and Lowery, *Understanding United States Government Growth;* Susan Tolchin and Martin Tolchin, *Dismantling America: The Rush to Deregulate* (New York: Houghton Mifflin, 1983); Thomas McGraw (ed.), *Regulation in Perspective: Historical Essays* (Cambridge, Mass.: Harvard University Press, 1981).

devastate the landscape without having to pay any restoration costs. Dereg-ulation now allows corporate executives to pad their paychecks with fringe benefits and perquisites without having to tell stockholders or tax collectors, an arrangement that one business journalist called "a license to steal."[67] Deregulation has enabled banks to increase customer-service fees at a time when their own computerized customer-service costs have declined. As one Congressional representative observed: "It is not the customers who are clamoring for more deregulation, it is the bankers."[68]

Business is not really committed to some abstract "free-market" prin-ciple. Regulations that enhance profits are supported and those that cut into profits are denounced. It is only in the latter case that the cry for de-regulation is heard throughout the nation's boardrooms. Business is con-cerned that public-service regulations might mobilize new constituencies, or redistribute income downward instead of upward, or increase the not-for-profit public sector of the economy. From the earliest days of the Re-public to today, the owning class has feared that government might become unduly responsive to popular sentiment, arousing mass expectations and eventually succumbing to demands that could seriously challenge the ex-isting distribution of class power and wealth.

To be sure, business is not without its interior divisions. Policies fre-quently benefit the wealthier firms at the expense of smaller ones. The howls of pain emanating from these weaker competitors are more likely to be heard than the quiet satisfaction of the giant victors. Small businesses usually have good cause to complain of government meddling, since most regulations are written to suit the corporate giants and are often excessively burden-some for the smaller enterprise. Government agencies more vigorously pursue their enforcement efforts against small companies because—unlike the big firms—they have less influence in Congress and can less afford to defend themselves in drawn-out litigation.[69]

Finally, I would suggest that much of the verbal opposition to govern-ment is a manifestation of the businessperson's adherence to the business ideology, the belief in the virtues of rugged individualism and private com-petition. That individuals might violate this creed in their own corporate affairs does not mean their devotion to it is consciously hypocritical. One should not underestimate the human capacity to indulge in selective per-

---

67. Jerry Knight in the *Washington Post*, September 26, 1983; see also Mark Green and Norman Waitzman, *Business War on the Law* (Washington, D.C.: Public Citizen, 1980).

68. Rep. Fernand St. Germain, chair of the House Banking Committee, quoted in *Washington Post*, April 12, 1984. On the deregulation of the airline industry, see John Nance, *Blind Trust* (New York: William Morrow, 1984). A Roper poll found that people who say government overregulates are consistently outnumbered by those who say it is not doing enough for consumer and environmental protection: *Washington Post*, November 10, 1981.

69. *New York Times*, July 2, 1977.

ceptions and rationales. These rationales are no less sincerely felt because they are self-serving. Quite the contrary, it is a creed's congruity with a favorable self-image and self-interest that makes it so compelling. Many businesspeople, including those who have benefited in almost every way from government contracts, subsidies, and tax laws, believe the advantages they enjoy are the result of their own self-reliance, efforts, and talents in a highly competitive "private" market. They believe that the assistance business gets from the government benefits the national economy, while the assistance others get is a handout to parasites.

What is needed is not an endless proliferation of regulatory units but a change in the conditions that demand so much regulation—that is, a different method of ownership and a different purpose for production. What is needed is a mobilization of public awareness and democratic force that will place people before profits, and redirect government authority to the service of public needs.

16

The Supremely
Political Court

Article III, Section I of the U.S. Constitution reads: "The judicial Power of the United States shall be vested in one supreme Court, and in such inferior Courts as the Congress may from time to time ordain and establish." The Supreme Court justices and all other federal judges are nominated by the president and subject to confirmation by the Senate. Federal judges have life tenure and can be removed from office only for misconduct and only through impeachment by the Senate.[1]

All three branches of government are sworn to uphold the Constitution, but the Supreme Court alone reviews the constitutionality of actions by the other two branches, at least in those cases brought before it. Nothing in the Constitution gives the Court this power of *judicial review,* but the proceedings of the Constitutional Convention of 1787 reveal that many delegates expected the judiciary to overturn laws it deemed inconsistent with the Constitution.[2] Of even greater significance is the Court's power of *judicial interpretation* to decide the intent and scope of laws as they are applied in actual situations. Our main concern here is with trying to understand the political role the Court has played in the struggle for and against democracy.

WHO JUDGES?

Some Americans think of the Constitution as a vital force, having an animation of its own. At the same time they expect Supreme Court justices to

---

1. The size of the Supreme Court is determined by statute, fluctuating over the years from six to ten members, and being fixed at nine since 1877.

2. Max Farrand, *The Framing of the Constitution of the United States* (New Haven, Conn.: Yale University Press, 1913), pp. 156–157. See Chief Justice John Marshall's argument for judicial review in the landmark case of *Marbury* v. *Madison* (1803).

be above the normal prejudices of other persons. Thus, they envision "a living Constitution" and an insentient Court. But a moment's reflection should remind us that it is the other way around. If the Constitution is, as they say, an "elastic instrument," then much of the stretching has been done by the nine persons on the Court, and the directions in which they pull are largely determined by their own ideological predilections. As Chief Justice Hughes pointedly remarked, "We are under a Constitution but the Constitution is what the judges say it is."[3]

By its nature, the Supreme Court is something of an aristocratic branch: its members are appointed rather than elected; they enjoy life tenure and are formally accountable to no one once in office; and they have the final word on constitutional matters. As intended by the framers, the Court's mandate is to act as a check on the democratic majority and as a protector of private contract, credit, and property. Generally speaking, in class background and political proclivity, the justices have more commonly identified with the landed interests than with the landless, the slave owners rather than the slaves, the industrialists rather than the workers, the exponents of Herbert Spencer rather than of Karl Marx. Over a century ago Justice Miller, a Lincoln appointee to the Court, made note of the judiciary's class biases: "It is vain to contend with judges who have been at the bar, the advocates for forty years of railroad companies, and all the forms of associated capital . . . All their training, all their feelings are from the start in favor of those who need no such influence."[4]

Through most of its history "the Court's personnel were recruited mainly from the class of corporate lawyers, so there was no shortage of empathy with the desires of expanding capitalism."[5] The process of legal education and professional training makes it unlikely that dissidents will be picked for the bench—and very few have been. The bar associations and law schools, and the foundations that finance the law journals, endowed chairs, and research grants in jurisprudence, are dedicated to fortifying not modifying the existing system of ownership and wealth. One study finds that the American Bar Association's quasi-official Federal Judiciary Committee, whose task is to pass on the qualifications of prospective judges at

---

3. Dexter Perkins, *Charles Evans Hughes* (Boston: Little, Brown, 1956), p. 16.

4. Quoted in Felix Frankfurter, *Mr. Justice Holmes and the Supreme Court* (New York: Atheneum, 1965), p. 54. Various justices, including Chief Justice Marshall, were slaveholders. They repeatedly protected the primacy of property rights in slaves, rejecting all slave petitions for freedom. In *Dred Scott* v. *Sandford* (1857), the Court concluded that, be they slave or free, Blacks were a "subordinate and inferior class of beings" without constitutional rights and that Congress had no power to exclude slaveholders and their chattel from the territories.

5. Russell Galloway, *The Rich and the Poor in Supreme Court History, 1790–1982* (Greenbrae, Calif.: Paradigm Press, 1982), pp. 163, and 180–181.

all federal levels, favors those whose orientation is conservative and supportive of corporate interests.[6] Generally, the acceptable range of politico-economic opinion for Supreme Court justices has been from ultraconservative to mainstream liberal. In most cases relating to major economic issues, there are well-articulated rationales supporting either a conservative or liberal viewpoint. How a justice or any other federal judge decides has less to do with objective inquiry than with his or her ideological preference. Both conservative and liberal ideologies, of course, accept the existing economic system as an unchallengeable given.

Occasionally a president will select someone for the Court whose behavior goes contrary to his expectations, but generally presidents have been successful in matching court appointments with their own ideological preferences. President Reagan was second to none in this endeavor, stocking more than half of the 744 federal judgeships with ideologically committed conservatives, mostly in their thirties and forties, who will be handing down decisions and shaping the law of the land into the second and third decades of the next century. As compared to his predecessor, Jimmy Carter, Reagan appointed very few Blacks, Latinos, or women. He also picked many more upper-class persons: 81 percent of his appointees had incomes of over $200,000 and 23 percent admitted to being millionaires.[7]

Reagan's successor, George Bush, appointed an additional 195 federal judges, usually youngish conservatives, including Clarence Thomas, a 43-year-old undistinguished archconservative to replace the great Thurgood

---

6. Joel Grossman, *Lawyers and Judges: The ABA and the Politics of Judicial Selection* (New York: Wiley, 1965). Whether appointed by Democratic or Republican presidents, judges are drawn preponderantly from highly privileged backgrounds: Sheldon Goldman, "Johnson and Nixon Appointees to the Lower Federal Courts: Some Socio-Political Perspectives," *Journal of Politics*, 34, August 1972, pp. 934–942.

7. Herman Schwartz, *Packing the Courts* (New York: Charles Scribner's Sons, 1988); Sheldon Goldman, "Reaganizing the Judiciary," *Judicature*, 68, April–May 1985, pp. 313–329. For some candidates, a conservative ideology seemed to have been the only qualification. Thus, the extremely conservative Daniel Manion, age forty-four, appointed to a lifetime position as federal appellate judge, was declared completely unqualified and lacking in a commitment to the Constitution by the deans of more than forty law schools: *New York Times*, July 25, 1986. For federal district court, Reagan picked an admitted admirer of the Ku Klux Klan, Jefferson Beauregard Sessions III. But the Senate refused to confirm him. In 1986 Reagan picked Justice William Rehnquist, the most conservative member of the Court, to be chief justice. During his confirmation hearings, Rehnquist was confronted with a segregationist memorandum he wrote as a law clerk. He claimed it was the opinion of the late Justice Robert Jackson (who had opposed segregation). Rehnquist was unable to refute eyewitness testimony that he harassed Black and Hispanic voters in Phoenix in the 1960s. Nor did he explain why he signed an anti-Semitic covenant for one of his homes. In 1972, he cast the deciding vote in *Laird* v. *Tatum* to dismiss a probe of Army intelligence—even though he had been directly involved in the case while serving in the Nixon administration. Thus, he protected himself from damage claims. Questioned about this violation of judicial ethics, he said he could not remember: *New York Times*, September 11 and 17, 1986.

"I'm happy to say that my final judgment of a case is almost always consistent with my prejudgment of the case."

Marshall on the Supreme Court. When Bill Clinton, a Democrat, became president, he had the opportunity to appoint more than one hundred vacancies and introduce some ideological diversity in the courts. As of February 1994, he had yet to fill most of these vacancies and seemed not likely to leave a strong liberal impress on the judiciary. His one Supreme Court appointee in 1993, Ruth Bader Ginsburg, when serving on a lower federal court, had voted more often with the conservatives than the liberals and continued to do so once on the Supreme Court.

CONSERVATIVE JUDICIAL ACTIVISM

It is said that the devil himself can quote the Bible for his own purposes. The Constitution is not unlike the Bible in this respect, and over the generations, Supreme Court justices have shown an infernal agility in finding constitutional justifications for the continuation of almost every inequity and iniquity, be it slavery or segregation, child labor or the sixteen-hour workday, state sedition laws or assaults on the First Amendment.

In its early days under Chief Justice John Marshall, the Court emerged as a guardian of property, declaring that a corporation was to be considered a "person" entitled to all the rights accorded persons under the Constitution.[8] The Marshall Court supported the supremacy of federal powers over the states. In *McCulloch* v. *Maryland* (1819) the Court forbade Maryland from taxing a federal bank and affirmed Congress's right to create a bank (a power not mentioned in the Constitution). Marshall argued that Article 1, Section 8, gave Congress the right "to make all laws necessary and proper" for carrying out its delegated powers. So was the groundwork laid for the expansion of federal power and the protection of corporate interests by conservative judicial activists like Marshall.

Much of the debate about the Supreme Court today centers on whether (a) the Bench should act "politically" and "ideologically" by exercising a liberal "judicial activism," vigorously supporting individual rights and social needs, or (b) employ a conservative "judicial restraint" by deferring to the other two branches of government and cleaving close to the traditional intent of the Constitution.[9] In practice, however, conservative justices are just as ideologically activist as liberal ones—if not more so. Only during a relatively few periods—most notably the 1960s—did the High Court become an active supporter of individual rights and economic reform on behalf of the poor. Through most of its history the Court has engaged in a *conservative* judicial activism in defense of wealthy and propertied interests.

Whether the Court judged the government to be improperly interfering with the economy depended on which social class benefited. When the federal government wanted to establish national banks, or give away half the country to private speculators, or subsidize industries, or set up commissions that fixed prices and interest rates for manufacturers and banks, or send Marines to secure corporate investments in Central America, or imprison people who spoke out against war and capitalism, or deport immigrant radicals without a trial, or use the United States Army to shoot workers and break strikes, the Court inventively found constitutional pegs that made such actions acceptable.

But if the federal or state governments sought to limit workday hours, set minimum wage or occupational safety standards, ensure the safety of

---

8. *Trustees of Dartmouth College* v. *Woodward* (1819). Here Marshall described the corporation as "an artificial being, invisible, intangible, and existing only in the contemplation of law"—but still a "person."

9. For example, see Justice William Brennan, "The Constitution of the United States," text of an address at Georgetown University, Washington, D.C., October 12, 1985 and Raoul Berger's response *Washington Post*, October 28, 1985; and the editorial in *Washington Post*, September 14, 1990.

consumer products, guarantee the right of collective bargaining, or in other ways offer protections against the powers of business, then the Court ruled that ours was a limited form of government that could not tamper with property rights and the "free market" by depriving owner and worker of "substantive due process" and "freedom of contract"—concepts elevated to supreme status even though the limitations claimed on their behalf exist nowhere in the Constitution.[10]

When Congress outlawed child labor, the Court's conservative majority found it to be an unconstitutional usurpation of the reserved powers of the states under the Tenth Amendment.[11] But when the states passed social-welfare legislation, the Court found it in violation of "substantive due process" under the Fourteenth Amendment.[12] Thus the justices used the Tenth Amendment to stop federal reforms initiated under the Fourteenth Amendment, and the Fourteenth to stop state reforms initiated under the Tenth. Juridically speaking, it's hard to get more inventive and activist than that.

The Fourteenth Amendment, adopted in 1868 ostensibly to establish full citizenship for Blacks, says, "No State shall make or enforce any law which shall abridge the privileges or immunities of citizens of the United States; nor shall any State deprive any person of life, liberty, or property, without due process of law; nor deny to any person within its jurisdiction the equal protection of the laws." Once again the Court decided that "person" included corporations and that the Fourteenth Amendment was intended to protect business conglomerations from the "vexatious regulations" of the states.

The Court's conservative majority handed down a series of decisions in the latter half of the nineteenth century and the early twentieth, most notably *Plessy* v. *Ferguson* (1896), which gave an inventive reading to the Fourteenth Amendment's equal protection clause. The *Plessy* decision enunciated the "separate but equal" doctrine, which said that the forced separation of Blacks from Whites in public facilities did not impute inferiority as long as facilities were more or less equal (which they rarely were). The doctrine gave constitutional legitimation to the racist practice of segregation.

Convinced that they too were persons despite the treatment accorded them by a male-dominated society, women began to argue that the Four-

---

10. "Substantive due process" was a judicial invention that allowed the Court to declare laws unconstitutional because they interfered with the liberty of corporations and individuals to wield their economic power as they saw fit. On this and the sanctity of contract, see *Allegeyer* v. *Louisiana* (1897), *Lochner* v. *New York* (1905), *Adair* v. *United States* (1908).

11. *Hammer* v. *Dagenhart* (1918). The Tenth Amendment reads: "The Powers not delegated to the United States by this Constitution, nor prohibited by it to the states, are reserved to the States respectively or to the people." See also *Carter* v. *Carter Coal Co.* (1936).

12. *Morehead* v. *New York* (1936).

teenth and Fifth Amendments applied to them and that the voting restrictions imposed on them by state and federal governments should be abolished. A test case reached the Supreme Court in 1875, and the justices unanimously decided that women were citizens but citizenship did not necessarily confer the right of suffrage.[13] The Court seemingly had made up its mind that "privileges and immunities of citizens," "due process," and "equal protection of the laws" applied to such "persons" as business corporations but not to women and persons of African descent.

Well into the New Deal era, the Supreme Court was the activist bastion of laissez-faire capitalism, striking down—often by slim five-to-four majorities—reforms produced by the state legislatures and Congress. The Great Depression of the 1930s made clear to many liberal policymakers that the federal government needed to revive a stagnant economy and initiate some modest measure of social justice. Justice Brandeis expressed this position clearly: "There will come a revolt of the people against the capitalists, unless the aspirations of the people are given some adequate legal expression. . . . we shall inevitably be swept farther toward socialism unless we can curb the excesses of our financial magnates."[14] From 1937 onward, under pressure from the public and the White House, and with the switch of one conservative justice to the side of the liberals, the Supreme Court began to accept the constitutionality of New Deal legislation.

CIRCUMVENTING THE FIRST AMENDMENT

While opposing restrictions on capitalist economic power, the Court supported restrictions on the civil liberties of persons who agitated against that power. The First Amendment says, "Congress shall make no law . . . abridging the freedom of speech, or of the press."[15] Yet, ever since the Alien and Sedition Acts of 1798, Congress and the state legislatures have passed numerous laws to penalize the expression of politically heretical ideas as "subversive" or "seditious." During the First World War almost two thousand prosecutions were carried out, mostly against anticapitalists who expressed

---

13. *Minor* v. *Happersett* (1875). The Fifth Amendment says, among other things, that no person shall be denied "due process of law." It applies to the federal government as the Fourteenth Amendment applies to the states. The Supreme Court also declared that women had no right to practice law: *Bradwell* v. *State* (1872).

14. Louis D. Brandeis, *Business: A Profession* (Boston: Small, Maynard, 1933), p. 330.

15. Proponents of free speech allow that libel and slander might be restricted by law, although even defamatory speech—when directed against public figures—has been treated as protected under the First Amendment: *New York Times Co.* v. *Sullivan* (1964) and *Time Inc.* v. *Hill* (1967).

opposition to the war, including the U.S. socialist leader Eugene Victor Debs.[16]

The High Court's attitude toward the First Amendment was best expressed by Justice Oliver Wendell Holmes in the famous case of *Schenck v. United States* (1919). Schenck was charged with attempting to cause insubordination among United States military forces and obstructing recruitment, both violations of the Espionage Act of 1917. Actually, he had distributed a leaflet that urged repeal of the draft and condemned the war as a wrong perpetrated by Wall Street. In ordinary times, Holmes reasoned, such speech is protected by the First Amendment, but when a nation is at war, statements like Schenck's create "a clear and present danger" of bringing about "evils that Congress has a right to prevent." Free speech, Holmes argued, "does not protect a man in falsely shouting fire in a crowded theater and causing a panic." The analogy is farfetched: Schenck was not in a theater but was seeking a forum to voice his opposition to policies that the Court treated as beyond challenge. Holmes was summoning the same argument paraded by every ruler who has sought to abrogate a people's freedom: these are not normal times; there is a grave menace within or just outside our gates; national security necessitates a suspension of democratic rights.[17]

More than once the Court treated the allegedly pernicious quality of a radical idea as certain evidence of its lethal efficacy and as justification for its suppression. When the top leadership of the Communist Party was convicted in 1951 under the Smith Act, which made it a felony to teach or advocate the violent overthrow of the government, the Court upheld the act and the convictions, arguing in *Dennis et al* v. *United States* that there was no freedom under the Constitution for those who conspired to propagate revolutionary movements. Free speech was not an absolute value but one of many competing ones. Justices Black and Douglas dissented, arguing that the defendants had not been charged with any acts or even with saying anything about violent revolution, but were intending to publish the classic writings of Marx, Engels, and Lenin. In any case, the First Amendment was designed to protect the very heretical views we might find offensive and fearsome. Safely orthodox ideas rarely needed constitutional protection.

---

16. One individual, who in private conversation in a relative's home opined that it was a rich man's war, was fined $5,000 and sentenced to twenty years in prison: Hearings before a Subcommittee of the Senate Judiciary Committee, *Amnesty and Pardon for Political Prisoners* (Washington, D.C.: Government Printing Office, 1927), p. 54. See also Charles Goodell, *Political Prisoners in America* (New York: Random House, 1973) and the more recent incidents in chapter 9 of this book.

17. Holmes made a similar argument in *Debs* v. *United States* (1919). Yet he was considered one of the more liberal justices of his day because in subsequent cases he placed himself against the Court's majority and on the side of the First Amendment: *Abrams* v. *United States* (1919), *Gitlow* v. *New York* (1925); also Richard Polenberg, *Fighting Faiths, The Abrams Case, the Supreme Court and Free Speech* (New York: Viking, 1987).

Six years later, fourteen more communist leaders were convicted under the Smith Act. This time, however, some of the hysteria of the McCarthy era had subsided and the Court's political make-up had shifted. So the justices virtually reversed themselves, ruling that the Smith Act prohibited only incitement to unlawful actions and not "advocacy of abstract doctrine." The convictions were overthrown. Justice Black added the opinion that the Smith Act itself should be declared unconstitutional because "the First Amendment forbids Congress to punish people for talking about public affairs, whether or not such discussion incites to action, legal or illegal."[18]

Freedom for Revolutionaries?

Opposed to Black's view are those who argue that revolutionaries violate the democratic rules of the game and should not be allowed "to take advantage of the very liberties they seek to destroy"; in order to preserve our freedom, we may find it necessary to deprive some people of theirs.[19] Several rejoinders might be offered.

First, as a point of historical fact, the threat of revolution in the United States has never been as real or harmful to our liberties as the measures taken to "protect" us from revolutionary ideas. History repeatedly demonstrates the expansive quality of repression. In the name of national security, revolutionary advocacy is suppressed, then "inciting" words, then unpopular doctrines, then "irresponsible" news reports, then any kind of criticism that those in power find intolerable. Americans were never "given" their freedoms; they had to organize, agitate, and struggle fiercely for whatever rights they won. As with our bodily health, so with the health of our body politic: we best preserve our faculties and liberties against decay by vigorously exercising them.

Second, the suppression is conducted by political elites who, in protecting us from "harmful" thoughts, are in effect making up our minds for us by depriving us of the opportunity of hearing and debating ideas with revolutionary advocates. An exchange is forbidden because the advocate has been silenced—which in effect silences us too.

Third, it is not true that anticapitalists are dedicated to the destruction of freedom. Much of the ferment in United States history instigated by socialists, anarchists, and communists actually augmented our democratic rights. The working-class agitations of the early nineteenth century wid-

---

18. *Yates et al.* v. *United States* (1957). Congress repealed the Smith Act in 1977.

19. For samples of this thinking, see the Vinson and Jackson opinions in the *Dennis* case; and Carl Auerbach, "The Communist Control Act of 1954," in Samuel Hendel (ed.), *Basic Issues of American Democracy*, 8th ed. (Englewood Cliffs, N.J.: Prentice-Hall, 1976), pp. 59–63.

ened the areas of dissent and helped extend the franchise to propertyless working people. The organized demonstrations against repressive local ordinances in the early twentieth century by the revolutionary-minded Industrial Workers of the World (the "Wobblies' free-speech fights") fortified the First Amendment against attacks by the guardians of wealth. The crucial role communists played in organizing industrial unions in the 1930s and struggling for social reforms, peace, and civil rights strengthened rather than undermined democratic forces. The antiwar protests against the Vietnam War challenged an immoral, illegal military action and tried to broaden the spectrum of critical opinion and information regarding U.S. foreign policy. It also inadvertently led to the enfranchisement of eighteen-year olds.

Fourth, progressive critics would argue that instead of worrying about some future menace, we should realize that freedom is in short supply in the present society. The construction of new socioeconomic alternatives would bring an increase in freedom, including freedom from poverty and hunger, freedom to share in the making of decisions that govern one's work and community, and freedom to experiment with new forms of production and ownership. Admittedly some freedoms enjoyed today would be lost in a revolutionary society, such as the freedom to exploit other people and get rich from their labor, the freedom to squander natural resources and treat the environment as a septic tank, the freedom to monopolize information and exercise unaccountable power.

In many countries, social revolutionary movements brought a net increase in the freedom of individuals, revolutionaries argue, by advancing the conditions necessary for health and human life; by providing jobs for the unemployed and education for the illiterate; by using economic resources for social development rather than corporate profit; and by overthrowing reactionary semifeudal regimes, ending foreign exploitation, and involving large sectors of the populace in the task of economic reconstruction. Revolutions can extend a number of real freedoms without destroying those that never existed for the people of those countries.

The argument can be debated, but not if it is suppressed. In any case, the real danger to freedom in the United States is from the undemocratic control exercised by those in government, the media, academia, business, and other institutions who would insulate us from "unacceptable" viewpoints. No idea is as dangerous as the force that would seek to repress it.

AS THE COURT TURNS

The Supreme Court's record in the area of personal liberties, while gravely wanting, is not totally devoid of merit. Over the years the Court has extended portions of the Bill of Rights to cover not only the federal government but state government (via the Fourteenth Amendment). Attempts by the states to censor publications, deny individuals the right to peaceful assembly, and weaken the separation between church and state were overturned.[20]

The direction the Supreme Court takes depends (a) on the pressures exerted by various advocacy groups and the political climate of the times, and (b) the political composition of the Court's majority. In the 1960s, fortified by the social activism of the wider society and a liberal majority of justices, the Court under Chief Justice Earl Warren took a liberal activist role. It ruled that a poor person had the right to counsel in state criminal trials and an arrested person had the right to a lawyer at the onset of police interrogation.[21] The Warren Court decided that malapportioned state legislative districts had to be redrawn in accordance with population distribution, so that voters in the overpopulated districts were not denied equal protection under the law.[22]

The Warren Court also handed down a number of landmark decisions aimed at abolishing racial segregation. The most widely celebrated, *Brown v. Board of Education* (1954), unanimously ruled that "separate educational facilities are inherently unequal" because of the inescapable imputation of inferiority cast upon the segregated minority group, made all the worse when sanctioned by law. This decision overruled the "separate but equal" doctrine enunciated in 1896 in the *Plessy* case.[23]

The law has always treated public assistance for the poor and the disabled as "privileges" which could be cut off at will. The Warren Court rejected the distinction between "rights" and "privileges" and held that persons who qualified for benefits had a protected "property" interest that could not be taken away without due process of law. "For the first time in the nation's history, the Court majority began to exercise initiative on behalf of the poor."[24]

While opening up new opportunities for democratic gains in civil liberties, civil rights, and protections for the poor, the Warren Court did not stray very far from the basic capitalist ideology shared by both liberal and conservative jurists, to wit: (a) firms may invest or disinvest at will and move elsewhere regardless of the hardship wreaked upon the surrounding commu-

---

20. See *Near* v. *Minnesota* (1931), *Dejonge* v. *Oregon* (1937), *McCollum* v. *Board of Education* (1948).

21. See *Gideon* v. *Wainwright* (1963); *Escobedo* v. *Illinois* (1964) and *Miranda* v. *Arizona* (1966).

22. In some states less than a third of the population elected more than half the legislators: *Baker* v. *Carr* (1962) and *Reynolds* v. *Sims* (1964). A similar decision was made in regard to congressional districts in *Wesberry* v. *Sanders* (1964).

23. See also the decision nullifying state prohibitions against interracial marriage: *Loving* v. *Virginia* (1967). Loving was the plaintiff's name.

24. Galloway, *The Rich and The Poor*, p. 163; *King* v. *Smith* (1968); *Sniadich* v. *Family Finance Corporation* (1969); *Shapiro* v. *Thompson* (1969); *Hunter* v. *Erickson* (1969).

nity and work force; (b) workers have no legal say in the direction of their company or the products of their labor—they must obey employer directives, even ones that violate the labor contract, pending completion of an often inadequate grievance process; and (c) most forms of worker self-protection, including wildcat strikes (work-stoppages that occur during the terms of a contract) and secondary boycotts are outlawed or heavily restricted.[25]

Packed with Nixon, Ford, Reagan, and Bush appointees, the Court has taken a decidedly rightward turn on a variety of crucial issues over the last two decades:[26]

Labor and business. In decisions involving disputes between workers and owners, the Burger and Rehnquist Courts almost always have sided with the owners, weakening labor's ability to organize and bargain collectively.[27] The conservative Court ruled that workers do not have the right to strike over safety issues if their contract provides a grievance procedure. This decision denied miners the right to walk off the job in the face of serious and immediate safety violations that management refused to remedy.[28] The Court decided that employers can in effect penalize workers for unionizing by closing down operations and denying them jobs. Companies could now unilaterally terminate a labor contract and drastically cut employees' wages by filing for "reorganization" under the bankruptcy law. And unions were denied the right to prevent members from quitting the union and crossing picket lines during a strike or when a strike seemed imminent.[29] College faculty unions were declared not covered by federal laws because teachers exercised a "managerial" function when recruiting for new faculty personnel.[30] The Court's conservative majority upheld state laws denying unemployment benefits to striking workers and a federal law denying them food stamps.[31] Management was given more power to change worker

---

25. Karl Klare, "Critical Theory and Labor Relations Law," in David Kairys (ed.), *The Politics of Law* (New York: Pantheon, 1982), pp. 65–88.

26. For general critiques, see Schwartz, *Packing the Courts;* David Kairys, *With Liberty and Justice for Some: A Critique of the Conservative Supreme Court* (New York: New Press, 1993); Herman Schwartz (ed.), *The Burger Years* (New York: Penguin, 1988).

27. For example, *Allied Structural Steel Co.* v. *Spannaus* (1978); *Lechmere* v. *National Labor Relations Board* (1992).

28. *Gateway Coal Co.* v. *United Mine Workers* (1974).

29. *First National Maintenance Corp.* v. *NLRB* (1981); *Pattern Makers' League of North America, AFL-CIO* v. *NLRB* (1985). In another blow to organized labor, it was decided that nonunion members who were required by labor contracts to pay fees equivalent to union dues could demand that none of their money be used for political activity: *Communications Workers of America* v. *Beck* (1988); *Lehnert* v. *Ferris Faculty Association* (1991).

30. *NLRB* v. *Yeshiva University* (1980). In fact, faculty spend almost all their time on their teaching and scholarship. By designating them "managers," the Court provided yet another example of judicial fabrication.

31. *Lyng* v. *International Union* (1988). In his dissent, Justice Thurgood Marshall noted that the true purpose of the law was to help management break strikes.

benefit standards and deny health benefits.[32] Companies could give preferential hiring to scabs who crossed picket lines, thereby further undermining organized labor's right to strike.[33]

Despite a law limiting water subsidies to farms of 160 acres or less and
to farmers who "live on or near the land," the Court held that large commercial farms, including ones owned by Southern Pacific and Standard Oil,
were entitled to the subsidies. In seeming violation of the Clean Air Act,
the Court said industries could expand in regions with the dirtiest air even
if it results in worsening pollution.[34] The Court upheld a lower federal
court ruling that allows employers to slash health insurance for workers
who develop costly illnesses. In effect, workers will have coverage only as
long as they don't use it for any serious illness—which undermines the
whole purpose of insurance.[35]

Economic inequality. The conservative majority on the High Court give
more consideration to the preferences of the rich than the needs of the
poor. By upholding laws that reduce welfare assistance, the conservative
jurists rejected the idea that aid to the poor was protected by due process.[36]
In seeming violation of the equal-protection clause of the Fourteenth
Amendment, the justices decided that a state may vary the quality of education in accordance with the amount of taxable wealth located in its school
districts, thus allowing just about any degree of inequality short of absolute
deprivation.[37] California's Proposition 13 limited tax increases on property
bought before 1975, so that persons with newly purchased homes carry tax
burdens almost 400 percent heavier than longtime owners. The Supreme
Court decided that the existence of a privileged class of property holders
did not violate equal protection under the law.[38]

---

32. *Public Employees Retirement System of Ohio* v. *Betts* (1989); *Pauley* v. *Bethenergy
Mines* (1991).

33. *Trans World Airlines* v. *Independent Federation of Flight Attendants* (1989).

34. Eric Nadler, "Supreme Court Backs Agribusiness," *Guardian,* July 2, 1980; *Chevron
USA Inc.* v. *National Resources Defense Council Inc. et al* (1984).

35. *Frank Greenberg Executor* v. *H & H Music Company* (1992).

36. *Dandridge* v. *Williams* (1970); *Rosado* v. *Wyman* (1970). On the failure of federal and
state courts to fulfill the promise of equality, see Charles Haar and Daniel Fessler, *The Wrong
Side of the Tracks* (New York: Simon & Schuster, 1986).

37. *San Antonio Independent School District* v. *Rodriguez* (1973). In *Kadrmas* v. *Dick-
enson Public Schools* (1988), the Court ruled that low-income families that could not afford
school-bus fees for their children were not entitled to free service because education was not
a fundamental right. In a dissent, Justice Thurgood Marshall accused the majority of sanc-
tioning discrimination against the poor.

38. *Nordlinger* v. *Hahn* (1992). This case offers another instance of judicial fabrication; the
Court decided the case on something neither side had argued, the stability of neighborhoods.
In a lone dissent, Justice Stevens called Proposition 13 a windfall for people who invested in
California real estate in the 1970s. It "establishes a privilege of a medieval character: Two
families with equal needs and equal resources are treated differently. . . ."

Civil liberties. In First Amendment cases the conservative majority usually has favored government authority over dissent.[39] The Bench allowed the U.S. Army to spy secretly on lawful civilian political activity, but prohibited civilians from openly bringing political literature and demonstrations to military posts.[40] The Court said that bans on political signs in public places were not a restriction on free speech.[41] The justices upheld a law requiring male college students to register with the Selective Service System if they want federal financial aid—a requirement that can be more successfully evaded by students who do not need aid.[42] In *Thornburgh* v. *Abbott* (1989), prison officials were granted almost a free hand in deciding what publications prisoners could receive, a censorship applied mostly against politically dissident literature. Students fared not much better when the Court ruled that high-school administrators had the authority to censor student publications.[43]

Red-baiting repression was given a boost when the Bench ruled that a Michigan state worker, who was denied a promotion because the police Red squad had a file on his politically active brother, could not collect damages. The Court decided that the worker could not sue the state because it was not a person, a decision that placed government's repressive acts above legal challenge by its citizens.[44]

Separation of church and state. The First Amendment reads in part: "Congress shall make no law respecting an establishment of religion, or

---

39. For example, reporters were denied a right to confidential news sources: *United States* v. *Caldwell* (1972); *Zurcher* v. *Stanford Daily* (1978). The conservative majority did uphold the right to criticize public figures even in objectionable ways: *Hustler Magazine* v. *Falwell* (1988); and the right to sue writers who fabricate quotations or significantly alter them in damaging ways: *Masson* v. *New Yorker Magazine* (1991).

40. See respectively *Laird* v. *Tatum* (1972) and *Greer* v. *Spock* (1976).

41. *Members of the City Council of Los Angeles et al.* v. *Taxpayers for Vincent et al.* (1984). The Court also repeatedly has restricted demonstrations and leafleting at shopping malls, for instance: *Clark* v. *Community for Creative Non-Violence* (1984).

42. *Selective Service* v. *Minnesota Public Interest Research Group* (1984). In order to apply for aid, any nonregistrant would be forced to incriminate himself.

43. *Hazelwood School District* v. *Kuhlmeir* (1988). The censored articles dealt with teenage pregnancy and with problems of children in divorced families. The conservative majority disregarded the precedent established by *Tinker* v. *Des Moines Independent School District* (1969), in which the Court had declared that school officials did not possess absolute authority over students and could not deny them their constitutional rights by confining their speech only to officially approved expression. In *Smith* v. *UC Regents* (1993), the Supreme Court of California took a big step toward suppressing political expression on college campuses by declaring that mandatory student fees are unconstitutional if they go toward supporting campus groups with political or ideological agendas.

44. *Will* v. *Michigan Department of State Police* (1989). On the Court's collusion with state repression, see Alexander Charns, *Cloak and Gavel: FBI Wiretaps, Bugs, Informers, and the Supreme Court* (Champaign, Ill.: University of Illinois Press, 1992). But by five-to-four majorities, the Court twice ruled that laws prohibiting flag desecration and flag burning violated the First Amendment, since such acts were a form of protest expression: *Texas* v. *Johnson* (1989) and *U.S.* v. *Eichman* (1990).

prohibiting the free exercise thereof." On the disestablishment clause, the Court has a mixed record. In *support* of the separation of church and state, it has ruled that (a) government has no business sponsoring prayer in the public schools, (b) states may tax the sale of religious books and artifacts by religious organizations, and (c) states have no right to require public schools teaching evolution to also teach Christian views of "creationism" (which argues that evolution never occurred and the world was made by God in six days).[45] In *violation* of the separation of church and state, the Court has long held that religious organizations can enjoy various exemptions from taxation—which narrows the tax base and increases everyone else's tax burden, forcing laypersons to indirectly subsidize religious bodies.[46] Even when religious groups have engaged overtly and actively in political issues, as has the Roman Catholic Church and some Protestant fundamentalist bodies on the abortion issue, the IRS allows them to retain their tax-exempt status.[47] In a five-to-four decision, the Court ruled that federal funds given to religious groups to promote chastity did not violate separation of church and state. In another five-to-four decision, the Court decided that the tuition, textbook, and transportation costs for private schools (including religious ones) were tax deductible.[48]

Criminal justice. In this area, the conservative Court of the last two decades has done little for individual rights. The *Miranda* rule, which forbade the use of police torture in obtaining confessions, was greatly weakened.[49] The Court ruled that persons who murder at the age of sixteen or seventeen can be executed for the crime and so can mentally retarded persons.[50] The justices decided that sentencing a mentally retarded thirteen-year-old to life was not a violation of the Eighth Amendment's prohibition against "cruel and unusual punishment,"[51] nor was a life sentence given to a man for three minor frauds totaling $230,[52] nor a life sentence without parole for

---

45. On public school prayer: *Engels* v. *Vitale* (1962); *School District of Abington* v. *Schempp* (1963); and *Wallace* v. *Jaffree* (1985). On sales tax: *Texas Monthly* v. *Bullock* (1989); *Swaggart Ministries* v. *California* (1990). On creationism: *Edwards* v. *Aguillard* (1987).

46. *Murray* v. *Curlett* (1963); *Lemon* v. *Kurtzman* (1971); *Walz* v. *Tax Commission* (1970).

47. David Burnham, "Alter the Catholic Church's Tax Status?" *New York Times,* July 29, 1988.

48. On chastity: *Bowen* v. *Kendrick* (1988). On tax deductions: *Mueller* v. *Allen* (1983).

49. In *Arizona* v. *Fulminante* (1991), the Court ruled that "the prosecutor's use of a coerced confession—no matter how vicious the police conduct may have been—may now constitute harmless error."

50. On executing teenagers: *Wilkins* v. *Missouri* (1989) and *Standford* v. *Kentucky* (1989). On executing the mentally retarded: *Penry* v. *Lynaugh* (1989).

51. *Massey* v. *Washington* (1991). The youth's older codefendent testified that Massey "was just there" and had not killed anyone.

52. *Rummel* v. *Estelle* (1980), a five-to-four decision. Here, Rehnquist argued that cruel and unusual punishment might be when someone is given a life sentence for "overtime parking." Such an example leaves room for nearly any kind of unjust sentence and reduces the

a first-time conviction of cocaine possession.[53] The prohibition against cruel and unusual punishment, the Court said in *Ingraham* v. *Wright* (1977), does not protect school children from corporal punishment even if the children have been severely injured by school officials. And the due process clause does not impose an obligation on the government to protect an individual from abuse from another individual, specifically a child from a parent.[54]

The Fourth Amendment protection against unreasonable searches and seizures was nearly obliterated when the Court upheld the police's power to conduct sweeping searches in private homes and on buses and to arrest individuals without a warrant and hold them without a court hearing.[55] By unilaterally rewriting specific rules set down by Congress, the conservative activists on the Court severely limited the ability of state prisoners to go to federal court with claims that their constitutional rights were violated. Prisoners who filed lawsuits to fight inhumane conditions now had to show that prison officials exhibited "deliberate indifference" to their rights. The justices did not explain how one could demonstrate such intent if the inhumane prison conditions themselves did not.[56] The Court denied a hearing to a man on death row because his appeal was founded not on a procedural flaw but on errors of fact, specifically additional evidence proving his innocence. In a dissent, Justice Blackmun bemoaned "this Court's obvious eagerness to do away with any restriction on the States' power to execute whomever and however they please" and called the ruling "perilously close to simple murder."[57]

Executive power. The executive is the home of the CIA, the Pentagon, and other national-security agencies that are instrumental in maintaining

---

Eighth Amendment protection to nothing. In *Solem* v. *Helm* (1983), a new five-to-four majority overturned *Rummel* and concluded that a life sentence for a series of minor crimes does constitute cruel and unusual punishment. On some of the Supreme Court's worst decisions, see Joel Joseph, *Black Mondays* (Bethesda, Md.: National Press, 1987).

53. *Harmelin* v. *Michigan* (1991).

54. *De Shaney* v. *Winnebago County Department of Social Services* (1989). The Court seems to think minors can fend for themselves. A law permitting children to testify behind a screen in sexual abuse cases—to make it less traumatic for them to appear in the same venue with their molesters—was declared unconstitutional: *Coy* v. *Iowa* (1988).

55. *Maryland* v. *Blue* (1990); *Florida* v. *Bostick* (1991); *County of Riverside* v. *McLaughlin* (1991).

56. On right to appeal: *McCleskey* v. *Zant* (1991) and *Keeney* v. *Tamayo-Reyes* (1992). On inhumane conditions: *Wilson* v. *Seiter* (1991). The Court reasoned that bad conditions that had accumulated through years of mismanagement, underfunding, and overcrowding were not litigable, since deliberate neglect could not be ascribed to a specific official.

57. *Herrera* v. *Collins* (1993). In *McNally* v. *United States* (1987), the Court did rein in the prosecutory power, making it more difficult to bring mail fraud charges against corrupt persons in government, the judiciary, and private business. Justice Stevens dissented, wondering "why a Court that has not been particularly receptive to the rights of criminal defendants" now protects "the elite class of powerful individuals who will benefit from this decision."

the domestic and global status quo. It is the branch most closely integrated with the military-industrial complex. Not surprisingly, the conservative-dominated Court has repeatedly affirmed the authority of the executive over the other branches and over individual rights. The Court ruled that the State Department could deny a passport to a former CIA employee who had written books exposing illegal CIA covert operations. Neither Congress nor the Constitution granted this power to the executive, but the Bench declared that in matters of "foreign policy and national security" the absence of an empowering law is not to be taken as a sign of congressional disapproval. By judicial fiat, the president now could do whatever he wanted in the absence of specific legislative prohibition.[58]

As part of a continuing pattern of deferring to presidential power in military and foreign affairs, the federal courts refused to hear cases challenging the president on such things as the undeclared war in Vietnam, the unprovoked U.S. invasion of Grenada, the imposition of embargoes on Nicaragua, the U.S. invasion of Panama, and the deportation of Haitian, Guatemalan, and Salvadoran refugees.[59] In a landmark decision the Supreme Court overturned the "legislative veto," a device used in over 200 laws in which Congress authorized the president to do something while retaining the right to negate his action by a simple majority decision. The Court ruled this was an infringement on the separation of powers, thus dealing Congress a serious blow in its attempts to hold the federal bureaucracy accountable.[60]

The electoral system. While unable to contravene earlier reapportionment cases, the conservative Court issued several decisions that nibbled away at the "one-person, one-vote" rule and allowed for greater population disparities among state and congressional legislative districts.[61] The Bench also decided that districts designed in an unusual shape to give North Carolina its first African American members in Congress since Reconstruction were a form of gerrymandering that violated the constitutional rights of White voters.[62] The Court decided that states could not prohibit corporations from independently spending unlimited amounts of their funds to

---

58. *Haig* v. *Agee* (1981) and *Regan* v. *Wald* (1984).

59. For instance, *John Conyers et al.* v. *Ronald Reagan,* denied January 20, 1984; *INS* v. *Elias Zacarias* (1992); also *Washington Post,* January 23 and February 1, 1992.

60. *Immigration and Naturalization Service* v. *Chadha* (1983). The so-called "legislative veto" enabled Congress to delegate authority to an executive agency and take it back if the agency did things that Congress had not intended. Some of us would argue that this is not a usurpation of power but a constitutional exercise of congressional oversight. Conservatives on the Supreme Court seem to think that "separation of powers" means that the executive is totally independent and accountable to no one.

61. *Mahan* v. *Howell* (1973) and *Davis* v. *Bandemer* (1986).

62. *Shaw* v. *Reno* (1993). The special design to ensure some Black representation in Congress did not deprive Whites from dominating almost all of North Carolina's congressional delegation.

influence the outcome of public referenda or other elections because campaign expenditures were a part of "speech" and the Constitution guarantees freedom of speech to business firms, which are to be considered "persons." Nor could limits be imposed on the amount that rich candidates spend on their campaigns or the amounts that "independent" PACs spend in presidential elections.[63] Thus the poor candidate and the rich candidate can both freely compete, one in a whisper and the other in a roar.

Abortion and gender discrimination. Cases that do not directly challenge corporate power or executive authority, including such issues as abortion and sex discrimination, have received mixed treatment by conservatives on the Supreme Court. Sometimes the moderate conservatives sided with the one or two remaining liberals to defeat the ultraconservatives.[64] Occasionally, even the ultraconservatives join in a liberal decision, as when the Court ruled unanimously that (a) sexual harassment on the job violated a person's civil rights, (b) a divorced woman cannot be denied custody of her children because of her remarriage to a man of another race, and (c) victims of sexual harassment can obtain monetary damages from the institution in which the harassment occurred.[65] The Court declared unconstitutional a requirement that women seeking abortions notify their husbands, but it ruled that underage women must obtain parental consent for an abortion.[66] And it upheld a Reagan-Bush administration rule prohibiting family-planning clinics that receive federal funds from providing abortion information to clients.[67]

The Supreme Court declared that federal courts have absolutely no power to stop antiabortion extremists from their campaigns of trespass, intimidation, and obstruction against abortion clinics.[68] In 1994, however, the Court did concede that abortion clinics could invoke the federal racketeering law to sue violent antiabortion protest groups for damages. This decision leaves abortion clinics with the task of proving that specific individuals and

---

63. *First National Bank of Boston* v. *Bellotti* (1978); *Citizens Against Rent Control et al.* v. *City of Berkeley et al.* (1981). Rich individuals also are allowed to spend any amount in an "independent" effort to elect or defeat any candidate: *Buckley* v. *Valeo* (1976).

64. For instance, two positive decisions on women's rights: *California Federal Savings and Loan Association* v. *Guerra* (1987) and *Roberts* v. *U.S. Jaycees* (1984).

65. See respectively, *Mentor Savings Bank, FSB* v. *Vinson* (1986); *Palmore* v. *Sidoti* (1984); *Franklin* v. *Gwinnett County Public Schools* (1992).

66. See respectively, *Planned Parenthood* v. *Casey* (1992) and *Hodgson* v. *Minnesota* (1990). The reasoning in the latter case seems to be that a young woman is not old enough to decide to get an abortion but she is old enough to become a mother; see also *Ohio* v. *Akron Center for Reproductive Health* (1990). In *Webster* v. *Reproductive Health Services* (1989), the Court gave states broad powers to impose restrictions on abortions, such as barring the use of public money, medical personnel, and facilities.

67. *Rust* v. *Sullivan* (1991). In 1993, Congress passed a law overruling the administrative rule and the Court's decision.

68. *Jane Bray* v. *Alexandria Women's Clinic* (1993).

organizations are conducting a nationwide campaign of intimidation, bombings, and other violent acts. One would think the local police and the federal government itself would take responsibility for moving against such violence without the clinics having to take on the task themselves.[69]

Affirmative action and civil rights. Justice Harry Blackmun explained in *University of California* v. *Bakke* that special measures had to be taken to correct the inequities of race relations in the United States: "In order to get beyond racism, we must first take account of race. There is no other way. And in order to treat some persons equally, we must treat them differently. We cannot . . . let the equal protection clause perpetuate racial supremacy." In 1987, the Court upheld affirmative action to redress a conspicuous imbalance in traditionally segregated job categories; employers could promote women and minorities ahead of White males, without evidence of prior discrimination.[70] Not long after, however, the justices began to retreat, making it more difficult to establish discrimination claims against employers, giving White males increased opportunity to challenge affirmative action, and sharply limiting the ability of state and local governments to reserve a fixed percentage of contracts for minority businesses.[71]

A five-to-four majority decided that if an employer asserts "business necessity" to justify a racist or sexist practice, the burden is on the worker to prove intent and show that the practice is not job-related.[72] Likewise, an African American on death row had to prove—in his own specific case—that racism was the cause of his conviction and sentence (something not easy to do). He could not claim discrimination just because people of color are consistently treated more harshly than Whites by the criminal justice system.[73]

The justices upheld the denial of tax-exempt treatment for schools that discriminate racially, but they also supported a Minnesota statute providing state income-tax relief for private schools, thus supporting a public subsidy to the "White flight" to private institutions.[74]

---

69. *National Organization for Women* v. *Scheidler* (1994).

70. *Johnson* v. *Transportation Agency, Santa Clara County* (1987).

71. *Lorance* v. *AT&T Technologies* (1989); *City of Richmond* v. *J.A. Crosson Co.* (1989); *Martin* v. *Wilks* (1989); *City of Richmond* v. *J.A. Crosson Co.* (1988).

72. *Ward's Cove Packing Co.* v. *Atonio* (1989). It is often impossible to demonstrate intent. We can see the effects of an action but usually can only divine the motive. This case overturned *Griggs* v. *Duke Power* (1971) in which the Court unanimously had ruled that job discrimination need not be intentional.

73. *McClesky* v. *Kemp* (1992). On the history of constitutionally sanctioned racism, see Mary Frances Berry, *Black Resistance, White Law*, updated (New York: Allen Lane/Penguin, 1994).

74. On denial of tax exemption: *Bob Jones University* v. *United States* (1983), but also the subsequent narrowing decision in *Allen* v. *Wright* (1984). On granting tax relief: *Mueller* v. *Allen* (1983).

In a county in Alabama, for the first time in recent memory, two African Americans were elected to the board of supervisors. The board responded by abolishing the power of individual supervisors to make decisions regarding their own districts and gave that power to the White-dominated board as a whole. The Supreme Court overruled the Justice Department and decided that this subterfuge did not constitute unfair treatment and did not violate the voting rights laws.[75]

The Supreme Court's right-wing ideological bias is reflected not only in the decisions it hands down but in the cases it selects or refuses to review. Federal district courts decide almost 300,000 cases a year. Appeals are made to the twelve U.S. Courts of Appeal, which annually handle some 30,000 cases. The Supreme Court, in contrast, hands down about 170 decisions a year. During the last two decades of conservative domination of the Court, review access has been sharply curtailed for plaintiffs representing labor, minorities, consumers, and individual rights. Powerless and pauperized individuals have had a diminishing chance of getting their cases reviewed, unlike powerful and prestigious petitioners such as the government and the giant corporations. State and federal prosecutors were able to gain a hearing by the High Court at a rate fifty times greater than defendants. Criminal defendants who could afford the legal filing fee were twice as likely to be granted review as were indigent defendants.[76] In choosing cases the way it does, the Court sends out a clear message to appeals courts about which convictions to uphold and which to overrule.

It has been argued that because its work load has so increased, the Supreme Court must perforce turn down greater numbers of cases. The truth is, while the number of lower-court appeals have indeed multiplied, the amount of time the Reagan-Bush appointees on the Court spent on deliberations and the number of cases they heard diminished by one-fourth as compared to the Warren Court.[77] It is hard to argue that the Court is increasingly overworked when in fact its conservative majority has been reducing the time spent on cases. Even if it were true that the Court is overburdened, this does not explain the evident class bias as to which cases are granted certiorari.

---

75. *Presley* v. *Etowah County Commission* (1992). This decision departed from earlier cases in which the Court was willing to apply the Voting Rights Act to various electoral subterfuges that worked with racist effect.

76. Janis Judson, *The Hidden Agenda: Non-Decision-Making on the U.S. Supreme Court* (University of Maryland, Ph.D. dissertation, 1986); *Los Angeles Times*, November 9, 1989; *Washington Post*, October 21, 1984. Among recent nondecisions, the Court refused to hear an appeal by pro-choice groups challenging the Catholic Church's tax-exempt status; it refused to challenge a U.S. Court of Appeals panel that overturned Oliver North's conviction for his role in the Iran-contra conspiracy.

77. *Washington Post*, October 1, 1990.

INFLUENCE OF THE COURT

A few generalizations can be drawn about the Supreme Court's political influence. More often than not, the Court has been a conservative force. For over half a century it wielded a probusiness minority veto on the kind of reform legislation that European countries had implemented decades earlier. It prevented Congress from instituting progressive income taxes, a decision that took eighteen years and a constitutional amendment to circumvent. It accepted racist segregation for almost a century after the Civil War and delayed female suffrage for forty-eight years. And it has prevented Congress from placing limitations on personal campaign spending by the rich.

By playing a crucial role in defining what is constitutional, the Court gives encouraging cues to large sectors of the public, including the Congress itself. Unable to pass a civil-rights act for seventy years, Congress enacted three in the decade after *Brown* v. *Board of Education*. With the law on their side, civil-rights advocates throughout the nation stepped up the pressure to make desegregation a reality. Likewise, the Warren Court's decisions protecting the rights of the poor opened a whole new field of welfare-reform litigation and was an inducement to various poor people's movements.

Since the Court can neither legislate nor enforce its decisions, it has been deemed the "least dangerous branch." But the Reagan and Bush years demonstrated that a militantly conservative Court bolstered by a conservative executive can exercise quite an activistic influence. Again and again the Court imposed its own tortured logic to cases, blatantly violating the clear language of a law and the intent of Congress. Or it upheld administrative regulations designed to negate a statute. When Congress tried to undo the Court's right-wing activism and reinstate the law as it was intended, President Reagan or President Bush would veto or threaten to veto the new measure. Unable to muster the two-thirds vote needed to override the veto, Congress would be thwarted. Thus, a conservative president, assisted by five or more right-wing activistic justices and one-third-plus-one of either the House or the Senate, could rewrite the law of the land and govern as it wanted.[78]

In reaction to the liberal activism of the Warren Court, conservatives have argued that the Court must cease its intrusive role and defer to the policymaking branches of government. But "judicial restraint" has been applied in selective ways. When conservatives in Congress, the White House, and certain state and local governments launched attacks against freedom

---

78. Herman Schwartz, "Second Opinion," *Nation*, June 17, 1991, p. 801. For specific examples, see the various cases cited in the previous section of this chapter.

to travel, labor rights, the right to counsel, and free speech, the conservative Court was a model of restraint and deferred to these agencies of government. But when it came to advancing a right-wing agenda, the Court's conservative majority has been downright adventuristic, showing no hesitation to rewrite much of the Constitution, rig the rules of the game, invent concepts and arguments out of thin air, eviscerate laws, treat congressional intent and precedence as irrelevant, bolster an authoritarian executive power, block economic and campaign reforms, roll back substantive political and economic gains, and undermine civil liberties, civil rights, and the democratic process itself (such as it is).

Like the Courts of earlier times, the present conservative-activist Court has played federal power against state power and vice versa to defend corporate-class interests. Thus it limited the federal government's ability to protect work conditions of employees, claiming an infringement of states rights under the Tenth Amendment, and then restricted the ability of states to limit business's spending power in referenda, claiming federal prerogatives under the First Amendment. In such cases, one hears little complaint from conservatives about the Court's activist usurpation of policy-making powers. A consistent double standard obtains. Judicial activism that strengthens authoritarian statism and corporate-class interests is acceptable. Judicial activism that supports democratic working-class rights and socioeconomic equality invites attack.[79]

One way to trim judicial adventurism is to end life tenure for federal judges, including the justices who sit on the Supreme Court. It would take a constitutional amendment, but it would be worth it. Today only three states provide life tenure for state judges; the other forty-seven set term limits ranging from four to twelve years.[80] Life tenure was supposed to shield the federal judiciary from outside influences and place it above partisan politics. Experience shows that judges are as political and ideological as anyone else. Their independence leaves them unchecked by anything but their own sense of propriety. A seven-year or ten-year term limit would still give a jurist significant independence, but would not allow him or her to remain unaccountable for life. Judges who exhibited a hostile view toward constitutional rights could be replaced. No ideologically partisan group could pack the courts for decades ahead. There would be more turnover and a greater possibility of more responsiveness to popular needs.

This is not to say that jurists are impervious to social realities. New social movements can affect the Court. The justices not only read the Constitution but also the newspapers. They not only talk to each other but to

---

79. For critical discussions, see Stephen Halpem and Charles Lamb (eds.), *Supreme Court Activism and Restraint* (Lexington, Mass.: D. C. Heath, 1982).

80. Doug Bandow, "End Life Tenure for Judges," *New York Times*, September 6, 1986.

friends and acquaintances. Few jurists remain untouched by the great tides of public opinion and by the subtler shifts in values and perceptions.[81] The Court is always operating in a climate of opinion shaped by political forces larger than itself. Popular pressure and term limitations may be our most immediate hope in restraining the powers of an oligarchic, elitist judiciary.

---

81. Even Chief Justice William Rehnquist admits as much. See his *The Supreme Court: How It Was, How It Is* (New York: Morrow, 1987).

17

Democracy
for the Few

A glance at the social map of this country reveals a vast agglomeration of interest groups and governing agencies. If this is what we mean by pluralism, then the United States is a pluralistic society, as is any society of size and complexity. But the proponents of pluralism presume to be saying something about how power is distributed and how democracy works. Supposedly, a pluralistic society works through democratic means to produce democratic outputs that benefit the populace. Thus, Ralf Dahrendorf writes: "The scene of group conflict has become a kind of market in which relatively autonomous forces contend according to certain rules of the game, by virtue of which nobody is a permanent winner or loser."[1] The government is not controlled by a monolithic corporate elite that gets what it wants on every question, the pluralists say. If there are elites in our society, they are specialized and checked in their demands by conflicting elites. No group can press its advantages too far and any group can find a way within the political system to make its influence felt. Government stands above any one particular influence but responds to many. So say the pluralists.[2]

---

1. Ralf Dahrendorf, *Class and Class Conflict in Industrial Society* (Stanford, Calif.: Stanford University Press, 1959), p. 67.

2. For early pluralist statements, see Earl Latham, *The Group Basis of Politics* (Ithaca, N.Y.: Cornell University Press, 1952); Robert Dahl, *Who Governs?* (New Haven, Conn.: Yale University Press, 1961); Nelson Polsby, *Community Power and Political Theory*, Rev. ed. (New Haven, Conn.: Yale University Press, 1980). A good collection of critiques of pluralism can be found in Charles A. McCoy and John Playford (eds.), *Apolitical Politics* (New York: Crowell, 1967); also Marvin Surkin and Alan Wolfe (eds.), *An End to Political Science: The Caucus Papers* (New York: Basic Books, 1970).

PLURALISM FOR THE FEW

The evidence offered in the preceding chapters leaves us with reason to doubt that the United States is a pluralistic democracy as described above. To summarize and expand on previous points:

Most government policies favor large investor interests at a substantial cost to the rest of the populace. Democratic struggles have won some real benefits for the pubic, yet assistance has not reached millions who are most in need, and no solution is in sight for the many social problems described in earlier chapters. There is a commodity glut in the private market and scarcity in public services. While the rich get ever richer, possessed with more money than they know what to do with, the majority of the populace lives in a condition of economic insecurity, struggling to make ends meet. While defense contractors at home and military dictatorships abroad fatten on the largesse of the U.S. Treasury, federal, state, and local governments go deeper into debt.

To think of government as nothing more than a referee amidst a vast array of "countervailing" groups (which presumably represent all the important interests within the society) is to forget that government best serves those who can serve themselves, granting hundreds of billions of dollars in tax cuts to the rich while cutting back on social services for the rest of us. There are reasons why important public programs fail to measure up to their promise. Often the allocations are meager while the problem is immense, as for instance with programs relating to poverty. Other times the expenditures may be substantial but the problem is deeply ingrained in the economic system itself, for example, job training for nonexistent jobs.

Power in America "is plural and fluid," claimed one pluralist.[3] In reality, power is distributed among entrenched, well-organized, well-financed, politico-economic conglomerates. Wealth is the most crucial power resource, and its distribution is neither "plural" nor "fluid." Not everyone with money chooses to use it to exert political influence, and not everyone with money need bother. But when they so desire, those who control the wealth of society enjoy a persistent and pervasive political advantage.

The pluralists have not a word to say about the pervasive role of political repression in American society, the purging and exclusion of anticapitalist dissidents from government, from the labor movement, the media, academia, and the entertainment world, along with the surveillance and harassment of protest organizations and public-interest groups. Nor do the pluralists give any recognition to the elitist nature of most professional institutions and of most governmental and nongovernmental policymakers.

---

3. Max Lerner, *America as a Civilization* (New York: Simon & Schuster, 1957), p. 398.

Pluralists seem never to allude to the near-monopoly control of ideas and information that is the daily fare of the news and entertainment sectors of the mass media, creating a climate of opinion favorable to the owning-class ideology at home and abroad. Nor are the pluralists much troubled by the rigged monopoly rules under which the two major political parties operate, and an electoral system that treats vast sums of money as a prerequisite for office.

The pluralists make much of the fact that wealthy interests do not always operate with clear and deliberate purpose.[4] To be sure, like everyone else, elites sometimes make mistakes and suffer confusions about tactics. But if they are not omniscient and infallible, neither are they habitual laggards and imbeciles. If they do not always calculate correctly in the pursuit of their class interests, they do so often and successfully enough.

Is the American polity ruled by a secretive, conspiratorial, omnipotent, monolithic power elite? No, the plutocracy, or ruling class, does not fit that easily refuted caricature. First of all, no ruling class in history, no matter how autocratic, has ever achieved omnipotence. All have had to make concessions and allow for unexpected and undesired developments. In addition, ruling elites are not always secretive. The influence they exercise over governing bodies is sometimes overt and sometimes covert, as we have seen. It is exercised through control of business and governmental leadership positions, interlocking directorates, and trusteeships, the elite membership of which, while not widely advertised, is public knowledge. However, these elites do often find it desirable to plan in secret, minimize or distort the flow of information, and develop policies that sometimes violate the law they profess to uphold. Examples aplenty have been offered in this book.

American government is not ruled by a monolithic elite. There are serious differences in how best to mute class conflict and maintain the existing system. Differences can arise between moderately conservative and extremely conservative capitalists, between large and small investor interests, and between domestic and international corporations—all of which lends an element of indeterminacy to policies. But these conflicts seldom take into account the interests of the working public. When push comes to shove, what holds the various elites together is their common interest in preserving an economic system that assures the continued accumulation of corporate wealth and the privileged life-styles of the rich and powerful.

Does this amount to a "conspiracy theory" of society? First, it should be noted that conspiracies do exist. A common view is that conspiracy is only the imaginings of kooks. But just because some people have fantasies of conspiracies does not mean that all conspiracies are fantasies. There was

---

4. Dahl, *Who Governs?*, p. 272. Also see Robert Dahl, *Modern Political Analysis* (Englewood Cliffs, N.J.: Prentice Hall, 1970).

the secretive planning of escalation for the Vietnam War as revealed in the Pentagon Papers; the Watergate break-in; the FBI COINTELPRO disruption of dissident groups; the several phoney but well-orchestrated "energy crises" that sharply boosted oil prices in the 1970s; the Iran-contra conspiracy; the savings-and-loan conspiracies; and the well-documented conspiracies to assassinate President John Kennedy, Martin Luther King, and Malcolm X, and the subsequent cover-ups.[5]

Ruling elites admit to conspiring in secret, without being held accountable to anyone: they call it "national security." But when one suggests that their plans (whether covert or overt) benefit the interests of their class and are intended to do so, one is dismissed as a "conspiracy theorist." It is allowed that farmers, steelworkers, or even welfare mothers may concert to advance their interests, but it may not be suggested that moneyed elites do as much—even when they actually occupy the decision-making posts. Instead, we are asked to believe that these estimable persons of wealth and position walk through life indifferent to the fate of their vast holdings.

Although there is no one grand power elite, there is continual cooperation between various corporate and governmental elites in every area of the political economy. Many of the stronger corporate groups tend to predominate in their particular spheres of interest, more or less unmolested by other elites.[6] In any case, the conflicts among plutocratic interests seldom work to the advantage of the mass of people. They are conflicts of haves versus haves. Often they are resolved not by compromise but by logrolling, involving more collusion than competition. These mutually satisfying arrangements among "competitors" usually come at the expense of the public interest—as when the costs of collusion are passed on to us in the form of higher prices, higher taxes, environmental devastation, and inflation. To be sure, the demands of the have-nots may be heard occasionally as a clamor outside the gate, and now and then something is tossed to the unfortunates.

One might better think of ours as a dual political system. First, there is the *public* system centering around electoral and representative activities, including campaign conflicts, voter turnout, political personalities, public pronouncements, official role-playing, and certain ambiguous presentations of issues that bestir presidents, governors, mayors, and their respective legislatures. Then there is the *covert* system, involving multibillion-dollar contracts, tax write-offs, protections, rebates, grants, loss compensations,

---

5. On the murder of John Kennedy, see the citations in chapter 9, footnote 88. See also Philip Melanson, *The Martin Luther King Assassination* (New York: Shapolsky, 1991); Mark Lane and Dick Gregory, *Murder in Memphis: The FBI and the Assassination of Martin Luther King* (New York: Thunder Mouth, 1993); Karl Evanzz, *The Judas Factor, The Plot to Kill Malcolm X* (New York: Thunder Mouth Press, 1992); George Breitman, Herman Porter, and Baxter Smith, *The Assassination of Malcolm X* (New York: Pathfinder, 1976).

6. Peter Bachrach, *The Theory of Democratic Elitism* (Boston: Little, Brown, 1967), p. 37.

subsidies, leases, giveaways, and the whole vast process of budgeting, advising, regulating, protecting, and servicing major companies, now ignoring or rewriting the law on behalf of the powerful, now applying it with full punitive vigor against heretics and "troublemakers." The public system is highly visible, taught in the schools, dissected by academicians, gossiped about by news commentators. The covert system is seldom acknowledged.

Along with the special interests of business firms, there is the overall influence exerted by business *as a system.* More than just an abstraction, business is a pervasive system of power, a way of organizing property, capital, and labor. Corporate business occupies a special position within the economic system; in a sense, it *is* the economic system. On major politico-economic issues, business gets its way with government because there exists no alternative way of organizing investment and production within the existing capitalist structure. Because business controls the very economy of the nation, government perforce enters into a uniquely intimate relationship with it. The health of the economy is treated by policymakers as a necessary condition for the health of the nation, and since it happens that the economy is in the hands of large interests, then presumably government's service to the public is best accomplished by service to these interests. The goals of business (high profits and secure markets) becomes the goal of government, and the "national interest" becomes identified with the systemic needs of corporate capitalism.

Since policymakers must operate in and through the corporate economy, it is not long before they are operating *for* it. In order to keep the peace, business may occasionally accept reforms and regulations it does not like, but government cannot ignore business's own reason for being, i.e., the accumulation of capital. Sooner or later, business as a system must be met on its own terms or be replaced by another system.

REFORM AND THE "MIXED ECONOMY"

Some writers mistakenly conclude that we have become a "postcapitalist" society with a "mixed economy" that is neither capitalist nor socialist. This view avoids consideration of whom government benefits when mixing itself with the economy. It blurs the class nature of policy outputs. Business elites know otherwise. They are capable of making class distinctions in public policy, supporting government services and regulations that benefit their interests, and opposing the ones that might benefit workers, consumers, the needy, and the environment.

Government involvement in the economy represents not a growth in socialism (as that term is normally understood by socialists) but in state-supported capitalism, not the communization of private wealth but the privatization of the commonwealth. This development has brought a great deal of government involvement, but a kind that revolves around bolstering the profit system, not limiting it. The giant corporations remain the sole conduit for most public expenditures. Be it schools or school lunches, submarines or space ships, harbors or highways, government relies almost exclusively on private suppliers. The government is not a producer in competition with business, but a giant purchaser of business products and services.

In capitalist countries, government generally nationalizes sick and unprofitable industries and privatizes profitable public ones. Thus, in 1986 the social democratic government in Spain nationalized vast private holdings to avert their collapse. After bringing them back to health with generous nourishment from the public treasure, they were sold back to private companies.[7] The same was done with Conrail in the United States. And a conservative Greek government privatized publicly owned companies such as the national airlines and the telecommunications system, both of which had been reporting continuous profits for several years.[8]

When a capitalist government takes over an enterprise, ownership is often only on paper, representing nothing more than a change from private stocks to public bonds owned by the same wealthy investors. When private capital sells its franchise to the government, it is usually for a nice price. "Ownership" in the form of a huge bonded debt—with all the risks and losses and none of the profits—are passed on to the public. Public ownership is not socialism unless it breaks the moneyed power of the investor class, so that the wealth of the enterprise as well as nominal ownership is in public hands.

The Limits of Reform

Defenders of the existing system assert that the history of "democratic capitalism" has been one of gradual reform. To be sure, important reforms have been won by working people. To the extent that the present economic order has anything humane and civil about it, it is because of the struggles of millions of people engaged in advancing their living standard and their rights as citizens. It is somewhat ironic to credit capitalism with the genius of gradual reform when (a) most economic reforms through history have been vehemently resisted by the capitalist class and were won only after

---

7. *New York Times*, January 6, 1986. Note how the bond issue for nationalized firms in France offered by the "socialist" government in France in 1981 attracted big investors: *Washington Post*, September 10, 1981.

8. James Petras and Chronis Polychroniou, "The *Times* in Greece," *Lies of Our Times*, May 1991, p. 6.

prolonged, bitter, and sometimes bloody popular struggle, and (b) most of the problems needing reform have been caused or intensified by capitalism.

We might ask: Why doesn't the future arrive? Why is fundamental change so difficult to effect? Why is social justice so hard to achieve? The answer is twofold:

First, quite simply, those who have the interest in fundamental change have not the power, while those who have the power have not the interest, being disinclined to commit class suicide. It is not that decision makers have been unable to figure out the steps for change; it is that they oppose the things that change entails. Officeholders are usually most receptive to those who have the resources to command their attention. In political life as in economic life, needs do not become marketable demands until they are backed by "buying power" or "exchange power," for only then is it in the "producer's" interest to respond. The problem for many unorganized citizens and workers is that they have few political resources of their own to exchange. For the politician, the compelling quality of any argument is determined less by its logic and evidence than by the strength of its advocates. The wants of the unorganized public seldom become marketable political demands; they seldom become imperatives to which officials find it in their own interest to respond, especially if the changes would put the officeholder on a collision course with powerful interests.

Second, the reason our labor, skills, technology, and natural resources are not used for social needs is that they are used for corporate gain. The corporations cannot build low-rent houses and feed the poor because their interest is not in social reconstruction but in private profit. State-supported capitalism cannot exist without state support, without passing its immense costs and inefficiencies onto the public.

Contrary to the view of liberal critics, the nation's immense social problems are not irrational offshoots of a basically rational system, to be solved by replacing the existing corporate and political decision makers with persons who would be better intentioned. Rather, the problems are rational outcomes of a basically irrational system, a system structured not for satisfying human need but magnifying human greed.

How can we speak of our politico-economic system as being a product of the democratic will? What democratic will demanded that Washington be honeycombed with high-paid corporate lobbyists who would regularly raid the public treasure on behalf of rich clients? What democratic mandate directed the government to give away more monies every year to the top 1 percent of the population, in interest payments on public bonds than are spent on services to the bottom 20 percent? When was the public consulted on Alaskan oil leases, interest rates, and agribusiness subsidies? When did the public insist on having unsafe, overpriced drugs and foods and an FDA that protects rather than punishes the companies that market them?

When did the American people urge the government to go easy on polluters and allow the utility companies to overcharge consumers? When did the voice of the people clamor for unsafe work conditions in mines, factories, and on farms? How often have the people demonstrated for multibillion-dollar tax breaks for the super-rich and a multibillion-dollar space shuttle high in the sky that leaves the rest of us more burdened by taxes and deprived of necessary services here on earth? What democratic will decreed that we destroy the Cambodian countryside between 1969 and 1971 in a bombing campaign conducted without the consent or even the knowledge of Congress and the public? When did public opinion demand that we wage a mercenary war of attrition against Nicaragua, or invade Grenada and Panama, or slaughter 100,000 Iraqis, or occupy Somalia, or support wars against popular forces in El Salvador, Guatemala, Angola, Mozambique, the Western Sahara, and East Timor, or subvert progressive governments in Chile, Indonesia, and a dozen other countries?

Far from giving their assent, ordinary people have had to struggle to find out what is going on. And when public opinion has mobilized, it is in the opposite direction, against the worst abuses and most blatant privileges of plutocracy, against the spoliation of the environment, and against bigger military budgets and armed interventions in other lands.[9]

DEMOCRACY AS CLASS STRUGGLE

The ruling class has several ways of expropriating the earnings of the people. First and foremost, as *workers,* people receive only a portion of the value their labor power creates. The rest goes to the owners of capital. On behalf of owners, managers continually devise methods—including speed-ups, downgrading, layoffs, the threat of plant closings, and union busting—to tame labor and intensify the process of capital accumulation.

Second, as *consumers,* people are victimized by monopoly practices that force them to spend more for less. They are confronted with increasingly exploitative forms of involuntary consumption, as when relatively inexpensive mass-transit systems are neglected or eliminated, creating a greater dependency on automobiles; or when low-rental apartments are converted in high-priced condominiums.

Third, over the last thirty-five years or so, working people, as *taxpayers,* have had to shoulder an ever larger portion of the tax burden, while business pays less and less. Indeed, the dramatic decline in business taxes has

---

9. The Gulf War against Iraq did stir jingo fervor once it began. But up to the eve of hostilities, despite the relentless interventionist propaganda hype of the major media, a majority of the U.S. public favored a diplomatic settlement rather than military engagement.

been a major cause of growth in the federal deficit. As we have seen, the deficit itself is a source of income for the moneyed class and an additional burden on taxpayers.

Fourth, as *citizens,* the people get less than they pay for in government services. The lion's share of federal spending goes to large firms, defense contractors, and big financial creditors. As citizens, the people also endure the hidden "diseconomies" shifted onto them by private business, as when a chemical company contaminates a community's groundwater with its toxic wastes.

The existing system of power and wealth, with its attendant abuses and injustices, activates a resistance from workers, consumers, community groups, and taxpayers—who are usually one and the same people, those whom I have been called "the democratic forces." There exists, then, not only class oppression but class struggle, not only plutocratic dominance but popular opposition and demands for reform.

There is a tradition of popular struggle in the United States that has been downplayed and ignored. It ebbs and flows but never ceases. Moved by a combination of anger and hope, ordinary people have organized, agitated, demonstrated, and engaged in electoral challenges, civil disobedience, strikes, sit-ins, takeovers, boycotts, and sometimes violent clashes with the authorities—for better wages and work conditions, a safer environment, racial and gender justice, and peace and nonintervention abroad. Against the heaviest odds, they have suffered many defeats but won some important victories, forcibly extracting concessions and imposing reforms upon resistant rulers.

Democracy is something more than a set of political procedures. To be worthy of its name, democracy should produce substantive outcomes that advance the health and well-being of the people. In the modern age, popular forces have come to consider their class demands for such things as jobs and old-age security to be as much a part of their democratic birthright as more formal political rights. Indeed many of the struggles for political democracy, the right to vote, assemble, petition, and dissent, have been largely propelled by the struggle for economic and social democracy, by a desire to democratize the rules of the political game so as to be in a better position to fight for one's socioeconomic interests. In a word, the struggle for democracy has been part of the class struggle against plutocracy.

Through the nineteenth century and into the twentieth, the propertied classes resisted the expansion of democratic rights, be it universal suffrage, abolitionism, civil liberties, or affirmative action. They knew that the growth of popular rights would only strengthen popular forces and impose limits on elite privileges. They instinctively understood, even if they seldom publicly articulated it, that it is not socialism that subverts democracy, but democracy that subverts capitalism.

The conservative agenda is to return to the days before the New Deal, to a country with a small middle class and an impoverished mass. As Paul Volcker, erstwhile chair of the Federal Reserve Board said: "The standard of living of the average American has to decline." [10] To bolster profits, government increases its support to business and eliminates the federal regulations that cut into business earnings. Wages are held down by forcing people to compete more intensely for work on terms increasingly favorable to management. Historically, this is done by eliminating jobs through mechanization, by bringing immigrant labor into the country, and by investing capital in countries that offer cheaper labor markets and other favorable terms.

Wages have been held down also by downgrading skilled workers and increasing the number of workers on the job market, thereby making them compete more desperately for whatever jobs are available and lowering the price of labor. In the 1980s the Republican administration eased child-labor laws, lowered the employable age for some jobs, and raised the future retirement age, thus increasing the number of workers competing for jobs.

Another way to depress wages is to eliminate alternative sources of support. Wage workers are made, not born. The historical process of creating people willing to work for subsistence wages entailed driving them off the land and into the factories, denying them access to farms and to the game, fuel, and fruits of the commons. Divorced from these means of subsistence, the peasant became the proletarian. Today, unemployment benefits and other forms of public assistance are reduced in order to deny alternative sources of sustenance. Public jobs are eliminated so that more workers will compete for employment in the private sector. Conservatives seek to lower the minimum wage for youth and resist attempts to equalize wages and job opportunities for women and minorities, so keeping women, youth, and minorities as the traditional underpaid "reserve army of labor" used throughout history to depress wages.

Still another way to hold down wages and maximize profits is to keep the work force divided and poorly organized. Racism has played an important divisive role, as the economic fears and anger of Whites are channeled away from employers and toward minorities and immigrants who are seen as competitors for scarce jobs, education, and housing. Racism has a deflationary effect on wages similar to sexism. When a large portion of the work force are underpaid because they are Black, Latino, or female, this holds down the price of labor and increases profits.

Rulers have often sought to mute popular grievances by conjuring up domestic radical enemies and foreign foes. For decades they filled the air with alarms about a global "Soviet Menace" that supposedly was out to

10. *Washington Post,* March 9, 1980.

enslave the world. With the demise of the Soviet Union, U.S. leaders continued to direct public attention to the supposed dangers beyond our shores in order to justify the profitable military-industrial establishment and win support for intervention against liberation movements that threaten the global corporate order.

When democratic forces mobilize to defend their standard of living, democracy proves troublesome to capitalism. So the ruling class must attack not only the people's standard of living but the very democratic rights that help them defend that standard. Thus, the right to strike and to bargain collectively come under persistent attack by both the courts and legislatures. The laws against minor parties are tightened and public funding of the two-party monopoly is expanded. Federal security agencies and local police, abetted by the courts, repress community activists and weaken many of the civil liberties and civil rights won in the past.

THE TWO FACES OF THE STATE

Some critics of capitalism believe that as the problems of the economy deepen, modern capitalism will succumb to its own internal contradictions; as the economic "substructure" gives way, the "superstructure" of the capitalist state will be carried down with it, and the opportunity for a better society will be at hand. This position underestimates the extent to which the state can act with independent effect to preserve the capitalist class. The state is more than a front for the economic interests it serves; it is the single most important instrument that corporate America has at its command. The power to use police and military force, the power of eminent domain, the power to tax, spend, and legislate, to use public funds for private profit, have access to limitless credit, mobilize highly emotive symbols of loyalty and legitimacy, and suppress political dissidents—such resources of the state give corporate America a durability it could never provide for itself. "The stability and future of the economy is grounded, in the last analysis, on the power of the state to act to preserve it." [11]

The state, however, is not merely a puppet of the capitalist class. As already noted, to fulfill its task of bolstering the capitalist system as a whole, it must sometimes resist particular corporate interests. The state is also the place where liberal and conservative ruling-class factions struggle over how

---

11. Gabriel Kolko, *The Triumph of Conservatism* (Chicago: Quadrangle Books, 1967), p. 302. The state also functions to stabilize trade arrangements among giant firms. Historically, "firms in an oligopolistic industry often turn to the federal government to do for them what they cannot do for themselves—namely, enforce obedience to the rules of their own cartel": Frank Kofsky, *Harry S. Truman and the War Scare of 1948* (New York: St. Martin's Press, 1993), p. 190.

best to keep the system afloat. The more liberal elements see that democratic concessions sometimes can be beneficial to the economic system—by keeping capitalism from devouring those who make and buy its products. If conservative goals are too successful, then the contradictions of capitalism intensify and so do its instabilities. Profits may be maintained and even increased for a time through various financial contrivances, but unemployment grows, markets shrink, discontent deepens, and small and not so small businesses perish. As the pyramid begins to tremble from conservative victories, some of the less myopic occupants of the apex develop a new appreciation for the base that sustains them. For many conservatives, however, too much already has gone to the people and into the nonprofit sector. Under conservative rule, demand may slump and the pie may not expand as swiftly as before but the slice that goes to the business class grows immensely.

The state's ability to act in the interests of the capitalist class is limited by several factors. First, government officials cannot always know what are the best policies for the corporate system, especially when particular interests need contradictory things such as immediate tariff protections and long-range free-trade agreements, or cutbacks in wages and growing consumer markets. Confusions and conflicts arise within the state that reflect the irrationalities of capitalism itself.

Second, serious market conflicts are likely to arise with economic competitors like Japan and Germany. As stagnation and unemployment become chronic conditions throughout the capitalist world, the competition between capitalist nations will intensify, posing problems for which the capitalist nation-state is not likely to find easy answers.

Third, the state must deal with capitalism's contradictions on capitalism's own terms—which is itself something of a contradiction, for the state rarely can get to systemic causes. Thus, government attends to toxic waste rather than to the modes of production and profit of the chemical and oil industries. It offers poverty assistance programs rather than dealing with the modes of investment and profit accumulation that create unemployment and poverty. The crises periods of U.S. capitalism are growing longer, and the recovery periods more shallow. Public indebtedness and unemployment are becoming more acute. Thus, twenty-five years ago a $20 billion deficit was considered serious; today it would be a fiscal triumph to get the annual deficit to below $100 billion. Twenty-five years ago, 5 percent unemployment and 4 percent inflation were thought to be real problems; today such rates are treated as quite acceptable.

The state best protects the existing class structure by enlisting the loyalty and support of the populace. To do so, it must maintain its own legitimacy in the eyes of the people. And legitimacy is preserved by keeping an appearance of popular rule and neutrality in regard to class interests. More important than the constraints of appearances are the actual power restraints imposed by democratic forces. There is just so much the people will take before they begin to resist. Marx anticipated that class struggle would bring the overthrow of capitalism. Short of that, class struggle constrains and alters the capitalist state, so that the state itself, or portions of it, become an arena of struggle that reflects the conflict going on in the wider society.

Having correctly discerned that "American democracy" as professed by establishment opinion makers is something of a sham, some people incorrectly dismiss the democratic rights won by popular forces as being of little account. But these democratic rights and the organized strength of democratic forces are, at present, all we have to keep some rulers from imposing a dictatorial final solution, smashing all democratic organizations so better to impose a draconian economy on the people and secure the dominance of capital over labor.

The vast inequality in economic power as exists in our capitalist society translates into a great inequality of social power. More than half a century ago the sociologist Max Weber wrote: "The question is: How are freedom and democracy in the long run at all possible under the domination of highly developed capitalism?"[12] That question is still with us. As the crisis of capitalism deepens, as the contradiction between the egalitarian expectations of democracy and the demoralizing thievery of capitalism sharpens, the state must act more repressively to hold together the existing class system.

Why doesn't the capitalist class in the United States resort to fascist rule? It would make things easier: no organized dissent, no environmental or occupational protections to worry about, no elections or labor unions. As of now, there is no need for such drastic measures since the dominant class is getting pretty much what it wants behind a democratic facade. In a country like the United States, the success of a dictatorial solution to the crisis of capitalism would depend on whether the ruling class could stuff the democratic genie back into the bottle. Ruling elites are restrained in their autocratic impulses by the fear that they could not get away with it, that the people and the enlisted ranks of the armed forces would not go along. A state that relies solely on its bayonets to rule is exposed as an instrument of class domination. It loses credibility, generates resistance rather than compliance, and ignites a rebellious and even revolutionary consciousness. Given secure profit margins, elites generally prefer a "democracy for the few" to an outright dictatorship.

Representative government is a very serviceable form of governance for capitalism, even if often a troublesome one, for it offers a modicum of liberty and self-rule while masking the class nature of the state. Rather than

---

12. H. H. Gerth and C. Wright Mills (eds.), *From Max Weber: Essays in Sociology* (New York: Oxford University Press, 1958).

relying exclusively on the club and the gun, bourgeois democracy employs a cooptive, legitimating power—which is ruling-class power at its most hypocritical and most effective. By playing these contradictory roles of protector of capital and "protector of the people," the state best fulfills its fundamental class role.

What is said of the state is true of the law, the bureaucracy, the political parties, the legislators, the universities, the professions, and the media. In order to best fulfill their class-control and class-dominating functions yet keep their social legitimacy, these institutions must maintain the appearance of neutrality and autonomy. To foster that appearance, they must occasionally exercise some critical independence and autonomy from the state and from capitalism. They must save a few decisions for the people, attempt to blunt popular agitations, and take minimally corrective measures to counter the more egregious transgressions against democratic appearances.

WHAT IS TO BE DONE?

Here are some of the things that need to be done to bring us to a more equitable and democratic society:

Reform the electoral system. To curb the power of the moneyed interests and lobbyists, minor-party as well as major-party candidates should be provided with public financing. In addition, a strict cap should be placed on campaign spending by all candidates and supporters, with no loopholes allowed. The various states should institute proportional representation so that every vote will count and major parties will no longer dominate the legislature with artificially inflated majorities. Also needed is a standard federal electoral law allowing uniform and easy ballot access for third parties and independents. We should also abolish the Electoral College to avoid artificially inflated majorities that favor the two-party monopoly and undermine the popular vote.

Encourage voter participation by having (a) universal, same-day registration and a government sponsored postcard registration campaign; (b) more accessible polling sites in low-income areas; (c) an election on an entire weekend instead of a work day (now usually Tuesday) so that persons who travel long distances and work long hours will have sufficient opportunity to get to a polling place. Also prohibit media projections of winners on election day prior to the closing of the polls.[13]

---

13. The District of Columbia should be granted statehood by Congress. As of now its 607,000 citizens are denied full representation in Congress and complete self-rule. They elect a mayor and city council but Congress and the president retain the power to overrule all the city's laws and budgets. Washington, D.C., remains one of the U.S. government's internal colonies.

Democratize our judiciary and do away with oligarchic court power. According to one poll, 59 percent of the citizenry favor popular election of Supreme Court justices and 91 percent want the terms of all federal judges to be limited.[14]

Democratize the media. The airwaves are the property of the U.S. people. As part of their public-service licensing requirements, television and radio stations should be required to give—free of charge—public air time to *all* political viewpoints, including dissident and radical ones. The media should be required to give equal time to all candidates, not just Democrats and Republicans. The power of money should not prefigure the range of political discourse. In campaign debates, the candidates should be allowed to speak for extended periods, not just sixty-second sound bites. And they should be questioned by representatives from labor, peace, consumer, environmental, feminist, civil rights, and gay rights groups, instead of just the usual politically limited media pundits.[15]

Cut military spending and accelerate peacetime conversion. The military spending binge of the last fourteen years is the major cause of our $4 trillion national debt, our runaway deficits, our decaying infrastructure, and our crushing tax burden. Military spending has transformed the United States from the world's biggest lender into the world's biggest debtor nation. To save hundreds of billions of dollars each year, we should cut the bloated, wasteful, and destructive "defense" budget by two-thirds over a period of a few years. The Pentagon now maintains a massive nuclear arsenal and other strike forces designed to fight a total war against a superpower enemy who no longer exists. To save additional billions each year and cut down on the damage done to the environment, the United States should stop all nuclear tests, including underground ones, and wage a diplomatic offensive for a nuclear-free world.

The U.S. also could save tens of billions of dollars if it stopped pursuing armed foreign interventions. "Power Projection" forces and most of the Navy's carrier battle groups could be eliminated with no loss of national security, along with the U.S. Central Command (formerly the Rapid Deployment Force).

The depressive economic effects of ridding ourselves of a war economy could be mitigated by embarking upon a massive conversion to a peace economy, putting the monies saved from the military budget into human

---

14. Survey by the *National Law Journal*, reported in *People's Daily World*, September 12, 1986.

15. The power of television to change the status of minor parties was dramatized in Brazil. In September 1989, Workers' Party candidate Luis Inacio da Silva, nicknamed Lula, had a 4 percent approval rating, and regularly was given unfavorable coverage by the media. With a daily free-time television rule in effect during the campaign, Lula's rating soared to 43 percent and he almost won the election: *New York Times*, December 14, 1989.

services and domestic needs. The shift away from war spending would improve our quality of life and lead to a healthier overall economy.[16]

Abolish the CIA and the national security state. Congress should drastically cut the budgets of national security agencies, limit their mandates to intelligence gathering, prohibit gangster covert actions against Third World social movements, and impeach those executive officers who fail to obey the lawful limits imposed on them. The power of the executive to act with criminally violent effect against various peoples, including our own, should be exposed, challenged, and stopped. The Freedom of Information Act should be enforced instead of undermined by those who say they have nothing to hide, then try to hide almost everything they do.

End U.S.-sponsored counterinsurgency wars against the poor of the world. Eliminate all foreign aid to regimes engaged in oppression of their own peoples. The billions of U.S. tax dollars that flow into the Swiss bank accounts of foreign autocrats and militarists could be better spent on human services at home. Lift the trade and travel bans imposed on Cuba and other countries that have dared to deviate from the free-market orthodoxy.

Reform taxes and wages. Reintroduce the progressive income tax for rich individuals and corporations—without the many loopholes and deductions that still exist. Also, strengthen the inheritance tax and introduce a tax on accumulated wealth rather than just income. At the same time, give tax relief to the working poor and other low-income employees. Reduce the regressive Social Security tax; it produces a yearly $50 billion surplus that is shifted into the general budget to be spent on all sorts of things other than pensions for the elderly.

Reform labor law. Abolish antilabor laws like Taft-Hartley. Provide government protections to workers who now risk their jobs when they try to organize. Prohibit management's use of permanent replacements for striking workers. Penalize employers who refuse to negotiate a contract after certification has been won. Repeal the restrictive "right to work" and "open shop" laws that undermine collective bargaining. And increase the minimum wage to a living wage level.

Repeal the North American Free Trade Agreement (NAFTA) and the General Agreement on Tariffs and Trade (GATT), which places national sovereignty in the hands of nonelective, secretive, international tribunals that can overrule the prolabor, environmental, and consumer laws of any federal or state government, and further undermine U.S. living standards.

---

16. Paul Blustein and John Berry, "Deep Pentagon Cuts Could Boost Economy's Fortunes," *Washington Post*, November 22, 1989; Ann Markusen, "Turning Off the War Machine," *New York Times*, November 22, 1992; see chapter 6 for additional references on conversion.

Improve agriculture and the ecology. Distribute to almost two million needy farmers the billions of federal dollars now received by rich agribusiness firms. Encourage organic commercial farming and phase out the use of pesticides, chemical fertilizers, and hormones.[17] Engage in a concerted effort at conservation and ecological restoration, including a massive clean up of the land, air, and water. Develop rapid mass transit systems within and between cities for safe, economical transportation, and develop electric and solar-powered vehicles to minimize the disastrous ecological

---

17. The latest atrocity is bovine growth hormone (BGH) sold by Monsanto Co. to induce dairy cows to produce abnormally high amounts of milk. The cows also suffer from increased infection and malnutrition. Greater feeding and health maintenance costs generally outweigh production increases, but Monsanto keeps pushing the $500 million biotech "wonder drug" on farmers. The FDA approved the drug and has decided not to ask dairies to label milk that contains BGH even though it may have harmful effects on consumers: *San Francisco Examiner,* February 3, 1994. Increased milk production through BGH will cost taxpayers $100 million a year in additional federal surplus purchases, mostly benefiting a few big dairy producers: *New York Times,* February 21, 1994.

effects of fossil fuels.[18] Phase out nuclear plants and initiate a crash program to develop thermal, hydro, tidal, and solar-energy sources.

Improve health care and safety. Institute a single-payer health-care system that provides comprehensive service to all and allows patients to go to the doctor of their choice, as does the system in Canada and elsewhere.[19] There is no reason to spend tens of billions more on health-care insurance (as proposed by President Clinton) when we already expend vastly more per capita than any other nation. Under single-payer health care, the billions of dollars that go as profits to hundreds of insurance companies would be used for medical treatment.

Thousands of additional federal inspectors are needed for the various agencies responsible for the enforcement of occupational safety and consumer protection laws. "Where are we going to get the money to pay for all this?" one hears. The question is never asked in regard to the defense budget or business subsidies. As already noted, we can get the additional funds from a more progressive tax system and from major cuts in big business subsidies and military spending.[20]

Revise fiscal policy. Government could end deficit spending by taxing the financial class from whom it now borrows. It must stop bribing the rich with investment subsidies and other guarantees, and redirect capital investments toward not-for-profit public goals. The national debt should be rescheduled, with full compensation to small bondholders and only minimal and partial compensation to large ones. The national debt is a transfer payment from taxpayers to bondholders, from labor to capital, from average people to the wealthy. Like Latin American peasants, U.S. taxpayers will be sacrificing their standard of living for generations to come to pay off wealthy creditors—as they are doing today.

Eliminate gender, racial and political injustice. End all racial and gender discriminatory practices in all institutional settings, including the law and the courts themselves. Vigorously enforce the law to protect abortion clinics from vigilante violence, women from male abuse, children from adult

18. Stanford Ovshinsky, president of Energy Conversion Devices, notes that a newly developed electric car now has a long driving range on a battery that lasts a lifetime, uses environmentally safe materials, is easily manufactured, with operational costs that are far less than a gas-driven car: correspondence, *New York Times,* July 20, 1993.

19. Consider health care in Hawaii. According to Dr. John Lewin, director of Hawaii's Department of Health, Hawaii's universal access plan is a "powerful cost containment strategy. If everyone has access to good primary care they will not need a $500 visit to the emergency room and there will not be as many surgeries or high-tech interventions": "Healthcare: How It Works in Hawaii," *People's Weekly World,* December 11, 1993, pp. 12–13.

20. The entire budget of the Consumer Product Safety Commission is equivalent to the price of running the Defense Department for one hour: *Washington Post,* February 2, 1989.

abuse, homosexuals and minorities from hate crimes and police brutality.[21] Release the hundreds of dissenters who are serving long prison terms on trumped-up charges and whose major offense is their anticapitalism.

Increase employment. Americans are working harder and longer for less.[22] Yet millions have no work at all. We should initiate a six-hour work day or a four-day work week with no cut in pay or a four-day work week with no pay cut and no compulsory overtime. Initiate a massive federal job program, putting people to work on the various undertakings mentioned above. Many important vital services are needed, and many people need work. A Works Project Administration (WPA), more encompassing than the one created during the New Deal, could employ people to reclaim the environment, build needed industries, affordable housing, and transportation, rebuild a crumbling infrastructure, and provide services for the aged and infirm and for the public in general.

People could be put to work producing goods and services in competition with the private market. The New Deal's WPA engaged in the production of goods, including manufacturing clothes and mattresses for relief clients, surgical gowns for hospitals, and canned meat, fruits, and vegetables for the jobless poor.[23] This kind of not-for-profit direct production to meet human needs brings in revenues to the government both in the sales of the goods and in taxes on the incomes of the new jobs created. Eliminated from the picture is private profit for those who live off the labor of others—which explains their fierce hostility toward government programs that engage in direct production.

Government for the few serves and subsidizes corporate interests at public expense. The policy changes listed above reverse that flow, transferring wealth from the private to the public realm, for human needs. None of these measures will prevail unless the structural problems of capitalism are themselves resolved. As social goals and investment targets are transformed to not-for-profit direct production, private capital will go on strike, so to speak; investors will refuse to invest and will close down production. What is needed then is public ownership of the major means of production and public ownership of the moneyed power itself—in a word, socialism.

But can socialism work? Is it not just a dream in theory and a nightmare in practice? Can the government produce anything of worth? As mentioned in an earlier chapter, various private industries (defense, railroads, satellite

---

21. In 1994, for the first time, the Justice Department ordered federal civil rights mediators to take up a case involving harassment and violence against gays: *New York Times,* February 19, 1994.

22. In 1960, one college graduate with a C average could earn enough to buy a three-bedroom house and support a wife and three children. Today it takes two childless adults working full time to afford rent on a one bedroom apartment: *Nation,* January 17, 1994.

23. Kim Moody, "Going Public," *Progressive,* July 1983, p. 20.

communication, aeronautics, and nuclear power, to name some) exist today only because the government funded the research and development and provided most of the risk capital. Market forces are not a necessary basis for scientific and technological development. The great achievements of numerous U.S. university and government laboratories during and after World War II were conducted under conditions of central federal planning and not-for-profit public funding.[24] We already have some socialized services and they work quite well when sufficiently funded. Our roads and water supplies are socialized, as are our bridges and ports, and in some states so are liquor stores, which yearly generate hundreds of millions of dollars in state revenues.[25]

We need public banks that can be capitalized with state funds and with labor union pensions that are now in private banks. The Bank of North Dakota is the only bank wholly owned by a state. In earlier times it helped farmers who were being taken advantage of by grain monopolies and private banks. Today, the Bank of North Dakota is one of the leading lenders of student loans in the nation and an important source of credit for farmers, ranchers, small businesses, and local governments.[26]

There are also the examples of "lemon socialism," noted earlier, in which governments in this and other countries have taken over industries ailing from being bled for profits, and nursed them back to health, testimony to the comparative capacities of private and public capital. In France immediately after World War II, the government nationalized banks, railways, and natural resources in a successful attempt to speed up reconstruction. The French telephone, gas, and electric companies were also public monopolies. Public ownership in France brought such marvels as the high-speed TGV train, superior to trains provided by U.S. capitalism, and the Minitel telephone computer, a communication-information service far in advance of anything offered by AT&T or other private companies in the United States.[27] The publicly owned railroads in France and Italy work much better than the privately owned ones in the United States (which work as well as they do because of public subsidies).[28]

---

24. Erwin Marquit, "The State, the Market and Socialist Pluralism," *Political Affairs*, May 1990, pp. 16–21.

25. In the mid-1980s, the state-owned liquor stores in Pennsylvania generated $750 million annually for that state's coffers: *People's Daily World*, December 9, 1986.

26. James Rowen, "Public Control of Public Money," *Progressive*, February 1977, pp. 47–52. Other states have considered creating state banks, but private banking interests have blocked enactment: *Washington Post*, March 18, 1984.

27. By late 1993, the conservative government in France was planning to deliver all publicly owned companies over to the mercies of the private market: *San Francisco Chronicle*, September 27, 1993.

28. See also Leland Stauber, *A New Program for Democratic Socialism: Lessons from the Market-Planning Experience in Austria* (Carbondale, Ill.: Four Willows Press, 1987).

The state and municipal universities in the United States are public and therefore "socialist" (shocking news to some of the students who attend them), and some of them are among the very best institutions of higher learning in the country. Publicly owned utilities in this country are better managed than investor-owned ones; and since they do not have to produce huge salaries for their CEOs and profits for stockholders, their rates are lower and they put millions in profits back into the public budget.[29] Then there is the British National Health Service, which costs 50 percent less than our private system yet guarantees more basic care for the medically needy.[30]

There is also what is called the "third sector" of the economy, consisting of more than 30,000 worker-run cooperatives and consumer goods co-ops, 13,000 credit unions, nearly 100 cooperative banks, and more than 100 cooperative insurance companies, plus about 5,000 housing co-ops, 1,200 rural utility co-ops, and 115 telecommunication and cable co-ops.[31] Socialists are not against private property, such as a home, a plot of land, and personal possessions, nor even small businesses if they are not used to exploit others. Nor are most socialists against modest income differentials or rewards to persons who make special contributions to society. Nor are they against profit, as long as the profit is used by and for the needs of society. The benefits as well as the costs of the economy should be socialized.

Conservatives in various countries do what they can to undermine public services by depriving them of funds and imposing punitive administrative measures. As the quality of the public service deteriorates, they then claim that it "does not work" and they move toward privatization. Conservatives in the USA have been doing this with the postal service and public education (including higher education). Privatization usually is a bonanza for rich stockholders but a misfortune for workers and consumers. The 1987 privatization of postal services in New Zealand brought a tidy profit for investors, wage and benefit cuts for postal workers, and a closing of more than a third of the country's post offices. Likewise, the privatization

---

29. Martin Espinoza, "The Public-Power Advantage," *Bay Guardian*, August 19, 1992, pp. 19–23.

30. *New York Times*, June 3, 1987. Although the Tory government imposed budget stringencies and centralized techniques on British health care "in order to squeeze economics from the system at the expense of quality," a majority of Britons still want to keep their socialized health service: ibid.

31. Gar Alperovitz in *Pegs Newsletter*, vol. 3, no. 1, n.d., p. 4; also Christopher Gunn and Hazel Dayton Gunn, *Reclaiming Capital: Democratic Initiatives and Community Development* (Ithaca, N.Y.: Cornell University Press, 1991); Kirk Scharfenberg, "The Community as Bank Examiner," *Working Papers*, September/October 1980, pp. 30–35. Construction trade unions have used pension funds to build low-cost housing and to start unionized, employee-owned contracting firms: David Moberg, "Potpurri of Union Capital Strategies," *In These Times*, April 29–May 5, 1987, p. 6.

of the telephone and gas industries in Great Britain resulted in soaring costs and lower quality service.[32]

If public ownership works, why are so many countries privatizing their industries? It is usually conservative governments that rush to privatize—because public ownership *is* working so well. If the not-for-profit public sector provides an ever expanding array of goods and services, what is left for the investor who profits from other people's labor? A growing public sector is potentially a great danger to corporate capitalism.

There is no guarantee that a socialized economy will always succeed. The state-owned economies of Eastern Europe and the former Soviet Union suffered ultimately fatal distortions in their development because of (a) the backlog of poverty and want in the societies they inherited; (b) years of capitalist encirclement, embargo, invasion, devastating wars, and costly arms buildup; (c) excessive bureaucratization and poor incentive systems; (d) lack of initiative in the service sectors and innovation in technology; and (e) a repressive political rule that allowed little critical expression and feedback. At the same time, it should be acknowledged that the former communist states transformed impoverished countries into relatively advanced societies.[33]

As the peoples in these former communist countries are now discovering, the "free market" means freedom mostly for those who have money and a sharp decline in living standards for everyone else. With "free-market reforms" came an inflation that diminished workers' real wages and dissolved their savings. Health and education systems have deteriorated. Unemployment, poverty, homelessness, crime, violence, suicide, mental depression, and prostitution have skyrocketed.[34] The breakup of farm collectives and cooperatives and the reversion to private farming has caused a 40 percent decline in agricultural productivity in countries like Hungary and East Germany—where collective farming actually had performed as well and often better than the heavily subsidized private farming in the West.[35]

---

32. On New Zealand: Les Winick, "Puffing Privatization," *Lies of Our Times,* April 1990, p. 18. On Britain: William Pomeroy, "Watery Grave for British Privatization?" *People's Daily World,* October 11, 1989.

33. Whatever else one wants to say about the erstwhile communist societies, they achieved what capitalism cannot and has no intention of accomplishing: adequate food, housing, and clothing for all; economic security in old age; free medical care; free education at all levels; and the right to a job—in countries that were never as rich as ours.

34. *Lies of Our Times,* January 1991, pp. 19–20; *Guardian,* May 22, 1991; *Washington Post,* September 29, 1991; *Democratic Journalist,* July 1991, p. 8. A Ukrainian miner says, "I prefer the Soviet Union to be back together again, a combination of the material gains of those years with the freedom of expression now": *New York Times,* July 17, 1993; also Fred Weir, "Time of Troubles," *In These Times,* March 7, 1994, pp. 30–31.

35. *Los Angeles Times,* January 29, 1994; Robert McIntyre, "Collective Agriculture in Eastern Europe and the Former Soviet Union," *Monthly Review,* December 1993, pp. 1–15. The post-communist "democratic" regimes have brought their own forms of political

Whether socialism can be brought about within the framework of the existing modern capitalist state or by a revolutionary overthrow of that state is a question unresolved by history. So far there have been no examples of either road to socialism in modern industrial society. The question of what kind of socialism we should struggle for deserves more extensive treatment than can be given here. American socialism cannot be modeled on the former Soviet Union, China, Cuba, or other countries with different historical, economic, and cultural developments. But these countries ought to be examined so that we might learn from their accomplishments, problems, failures, and crimes. Our goal should be an egalitarian, communitarian, environmentally conscious socialism, with a variety of participatory and productive forms, offering both security and democracy.

What is needed to bring about fundamental change is widespread organizing not only around particular issues but for a socialist movement that can project both the desirability of an alternative system and the possibility

---

repression; see Michael Parenti, "Yeltsin's Coup and the Media's Alchemy," *Lies of Our Times,* January/February 1994, pp. 11–14.

and indeed the great necessity for democratic change. There is much evidence—some of it presented in this book—indicating that Americans are well ahead of the existing political elites in their willingness to embrace new alternatives, including public ownership of the major corporations and worker control of production. With time and struggle, as the possibility for progressive change becomes more evident and the longing for a better social life grows stronger, we might hope that people will become increasingly intolerant of the monumental injustices of the existing capitalist system and will move toward a profoundly democratic solution. Perhaps then the day will come, as it came in social orders of the past, when those who seem invincible will be shaken from their pinnacles.

There is nothing sacred about the existing system. All economic and political institutions are contrivances that should serve the interests of the people. When they fail to do so, they should be replaced by something more responsive, more just, and more democratic. Marx said this, and so did Jefferson. It is a revolutionary doctrine, and very much an American one.

Index